Person, Self, and Experience

PERSON, SELF, AND EXPERIENCE

Exploring Pacific Ethnopsychologies

Edited by

Geoffrey M. White and John Kirkpatrick

UNIVERSITY OF CALIFORNIA PRESS
Berkeley   Los Angeles   London

University of California Press
Berkeley and Los Angeles, California

University of California Press, Ltd.
London, England

Copyright © 1985 by The Regents of the University of California

Library of Congress Cataloging in Publication Data

Main entry under title:

Person, self, and experience.

   Includes index.
   1. Ethnopsychology—Congresses.   2. Oceanians—Psychology—Congresses.
I. White, Geoffrey M.   II. Kirkpatrick, John, 1949–   .
GN502.P46   1985   155.8   84–28104
ISBN 0–520–05280–3

Printed in the United States of America

1 2 3 4 5 6 7 8 9

Contents

Part IV. Epilogue

Preface

This book has evolved through a working session, in 1981, and a formal symposium, in 1982, at the annual meetings of the Association for Social Anthropology in Oceania. We are grateful to the Association and our fellow members for many stimulating conversations and an excellent context for our work. In the two sessions and through the circulation and mutual criticism of the papers we were able to formulate our concerns and clarify many ideas. We benefited from the contributions and criticism of participants who are not represented herein. Allan Hanson, Michael D. Lieber, Susan Montague, P. B. Roscoe, Theodore Schwartz, Martin G. Silverman, and William Thurston presented papers. Robert I. Levy and Ward Goodenough, in 1981 and 1982, respectively, contributed as interested critics. We benefited greatly from the suggestions and overview provided by Michelle Z. Rosaldo in 1981. We deeply regret her death, and wish to dedicate this volume to her.

The organizational divisions of this work are intended only as suggestive groupings, not as definitive themes. Each of the chapters casts a wide net in its approach to ethnopsychology, intersecting in certain respects with each of the others.

We would like to thank Jenny Ichinotsubo and others at the East-West Center for their patient assistance with typing and clerical support.

Finally, we want to note that we have shared equally the tasks of editing this volume and writing its introduction. The ordering of our names was decided by a coin toss.

Part I
Introduction

1

Exploring Ethnopsychologies

John Kirkpatrick and Geoffrey M. White

Anthropologists working with Pacific peoples have long been interested in psychological issues. Rivers studied perception in the Torres Strait in 1898–99. Malinowski (1927) attempted to test and rethink Oedipal theory from his Trobriand data. Gregory Bateson developed his notions of ethos ("a culturally standardized system of organization of the instincts and emotions") and eidos ("a standardization of the cognitive aspects of the personality") in explicitly psychological terms in his study of the Iatmul *naven* ceremony (1956:118, 220). Culture and personality studies were grounded largely on research by Mead in Samoa (1928*a*, 1928*b*) and New Guinea (1930, 1935), and on Linton's analysis of Marquesan culture (in Kardiner 1939). Mead also addressed Piagetian claims in her work on Manus (1932). Gladwin and Sarason (1953) provided, in a study of Trukese personality using projective tests, an example of interdisciplinary collaboration. The bulk of recent work in the Pacific has focused on social organization and cultural codes, although general accounts of culture and personality covering entire regions have emerged (Levy 1969; Langness and Gladwin 1972; Schwartz 1973) and authors such as Levy (1973), Howard (1974), and Hutchins (1980) deal skillfully with questions of affect, motivation, and cognition.

Why, then, a book *exploring* ethnopsychologies? The answer has to do in part with new analytical approaches, in part with the assumptions and limitations of previous work. Culture and personality studies drew on existing theories of personality, usually psychoanalytic in persuasion (but see Whiting 1941 for a social learning approach), to formulate research topics and guide ethnographic observation. The goal in many studies was to use personality variables to interpret behavior and explain sociocultural institutions (e.g., Kardiner 1939; DuBois 1960; Spiro 1961). But the various theories of personality used in this way generally rely upon a model of the person in which individual motivational constructs (whether Freudian defenses, Malinowskian needs, or Murray's personality types) are the primary locus of organization in behavior. As a result, cultural data are analyzed as expressions of individual needs, motives, or behavioral dispositions—Benedict's (1934) "personality writ large." As Nisbett and Ross (1980) note, the heavy reliance on motivational explanations in psychoanalytic theory may be a reflection of the common tendency to overextend the attribution of intentions and motives in explaining the behavior of others. Much less attention has been paid by Westerners, scholars and laymen alike, to processes of interpretation whereby personal experience and behavior are seen to be relevant to the culturally constructed concerns of persons and communities. Nor do we know much about the questions people in other cultures ask about psychological matters, or the theories they draw on in formulating their answers.

The ethnopsychological approaches represented in this volume differ from the culture and personality perspective in several respects. First of all, we find that we cannot *assume* we know the cultural significance of data on, for example, religious beliefs or styles of interpersonal communication. Hallowell's (1955) notion of a "behavioral environment," in which objects, actions, and events gain behavioral significance through a process of cultural interpretation, highlights the problem of determining just what behavior is all about—a research question that is logically prior to attempts at explanation. The authors of this volume seek to understand and describe the cultural significance of social and psychological events as they are actively interpreted in social context. The locus of observation, then, shifts from individual behavior to the conceptual and interactive processes used to construct social meaning in everyday life.

We agree with the psychodynamic view that not all that is cultural is recognized or expressed. Yet, until we are able to understand just how, and in what contexts, people do formulate conscious interpretations of social experience, we are left with no way to demarcate either the extent or the behavioral significance of the culturally ineffable. In response to the influential work of Miller, Galanter, and Pribram (1960), psychologists (and anthropologists concerned with cognition, e.g., Wallace 1970) expanded their approaches to human cognition and decision making to show linkages between folk conceptual models and personal action. The chapters that follow are also concerned with these linkages, but draw their data from particular social and cultural contexts that show the importance of ethnopsychological formulations as a basis for active participation in social life.

We hold that comparative work aimed at the elucidation of ethnopsychological principles in different cultural contexts will help to provide a vantage point on some of the most basic, and usually invisible, assumptions guiding theory building in social science. (See Lutz, chap. 2, and Howard, chap. 11, for further discussion.) We expect to find both convergence and divergence between cultural practices and scientific theories. Convergences are evident in, for example, Wallace's (1958) account of dream interpretation among the Iroquois, reminiscent of psychoanalysis, and White's (chap. 9) description of a psychosomatic theory of illness on Santa Isabel.

However, the following chapters show much variability in the central tenets and uses of folk models of personality, thinking, and feeling. Such variability suggests that uniform psychological constructs can be applied cross-culturally only at the risk of minimizing or misconstruing the insights and concerns of participants. This risk often went unobserved in earlier studies, as Caughey (1980:175) notes:

> Much of the early ethnographic work which paid attention to personality concepts in other cultures was based on a sympathetic feeling for local personality appraisal. Thus Mead (1935:171) describes the Mundugumor "ideal personality" with a list of English expressions whose relationship to Mundugumor personality concepts remains unclear. In later work as well, there is little tendency to see the meaning of personality terms as a problem. Where the subjects' terms are reported at all they are often described simply by equating the local label with an English gloss whose meaning is taken to be obvious in itself and approximately equivalent to that of the subjects' term. This tendency is linked to the assumption, often quite explicit, that a single universal mode of personality appraisal underlies different ethnopsychologies.

Not only personality, but emotion, cognition, and other aspects of psychological functioning have been treated similarly. For example, the opposition of shame and guilt has been recurrently invoked by anthropologists to characterize the psychological functioning or ethnopsychology of the peoples studied. The notion of "shame cultures" reached its clearest expression in Benedict's work on Japan (1946). Since that time, anthropologists and others have continued to be interested in Japanese understandings of shame and their relation to personality and affect (DeVos 1973; Doi 1973; Lebra 1976). Ideas about guilt and shame have passed from anthropologists to a wider audience (e.g., Dodds 1951; Redfield 1975): (1) guilt and shame are important bases for social control of persons; (2) these controls are differentially distributed in different societies; and (3) it is useful to distinguish shame cultures and guilt cultures. However, these ideas drastically simplify the interrelations of experience, cultural coding, and social control (Singer 1953). For us, the crucial question is whether they can serve to bring together information about action, emotional expression, and experience precisely. How well can one characterize an ethnopsychology by saying that shame—or guilt, or any other English term for an emotion used to capture foreign ideas and experiences—is dominant in a culture?

A first response is to note the indeterminacy of the formulation: in a shame culture, do people express shame often, feel it often, or feel it only at crucial moments of deviation from cultural ideals? Only in the first case (in which people frequently express shame) is an ethnopsychological concept foregrounded. The latter cases of "shame culture" deal with a relation between persons and their social environment, usually without specifying the contexts or discourses in which that relation is inculcated and elaborated. Examples of more precise analyses of cultural formulations of "shame" in interactive settings are offered in particular studies such as Bourdieu's (1966) account of sequences of challenge and riposte in Kabylia, and Schieffelin's work (1979, 1982) on socialization through teasing and shaming among the Kaluli. Bourdieu shows honor and shame to be at issue in a wide range of interactions, and to be negotiated in orderly ways. He deals in some detail with the ways questions of honor arise, and hence he situates general statements, self-evaluations, and accounts of actors in relation to a regular social practice. We find the value of this study to be grounded in its depiction of the contexts and procedures for questioning and asserting honor in Kabylia. Bourdieu explicates a view of Kabyle men as "those who confront others" (1966:232), but this is achieved ethnographically, not by reliance on general notions of honor and shame. Similarly, Schieffelin specifies the interactive routines in Kaluli social life in which shame functions, and the action strategies available for participants in shaming interactions. The quality of the description and analysis make "shame" a useful category in understanding the Kaluli, precisely because it is ethnographically situated.

"Shame cultures" can be found nearly everywhere. As Kroeber (1948:612) noted, this testifies above all to the exceptional status of the opposed case, "conscious sinfulness," among Anglo-Saxon Protestants. The prominence of shame also reflects the practice, probably universal in human cultures, of characterizing affective experience in relation to interactional contexts. Even if contextual bases of affect are universally recognized, we doubt if these are the sole means for construing persons' states in any culture. (No culture is only a "shame culture.") We doubt, then, whether any people depends exclusively on a single, uniform mode of ethnopsychological interpretation. Different sorts of behavior are noted in different circumstances, depending, for instance, on situation, the intentions of the observer, or biographical facts known about the observed. Furthermore, different concepts and models (such as personality, intention, or emotional state) are used, separately or together, to formulate inferences from behavior. (Sapir [1949] offers classic examples.) We have no reason to expect that the situations in which members of one culture make personality appraisals, the evidence they call on to make them, and the categories they draw on to map the variety of recognized personalities correlate closely with those of members of another culture. (For instances of noncorrelation, see Hall 1976 and Bateson 1972:99ff.)

In this thicket of problems, some researchers may choose to cut their way out, avoiding questions of interpersonal assessment and ethnopsychological variance altogether. Culturally variable processes can be excluded or reduced to quantified aspects of a controlled experiment. The drawback of these research strategies is a failure to learn much about ordinary social or psychological events as experienced by enculturated human beings, and about the insights into psychological functioning found in other traditions.

We choose a different route, that of exploring, with ethnographic description and analysis, the procedures and categories used by actors to assess persons and situations. We find, in our experience of diverse cultures and in accounts such as those of Hallowell (1955, 1976), Geertz (1973, 1976), Keeler (1983), LeVine (1980), Levy (1973), Read (1955), Rosaldo (1980), M. Strathern (1968), A. Strathern (1975, 1981), and Straus (1977), ample evidence that interpersonal assessments vary from culture to culture. We do not expect to be able to map all the cognitive procedures involved in such assessments at this point, but we are certain that adequate models of those procedures cannot be developed without extensive study both of cultural codings of personhood, action, and situations, and of social practices of talking about actors and action. Moreover, we expect that studies of the organization of interpretive routines in the form of classification, metaphor, inference, and other orderings are necessary if we are eventually to understand the economy with which the cognitive work of interpersonal assessment is accomplished.

Several essays on the relationship of culture to self and affect have recently appeared (Heelas and Lock 1981; Lee 1982; Shweder and LeVine 1984). Theoretical statements about the interrelations of cultural categories and experience abound, although the rich accounts of social life needed to inform and test them are harder to find. We see this volume as helping to rectify that imbalance, and as suggesting analytic strategies for dealing with both the orderliness and the complexity of people's situated uses of psychological concepts. The objectives of this book are to document practices of understanding persons in a sample of Pacific cultures, to develop analytical strategies for making explicit important relations among concepts used in those practices, and to assess the role those practices and concepts play in social life. In the process we hope to show that the study of ethnopsychologies can be a fruitful collaborative enterprise with results pertinent to larger questions posed by anthropologists and psychologists.

The ethnographic chapters of this book take particular cultures and societies as frames of reference, dealing with such matters as the definition and interrelation of anger, grief, and shame among the Kaluli of Papua New Guinea (chap. 5). These are all written on the basis of extended fieldwork conducted in the local language. The authors situate ideas of personhood, shame, and the like in relation to social organizations and universes of discourse in which they are pertinent to actors. The authors differ in their topical emphases, their strategies for identifying major components of ethnopsychology, and their perspective on links between those components and the rest of social life. One chapter deals with early childhood development; another emphasizes practices of "disentangling" emotional conflict; yet another brings out abstract ordering principles of world view—but all deal with the definition of personhood and the cultural recognition of interpersonal variation. The authors of all the chapters agree on the need to view ethnopsychology in detailed social and cultural contexts, and on the fruitfulness, in relation to wider analytic concerns, of studying ethnopsychology in the Pacific.

Most of the ethnographic chapters were first presented at meetings of the Association for Social Anthropology in Oceania. At those meetings, we tried to identify common ground for work on ethnopsychology, and to distinguish fruitful strategies for research. As a result, the ethnographic chapters are not merely reports. They include explicit accounts of perspectives on ethnopsychology, as well as findings and analysis. In writing this introduction, we draw in part on the insights and arguments that emerged in the meetings.

In the rest of this chapter, we sketch a background for the studies that follow. We define ethnopsychology as a topic for both ethnographic and comparative work, and discuss some of the major ideas used by anthropologists to formulate accounts of ethnopsychologies. Problems of method are briefly reviewed, and the ways that the authors of the following chapters have confronted and dealt with such problems are identified. Some of the findings of those chapters are noted, so as to suggest the import of ethnopsychologies for our understanding of culture and social life.

THEORETICAL CONSIDERATIONS

We take ethnopsychologies to be cultural understandings of personal identity, action, and experience. Following Hallowell's (1955) lead, we recognize self-awareness as a human universal. Along with it, awareness of similarities among persons and of shared involvements and propensities crosscutting the distinctiveness of selves also seems universal. These apperceptions are basic parameters of the psychological aspect of cultures, not of ethnopsychology per se. This is because, as Hallowell's argument implies, the definition of self can occur in and through any domain or element of a culture. We wish to focus attention on a more restricted topic: cultural formulations of persons, personal action and experience, and the interactive practices through which such formulations are conveyed in social life. (We view persons and selves as shaped by processes of cultural definition and as interrelated but distinct. We do not attempt to define "self" here; for approaches to that problem, see chaps. 2, 4, and 8.) We note particularly that the interpretive work of folk psychology depends, as the notion of "psychology" implies, upon an organized body of knowledge for its coherence and communicability. Hence, we repeatedly ask, Upon what presuppositions, and through what course of reasoning, do cultural formulations of experience rely for their intelligibility and effectiveness?

Persons are points of intersection between the subjective and the social. Here we follow Durkheim (1898), but only to an extent. We take persons to be, first, cultural elements, topics of knowledge and discourse. Persons are constructs deemed capable of experience, will, action, identity, and the like. Actual beings may be treated as persons in a culture, but we do not take them to be persons by definition. Indeed, not all humans need be persons in a culture, nor are all persons likely to be human. (See Hallowell 1960 and Straus 1977 for exemplary cases.) Persons are cultural bases for formulating and exploring subjective experience. Equally, persons are recognizable as elements of social life, as occupying social statuses and participating in social groups and events. In a particular culture, the field of human action may be either extensively or minimally coded as social, that is, as orderly by virtue of persons' involvement in an institutional and moral universe that stands apart from their identities and capacities as persons.

We do not wish to define the bounds of the personal and the social by fiat, but to explore them. Similarly we do not claim particular experiences or attributes of persons to be by definition central to personhood and subjectivity. We hope to learn on what foundations personhood may be erected in different cultures.

Cultural Formulations of the Person: Personage/ Person/Individual

In a classic paper, Mauss (1938) suggested that cultural conceptions of social actors have evolved from a view of the person as enacting a determinate ritual role to modern Western ideas of the individual. For comparative purposes, this model can be used without its evolutionary phrasing and further specified in several ways (see Rorty 1976, and Fajans, chap. 10, for examples). This model hinges on our sense of the social and the individual as opposed, as does the shame/guilt duality discussed above (see also chap. 2). Its ideal types, however, have the advantage of synthesizing expectations and values in a way that may capture much of the orderliness of an ethnopsychology.

Thus, in chapter 10, Fajans uses the term "person" in a technical sense, as an embodied actor of roles, and argues that the Baining understand themselves as persons in this sense. Her argument is more extensive: she shows how Baining structure their interactions so as to validate this view and how actors who cannot be so coded find themselves experiencing disorder or deprivation. Fajans also shows how such discordant experiences are remembered in ways that, over time, condense them into images of disorder.

The argument, then, is not simply that Baining are or see themselves as actors of a particular sort, but that their social world is organized to support this view. Furthermore, their understandings of experience set apart events that do not fit easily within this perspective and hence are not to be integrated with normal estimations of self and other. Much like Bourdieu, Fajans uses a general topic and theoretical distinctions as a point of entry into, and a synthesizing image of, the cumulative impact of social practices and cultural codings. She shows the Baining as working to construe themselves as persons (in her sense), not simply to be persons, and hence depicts the tension between ideal images and the evidence of divergence from ideals which emerges in Baining life.

We suggest that, for cross-cultural analysis, it is not the Maussian categories so much as the problem of accommodating reality to valued images of humanity which can usefully serve as a basis for comparative study. After all, in many cultures persons are valued as conforming to well-known social routines, and discretion about slips or confusions in performing is enjoined: ideals of personhood approximate Mauss's notion of the person, and social life can be viewed as confirming such ideals as realistic. The threats to ideal images which actors face vary widely, however, and these deserve attention along with the images they challenge.

In any event, the ability of members of a society to embrace ideals conditionally—as applying in many situations but not all, as ideals that fallible humans can only sometimes meet, or as ideals that must be upheld because humans are tempted to reject them, with disastrous consequences— must be recognized. Riesman (1977:122) offers an example worth keeping in mind:

> In Jelgoji, the verb *pulaade* is used to say "to behave like a Fulani," "to act Fulani." One day when I had done something considered by the Fulani as characteristic of their own behavior . . . they said to me, "*Ada puloo joonin,* Pool (You are acting Fulani now, Paul)." In the same way, the Fulani use this verb in speaking of themselves. For instance, if someone is invited to eat something and refuses, they might say to him, "*A pulotoo na? Taa puloo. Waru faa nyaamen.* (Are you acting Fulani? Don't act Fulani. Come, let's eat.)"

> The existence of such expressions suggests two things. First . . . "typically Fulani" behavior is often thought of by the Fulani themselves to be a role which one plays. Second, there are social situations where this Fulani behavior is not appropriate.

Clearly the Fulani person is deemed properly able to be more than Fulani. An analysis of "acting Fulani" would tell us far less about persons than about their perceived abilities to participate in some, but not all, social spheres.

A separate issue relevant to attempts to portray ethnopsychologies in terms of images of the person has to do with our tendency to assume that all psychological matters pertain to the single person. We find it hard to think otherwise, but note, especially in Oceania, evidence for other views. As Lutz notes, many attitudes are shared on Ifaluk (chap. 2): they are expectably and properly in '*our* insides,' not those of a solitary person. Discussions among the contributors to this volume and with other Oceanic ethnographers lead us to suspect that we record, recall, and analyze such matters as compassion and shame as aspects of particular persons when they may be enunciated as shared or generalized in a social network. The possible implications are extensive. If, for example, children in a hypothetical society are socialized with repeated warnings that "we (inclusive) are ashamed," they may learn the behavior expected of shame cultures—but they learn through being singled out not as deviant persons but as actors whose deviant actions are discordant with their membership in a larger affective and normative unit. In this case, "the person" may not map culturally valued units so much as points of potential disjuncture from such units, and "shame" may be less a personal feeling, and more a connective tissue in a social unit.

More realistically, our assumption that psychological matters pertain to particular persons may blind us to the recognition, in other cultures, of varied units capable of psychological experience. The problem is not so much one of whether the person is a cultural unit with experiential capacities, but whether other units—the family, the community, and even the land—may have similar, but distinct, capacities and means of articulating them. It is likely that the Marquesan saying that "the land becomes weird" at the death of a chief (Kirkpatrick 1981:453) and the Zapotec talk of the land as "sad" in times of poverty (Selby 1974:24) involve no claim that the soil has affective reactions, only a figurative usage. Such statements deserve scrutiny, however, as possibly following from ethnopsychological tenets, not immediate dismissal because we only view individuals as psychological entities. Detienne and Vernant (1978) have shown that the Greek notion of *metis* 'cunning intelligence' can be explicated fruitfully by relating Greek accounts of gods, heroes, citizens, and even octopi. An analysis of more restrictive scope would risk being puzzled by the wily Odysseus.

Individualistic vs. Sociocentric Ideologies

We have stressed that analyses focusing on notions of valued person-hood may provide summary images of ethnopsychological themes. They thus succeed by bringing out both ideals and recognized varieties of personal existence, by depicting a cultural universe of possibilities, not just a single standard. Discussions of world view or ideology may combine a focus on the person and this broad perspective, as in recent accounts of sociocentric or relational views of the person (Gearing 1970; Selby 1974, 1975; Shweder and Bourne 1982). An account of a social ideology of a people also can include the data—disvalued images, threats to personhood, psychological units other than the individual—that we noted as needed but potentially minimized in accounts of the image of the person.

Dumont (1970a, 1970b, 1977, 1978) has developed theoretical argu-ments for taking ideology to be the central subject matter of anthropology. He sees much of the difficulty Western scholars experience in comprehend-ing Indian institutions as stemming from a simultaneous failure to give due weight to Hindu ideology and a reliance on individualistic Western notions in formulating analytic questions and tools. Critical of individualistic as-sumptions, he writes at times as if a simple dichotomy exists between individualistic Western ideology and all other world views, in which the social whole, not the individual, is the focus of value (1970a:9). This is to treat Hindu, Zapotec, Fox, and many other cultures as alike, and alike above all in lacking Western philosophical assumptions.

Dumont, however, also holds out the promise of a more differentiated comparison, a comparison of ideologies according to their foci of value (individual or whole) and means of articulating a totalizing world view. A research program along these lines would ideally identify cultural formula-tions of the person as similar or different in their place in ideological wholes and in their symbolic constituents—but such a program is far from being realized (cf. Dumont 1978). (For ethnographically based models of ideolog-ical wholes, see Augé 1975 and Kirkpatrick 1983.)

Recent works on ethnopsychologies have shown that holistic ideologies may be person-oriented: Rosaldo (1980) and Straus (1977) offer detailed examples. In this volume, White (chap. 9), Poole (chap. 6), and Kirkpatrick (chap. 3) show how persons may emerge as distinct, autonomous agents in culturally specified circumstances. More work of this sort is needed if the ideological ordering of aspects of personhood is to be understood in more precise ways than currently exist.

In reviewing several approaches to ethnopsychology, we intend to depict a confluence of research problems, not a failure of competing paradigms. Differences of method and theory separate cognitive, symbolic, and psychological anthropologists. Authors of chapters in this volume owe allegiance to all three of these anthropological traditions. We see the differences among them as gaps to be crossed, not defended. (See Colby, Fernandez, and Kronenfeld 1981 for further discussion.) Ethnopsychology is a point at which convergence is possible. The chapters that follow span a variety of approaches, ranging from attempts to understand ethnopsychological formulations within the context of whole systems of ideology (Fajans, chap. 10, and Kirkpatrick, chap. 3) to analyses focusing on particular events or contexts of activity in order to explicate a more limited field of inference (Black, chap. 7, and White, chap. 9). The meeting ground for the authors in this volume, however, is in their concern with the salience of cultural knowledge of persons for understanding social events, and in their use of the data of everyday talk and interaction to investigate the organization and coherence of that knowledge. Furthermore, each author in some way notes his or her place, as investigator, in the analysis, indicating that ethnopsychological research necessarily involves a reflexive posture vis-à-vis the work of ethnography (see Crapanzano 1981; LeVine 1983). It seems to us that a range of approaches can be brought to bear on ethnopsychological data, for a variety of symbolic orderings are to be found in cultural formulations of persons, experience, and interpersonal activity.

APPROACHES AND METHODS

Given the central place of conceptual structures and interpretive routines in our approach to ethnopsychology, issues of linguistic meaning and translation are of particular importance in the task of ethnographic description. Much of our data is in the form of talk about persons, actions, and events, so understanding what is being said (whether to the ethnographer or in more natural discourse) is a minimal requirement of ethnopsychological research. In addition, however, we must go beyond simply understanding and describing what is said, and demonstrate how we formulate our interpretations. The following chapters show that this requires making explicit cultural assumptions that often go unspoken and social practices that often go unrecognized, but that make ordinary speech interpretable, pertinent, and socially forceful (Tyler 1978; Rabinow and Sullivan 1979; Keesing 1979; D'Andrade 1984*a*). Equally, strategies for translation need to be made explicit; several strategies are identified in later chapters.

The interest in language as an avenue to the analysis of conceptual structures will remind many readers of the work of ethnoscience. However, differences between the approaches to ethnopsychology represented here and those of traditional ethnoscience are instructive. The dominant emphasis in ethnoscience was the study of category systems expressed in terminologies such as kin terms or plant names. By examining the referential function of words used to name things, it has been possible to map the shape and organization of native systems of classification. The lexical approach of ethnoscience is based on ideas about the relation of language and thought which were well articulated by Leibniz in his *Nouveaux Essais sur l'Entendement* two hundred years ago: "I truly think that languages are the best mirror of the human mind and that an exact analysis of the signification of words would make known the operations of the understanding better than would anything else" (cited in Kretzmann 1967:381). Leibniz's interest in the "signification of words" reflects the ethnoscience focus on terminology and the categories they designate, a focus that has been most productive in areas of experience where identification and classification are important functions of language, as in the recognition of plant types or the diagnosis of disease.

However, the methods of referential semantics do not take us very far in understanding ethnopsychological vocabulary such as words for emotions or social actions. The contrasts between ethnopsychology and ethnobotany, for example, reveal some of the difficulties. Work on the latter has concentrated on the recognition, in different cultures, of plant species or varieties, and relations among species. Much debate concerns the adequacy of taxonomic and prototype models for representing cultural knowledge (Berlin, Breedlove, and Raven 1973; Hunn 1976; Dougherty 1985), but scholars agree on the centrality of speciation as a problem for ethnobotanical study. One practical advantage of this focus should be obvious. The ethnobotanist can find plants, preserve them, and show them to informants and, later, to botanists. He or she thus can compare several folk identifications with academic ones. We are not so lucky: we cannot preserve psychological specimens to be identified by informants and academic specialists. Nor do we have reason to expect that informants and academics perform comparable operations in identifying our hypothetical specimens.

When a person identifies plants, his or her action can be treated as a case of identifying a member of a known domain: types of plants. When a Marquesan sees a person as *vivi'io,* a Baining sees that person as *awumbuk,* and an American ethnographer suspects the person feels "lonely": each makes reference to a culturally specific domain. *Vivi'io* is, roughly, a frustration of what should be an active attitude of the person to others, an attitude frustrated by others' absence; *awumbuk* is, in Fajans's phrase, "a social hangover"; loneliness, Americans tell us, is a feeling internal to the subject. In this example we presume that members of each culture find a person's attitude comprehensible, and all make similar inferences about prior events—the subject has been left alone. These similarities attest to widespread concerns of human beings, but *not* to shared procedures and models for labeling, grouping, and dealing with those concerns. (Ethnoscience may face similar difficulties. For an account suggesting the problems raised by an analytic focus on speciation in one ethnographic situation, see Feld 1982, chap. 2.)

The diversity of cultural models for psychological elements and events derives in part from a functional complexity widespread among ethnopsychologies. Their terms do not simply refer. They carry evaluative force and participate in systematic allocations of moral value. Also, the use of an ethnopsychological term may say as much about the speaker, or the speaker's relation to the topic, as about the topic alone. (The Marquesan *mea ka'oha* and Ifaluk *gafago* 'object of concern/compassion' both may highlight aspects of the referent but point more surely to the speaker's attitude.)

We do not deny the existence of psychological universals. We stress, however, the point that ethnopsychological judgments are made in terms of specific cultural theories and metaphors. It may well be the case that Marquesans all see vivi'io where Americans all see loneliness—but they both actively construct an interpretation, rather than simply record a psychological reality independent of cultural coding.

The implications of the last point are not easily assessed. Here the analogy to ethnoscience may serve as a useful guide. Folk categories are not equivalent to scientific ones, or to groupings of natural facts. Yet folk category systems do accomplish detailed mappings of the world. What is more, apparently exotic folk categories can be shown to synthesize complex empirical data, and even ecological wisdom. For instance, the prohibited species listed in Leviticus, animals that either chew the cud or have cloven hooves, but not both, are less well adapted to desert and grassland ecologies than species with both attributes. Hunn (1979:114) argues that "the animal anomalies are not independent creations of a cultural system imposed on natural chaos, but rather reflect creative human reactions to the perception of empirical correlations in the natural environment." The recognition that cultural systems involve creative synthesis does not conflict with a view of them as capturing truths about the world. But which truths? We submit that, because of the complexity of ethnopsychological realities, this last question cannot be adequately answered by a simple generalization, at least not at this point. Instead, the opportunity arises to discover a variety of empirical correlates of folk wisdom, and then to search for their common features. We expect both specific cultural syntheses and the cross-cultural commonalities of ethnopsychologies to demarcate facts of concern to humans. We do not, however, expect the terms of any one ethnopsychology to identify precisely the field of concerns on which ethnopsychologies converge. Thus, Murphy (1976) has argued that recurrent patterns of disturbed behavior typical of schizophrenia are recognized and labeled as abnormal in cultures as diverse as Eskimo or Yoruba. Although these observations point to an important area of common concerns and similar percepts (of, we assume, biologically similar phenomena), they do not tell us enough about the cultural constructs being compared to say anything significant about commonalities in either the interpretation or the experience of schizophrenia.

Ethnopsychological vocabulary is used to talk about personal and social experience, not to identify or classify "objects" separable from their cultural contexts. Although investigations of the perception and categorization of mental disorder have described the important social consequences of "labeling" someone crazy (Waxler 1974), such labeling is in practice less a matter of perception and naming than a complex interactive process of interpretation and evaluation. Furthermore, this process is based on a broad range of cultural knowledge about persons and behavior which is not likely to form a finite set of attributes carving out a bounded domain (White 1982). Hence the methods of referential semantics, such as componential analysis, are of limited use in this regard. As a number of authors in this volume demonstrate, an ethnographic understanding of what Tobian notions of 'ghostly behavior'; Ifaluk *bush* 'crazy', 'incompetent'; Baining *akambain* 'crazy,' 'wild,' 'drunk'; or Marquesan *koea* 'crazy' are all about does not involve mapping a system of classification so much as explicating cultural models that are used to reason about, evaluate, and manage social experience.

Lexical studies have shed some light on cultural understandings of personal identity and experience (D'Andrade 1985b; Gerber 1976; Lutz 1982; White 1980). It is often possible to identify a corpus of words that serve similar functions in describing personal dispositions (personality terms) or affective processes (emotion words), but a careful analysis of the meanings of such words quickly takes the investigator beyond any neatly bounded domain of "individual traits" or "affective states" which could be labeled, compared, and contrasted in an effort to arrive at native definitions. Thus, an investigation of the domain of personality descriptors in Santa Isabel leads White (1980; chap. 9) to the conclusion that they derive their meaning primarily from understandings about processes of interpersonal interaction. Gerber (1976) and Lutz (1982) find that emotion words in Samoa and Ifaluk are organized by similar interpersonal themes and encode cultural knowledge about specific social relations and situations (chaps. 4 and 2). The authors in this volume repeatedly analyze emotion words (with the caveat that "emotion" is a poor label for specific cultural concepts at issue) for what they say, implicitly or explicitly, about interactive situations.

Some analysts treat emotion words as labels for physiological states or related facial expressions. They can find, in different cultures, highly replicable human abilities to typify certain behavioral displays (Ekman 1973). We view emotion words differently, as guideposts to cultural knowledge about social and affective experience. The recognition of a behavioral display as meaningful depends on inferential processes that mediate perception and categorization. The cultural meaning and behavioral implications of emotions depend, we submit, far more on such reasoning about social contexts of emotion than on classification of a few displays (cf. Averill 1980).

Some aspects of folk reasoning about the interactive significance of affect are probably universal (see Gerber, chap. 4). Yet wide variability, from culture to culture, is evident in such reasoning. The settings people of different cultures take to be normal or general contexts of affective experience differ widely, as the differences between the context of honor in Kabylia, American notions of normal interaction, and A'ara concerns with vulnerability to spiritual power (chap. 9) suggest. Some descriptors are identified with particular culturally specified settings, often ones that are marked by their deviation from expectations of normal interaction. To go back to our earlier example, "loneliness," *vivi'io,* and *awumbuk* differ largely in the ways the situation of an isolated person is understood to be problematic in American, Marquesan, and Baining culture.

The area of experience which Americans refer to as emotion, then, is a good example of the difficulties, and the promise, of using lexical data sets to study ethnopsychological understandings. While emotion concepts may serve an important classificatory function in identifying affective states of self or other (see Schachter and Singer 1962), they may also constitute key inferential links in interpretations of motivation and interpersonal process. Hence it seems possible and fruitful to study the negotiation of emotions as culturally defined elements in social life, leaving to the side questions of their biological basis or the panhuman reality of affect. (Gerber chooses to deal with such questions in her chapter 4, while others do not. This difference is a matter of approaches and priorities, not of firm theoretical positions.)

By examining the role of specific emotion concepts in forming behavioral interpretations, the ethnographer may glimpse unspoken cultural assumptions about social process (see Rosaldo 1980; Myers 1979). An important ethnographic task, then, is to delineate the conceptual structuring of these underlying assumptions in the form of interpretive schemata, however fragmentary or partial. Perhaps one of the reasons for the lack of progress in ethnopsychological research since Hallowell's pioneering work is the lack of analytic constructs to identify and represent the types of conceptual apparatus used in ethnopsychological discourse and to link them to situated social activities.

Anthropologists and psychologists have explored many forms of symbolic relationship: oppositions, classificatory structures, metaphors, functional orderings, scripts, and plans, among many others. Particular anthropological traditions have been preoccupied with the study of different sorts of ordering and of different social contexts in which such orderings may be found. The relations between those orderings in human social life and cognition have not been extensively explored. Thus Turner (1967) has shown how the *mudyi* tree (*Diplorrhyncus condylocarpon*) can serve as a condensed ritual symbol, in which a range of oppositions are implicated for the Ndembu. An ethnobotanist conceivably might show how Ndembu distinguish it from other trees, placing it in a taxonomic model of ethnobotanical knowledge. But the question remains: how is folk knowledge of the mudyi tree organized in human minds so that it provides a basis for intersubjective understanding, communication, and action in a variety of contexts?

Ethnopsychologies offer a fertile ground for the study of practical reasoning. They may be implicated in both formal contexts and everyday ones, in both specialized and widespread cultural knowledge. People often deal with ambiguity and uncertainty in using their knowledge of social experience and may have to rationalize, justify, or defend their talk about such matters. It is not only in such formal settings as litigation that they must enunciate the reasoning behind their claims about the world. In this volume, the organization of folk knowledge in practical reasoning is studied from several perspectives.

Key Words and Metaphors

Each of the authors in this volume explicates the meanings and uses of certain key vernacular terms and phrases to describe aspects of ethnopsychological interpretation. They take diverse approaches to this task, but generally agree that the vocabulary in question does not function primarily to "classify" social reality in terms of taxonomic schemata consisting of categories related through contrast and inclusion. Rather, by focusing on frequently used words that point to salient cultural notions, such as Bimin-Kuskusmin *finiik* (chap. 6), Marquesan *ka'oha* (chap. 3), or Baining *akambain* (chap. 10), the ethnographer is able to track inferential pathways through webs of associative knowledge which underly the terms' various meanings and uses. In her approach to the Ilongot key word *liget* 'passion', Rosaldo (1980:24) has put the case eloquently:

> We can learn about Ilongot life by using words like *liget* as an initial text, not because Ilongots "classify" a person wild with rage in terms that, unlike ours, refer as well to energetic farmers—but rather because a proper understanding of what *liget* means requires us to look beyond the word itself to sentences in which it is employed, images through which it is invoked, and social processes and activities that Ilongots use it to describe. By so "interpreting" the meanings presupposed by certain terms one can, I think, begin to translate cultures, and in particular, come to grips with motivational patterns that are to be discovered neither in classificatory nouns nor in outlandish "symbols."

Because ethnopsychological concepts are abstract and complexly structured, they require the sort of open-ended approach outlined by Rosaldo which allows the ethnographer to discover a word's meanings and ambiguities in a variety of contexts and uses. Where there are areas of language use in which certain words function in similar ways, it may prove useful to explore relations of contrast and similarity among terms that can be meaningfully compared, such as words used to talk about emotions or to describe personal behavioral propensities. Lexical data such as those cited by Gerber (chap. 4), Lutz (chap. 2), and White (chap. 9) have heuristic value in ferreting out clusters of similar terms or linguistic oppositions which form bipolar conceptual dimensions. Somewhat similar but less formalized strategies are used in other chapters, notably in Poole's discussion of clusters of key Bimin-Kuskusmin emotion words (chap. 6) and Kirkpatrick's analysis (chap. 3). The latter is not only able to describe distinct types of accounts of engagement in action used by Marquesans but he also shows their interrelation in a model of underlying assumptions.

Quinn provides another example of the analysis of key words in her study of Americans' understandings about marriage. From the vantage point of ethnopsychology, this work is interesting because it demonstrates, with examples familiar to members of American culture, that some of our most basic social institutions are built on cultural understandings about persons, emotions, and human relationships (cf. Schneider 1968).

Quinn finds that a number of words such as 'commitment,' 'relationship,' and 'love' recur frequently in informants' conversations about marriage. Each is semantically complex and may be used in several distinct syntactic contexts to express different meanings. Conceptual analysis of the key word 'commitment' shows that it is used particularly to express three related senses, PROMISE, DEDICATION, and ATTACHMENT. Quinn's (1982:793) discussion of the ATTACHMENT notion reveals its ethnopsychological underpinnings:

> The attachment is not intellectual . . . its overriding sense is rather that of emotional attachment. In American folk psychology, two people do become emotionally attached or grow more emotionally attached over time, as they engage in a joint pursuit of goals as important, effortful and remote as making a family; making the marriage work; struggling to figure out what it is about or where each other is; or helping each other "through the good times and the bad times." In sum, the word "commitment" tells a complex story about American marriage.

Quinn's approach is in line with the work of many others (e.g., Sapir and Crocker 1977) who argue that metaphor is an important means of conceptualizing social and psychological experience, and that close attention to metaphorical usages can be an important source of evidence about the structure of ethnopsychological concepts. The investigation of ethnopsychological metaphors may be particularly fruitful if one takes the expanded view of metaphor recently espoused by Lakoff and Johnson (1980) which does not make a sharp distinction between "literal" and "metaphorical" language, but rather sees much of ordinary language as metaphorical extensions of concepts that are more closely grounded in physical experience.

The authors in this volume discuss numerous metaphors that formulate social or psychological concepts in terms of images drawn from bodily experience, perception, and the physical environment. Points of cross-cultural convergence as well as divergence in the construction of ethnopsychological metaphor are noted. For example, both Gerber (chap. 4) and White (chap. 9) describe the use of spatial operators such as HIGH/LOW or ABOVE/BELOW to represent social positioning and interactive traits. And Lutz (chap. 2) notes a contrast in developmental metaphors such that the Ifaluk speak primarily about an increase in quantity of thoughts and emotions, whereas the Bimin-Kuskusmin (chap. 6) use images of direction and solidification. Concepts of physical experience or perception do not represent psychological concepts simply on the basis of broad evaluative connotations (i.e., because both are seen as "good" or "bad"), but rather do so on the basis of more specific semantic similarities in the types of attributes, relations, or inferences which they encode. Thus, when A'ara speakers say that social actions cause 'pain' or 'hurt' someone, those actions are characterized and evaluated as harmful, with further implications that the person who has been threatened with harm will take corrective action. In this way, knowledge about bodily experience, and physical goal-oriented activity can be elaborated in a model for thinking, moralizing, and problem solving in social experience.

The grounding of abstract social or psychological metaphors in more immediate or clearly delineated experience with the physical world may provide a basis for cross-cultural similarities in figurative ethnopsychological language (see Brown and Witkowski 1981). Asch (1958) began a comparative investigation of psychological metaphor twenty-five years ago, observing, for example, intriguing parallels in the use of adjectival oppositions such as sweet/sour to describe persons in six languages. The analyses in this volume show that direct comparisons of metaphorical usages of words will require careful explication of culture-specific meanings which go well beyond a simple juxtaposition of English glosses. Much more work on both metaphorical images and forms of metaphorical construction will be necessary before the problems of translation can be routinized.

The potential richness of metaphor as a source of ethnopsychological data lies in the fact that the application of words from one domain of experience to another makes available selected pieces of an organized knowledge structure appropriate to one kind of experience for use in conceptualizing, evaluating, and acting in another domain. In both the Hawaiian and A'ara cases (chaps. 8 and 9), metaphors of being 'tangled' and 'blocked' are used to describe states of emotional and social conflict which point to culturally institutionalized means of 'disentangling' or 'setting right' the conflict. The A'ara metaphors of 'tangled' and 'blocked' are an effective means of conceptualizing the premises of a folk theory that explains failure and misfortune in terms of socioemotional conflict. By symbolizing conflict in images such as a tangled fishing net or a blocked path—physical conditions interfering with the completion of everyday tasks—social or psychological conflict is represented as something that may also impede goal-directed activity such as curing or hunting. Moreover, these images carry the implication that some effort, of the painstaking sort appropriate for untangling knotted ropes or clearing away obstructions, is necessary in order to attain desired goals.

Folk Theories and Inference

Ethnopsychological formulations of persons and social events implicitly select, highlight, and shape those aspects of behavior which are consistent with prior cultural models—models that specify what is culturally plausible in social life (see, e.g., Shweder and D'Andrade 1980). Indeed, one of the central features of ethnopsychological interpretation is that it does not follow from discrete or isolated bits of folk wisdom, but is based on an *organized* body of understandings. (Chaps. 3 and 5 are especially concerned with the coherence of ethnopsychological understandings.) Furthermore, these understandings do not simply represent an assemblage of behavioral facts. Rather, they are actively used to draw inferences that go beyond the data of interactive events to create social meaning. In other words, using cultural assumptions about what follows from what in social life, the folk "psychologist" formulates, through inference, "hypotheses" that represent explanations or predictions about the course of social behavior. The analogy of organized cultural understandings to a set of premises which form a more or less coherent folk theory provides an important basis for our approach to ordinary interpretations of behavior as a folk "psychology." However, by extending the notion of psychology to the domain of commonsense interpretations, we have ourselves created a metaphor that both captures and distorts the phenomena we seek to investigate.

The folk psychologist could be seen as a subspecies of ethnoscientist who is busily classifying and hypothesizing about social experience in order to formulate and test theories that will best predict and bring order to his or her observations. Indeed, much of the work in social psychology, deriving from Heider's (1958) pathbreaking investigations of "naive psychology" and subsequent work on attribution theory, has used a model of the person very similar to this characterization of the ethnoscientist. Thus, Kelley (1967) proposed that people make causal inferences in much the same way that scientists do, by noting correlations between the effects of social action and its possible causes. It is not surprising, perhaps, that recent cognitive research in this tradition shows consistent shortcomings in people's ability to make accurate assessments of behavior, because of reliance on preexisting knowledge structures and a few heuristic principles rather than the rules of probability and logic (Nisbett and Ross 1980). While it is useful to understand the types of inferential strategy which may systematically shape commonsense reasoning, this view of the person as an "intuitive scientist" tends to obscure the point that ordinary social discourse is less concerned with accuracy alone than with the construction of an intersubjective world of action and moral judgment. Within such a culturally constructed universe of discourse, accuracy is much less at issue than matters of coherence and plausibility, as defined by those same models which produce cognitive "mistakes."

The approach to social cognition as implicit or intuitive science may have important methodological consequences. Attempts to assess the predictive adequacy of the folk psychologist have relied on experimental ma-nipulations of problems and questions in order to demonstrate *departures* from fixed standards of inference (Tversky and Kahneman 1977; Wason and Johnson-Laird 1972). This type of experimental elicitation presumes that the substance of a problem is independent of the inferential strategy used to think about it. However, cross-cultural research shows that pro-cesses of reasoning and problem solving are frequently tailored to par-ticular purposes, activities, or contexts (Laboratory of Comparative Human Cognition 1978). These findings suggest that attempts to discover patterns of ethnopsychological inference should begin with the question: What are people trying to do when they attempt to explain or "predict" behavior?

Cultural theories and inferences are used in a wide variety of social contexts for interpreting, rationalizing, defending, encouraging, scolding, or any of a limitless number of culturally formulated purposes. The con-cerns of the scientist with logical consistency and predictive accuracy, while they may be implicit in some cases, are rarely voiced as explicit frames for ethnopsychological discourse. By viewing people as intuitive scientists and studying their responses to questions posed in experimental situations, it is difficult, if not impossible, to understand the structure and operation of folk theories. As Frake (1977:3) has written:

> Perhaps instead of trying to devise provocative questions and other instruments to persuade people to talk about things they do not ordinarily talk about in that way, we should take as a serious topic of investigation what people in fact talk about, or, better, what they are in fact doing when they talk.

The studies in this volume begin to identify some of the naturally occurring topics of ethnopsychological discourse in the daily lives of people in several Pacific societies. One of the questions we may ask in extending our metaphors of "ethnopsychology" and "folk theory" is, What aspects of social experience engender more deliberate or explicit attempts at expla-nation? In other words, In what contexts do cultures provide organized bodies of knowledge which are put to recognized use in causal reasoning, whether personal, social, natural, or otherwise? By posing these questions, investigators may identify those areas of experience associated with ordinary explanations in natural discourse.

Among the areas of cultural concern which are discussed by authors in this volume as topics for ethnopsychological reasoning are: illness, de-viance from normal behavioral patterns (e.g., craziness, suicide, drunken-ness, or possession), life-cycle changes, death, injury, and success or failure in important goal-oriented activities such as gardening or fighting. Each of these areas of experience consists of behavioral events that contrast with what is normal or desirable, and, as a result, require definition and interpretation. These processes of interpretation may serve to formulate identities and relations within the social order, as in the case of developmental changes in identity, or they may demarcate the margins of the social order as a whole, as in the case of various forms of deviance. It is those areas of significant personal or social concern, characterized by uncertain or potentially harmful consequences, which are likely to be the focus of culturally organized folk theories. This type of knowledge, then, becomes the conceptual basis for action in explaining and dealing with problematic events. Perhaps because such events are matters of social concern and activity, they also tend to evoke public discourse, as interpretations are posed and counterposed in an effort to arrive at plausible explanations and, in some cases, at decisions about how best to resolve the situation.

The explicit theorizing characteristic of folk explanations of illness or deviance is an important source of insight into ethnopsychological inferences, particularly because it may bring into focus assumptions about normative or desirable patterns of behavior which often go unspoken. Another area of social life which often gives rise to ethnopsychological discourse, although perhaps not in the form of explicit folk theories, is that of social conflict and moral transgression. White (1985), Lutz (chap. 2), and Black (chap. 7) note that ethnopsychological vocabulary is frequently lopsided in its lexicalization of negative emotions or behaviors associated with interpersonal conflict. This lopsidedness reflects a point that is made in some way by each author in this volume—that is, that ordinary interpretations of social experience do not simply describe, measure, or represent behavior, but rather are concerned with evaluating and drawing out moral implications. Interpretive judgments of action also affect others and engage them in interaction.

Understanding what is being done in ethnopsychological discourse requires attention to social situations as occasions for particular kinds of culturally constructed activity. Interpretations and evaluations of everyday interaction are voiced in a wide spectrum of occasions, ranging from informal gossip and conversation to more formal or ritualized situations such as the A'ara "disentangling" (chap. 9), the Hawaiian *ho'oponopono* (chap. 8), and the Trobriand land litigation studied by Hutchins (1980). Focused ethnographic investigations of situated discourse should prove to be a fruitful source of insight into the conceptual organization of ethnopsychologies as well as the social organization of talking about persons and social events.

The following chapters are arranged according to their scope, rather than by ethnographic area. Chapters 2 through 6 are broad studies of emotion categories and the formulation of identity in social process. They have varied orientations and goals, but are similar in approaching their topics with surveys of the range of experience attributed to actors. In Chapters 7 through 9, particular events and topics emerge as foci for study: a case study of self-destructive behavior, processes of alleviating social and emotional disorder, and displays of anger and power. Chapter 10 synthesizes these two approaches nicely, for Fajans studies experiences of social disengagement yet integrates them into a larger model of the functioning of emotion categories and the like in a total social system.

Ito (chap. 8), Kirkpatrick (chap. 3), and Gerber (chap. 4) deal with Polynesian societies (Hawaii and the Marquesas in Eastern Polynesia, Samoa in the west). Lutz (chap. 2) and Black (chap. 7) deal with Micronesian atoll societies. The other ethnographic chapters are based on work in Melanesia, Schieffelin (chap. 5) and Poole (chap. 6) dealing with inland groups of New Guinea and Fajans (chap. 10) and White (chap. 9) dealing with island societies. These divisions suggest some commonalities and mask others. Certainly the emphasis on personal vulnerability evident in accounts of Bimin-Kuskusmin and A'ara has a Melanesian flavor, as does the Kaluli posture of assertion, echoed in Bimin-Kuskusmin. But many concepts, assumptions, and interpretive procedures are not restricted to one area or another. Notions of "concern" are salient from the Marquesas to Ifaluk. The assumption that sociability and relatedness underlie personal existence is exemplified among the Baining and Hawaiians, at opposite ends of the Pacific, and found more generally in notions of selfhood as fundamentally interpersonal. Attempts to dispel emotional conflict are institutionalized in Santa Isabel hamlets and Honolulu apartments. Again, such developmental themes as the emergence of shame from fearlike sensations are found in many of the case studies. We suspect that some recurrent emphases—views of emotions as more true or real in performance than if merely internal (see especially chap. 5) and presuppositions of human sociability—are widespread in the Pacific area. Whether these commonalities are areal ones, typical of small-scale societies, or panhuman themes will only be clear after much more research.

The diverse methodological approaches embodied in different chapters of this volume cover much of the range of approaches to ethnopsychological interpretation which seem fruitful. In line with our intent, to demonstrate the pervasiveness and interconnectedness of ethnopsychological formulations in social life, these chapters are generally broad in scope and do not deal solely with a single concept or interactive scene. Some contributors focus on a few situations, treating experience as contextually grounded, above all. Others place more emphasis on broad cultural understandings, treating situated interactions as scenes for the realization of central concepts and recurrent interpretive routines. Some view ethnopsychologies as needing explication in terms of holistic systems. Others emphasize the confluence of recurrent interpretive strategies, cultural codes, uncertainty, and human creativity in persons' acts of making sense.

Case studies, as in Black's account of an attempted suicide (chap. 7), demonstrate the effectiveness of focusing observation on events that stimulate people to formulate their assumptions about persons and social behavior. At the other methodological extreme, explicit models of ideology (chap. 3), of the structuring of social process and interpretation (chap. 10), and of the interaction of biological and cultural components of emotions (chap. 4) can function as formal semantic inquiries do, to uncover connections that may go unmentioned in social life. We offer no single method for discerning how people make sense of their own, and others', personhood. Instead, we wish to show the fruitfulness of diverse methodologies and the necessity of approaching ethnopsychological interpretation through accounts grounded in ordinary language and everyday events. We hope to learn not only, as Frake (1964) teaches us, how to ask for a drink but how people come to intend to live their lives.

ACKNOWLEDGMENTS

This chapter has profited greatly from many of the ideas and insights that emerged from discussions with the contributors to this volume and others who participated in the ethnopsychology symposia at the annual meetings of the Association for Social Anthropology in Oceania. We would also like to acknowledge the thoughtful criticisms and comments on this chapter given by Ray Fogelson and Donald Tuzin, although we alone are responsible for its content.

REFERENCES

Asch, S. E.
    1958   The Metaphor: A Psychological Inquiry. *In* Person Perception and Interpersonal Behavior. R. Tagiuri and L. Petrullo, eds. Pp. 86–94. Stanford: Stanford University Press.
Augé, M.
    1975   Théorie des pouvoirs et idéologie. Paris: Hermann.
Averill, J. R.
    1980   A Constructivist View of Emotion. *In* Emotion: Theory, Research and Experience. R. Plutchik and H. Kellerman, eds. New York: Academic Press.
Bateson, G.
    1956   Naven. Stanford: Stanford University Press. Rev. ed.

1972   Steps to an Ecology of Mind. New York: Ballantine.
Benedict, R.
1934   Patterns of Culture. Boston: Houghton Mifflin.
1946   The Chrysanthemum and the Sword. New York: World.
Berlin, B., D. E. Breedlove, and P. H. Raven
1973   General Principles of Classification and Nomenclature in Folk Biology. American Anthropologist 75:214–242.
Bourdieu, P.
1966   The Sentiment of Honour in Kabyle Society. *In* Honour and Shame: The Values of Mediterranean Society. J. G. Persitany, ed. Pp. 191–242. Chicago: University of Chicago Press.
Brown, C. H., and S. Witkowski
1981   Figurative Language in a Universalist Perspective. American Ethnologist 8:596–615.
Caughey, J. L.
1980   Personal Identity and Social Organization. Ethos 8:173–203.
Colby, B. N., J. Fernandez, and D. B. Kronenfeld
1981   Towards a Convergence of Cognitive and Symbolic Anthropology. American Ethnologist 8:422–450.
Crapanzano, V.
1981   Text, Transference and Indexicality. Ethos 9:122–148.
D'Andrade, R. G.
1984   Cultural Meaning Systems. *In* Culture Theory: Essays on Mind, Self and Emotion. R. A. Shweder and R. A. LeVine, eds. New York: Cambridge University Press.
1985   Character Terms and Cultural Models. *In* Directions in Cognitive Anthropology. J. Dougherty, ed. Urbana: University of Illinois.
Detienne, M., and J. P. Vernant
1978   Cunning Intelligence in Greek Culture and Society. Janet Lloyd, trans. Atlantic Highlands, N.J.: Humanities Press. (Original French edition published in 1974.)
DeVos, G. A.
1973   Socialization for Achievement. Berkeley, Los Angeles, London: University of California Press.
Dodds, E. R.
1951   The Greeks and the Irrational. Berkeley: University of California Press.
Doi, T.
1973   The Anatomy of Dependence. John Bester, trans. Tokyo: Kodansha.
Dougherty, J. (ed.)
1985   Directions in Cognitive Anthropology. Urbana: University of Ilinois.
Dubois, C.
1960   The People of Alor. Cambridge: Harvard University Press. Rev. ed.
Dumont, L.
1970*a*   Homo Hierarchicus. Mark Sainsbury, trans. Chicago: University of Chicago Press. (Original French edition published 1966.)
1970*b*   Religion/Politics and History in India. Paris and the Hague: Mouton.

1977   From Mandeville to Marx. Chicago: University of Chicago Press.
1978   La Communauté anthropologique et l'idéologie. L'Homme 18:83–110.
Durkheim, E.
1898   Représentations individuelles et représentations collectives. Revue de
        métaphysique et de morale 6:273–302.
Ekman, P.
1973   Cross-Cultural Studies of Facial Expression. In Darwin and Facial
        Expression. P. Ekman, ed. New York: Academic Press.
Feld, S.
1982   Sound and Sentiment: Birds, Weeping, Poetics and Song in Kaluli Ex-
        pression. Philadelphia: University of Pennsylvania Press.
Frake, C.
1964   How to Ask for a Drink in Subanun. American Anthropologist 66 (pt.
        2):127–132.
1977   Plying Frames Can Be Dangerous: Some Reflections on Methodology
        in Cognitive Anthropology. The Quarterly Newsletter of the Institute
        for Comparative Human Development 1:1–7.
Gearing, F.
1970   The Face of the Fox. Chicago: Aldine.
Geertz, C.
1973   Person, Time and Conduct in Bali. In The Interpretation of Cultures.
        Pp. 360–411. New York: Basic Books.
1976   "From the Native's Point of View": On the Nature of Anthropological
        Understanding. In Meaning in Anthropology. K. H. Basso and H. A.
        Selby, eds. Albuquerque: University of New Mexico Press.
Gerber, E.
1976   The Cultural Patterning of Emotion in Samoa. Ph.D. diss., University
        of California, San Diego.
Gladwin, T., and S. B. Sarason
1953   Truk: Man in Paradise. Viking Fund Publications in Anthropology, no.
        20. New York: Wenner-Gren Foundation.
Hall, E. T.
1976   Beyond Culture. Garden City, N.Y.: Doubleday Anchor.
Hallowell, A. I.
1955   Culture and Experience. Philadelphia: University of Pennsylvania Press.
1960   Ojibwa Ontology, Behavior, and World View. In Culture in History.
        Stanley Diamond, ed. New York: Columbia University Press.
Heelas, P., and A. Lock (eds.)
1981   Indigenous Psychologies: The Anthropology of the Self. London:
        Academic Press.
Heider, F.
1958   The Psychology of Interpersonal Relations. New York: J. Wiley and
        Sons.
Howard, A.
1974   Ain't No Big Thing: Coping Strategies in a Hawaiian-American Com-
        munity. Honolulu: University Press of Hawaii.

Hunn, E.
1976   Toward a Perceptual Model of Folk Biological Classification. American Ethnologist 3:508–524.
1979   The Abominations of Leviticus Revisited. *In* Classifications in their Social Context. Roy F. Ellen and David Reason, eds. Pp. 103–116. London: Academic Press.
Hutchins, E.
1980   Culture and Inference: A Trobriand Case Study. Cambridge: Harvard University Press.
Kardiner, A.
1939   The Individual and his Society. New York: Columbia University Press.
Keeler, W.
1983   Shame and Stagefright in Java. Ethos 11:152–165.
Keesing, R.
1979   Linguistic Knowledge and Cultural Knowledge: Some Doubts and Speculations. American Anthropologist 81:14–36.
Kelley, H. H.
1967   Attribution Theory in Social Psychology. *In* Nebraska Symposium on Motivation. Pp. 192–238. Lincoln: University of Nebraska Press.
Kirkpatrick, J.
1981   Appeals for 'Unity' in Marquesan Local Politics. Journal of the Polynesian Society 90:439–464.
1983   The Marquesan Notion of the Person. Ann Arbor: UMI Research Press.
Kretzmann, N.
1967   History of Semantics. *In* The Encyclopedia of Philosophy 7:358–406. New York: Macmillan.
Kroeber, A. L.
1948   Anthropology. New York: Harcourt, Brace.
Laboratory of Comparative Human Cognition
1978   Cognition as a Residual Category in Anthropology. Annual Review of Anthropology 7:51–69.
Lakoff, G., and M. Johnson
1980   Metaphors We Live By. Chicago: University of Chicago Press.
Lebra, T. S.
1976   Japanese Patterns of Behavior. Honolulu: University Press of Hawaii.
Lee, B. (ed.)
1982   Psychosocial Theories of the Self. New York: Plenum.
LeVine, R.
1980   Adulthood among the Gusii of Kenya. *In* Themes of Love and Work in Adulthood. Neil J. Smelser and Erik H. Erikson, eds. Cambridge: Harvard University Press.
1983   The Self in Culture. *In* Culture, Behavior and Personality. Revised Edition. Chicago: Aldine.
Levy, R. I.
1973   Tahitians: Mind and Experience in the Society Islands. Chicago: University of Chicago Press.

Lutz, C.
   1982   The Domain of Emotion Words on Ifaluk Atoll. American Ethnologist
           9:113–128.
Malinowski, B.
   1927   Sex and Repression in Savage Society. London: International Library of
           Psychology, Philosophy and Scientific Method.
Mauss, M.
   1938   Une catégorie de l'esprit humain: la notion de personne, celle de 'moi'.
           Journal of the Royal Anthropological Institute 68:263–281.
Mead, M.
   1928a   Coming of Age in Samoa. New York: Morrow.
   1928b   The Role of the Individual in Samoan Culture. Journal of the Royal
           Anthropological Institute 58:481–495.
   1930   Growing Up in New Guinea. New York: Morrow.
   1935   Sex and Temperament in Three Primitive Societies. New York: Mor-
           row.
Miller, G. A., E. Galanter, and K. H. Pribram
   1960   Plans and the Structure of Behavior. New York: Holt, Rinehart and
           Winston.
Murphy, J. M.
   1976   Psychiatric Labeling in Cross-Cultural Perspective. Science 191:1019–
           1028.
Myers, F. R.
   1979   Emotions and the Self: A Theory of Personhood and Political Order
           among Pintupi Aborigines. Ethos 7:343–370.
Nisbett, R., and L. Ross
   1980   Human Inference: Strategies and Shortcomings of Social Judgment.
           Englewood Cliffs, N.J.: Prentice-Hall.
Quinn, N.
   1982   "Commitment" in American Marriage: A Cultural Analysis. American
           Ethnologist 9:775–798.
Rabinow, P., and W. Sullivan (eds.)
   1979   Interpretive Social Science. Berkeley, Los Angeles, London: University
           of California Press.
Read, K. E.
   1955   Morality and the Concept of the Person Among the Gahuku-Gama.
           Oceania 25:233–282.
Redfield, J. M.
   1975   Nature and Culture in the Iliad. Chicago: University of Chicago Press.
Reisman, P.
   1977   Freedom in Fulani Social Life: An Introspective Ethnography. Chicago:
           University of Chicago Press.
Rorty, A. O.
   1976   A Literary Postscript: Characters, Persons, Selves, Individuals. *In* The
           Identities of Persons. Amelie O. Rorty, ed. Pp. 301–324. Berkeley, Los

Angeles, London: University of California Press.

Rosaldo, M. Z.
1980   Knowledge and Passion: Ilongot Notions of Self and Social Life. Cam-
        bridge: Cambridge University.

Sapir, E.
1949   The Emergence of the Concept of Personality in a Study of Cultures.
        In Selected Writings of Edward Sapir. David G. Mandelbaum, ed. Pp.
        590–600. Berkeley: University of California Press.

Sapir, J. D., and J. C. Crocker (eds.)
1977   The Social Use of Metaphor: Essays on the Anthropology of Rhetoric.
        Philadelphia: University of Pennsylvania Press.

Schachter, S., and J. E. Singer
1962   Cognitive, Social and Physiological Determinants of Emotional State.
        Psychological Review 69:379–399.

Schieffelin, B.
1979   Getting It Together: An Ethnographic Approach to the Study of the
        Development of Communicative Competence. *In* Developmental Prag-
        matics. E. Ochs and B. Schieffelin, eds. New York: Academic Press.
1982   How Kaluli Children Learn What to Say, What to Do and How to Feel.
        New York: Cambridge University Press.

Selby, H. A.
1974   Zapotec Deviance. Austin: University of Texas Press.
1975   Semantics and Causality in the Study of Deviance. *In* Sociocultural
        Dimensions of Language Use. Mary Sanches and Ben G. Blount, eds.
        Pp. 11–24. New York: Academic Press.

Shweder, R. A., and E. J. Bourne
1982   Does the Concept of the Person Vary Cross-Culturally? *In* Cultural
        Conceptions of Mental Health and Therapy. A. J. Marsella and G. M.
        White, eds. Pp. 97–137. Dordrecht: D. Reidel.

Shweder, R. A., and R. G. D'Andrade
1980   The Systematic Distortion Hypothesis. *In* Fallible Judgment in Be-
        havioral Research: New Directions for Methodology of Social and
        Behavioral Science, no. 4. R. Shweder, ed. San Francisco: Jossey-Bass.

Shweder, R. A., and R. A. LeVine (eds.)
1984   Culture Theory: Essays on Mind, Self and Emotion. New York: Cam-
        bridge University Press.

Singer, M.
1953   Shame Cultures and Guilt Cultures. *In* Shame and Guilt. Gerhart Piers
        and Milton Singer, eds. Springfield, Ill.: Charles G. Thomas.

Spiro, M. E.
1961   An Overview and Suggested Reorientation. *In* Psychological Anthropol-
        ogy: Approaches to Culture and Personality. F. L. K. Hsu, ed. Pp.
        459–492. Homewood, Ill.: Dorsey Press.

Strathern, A. J.
1975   Why is Shame on the Skin? Ethnology 14:347–356.

1981   Noman: Representations of Identity in Mount Hagen. *In* The Structure of Folk Models. L. Holy and M. Stuchlik, eds. ASA Monograph no. 20. Pp. 281–303. London: Academic Press.
Strathern, M.
1968   Popokl: The Question of Morality. Mankind 6:553–562.
Straus, A. S.
1977   Northern Cheyenne Ethnopsychology. Ethos 5:326–357.
Turner, V.
1967   The Forest of Symbols. Ithaca: Cornell University Press.
Tversky, A., and D. Kahneman
1977   Causal Schemata in Judgments Under Uncertainty. *In* Progress in Social Psychology. M. Fishbein, ed. Hillsdale, N.J.: Erlbaum Press.
Tyler, S.
1978   The Said and the Unsaid: Mind, Meaning and Culture. New York: Academic Press.
Wallace, A. F. C.
1958   Dreams and Wishes of the Soul: A Type of Psychoanalytic Theory Among the Seventeenth Century Iroquois. American Anthropologist 60:234–248.
Wason, P. C., and P. N. Johnson-Laird
1972   Psychology of Reasoning: Structure and Content. Cambridge: Harvard University Press.
Waxler, N. E.
1974   Culture and Mental Illness: A Social Labeling Perspective. Journal of Nervous and Mental Disease 159:379–395.
White, G. M.
1980   Conceptual Universals in Interpersonal Language. American Anthropologist 82:759–781.
1982   The Ethnographic Study of Cultural Knowledge of "Mental Disorder." *In* Cultural Conceptions of Mental Health and Therapy. A. J. Marsella and G. M. White, eds. Pp. 69–95. Dordrecht: D. Reidel.
1985   'Bad Ways' and 'Bad Talk': Interpretations of Interpersonal Conflict in a Melanesian Society. *In* Directions in Cognitive Anthropology. J. Dougherty, ed. Urbana: University of Illinois.
Whiting, J. W. M.
1941   Becoming a Kwoma. New Haven: Yale University Press.

Part II
Identity, Emotion, and Social Process

2

Ethnopsychology Compared to What? Explaining Behavior and Consciousness Among the Ifaluk

Catherine Lutz

INTRODUCTION

The description of ethnopsychological knowledge systems is based on the premise that people in every society have developed some shared understandings surrounding aspects of personal and social life, aspects that for heuristic purposes may be termed 'psychological'. As has been the case in the study of indigenous conceptualizations of such things as plants, history, and medicine, however, it has been necessary to recognize the danger (which is involved in naming a domain) of setting rigid or a priori boundaries to indigenous thought systems. Although we may find the rubrics of 'ethnopsychology', 'ethnosociology', or 'ethnoepistemology' useful starting points for ethnographic analysis given our understandings of the "domains" of knowledge, boundaries separating such fields may be nonexistent or differentially construed in other cultural systems. Most of the chapters in this volume, in fact, demonstrate the interpenetration of concepts of the person with virtually every other aspect of cultural knowledge, from that concerning the division of labor to that of the political arena. The term 'psychology' is appropriate, however, insofar as we are concerned with cultural constructions of particular persons as well as of human nature. I will begin, then, with the definitional premise that ethnopsychology is concerned with the way in which people conceptualize, monitor, and discuss their own and others' mental processes, behavior, and relationships. All ethnotheories explain some aspect of variability in the world; ethnopsychologies explain inter- and intrapersonal variation, and they both construct and result from people's observations of changes in consciousness, action, and relationships.

Ethnopsychological knowledge in human cultures has been related to the necessities of prediction and morality. In the first case, theories about human nature and human variation enable people to make "inferences about the interrelation of actors' goals, intentions, and abilities" and "to formulate probable courses of social action" (White 1980:767). In this way, ethnopsychological theory makes the behavior of others more predictable. Predictability, in turn, facilitates the coordination of plans and behavior, thereby enhancing the possibility of social order. The existence of ethnopsychological theory is also required by Hallowell's argument that self-awareness and concepts of the person are universal, while at the same time being cultural phenomena (Hallowell 1955, 1960). Without some notion of the self as distinct from other selves and objects, the creation, perception, and enactment of a human social and moral order would be impossible. However, cultural variability appears to exist not only in the contents of self-awareness and person concepts but also in the degree to which this awareness is itself monitored, emphasized as salient, and explicitly discussed in everyday discourse.

This chapter examines the ethnopsychology of the Ifaluk of Micronesia and suggests links between their interpretive system, cultural values, and material conditions. In the limited space available and in the interest of broad and maximal comparability with the other Oceanic ethnopsychologies represented in this volume, only a bare and abstract outline of what is a rich, varied, contextualized, and changing body of knowledge can be presented. It is particularly disappointing to have to set aside presentation of many of the accounts of events and statements and behavior and omissions which are the source of most of the ethnographic statements made here. Ifaluk ethnotheory is more than simply a set of propositions about experience. As Wallace has pointed out, an ethnopsychological frame of reference "is not merely a philosophical by-product of each culture, like a shadow, but the very skeleton of concrete cognitive assumptions on which the flesh of behavior is hung" (1970:143). Before going on to describe this knowledge system, several methodological issues need to be raised. These include the role of comparison in ethnopsychological description and evidence for the existence of indigenous psychologies.

Compared to What? Academic Psychology
as Ethnopsychology

Anthropological description usually operates by means of implicit rather than explicit contrast of the culture of the observed with the culture of the observer. The general tendency to leave this contrast an implicit one has roots in diverse epistemological and theoretical assumptions that cannot be examined here. However, it should be noted that both psychological and ethnopsychological anthropology have likewise failed to engage in an explicit discussion of the question, Compared to what? That nonreflexive approaches have been predominant is not surprising if one notes both the historical and cultural traditions in which the study of society arose as well as George Herbert Mead's insight that consciousness of others necessarily precedes consciousness of self. Thus, historically, the anthropological encounter is first construed as a question about the other before it can be seen that "the others and the self arise in the social act *together*" (Mead 1932:169; emphasis added; also see Crapanzano 1980).

Traditional culture and personality studies have described non-Western[1] peoples within the framework of an implicit comparison with Western psychological and behavioral norms. If, for example, the handling of children in one culture is described as 'indulgent', that statement is equally one about the nonindulgence of Euro-American children. If the Japanese are said to be quick to 'shame', that is also a description of how the ethnographer does *not* see her or himself. In attempting to examine the unspoken comparisons involved in studies that portray themselves as either scientific psychology or ethnopsychology, the first question that arises is, To what exactly are we comparing other cultures' psychologies? The Western anthropologist obviously draws on her or his own folk theory. The task for a comparative ethnopsychological approach, then, is to identify the sources and varieties of ethnotheory in the cultures of both the observed *and* the observer. (My use of single quotes for Western theoretical terms is intended to highlight the point that terms from a particular cultural tradition, not a culture-free science, are being used.)

While sometimes criticizing the lack of a cross-cultural perspective in academic psychology, anthropologists have nonetheless tended to see it as a Science dealing with real underlying psychological processes. There is much evidence, however, that the concerns, research questions, and unexamined first assumptions of academic psychologies are deeply rooted in the cultural traditions in which they arise. This relationship has been demonstrated in the areas of developmental psychology (LeVine 1980:77–81), cognitive psychology (Goodnow 1976), including Piagetian theory (Buck-

Morss 1975) and the psychology of intelligence (Lutz and LeVine 1983), trait psychology (D'Andrade 1974), psychiatric diagnosis (Gaines 1982), and social psychology (Gergen 1973, 1979). Nonetheless, academic psychology in the United States is a distinct historical institution whose current degree of integration with lay ethnopsychology is an empirical question. As Sanjek (1978) has noted, in literate cultures with a centralized state the official-legal taxonomy and, we may add by extension, the varieties of "official" psychology are not necessarily coterminous with the popular taxonomy. The examination of ethnopsychology would then involve looking at both written and unwritten psychologies and at the contexts in which the various systems of meaning interact.

As Geertz (1976), Straus (1977), Rosaldo (1980), and others have pointed out, our Western ideas and intuitions about the nature of the person may be cross-culturally unique. Many of the ethnopsychological categories and dichotomies with which Western cultures have been concerned are reflected directly in current academic discourse—psychological, anthropological, and otherwise. The dichotomies include especially the sharp opposition of the individual to the social which is reflected in the existence of the separate disciplines of psychology and anthropology; the concern with a subjective versus an objective reality evident in the distinction between ethnopsychology and psychology; the analytic separation of thought and action (Jenkins 1981) evident in the distinction between 'competence' and 'performance' and in the myriad debates and the boundaries between cognitive and behavioral psychology; the separation of the rational and cognitive from the irrational and emotional exemplified in the common assumption that problem solving and information processing fall exclusively within the cognitive domain; and, finally, the dimension that runs from the private to the public evident in the ethos and methods of clinical psychologists on the one hand and cognitive and experimental psychologists on the other.[2]

One slightly more detailed example can illustrate this point further. Academic psychology has taken English emotion words (such as 'fear', 'love', 'anger', and 'disgust'), has reified what are essentially American ethnopsychological concepts, and has accepted them, often unquestioned, as the conceptual apparatus of scientific inquiry. Given this limited cultural base, it would be surprising if the emotions, exactly as distinguished, conceptualized, and experienced in American society, emerge as universals. Exactly this has been assumed, however, and then 'proven' by Western researchers (Ekman 1974; Sorenson 1976). While it has been considered of great importance to ascertain whether some non-Western peoples 'feel guilt', the question does not arise as to whether Americans experience the New Guinea Hageners' emotion of *popokl* 'outrage over the failure of others to recognize one's claims' (Strathern 1968) or whether they are deficient in the ability to experience the Ifaluk emotion of *fago* 'compassion/love/sadness'.[3]

Further Methodological Considerations in Ethnopsychological Description

The methods that can be used to investigate and describe ethnopsychological theory are neither less varied nor, as Rosaldo has pointed out (1980:62), more complex than those which can be used to investigate other aspects of culture. The task of ethnopsychological study is to examine both what people say and do in everyday life which indicates that a cultural knowledge system for interpreting self and other is at work.

The ethnographer's acquisition of language skills is the first and most significant way in which the learning of ethnopsychological knowledge takes place. Several aspects of language are methodological entrées into such cultural knowledge systems. First, the lexicon of the self and interaction provides evidence about the concepts underlying ethnopsychological understanding. In the present study, the question of the meaning and translation of those terms was taken as the primary and logically prior question. The similarities and differences between, for example, the Ifaluk state term *fago* and the English terms 'compassion', 'love', and 'sadness' are at the core of ethnopsychological description/comparison (Lutz 1980). Also of methodological interest is the centrality or salience of particular ethnopsychological concepts within the wider cultural system. Quinn (1982) has shown the value of an analysis of the key words of particular knowledge domains in demonstrating the range and depth of meaning such words can communicate. In describing ethnopsychological concepts, it is of particular importance to note the salience or resonance of particular words within the knowledge system.

Beyond the lexicon of the self, the metaphors and modifiers used in talking about human functioning are important routes to an understanding of ethnopsychological conceptualizations. Lakoff and Johnson (1980) have argued that metaphors constitute one of the most fundamental ways in which people understand the world. By linking experience-near concepts, such as the spatial and ontological, with experience-far concepts (Geertz 1976), understanding is enabled or enhanced. As ethnopsychological concepts are often abstract to a degree that plants and colors are not, metaphors will frequently be used in attempts to understand and communicate the experience of self and other.

Finally, and perhaps more problematic, is the ethnopsychological proposition (Lutz, in press). Words descriptive of self and other constitute the primary elements from which ethnopsychological statements are built. These statements may be heard in natural conversation, or they may be presented to the ethnographer. They may be either general in form—"Some people are hot-tempered"—or particular—"She will go crazy if you hit her." Speech is naturally shorthand, however; there are many unspoken assumptions involved in conversations about self and others. These assumptions serve as the basis on which the hearer (including the ethnographer) makes sense of discourse. Thus, ethnopsychological knowledge is evident both in what is said and in what is not said (Tyler 1978). Since the inferences people make upon hearing a statement are based on culturally provided knowledge (Hutchins 1980), the attempt to understand why one statement (or action) follows the next is a crucial method for the study of ethnopsychology. Where some of the most vexing methodological problems arise is in validating our descriptions of implicit ethnopsychological propositions. An overly quick move to examine the supposedly implicit ethnopsychology of a people runs the danger of becoming culture and personality in a new guise, with our own ethnopsychological inference-making abilities taking over. However, the use of implicit knowledge can be convincingly demonstrated by reference to commonly occurring sequences of verbal and nonverbal behavior in everyday contexts.

In what contexts are ethnopsychological propositions evident? Black (1978) has pointed out that we observe ethnopsychology in the course, particularly, of public attempts to modify deviant behavior, as, for example, during dispute settlement. Given the ubiquity of deviance and of concern with defining and dealing with it, this is a particularly important theoretical and methodological framework for examining ethnopsychologies. Black has also pointed out here (chap. 7) that it is the negotiation of meaning that is observed by the ethnographer. What is usually at debate, then, is not the validity of the ethnopsychological tenet itself but rather the applicability of particular propositions about self and other *to a particular case.* This is not to say that ethnopsychological propositions are absolute, unchanging, or unambiguous 'rules' to which people unambivalently subscribe; culture is obviously structured by events as well as structuring them. In observing the negotiation process, we can attempt to discover both the criteria for making decisions about the applicability of widely shared propositions as well as the emergence of ethnopsychological meaning.

Additional methodological issues include the description of cultural and cognitive diversity in this domain and elucidation of the uses of ethnotheory, or the contexts in which it is produced and the purposes for which it is used. Questions of method surround the following aspects of particular ethnopsychological propositions: (1) the degree to which they are shared by all or some members of the community; (2) the historical context, or the manner in which propositions develop and change in tandem with changing environmental conditions and resultant changes in the issues that the domain must address; (3) the restriction of their expression or the change in their meaning in some particular contexts within a society as opposed to others (Kirk and Burton 1977; White 1978); and (4) the degree to which they are salient and in daily use or, conversely, a post hoc response (however culturally appropriate) to the ethnographer's concern with the subject.[4] Each of the above issues can fall under the rubric of the ecology of ethnopsychological knowledge insofar as they all concern its context-sensitive appearance. The systematicness with which the ecology of inter-personal behavior has been researched (Whiting and Whiting 1975) needs to be duplicated in this realm.

SOME IFALUK SETTINGS

Ifaluk atoll, with a population of 430, is located nearly 500 miles from both Yap and Truk in the West Caroline Islands of Micronesia.[5] A person on Ifaluk typically has been born and will die within the bounds of the atoll's one-half square mile. If female, she has probably never left the island. For a male the boundaries of experience may extend much farther as a result of sailing trips to nearby atolls, labor on other, more distant Micronesian islands, or attendance at high school on the atoll of Ulithi. A person is born in one of the atoll's four villages, but may shift homestead and village residence several times over the life course—at the age of about three if she or he is adopted and at marriage if male, as postmarital residence is matri-local. Each person is born into her or his mother's clan. Four of the atoll's clans are headed by hereditary chiefs, and each person knows her or his clan, lineage, and individual ranking in relation to others.

At the age of twenty-five a woman lives in a household that probably consists of about thirteen people, including her parents, her sisters (both uterine and adoptive) and their husbands, unmarried brothers, and several of her children and her sisters'. Some of her brothers' children and those of more distant kin have also likely been adopted into the household. Her husband, older sons, and, occasionally, her brothers will fish for her. All of the males in her village may fish together on occasion, and some of the fish will be sent to her homestead. On most days, the males of her household are to be found in the shoreside canoe houses making rope, working at canoe building, or planning communal work.

The woman spends much time at the task of cultivating taro in the several patches of interior swamp that she owns. Otherwise, she will be found preparing food, including breadfruit, coconut, and rice (the latter sent as typhoon relief by the U.S. government), as well as taro and fish, or weaving clothes. The cloth that she weaves will be either for her own wear or for offering on occasions such as funerals. On most days, she sends her toddlers with her husband to the canoe house; her infant may be with her or at the home of the adoptive parents for the daylight hours. By sunset, other members of the household have returned. After dinner, the remainder of the evening is spent in the telling of both new and old stories.

PERSON, SELF, AND OTHER: CATEGORIES OF AGENTS AND VARIATION IN CONSCIOUSNESS

In the initial definition of ethnopsychological knowledge, variation in behavior and consciousness within and across persons was presented as the object of ethnotheoretical explanation. It will be helpful to begin, then, by describing the class of actors whose behavior is explained in everyday life. Second, the universal distinction between self and other can be explored by an examination of differences in ways of speaking about the two.[6] And finally, variation in conscious experience within the individual is noted in Ifaluk ethnotheory and can be described as an aspect of self-awareness.

Personhood

There are three fundamental categories of actors in the behavioral environment of the Ifaluk: *yaremat* 'human persons', *yalus* 'spirits', and the Catholic God (also called yalus, or, more occasionally, *got*).[7] The 'human person' is said to first come into existence at about the sixth or seventh month after conception, as it is at this point that a miscarried fetus first looks physically human. The term *yaremat,* however, does not refer to this period in contrast to the earlier fetal period; rather, the contrast is drawn between 'human persons' and 'spirits'. There is great concern to distinguish any particular actor as a member of one of the two categories. This is indicated by the question frequently asked in legends by protagonists in their encounters with others, "Are you a spirit or are you a human person?" A very few anomalous individuals who are not considered to fall clearly into one category (e.g., an albino woman) have been the topic of much discussion and some anxiety. The need to distinguish between human persons and spirits follows from differences in what one can expect from encounters with each of the two.

The spirit differs from the human person primarily in terms of power and intentions. Although particular spirits may be either benevolent or malevolent, named or unnamed, ancestors or not, in general they are much more likely to intend harm or cause fright than are humans. They do, however, share many of the motivations and traits that the latter can have: they can be envious, righteously indignant, or compassionate, and, in the case of ancestor spirits, retain the personal characteristics that they were identified as having when alive. The Catholic God, in contrast, can be expected to consistently behave in an exemplary way that epitomizes Ifaluk values of sharing, concern for the welfare of others, and benevolent authority. In these respects, God is conceptualized as being motivated in much the same way as are chiefs on the island.

Although people make attempts to minimize contact with spirits, the thoughts and feelings of both human and nonhuman actors are believed to be fairly easily transmitted and to readily affect others. The special power of the spirits means that such interpsychic communication and influence tend to run in one direction—that is, from spirits to humans. Spirits are known to cause certain types of dreams as well as certain illnesses. The arena of illness and the arena of the dream are not enclosed within the self (although it is the self which is aware of them), and spirits can therefore freely enter those arenas and influence the course of events. As will be seen, other human persons can likewise cross what are considered private and less penetrable boundaries in Western conceptions.

The term *yaremat* is most frequently used in simple reference to individuals, as in "Who are those two human persons over there?" The term is also used rhetorically in situations where an individual feels that she or he has not received the treatment to which all persons are entitled. Thus, in one case, a person who had not been asked to share in the consumption of food by some people nearby asked a sympathetic listener, "Aren't I a human person?" 'Human persons' are not, therefore, simply the class of human agents; they are also the class to which certain types of behavior, including particularly nurturant and other inclusionary practices, *should be* accorded. Although there are recognized varieties of people, some of whom are seen as having mild to severe character and performance defects, ideally each would be considered a 'human person'.

Within the class of persons, then, how are self and other distinguished? The point at which the self stops and the other begins is neither fixed nor conceptualized as an impermeable wall. It is considered natural that one person's thought should influence another's. People are frequently characterized as 'following the thoughts/feelings' of others; in so following, they take on the attitudes, angers, or plans of the other. Similarly, the sources of behavior are seen as multiple and interpersonal and are not to be found exclusively at any independent or central part of the self. Although, as will be seen, a very important source of behavior is the individual will, the

mature self is one that is moved quite directly by others. Pronoun forms
in language can take on psychological and symbolic importance as markers
of the boundary and relations between self and others (see White, chap. 9).
Through these forms, people on Ifaluk place strong emphasis on perceived
or desired similarities between self and other. In relation to agentive pronouns, most striking is the frequent use of 'we' (inclusive) where 'I' might
have been used in American English discourse. In one of the initial weeks
of my stay on the island, I asked a group of young women visiting my
hut, "Do you [all] want to come with me to get drinking water?" Faces
fell, and I realized with later experience and reflection that my pronouns
were at fault, failing, as they did, to simply assume an isomorphism between
myself the speaker and the hearers. The usual and more correct form of the
question above would be, "We'll go get water now, O.K.?" The use of the
first person plural is nearly as common as that of the first person singular
in statements about mental events. On observing something unusual, a
person would be more likely to say, "We [speaker and listener] don't know
what's going on here" than "I don't know what's going on here." "We are
worried" is as likely to be heard as "I am worried." In the case of the
emotion word *fago* (compassion/love/sadness), the use of the first person
plural is more common than that of any other pronoun.

First person pronouns are, by definition, egocentric; they are used by
the speaker to frame all statements from his or her own viewpoint. When
the 'we' rather than the 'I' form is used, as it frequently is on Ifaluk, this
is strong evidence that the relevent viewpoint is taken to be that of the
group rather than the individual. The implications of this distinction may
be variable across contexts and cultures using the same pronoun forms. For
example, in the case of the use of the term 'compassion/love/sadness',
which refers to a very socially desirable emotion, to say "I feel compassion/
love/sadness for that person" may risk the interpretation of that statement
as a boastful one, which puts the self apart from and above others. In
another of the above examples, to say "I am going to get water" may
communicate an intention of striking out on one's own, without regard for
the needs of others, either for water or for companionship. It could also
result, in fact, in one's going for water alone, a prospect associated with
'boredom', 'loneliness' (people are assumed to virtually always want the
company of others), or 'fear' (of ghost encounters). Although the "interconnectedness" of self and other which White (chap. 9) infers from A'ara
pronoun use may be seen as an aspect of each of the examples here, a further
differentiation, by the context of statements of this sort, reveals how several
ethnopsychological 'principles' can interact in producing the linguistic
forms.

   The relation between selves and material objects is another potentially salient one (Csikszentmihalyi and Rochberg-Halton 1981), and ethnopsychological propositions may emerge as people address the problem in their everyday lives. The values and practices surrounding property ownership on Ifaluk stress egalitarianism and sharing. A person smoking a cigarette will pass it around to as many people as are present. Any great show of magnanimity in sharing is frowned upon, however, as this putting forward of self is seen as denigrating to the other. Any behavior that appears to make a gift out of what is seen as a shared resource is condemned, suggesting as it would that the item was given freely as a matter of choice. Rather, the item should be seen and treated as something that was 'ours' rather than 'mine' to begin with. Food, in particular, is invariably spoken of as 'our food'. But things that everyone possesses to an adequate and equal degree are generally not shared; these would include such things as clothing and bush knives. Such objects take on a special significance in marking out areas of autonomy and assertion of self.[8] Unlike time, labor, or food, these things can be disposed of only by their owner. This aspect of Ifaluk self-awareness was particularly dramatized by the exaggerated extent to which one of the mentally ill men on the island used the possessive during a visit to the house I occupied. His entire conversation consisted of a listing of his possessions, pointing out with emphasis "*my* lighter, *my* knife, *my* basket."

   There are also wider symbolic meanings involved with possessions. Consumable items such as food and tobacco, which are commonly shared and referred to as 'ours', are strongly tied into sociability and affect. To say that we eat together is to say that we are intimates. Clothing, however, not only marks off the physical boundary of the person but also connotes sexuality. Certain terms for male and female clothing, for example, are taboo in mixed company, and clothing should not be seen by those of the opposite gender when it is not being worn. In some respects, sexuality is seen as divisive, possibly creating competition and jealousy as opposed to sociability.

   Although people talk about themselves and others in ways that assume similarities and easy communication between them, it is nonetheless possible to identify differences in the ways in which self and other are spoken about. Other persons are sometimes described by a term from the domain of words for enduring characteristics of persons (see below),[9] although only a small number of the trait terms are used with any regularity for this purpose. By contrast, it is extremely rare to hear people talk of themselves in terms of their own traits or mannerisms. The more frequent descriptions of both self and others focus on the immediate situational sources of action, as in, for example, "She didn't invite me to her birthing because she followed the advice of her husband" or "The child walked away because he is irritated."

Talking about 'Our Insides'

With this outline of the nature of the person and the self-other distinction as it is seen and expressed, we can go on to ask in more detail about the nature of self-awareness, which has been defined here not only as awareness of a distinction between self and other but as awareness of variation in conscious experience. 'Introspection' is the term most frequently used in English for self-examination and its resultant self-awareness. As ethnopsychological knowledge arises in the context of goals, it should first be pointed out that introspection is valued only for certain purposes rather than as an end in itself. In contrast to our own notion of introspection as a potential voyage of 'self-discovery', valid in its own right and as a key to self-knowledge, the Ifaluk stress the moral self-monitoring role of introspection. People are often explicitly advised to "separate the good and the bad" in their minds in order to behave correctly; this requires a type of introspection. Absent is the notion that one should 'know oneself' on basic principle or that one *can* even know oneself outside of the moral and social constraints that sometimes make introspection necessary. The asocial definition of thought and its positive evaluation in Euro-American culture give introspection connotations not found among the Ifaluk, given their conceptions of the person. As will be seen, thinking is in fact sometimes seen as more troublesome than not, and people are advised in such cases to avoid introspection or dwelling on a thought. Of a girl who was homesick for her brother on another island and who went off alone to cry and to think about him, I was told by a somewhat exasperated observer, "She *wants* to think about him."

At the core of Ifaluk ethnopsychology is a set of beliefs about the structure of persons which portray them as undivided entities. In marked contrast to Western ethnopsychology, sharp distinctions are not made between thought and emotion, between the head and the heart, or between a conscious and an unconscious mind. Although some other distinctions can be and are made, both theory and use place more emphasis on the essential internal unity of the person than on her or his compartmentalization. This unity is evident in the way people talk about 'their insides'.

Niferash 'our insides'[10] is the one most general term used to describe the self and it is used to talk about both physiological and psychological structures and functions. 'Our insides' include thoughts, feelings, wishes, desires, illness, and physical sensations. To say "My insides are bad" (Ye ngaw niferai) may mean either that one is feeling physically bad or experiencing bad thoughts and emotions, or both. The exact meaning, as with the English phrase "I feel bad," is determined by context.

There are two primary terms used to describe aspects of 'our insides'— *nunuwan* 'thought/emotion' and *tip-* 'will/emotion/desire'. The following attempt to describe their meanings should *not* give the impression that the terms are seen as referring to two distinct 'entities'. In response to my questions about the differences between the two terms, people most often began with the statement that the two were very similar. Tip- and nunuwan are difficult to distinguish from each other because they are seen as referring to aspects of the same phenomenon. *Nunuwan* refers to mental events ranging from what we consider thought to what we consider emotion. Although the first and tentative translation that nunuwan brought to mind was 'thought', the inadequacy of that gloss soon became evident. The Ifaluk see mental events as value-laden, ideally moral stances, and they do not, for this reason, separate evaluative and emotional responses from nonevaluative and cognitive responses to an environmental event. Thus, *nunuwan* may be translated as 'cold through hot thought', 'hot through cool emotion', or, more simply, as 'thought/emotion'. The following field note entries illustrate the range of uses of the term:

> D. says that people who tease others and children who throw rocks at others do so because their nunuwan is bad.

> B. says that some people are short-tempered because their nunuwan is not good. Their nunuwan is not long.

> R. [a woman whose son had just died] asked for L.'s infant in adoption. Although the baby has already been promised to someone else, L. said, "Our nunuwan will be good if we give the infant to R."

> T. said that if we have bad nunuwan, we will have bad insides, and if we have good nunuwan, we will have good insides.

> [I was] sitting on the ocean side of the island with T. and after some silence she said, "I have lots of nunuwan when I look out over the sea" and then talked about how she doesn't know what she's going to do about adopting out her son who's been promised to a woman on [a distant island].

> A. said that R. [a pregnant woman] has lots of nunuwan because the health aide is leaving on the next ship which is coming, and she [R.] nunuwan that there will be trouble with the delivery of the baby.

It is not simply that thought evokes, or is accompanied by, an emotion; the two are inextricably linked. *Nunuwan* is included in the definitions of various words we would consider emotion words. For example, *yarofali* 'longing/missing' is the state of "continually nunuwan about [for example] one's dead mother." The emotion words themselves may be used to describe nunuwan when the latter is used as a noun, as in the example, "My thoughts/emotions are justifiably angry" (Ye song yaai nunuwan).

As several of these examples illustrate, nunuwan is heavily implicated in morality and maturity. A mature, exemplary person is sometimes characterized as one who has "many nunuwan" (although the same turn of phrase can also refer to the state of being burdened with many thoughts and feelings and attendant indecisiveness). Children and the mentally ill, in contrast, are said to have "only one nunuwan." Deviant behavior may also result from a dearth of nunuwan; in explaining the morally reprehensible behavior of one particular woman, someone told me, "She doesn't nunuwan behind her. She doesn't nunuwan that people will be justifiably angry at her, and so she just does what she wants. She thinks[11] that her nunuwan is the same as [other people's] nunuwan, [but it is not]."

Tip- 'will/emotion/desire' is the second major term descriptive of 'our insides'. This concept is similar to that of nunuwan, but is distinguished by its stronger connotations of desire and movement toward or away from an object. Like the Western concept of will, tip- implies preference and independent choice. A typical definition is the following: "Our tip- is what we want, like to chat with someone or to go visit another village." One of the most common uses for tip- in daily conversation occurs in the context of rank and obedience. Superordinates are regularly asked for permission to do something. If the elder knows of no rule or has no preference to the contrary, he or she will say, "Ye shag tipum,"[12] which is literally "It's just your will," or, in other words, "[In the absence of external constraints], it's up to you." Where social rules or values are not at stake, the person's tip- is granted free shrift. Tip- is not seen as intrinsically dangerous, however; individual will or desire is not seen as inherently antisocial or as necessarily amoral. Rather, it is one of the most important sources of action of all kinds. One's tip- may motivate conversation, dancing, or working in the taro gardens. But personal preference can by no means be the only thing a person considers in making a choice. Failure to behave correctly may be attributed to tip-. For example, a young girl of eight was scolded for failing to go visit her sick relative, and was told that her behavior (and the possible consequences) were due to her tip-.

Tip- is at once the capacity for emotion and the capacity for will. As is the case with nunuwan, one's tip- may be characterized as 'happy' or 'angry'. The fusion of emotion and will in tip- is not the result of a failure to differentiate the concept; rather, the concept is a seamless one because the act of desiring or willing something implies for the Ifaluk either its fulfillment or frustration. The individual will may be thwarted or not. Emotion is not produced as a result—it is inherent in the experience of tip-.

'Thought' and 'will' are not adequate translations for *nunuwan* and *tip-,* respectively, because neither of the latter are seen as emotionally neutral. Both are motivating, and thus help in accounting for behavior. The fact that the Ifaluk distinguish at all between the overlapping categories of tip- and nunuwan indicates, I believe, their concern with a distinction between unsocialized, unmanipulable, or idiosyncratic mental events and socially generated mental events. *Tip-* refers to those aspects of the self seen as more fully one's own. That these concepts are seen in this way may also be indicated by the fact that only *tip-,* and not *nunuwan,* takes a direct possessive suffix. The possessive suffix, taken also by body part and kin terms, may occur for items that are more tightly bound up in personal identity. Moral decisions and choices are more in the province of nunuwan, and 'social intelligence' (*repiy*) is associated more with nunuwan than with tip-. As people are not considered to be fundamentally antisocial, however, what people desire, or their tip-, is neither immoral nor amoral.

Other aspects of 'our insides', and ones that are distinguished from both nunuwan and tip-, are the states of hunger (*pechaiy*), pain (*metagi*), and sexual sensations (*mwegiligil*). These latter states are considered to be universal and unlearned human proclivities. Although their occurrence can lead to thoughts and feelings, they are considered an entirely different class of events from the latter. The Ifaluk further distinguish between these three states of physical sensation and the corresponding desires or drivelike states that follow upon the sensations. These include 'wanting food' (or a particular food) (*mwan*), 'wanting pain to end' (*gar*), and 'horniness' (*pashu*).

There appears to be considerable variation in the conceptions Oceanic peoples have of the place of physical processes in relation to mental or social ones. While many appear to use disrupted physical process (illness) as an idiom for talking about wider-ranging disruptions in psychosocial life, the use of normal physical process in metaphorical or literal understandings of mental or social process seems more variable. For example, the Baining (Fajans, chap. 10) experience hunger as a sentiment rather than as a physical sensation; although food is closely tied into sociability among both the Ifaluk and the Baining, the Ifaluk associate the sharing of food, rather than the consumption of it, with ties between people. The Tobians described by Black (chap. 7) share many cultural features with the Ifaluk, but nonetheless appear to be much more reticent in speaking about such physical states, with the fear being that such revelation would lead to manipulation (Black, personal communication). People on Ifaluk frequently and openly talk about hunger and pain, both as feeling states and as their associated drive states. This is not considered an embarrassing eruption of the natural into the cultural arena, but rather as a natural state of affairs over which no one is expected to have control.

It is now necessary to contextualize more fully these aspects of the person in the kinds of statements in which they are found in daily life. In particular, the metaphors that are in common use to describe normal and abnormal psychosocial functioning will shed light on the way in which the processes of the person and of self–other interaction are conceptualized.

'Thoughts/emotions' are often spoken of as 'coming out' or 'coming up' from 'our insides'. The spatial metaphor here is consistent with the traditional view of thoughts and desires as originating in the gut. When these things 'arise' within the person, they are then 'followed'—that is, people act in accordance with them. Thus, the relationship between mental occurrences and behavior is conceptualized as relatively nonproblematic in normal adults. The term *nunuwan* is appropriately glossed as 'thought/emotion' in part because the concept entails what we mean when we speak of 'emotion' in contrast to 'thought', which is to say, a mental event that strongly motivates behavior as opposed to one that does not.

The 'thoughts/emotions' of a person, as already noted, are also sometimes said to be 'followed' by others. This may occur because the other naturally wishes to 'follow', or because a specific request has been made, as in the form, "Sweetheart [a polite form commonly used in making requests], you will follow my thoughts/emotions." After the woman who was my adoptive mother in the field found that a close relative had given birth without her being asked to attend, she asked me to "follow [her] justifiable anger and so not visit the confined mother and infant." The implication is always that the 'follower' will behave in keeping with the other's thoughts and emotions and with the definition of the situation which they imply. The leader-follower image evoked here is a powerful one in the context of the value placed on obedience in all aspects of Ifaluk life. A request of this kind, like all requests, is taken seriously; it is also taken as a sign of desired intimacy between self and other.

Speech is attributed great power and importance throughout Ifaluk culture. It is seen as the primary vehicle for the enculturation of children; the chiefs, in speaking at periodic islandwide meetings, believe that their words exhorting the people to act ethically will result in behavior change; spoken prayers are one of the aspects of Christian ritual which has been most enthusiastically adopted; and great value is placed on the use of good or polite talk in interaction with others. Such talk is considered to be at the root of pleasant social relationships, one of the most important bases for compliance with requests, and a mark of fine character.

Consistent with those attitudes toward language and toward the 'following' of 'thoughts/emotions' is the view that the overt expression of mental events is a mark of maturity. Children and the mentally ill are said to be marked by problems with such expression. It is said that they do not talk about their 'thoughts/emotions' and that "their insides do not leave them." [13] Here the act of expression is metaphorically conceptualized as a physical act, with the internal event spoken of as a separate entity with independent movement. Mature people, in the Ifaluk view, verbally express what they are thinking and feeling. The mature are also capable of *ridding* themselves of unwanted thoughts and feelings, and this is said to be done primarily through verbalization of what is occurring in 'one's insides'.

Internal processes are seen as taking their significance in relation to social processes. The 'psychological' event is neither denied in favor of the social nor is it defined outside of the social; as 'thought/emotion' is defined as a truly *psychosocial* fact, so is expression seen as serving psychosocial goals. Expression is allowed and encouraged, although neither as an aggrandizement of the self nor as a praiseworthy expression of a unique self. Expression is seen instead as a natural concomitant of an external event, while the lack of expression is seen as a possible precursor to illness or as a sign of mental incapacity.

There is one important exception to the general permissiveness in expression. There is an absolute sanction against the physical expression of inner events in violence or, to an important but lesser extent, in loud or impolite words. For this reason, it is said that a person may not look 'angry' or 'irritated', but may still have 'angry thoughts/emotions'. Men, in particular, should and do suppress their 'anger'. The term for this suppression is *goli,* which is literally 'to hide'. One may also 'hide' laughter or tears in an inappropriate situation, but such masking is observable to others. The object of keeping a state an internal one is not to conceal the fact that one is experiencing a particular emotion, but rather to avoid conflict or other unpleasant social consequences. In general, however, there is little emphasis on the masking of emotion. It is frequently said that one can always tell what the internal state of the other person is, either from facial, gestural, or situational cues. The role of speech looms large here as well, as indicated by the answer to my frequent question about how one can tell if a person is experiencing X; the response was often, "She or he tells you." Occasionally, however, people would protest, to my questioning, that "we cannot see our insides" and so cannot be absolutely sure about what is going on there, and particularly so in the case of others' insides.

There are several other ideas in common use which point out the importance of ridding oneself of unpleasant or disruptive 'thoughts/emotions', and the role of the will in expediting this. 'We divide our heads'

(Gish si gamaku chimwash) is a phrase that is both an aphorism and a form of advice that is given, primarily by and to men, when someone is experiencing potentially socially disruptive 'thoughts/emotions'. It is, they say, as if there were two halves to the brain, one good and one bad. People are advised to separate the good from the bad, or 'divide the head', and then to 'throw away' disruptive 'thoughts/emotions'. This latter is universally the advice to the troubled, while at the same time advice is given to verbally express one's 'thoughts/emotions' as a preliminary step to ridding oneself of them.[14]

When troubled by unpleasant 'thoughts/emotions', it is said that the latter will not 'leave my insides'. When some problem or conflict results in such a situation of unresolved unpleasant 'thought/emotion', the person involved will go to another with the expressed purpose of "saying my thoughts/emotions so that they will leave me." Similarly, when one is experiencing grief over a death or homesickness, the advice given is to stay among people so that one will not 'think/feel' about the loss.

To express one's 'thoughts/emotions' verbally, therefore, is both a sign of intelligence, as this is the natural course of events, and the route to relief of the unpleasantness of those mental states. Although the will would appear to play a part in this process, by enabling the self to 'divide the head', the emphasis is more on control of behavior than of 'thoughts/emotions'. Although the latter are never bad in and of themselves (as they may be in the West with its concepts of sin and 'evil thoughts'), they can be disruptive and uncomfortable, and may cause illness in the self or others. What is important and valued, however, is to prevent the 'thoughts/ emotions' from leading to aggressive or socially disruptive behavior. The individual will, in ethnopsychological thought, can play a primary role in preventing this.

The Body

Any discussion of conceptions of the person must touch on the role the body plays within the system. Is the body a little-valued 'container' for more metaphysical and consequential events? Is it one of the aspects, and/or perhaps the only aspect, of persons which distinguishes them on a continuing basis from others? On Ifaluk, as elsewhere, the body's structure and well-being are seen to be involved in an inseparable and systematic way with psychosocial well-being. What we might call 'the emotional mind' of Ifaluk ethnopsychology is solidly embedded in moral and social life, on the one hand, and in the physical body, on the other.

The physical structure of 'our insides' is divided into the *ubwash* 'our upper torso', which includes the heart and liver, and *sagash* 'our gut/our stomach', which includes the stomach and abdominal region. The heart, liver, and stomach, as well as the brain, are implicated in ethnopsychological beliefs about the origin of specific psychological and physical processes, beliefs that have undergone much change through the influence of Japanese and American ethnopsychologies. Traditionally, all 'thought/emotion' (nunuwan) and 'will/emotion/desire' (tip-) were believed to be experienced in the 'gut', and most people, especially older adults, speak of thoughts and emotions as being located there. The Japanese colonialists, however, constantly told the island boys who attended their schools in the prewar period to 'use their heads'. There may also have been a period, during the Spanish colonization, when the heart was more often seen as the seat of 'thoughts/ emotions'. One term for the heart (*corason-*) is a variant of the Spanish, and this idea is also prevalent today. Many younger people, and most especially the men, now include the brain as one of the seats (and sometimes as the only seat) of 'thoughts/emotions'. There is much diversity of opinion, however, including the following post hoc synthesis given by a woman in her twenties: "It is uncertain whether 'thoughts/emotions' (nunuwan) and 'will/emotion/desire' (*tipash*) come from the heart along a large vein to the brain, which then sends them out so that we speak." The liver is also implicated in thought and emotion, specifically in relation to *rus* 'panic/ fright/surprise', which is said to cause the liver to jump.

The links between emotional–mental and physiological functioning are explicitly spoken about by the Ifaluk. The 'gut', as the traditional seat of thought, feeling, and will, is seen in a very real sense as the link between mind and body or, more accurately, as the core of the self in both its physical and mental functioning. Food, which holds a primary place in the Ifaluk value system (see Burrows and Spiro 1953), is the foundation for both physical and emotional states, positive and negative. The presence of plentiful fish or taro is often the occasion for exclamations of "Our insides are good," by which is meant both good mood and good physical feeling. Food provides by far the greatest satisfaction, and its lack produces the greatest upset.

Appetite is the one physical function most often seen as symptomatic of physical or emotional upset. Loss of appetite occurs for many reasons including homesickness, fear, and weariness. "Food does not taste sweet" when one is upset; when one has many 'thoughts/emotions' and is unsure about what will happen in the future, one feels "full from thoughts/emotions" and loses appetite. Such explanations are often sought for weight loss in others, as exemplified by the following incident. A young woman had become thin, which was attributed to different causes by various individuals. One woman said it was due to her having many 'thoughts/ emotions' because she had much work to do, yet her adoptive daughter constantly whined and needed to be carried. Another woman, however, said that her weight loss was due to her being 'lovesick' over her brother, who had gone away to school on Ulithi.[15] The stomach area is also seen as the region of the body first affected by strong negative thoughts and emotions. Extreme grief over a death or loss is often described as 'my gut is ripping'. Those who are experiencing such loss are advised not to 'hate your gut'; what is implied here is that the sufferer should 'feel compassion' for himself and follow traditional advice for alleviating the state of grief (e.g., stay among people).

Emotion, thought, and body are seen in ethnotheory as intimately linked via their role in illness. Emotional upset and physical illness are conceived of and treated in parallel ways. Both illness and unpleasant 'thoughts/emotions' can consist of disruptions 'in our insides'. In both cases the internal phenomena must be drawn out and expressed, as it is said that both illness and 'thoughts/emotions' must 'come out' in order to alleviate the trouble they can cause. In addition, emotion that is not expressed may cause illness. One term, *gachip*, is used in talking about therapy for both kinds of problems; in the case of emotional upset, it means 'to calm down' and in the case of illness, 'to cure'.

Individuals are constantly advised to 'throw out' their thoughts in order to avoid illness. At funerals, relatives of the deceased are advised to 'cry big' to avoid later illness. This advice is meant to be taken sequentially; that is, the grieving person should scream and wail for the twenty-four hours of the funeral and subsequently stop thinking about the deceased, or risk becoming ill. At the funeral of a five-year-old, I was also advised to 'cry big'. Observing my somewhat surreptitious tears, several people approached me and said, "You should not cry like this [imitating my stifled style and stiff posture] but should cry big, or you will be sick." The father of the child was told that he should not 'think/feel' about the dead child as he would then not be able to take care of his other children. The ability to throw away these bad 'thoughts/emotions' is a sign of 'social intelligence', but this should only be done after the intense mourning of the funeral period has acted as a prophylactic against possible illness. The mother of the child in the case above became ill after the funeral with headaches and numbness in her arms and legs. This was diagnosed (by the island's health aide) as being due to her 'thinking/feeling' about the dead child. This woman had in fact been the one close relative who had not 'cried big' for extended periods at the funeral.

Emotion in the self can cause illness in the other as well. This most often occurs between the confined mother and infant and between relatives who are living on two different islands. Those who are homesick for another will cause the latter to become ill if they continue to focus their 'thoughts/emotions' on the missed person. Such homesick people may themselves become ill, through loss of appetite as described above, or, as in several reported recent cases, they may become 'crazy' (bush). Counsel to an individual who is homesick will take the following general form: "Don't cry [although crying out of homesickness is not frowned upon]. Forget those thoughts of your relatives. You will soon see them again. If you continue to feel homesick, your relatives will know this, and they will become sick."

This process in the confined mother-infant pair is somewhat more complex. An infant will become sick and cry excessively if its mother has 'bad thoughts/emotions'. It is said that "it is like the baby knows the 'thoughts/emotions' of its mother and becomes *nguch* 'sick and tired/bored' of the mother." The confined mother is particularly susceptible to the latter emotion, and this may lead to 'irritability' or 'hot temper'. She may also be more likely to experience *waires* 'worry/conflict' about work around the house or garden which may be going undone. All of these 'thoughts/emotions' in the mother may result in the child's becoming sick and *tangiteng* 'frequently crying'. The child is given *taffeyalgos* 'medicine for gos',* with *gos* being the name of the condition of both the mother and the child.[16] The spirits may also be involved in causing a mother to become 'hot-tempered', resulting in the infant's sickness. The following case illustrates this.

> H. [an old man] heard his next door neighbor's infant son crying at night. The infant's crying was recognizable as *semat tang* 'some different crying' and was said to be due to the spirits of the infant's mother's mother's brother and mother's mother. It was said that these spirits *riglog lan yaal nunuwan* "ran into the thoughts/emotions of" the mother and had been causing her to be 'hot-tempered' and quarrel with her husband. M. said in partial explanation of the mother's irritability that it was difficult because there is no one to take the infant when she wants to go work in the taro patch. H. [the old man] made 'spirit medicine' for the infant.

This set of ethnopsychological beliefs serves as warning to people in the household and other relatives of the confined mother; it is their responsibility to see that work is done around the house and garden and that the mother is occasionally relieved of caretaking for the infant. It should also be noted that the mother with negative thoughts and emotions is not blamed for the infant's subsequent illness so much as are other relatives around her, including the spirits of deceased relatives. Blame is attributed quite explicitly in these cases, with it being said that, for example, "her sister did not think/feel about [the confined mother], that she needed help with the infant," and so illness resulted. This is but one example of the general principle that the mental state of *any* mature individual is seen as having fundamentally social roots. Others can then be held responsible for the social conditions that have produced the state. In so talking about the relation between emotion in self and other, the Ifaluk emphasize that their emotional lives *are* their social lives.

EXPLAINING AND EVALUATING BEHAVIOR

The question of the origins of behavior must be problematic to some extent in every society. This issue is not a philosophical one, but arises in the context of the goal of changing behavior that transgresses cultural norms and of duplicating behavior that exemplifies them. The behaviors that are seen as worthy of explanation are those identified as deviant, as Black (chap. 7) points out; they are 'marked' in relation to generally unspoken notions of normalcy (Fajans, chap. 10). Although ethnotheoretical ideas about the causes of behavior are elaborated particularly around negatively evaluated behavior, they also occur in relation to praiseworthy behaviors. The universal evaluative dimension of perception (Osgood, May, and Miron 1975) is evident in the state, trait, and behavioral descriptors in use on Ifaluk and elsewhere (e.g., White 1980). The strong evaluative loading on terms for feeling and acting indicates that the role of ethnopsychology is not simply to describe and explain but also to evaluate behavior vis-à-vis cultural values, and thereby begin to exercise some control over that behavior. Although cultures will vary both in terms of the sheer number and range of behaviors lexicalized and evaluated and in terms of the emphasis on control (as opposed to a more laissez-faire attitude toward state or behavior change), the recognition of at least some degree of interpersonal behavioral variation will necessitate both explanations and sanctions. Both vices *and* virtues are outlined because some control over the occurrence of both will be universally desirable.

Causality in Behavior

Most everyday explanations of behavior on Ifaluk are concerned with the situational causes of particular acts and their associated mental states. Emotion states are often the medium by which people talk about those situations, as particular situations are necessarily linked to particular emotions (see Lutz 1982*a*) that are linked to particular actions.[17] The first question unexpected behavior raises often concerns the incongruity between the situation and an emotion. Sitting by the channel that separates two islets of the atoll, the woman I was with noted another woman wading across with her baby in her arms. She called out, "Why don't you have him in a carrying basket? Won't you be regretful if it rains?"

A person's behavior is not, however, attributed to either wholly external or wholly internal sources (as the terms 'situation' and 'emotion' connote). The cause of behavior is not conceptualized as located in an inner wellspring so much as in environmental triggers. The most important facets of these situations, moreover, include the behavior of other actors. Typically, statements about the cause of behavior would take the form, "He did X, and so I did Y," or (in explaining others' behaviors), "He did X, and so she did Y." When the question arose, for example, why a particular young girl had not come to visit her biological parents for some time, it was said that "she is afraid/anxious that her younger brother would hit her."

The extent to which other people are sometimes seen as the ultimate source of one's own behavior often means that the responsibility (i.e., the cause and therefore occasionally the blame) for one's internal state lies with the other. Many of the emotion words can, with the addition of a causative prefix (*ga-*), be used to talk about the causes of both emotion and behavior. *Ye gasongayei* 'He made me justifiably angry', *Ihre gametagayei* 'They caused fright in me', and *Ye gafago* 'She is needy', or, literally, 'She causes compassion' are examples of statements that are very frequently heard. The mature person, it has been noted, expresses her internal states. The state is itself seen as having a reasonable situational explanation. Thus, the person who leaves his valuable possessions out in view of visitors is to blame when someone becomes *bosu* 'excited/jealous' as an inevitable result. The host in such a case would be criticized by saying he was *gabosu* 'showing off', or, literally, 'causing excitement/jealousy'.

Other types of explanation for behavior exist. The concept of *tip-* described earlier is used to talk about the willful aspects of the person. An individual's 'will/emotion/desire' is occasionally spoken of as the reason for an action: "Why is she making breadfruit instead of taro?" "It was her *tip-*." As the thoughts and emotions of others can have a powerful influence on one's own behavior, such influence is often taken as a satisfactory explanation for someone's actions. In one such case an older man was leaving to visit another island despite the advanced state of his daughter's pregnancy. As kin should ideally fear for their relative's life at the time of birthing, and as they should want to render help to the new mother—that is, as the man's actions did not correctly correspond to the situation—his behavior required explanation. It was decided, after much discussion, that he had "followed the nunuwan" of his wife (who was his second spouse and not the mother of the pregnant woman).

The concept of bush ('crazy, incompetent') is used in a wide variety of contexts to explain the actions of some people. 'Craziness' is the opposite

of repiy ('social intelligence') (see Lutz and LeVine 1983 for a description
of this concept); it is used to refer to any behavior that gives evidence of a
lack of mental and social competence. Thus, a 'crazy' person is one who
does not behave in ways that indicate she has correctly perceived the nature
of the situation she is in and so does not feel, think, or act appropriately.
A person may be 'crazy' in several senses. Some people are born 'crazy';
although their primary failing is their inability to perform adult work, they
also often engage in much otherwise inexplicable behavior such as violence,
shouting, or a lack of table manners. There have been cases in the past in
which a person was said to have 'gone crazy' for months or even years,
and then returned to a 'socially intelligent' state. In some cases, the cause
of the episode was said to have been a strong emotional experience, such
as 'homesickness' or 'panic', although in other cases there appeared to be
some reluctance to talk about the reasons behind it.

People who are otherwise 'socially intelligent' may sometimes do
things that earn them the label of 'craziness' on a very short term or even
metaphorical basis. For example, a woman who left her son at her household for much of an afternoon in order to engage in the much-maligned
activity of 'walking around' (which implies strutting around and a failure
to do one's work) was disparagingly called 'crazy'. Thus, the term can be
used to describe anyone who is behaving in an irrational and unadult
manner. To say that someone is 'crazy' is to say that his behavior has no
other reasonable explanation; it is also to at least temporarily write that
person off as one whose behavior is beyond the pale.[18]

The spirits can, in extreme and rare cases, cause the behavior of an
individual. I observed this only once, in the case of a young man whose
serious illness had been diagnosed as spirit caused. One afternoon, after a
week of illness, his arms began to sway up from his sides and he began to
talk "as if he were crazy." Unlike true 'craziness', however, his behavior
was explained as being due to the entry of a spirit into his body and its
control of his insides.

A final type of explanation for behavior is one made in terms of
enduring personal traits such as 'hot temper' or 'calmness'. These will be
explored after a discussion of ideas about child development.

The Ethnopsychology of Development

Examination of the life course can make two important contributions
to the description of an ethnopsychology. First, the course of development
is explicitly conceptualized, classified, and explained in most, if not all,
societies. These notions about development frequently point out the infant

or child as not yet fully a person. The ways in which children and adults are seen to differ will often reveal important ethnotheoretical dimensions that might otherwise go undiscovered. In addition, the process by which development is thought to occur is revealed in talk about the life course, including conceptions about which human behaviors are changeable and about how that change may be caused. Such conceptions thereby often point to the hypothesized origins of behavior. Ethnotheories of human development also recognize divergent outcomes, such that behavior and other aspects of personhood vary within and across adults. This variation may be explained with trait or behavioral descriptors—which are fundamentally statements of values.

Second, an examination of the life course reveals the ways in which a culturally specific self-awareness is built up. Following Hallowell (1955), we may ask about the behavioral environment of the emerging self. Via the efforts and example of the socializing other, the child begins to construct a self. The acquisition of ethnopsychological notions is a process that can be observed in both verbal and nonverbal communicative acts.

On Ifaluk, there are strong tabus against speaking of the unborn as a *sari* 'child'. It was formerly tabu to speak also of one who was stillborn, or one who died in the birth hut, as a 'child'. Rather, one said in such an event, "The water has been thrown out"—and the infant was buried without tears or ceremony. The Catholic missionaries, however, encouraged grave-yard burials for these fetuses and very young infants and there is now some mourning at a birth hut death.

Naming practices can provide insight into a people's ethnopsychology: in the act of linking a person with a label, the individual is particularized or identified in relation to other persons (see Goodenough 1965). The name may symbolize the location of the person in space and time and in relation to other objects in the environment (Geertz 1973). The Ifaluk name the infant (and begin to refer to it as a 'child') only after the mother has returned from the birth hut after a ten-day period of seclusion. Although the infant has been a 'person' (yaremat) since several months prior to birth, it is at this point, after the period of greatest life threat is passed, that children gain their full social identity. It is better that a newborn who dies does so nameless; without a name, it is said, there is less to forget. Names are given to the child by any one or more persons (kin or otherwise) who have taken an interest in the child. A name is frequently provided by the child's adoptive mother or father if there is one. The act of name giving is seen as an important statement of connection with the infant, and people will often give accounts of the origins of their names. The linguistic label itself is always unique, as a name can never be that of an ancestor (to mention the name of an ancestor is to call forth her or his spirit). Each syllable, however, may be taken from the name of a different ancestor. Thus, naming is seen as creating a bond between the child and both the creator of the name and the ancestors whose names were in part used.

From the earliest period infants are capable of certain emotions, but in general they must be protected from them. Concern with infants' states begins from birth. At one delivery, the first two comments about the infant were "It's a girl" and "It's hot-tempered." Infants may 'feel good inside', be 'hot-tempered', or experience rus ('panic/fright/surprise'), a state that has serious implications. In excess, this state can lead to illness. Parents therefore make serious attempts to protect the infant from it by avoiding loud noises and rough handling of the child, and by placing a wad of cloth close to the child's chest while it sleeps.

Crying is considered the primary way in which children express their needs. It is to be avoided at all costs, and mothers sleep in close contact with infants to anticipate their cries. Infants who cry while lying down are first assumed to be uncomfortable due to the impressions being made in their skin by the cloth or mat on which they are lying. If moving children to another position does not stop the crying, they are held and fed until they sleep. Infants are bathed if their cries are interpreted as meaning that they are hot and uncomfortable.

Until they reach the age of five or six, the most fundamental ethno-psychological fact about children is that they are socially incompetent or 'crazy' (bush). As noted above, they share this label with the mentally retarded and mentally ill, the deviant, and the senile. Young children, being 'crazy', are not considered responsible for their actions. Children are considered not to know right from wrong, and the resultant aberrant behavior must, therefore, be ignored or tolerated. From about one year of age onward, however, children may be called *gataulap*. This term can be glossed as 'naughty', as it connotes bad behavior, but behavior that, being more or less expected of someone at that age, is more annoying than reprehensible. Infants at the crawling stage may be 'naughty' if they climb up onto things or touch objects, but the quintessential 'naughty' child is the toddler. 'Naughty' toddlers empty out adults' personal baskets, and touch knives or thread. At three years, they run around, throw things, or hit others, or are always whining to be given something like a knife or basket.

It is near the age of weaning, at two years, that adults must begin to *garepiy* their children 'cause them to become socially intelligent', despite the fact that their educability is seriously limited. Learning theories on Ifaluk give a prominent role to both the parents (adoptive and biological) and peers. Bad behaviors are said to be most frequently learned from peers, although it is the parents' responsibility to counteract the bad example of children's age-mates. Although children are believed to learn through watching the behavior of others, a very important stress is placed on their ability to hear and to listen. The older weaned child is sometimes instructed on proper behavior through parents' stylized 'preaching' (*folog*). In these lectures, an axiom of proper behavior is gone over quietly but repeatedly. Obedience is highly valued, and children are believed to obey *when* and *because* they listen and understand language; intention and knowledge become virtually synonymous in this system. It is assumed that correct behavior naturally and inevitably follows from understanding, which should follow from listening. Although the concept of independent will is not absent (this is represented in the concept of tip-), the greatest stress is placed on the connections between language, listening, understanding, and correct behavior.

Physical punishment does not play a prominent role, either in the ethnotheory of learning or in practice. Lecturing is preferred to spanking, in line with the important roles given speaking and listening. It is said that children who are hit, rather than spoken to, may 'go crazy'. Physical punishment may be a source of great embarrassment to parents when they engage in it, as gentleness in all matters is highly valued. Children are also said to learn by the examples given through socialization techniques. Those who are hit, and who are not spoken to politely, will grow up to be short-tempered and will not know how to engage in 'good speech', or polite talk. There is also some fear expressed that children who are hit and shouted at may aggress against their parents in return, or possibly even kill themselves.

Children are first considered 'socially intelligent'—that is, they are seen as capable of a significant number of 'thoughts/emotions'—as they approach the age of six. In contrast to the Bimin-Kuskusmin (Poole, chap. 6), who use metaphors of directionality, solidification, and straightening to talk about the development of social sense in children, the Ifaluk speak primarily about an increase in the quantity of 'thoughts/emotions' and about their value (good or bad) as they occur across childhood. 'Social intelligence' consists of both the knowledge *and* the performance of mature and valued behaviors such as subsistence work, respect toward the more highly ranked, and 'compassion' for others, which are now expected of the child. The amount of time which parents spend casually instructing and formally 'preaching' goes up dramatically. Adults believe their words will now have an important effect on children, although in the first few years of being 'socially intelligent' children are believed to forget parts of the lectures. If children have not been periodically lectured during the earlier years, it is said that they will not be 'used to' such lectures. They will, therefore, become 'hot-tempered' when they are lectured at a later age.

When children reach the age of 'social intelligence' they are considered capable of learning some adult economic tasks. At this time as well, certain trait and behavior labels first become applicable to the child. Foremost among these is *gagu* 'laziness'. The state of *fago* ('compassion/love/sadness') is fully possible in the child beginning only at this period. The things that constitute 'naughtiness' change from the younger years. They now include being loud and disruptive at school, being uncooperative around the household, and causing younger children to be noisy by getting them excited or by making them laugh. In the latter instance, children begin to learn that they are responsible for the emotional states of others.

The development of individual differences is believed to arise out of the various forces at work on the child. All children are believed to be basically the same until they become 'a bit socially intelligent'. Young children have only one 'thought/emotion', which is to eat. When they reach the age of two, they begin to very slowly acquire more and varied notions. It is consequently only then that individual differences arise, as the number and nature of these 'thoughts/emotions' begin to diverge in different people. Among the several factors said to cause differences are gender and sibling order.[19] *Lalongaw* 'bad-hearted, jealous' and *tangiteng* 'frequently crying' children are recognized as different from others and are seen as particularly troublesome. 'Bad-heartedness' is a highly disvalued trait in both children and adults. Children are not born 'bad-hearted', but may become so when, for example, a new child is born and sibling rivalry occurs. I was told that the child "wants to be alone with the mother, and thinks that only the infant will be cared for by her." 'Bad-heartedness' is only possible in children once they are somewhat 'socially intelligent' and are capable of thinking such thoughts. 'Frequently crying' children are dealt with by encouraging them to verbalize their internal states. If they cry because someone has taken something from them, they are told to go and ask for it back; the verbal expression and action should substitute for tears.

The most important point of discontinuity in the life cycle in Ifaluk ethnotheory occurs with the gaining of 'social intelligence' at around age six. Although still called 'children', in many respects they are treated just like adults. While it is considered silly to try and converse with a child before that point, the 'socially intelligent' person of any age is incorporated in group conversation. In contrast to the more differentiated marking of stages and the particular elaboration of ideas about the nature of teenagers among Marquesans (Kirkpatrick, chap. 3), the Ifaluk downplay changes that occur in early and later adulthood. When 'elder' status is reached, however, sometime in the late forties or early fifties, certain personal traits are said to become more prominent in some people.

It is said that older persons are more likely to be *garusrus* 'easily and often frightened' and are also more likely to be *metau* 'playfully happy'.

Although senility is known and named, it is not considered to be a necessary or common concomitant of old age. Neither is physical debilitation considered to naturally follow aging, although the many seventy-year-olds who continue to work in the taro fields and climb coconut trees are seen as commendable.

Just as daily discussions on Ifaluk about the varieties of living persons elucidate some of the most important dimensions of personhood, so do deaths become "occasions for dramatic public statements about the meanings of particular lives and of life in general" (LeVine 1982:26). The Ifaluk mourn each death massively, with wailing and sung laments that tell of the pain of bereavement and the beauty or skills of the lost one.

> I will lose my mind with missing her.
> She was like a flower,
> Like the quick-growing tumeric;
> She grew fast, but no sooner grown than she died.
> To her mother she was like a flower;
> I wanted to wear her in my hair;
> But she has died and left me.
> I am worn with sorrow.[20]

People do not simply die; they "die away from" the living. The loss of the elderly is said to be no less painful than the loss of children. My question of whether the imminent death of an eighty-year-old woman would be seen as putting her out of her misery was greeted with some incredulity; the death of a person of any age tears a hole in a wide-ranging network.

Death is the point at which persons become spirits. It is as spirits that the deceased are dealt with from then on, and people reminisce little about them as persons; tabus on speaking their names support this practice. Although it is believed that those who have been good during their lives will become good spirits and those who have been bad will become bad spirits, these two prospects are not seen as reward and punishment so much as a continuation, in another form, of life as it was led in this world. Relatives who have died will be seen in the next world, and this fact is often given as counsel to those who are grieving over the death of another.[21] The exception to this is accidental or sudden death, which is a 'bad death' as the deceased will become a particularly malicious spirit. The prospect of such a death for the self or another is especially feared.[22] Death, both accidental and otherwise, stirs up the spirit world for a period, and leaves the living both fearful and lonely.

In sum, on Ifaluk ethnopsychological beliefs about development are related to parental goals about the type of child desired (Lutz 1983). The good child is depicted in ethnopsychology as one who has the correct emotions, as well as the correct behaviors. Children should grow up to work well and consistently, and not be lazy or short-tempered. The child should grow into 'social intelligence', which is to say, able to think, feel, and behave like an Ifaluk person. A more detailed discussion of those qualities that are valued follows.

Interpersonal Variation and Conceptions of the Good

To speak of one set of terms which the Ifaluk use to talk about inter-personal variation as 'personality' traits is misleading insofar as it connotes the range of ideas associated with that term in English, including ideas about the importance of traits in explaining much of the everyday behavior of individuals. Although the Ifaluk ethnopsychology of traits shares several notions with Western theory, such as a belief in the origins of some traits in early experience and learning, the emphasis is on explaining behavior rather than explaining individuals. In indigenous theory, people do have tendencies to feel, think, and behave in certain predictable ways, but in practice, it is only in exceptional cases that people are consistently or permanently identified with particular trait terms. Goodenough has iden-tified this same phenomenon on Truk, and he has noted that the permanent ascription of invidious labels to a large proportion of the population of nonmobile face-to-face communities may be counterproductive for con-tinued cooperation within such groups.[23] On Ifaluk, trait terms are used to explain and evaluate behavior only when it cannot be explained by solely emotional, which is to say, situational, criteria. Thus, the ideal explanation is one that appeals to what the Ifaluk see as universal human proclivities rather than particularistic ones. The latter are, however, sometimes neces-sary. While both state and trait terms are evaluative (and interrelated by their common reference to the same cultural value system), the use of trait terms may be less compatible with the goal of *changing* than of simply identifying or labeling behavior.

To use a trait term on Ifaluk is, almost invariably, to make a moral statement. In speaking about other people, both in interviews and in the daily round of conversation, the Ifaluk consistently speak in the same breath of the Good and the Bad (traits) and the emotions.[24] Many traits are defined by the dominance in a person of a particular emotional style, while the behavioral implications of both temporary and permanent personal states are explicitly judged by the criteria of cultural values. Two logical state-ments can describe the broad outlines of Ifaluk beliefs about the connections between their values, traits, and emotions:

1. The good person is 'calm' (*maluwelu*) and 'afraid/anxious' (*metagu*) and is not 'hot-tempered' (*sigsig*).
2. The bad person 'misbehaves' (*gataulap*), is not 'afraid/anxious', and is 'hot-tempered'.

The highest compliment that can be paid to a person is to say that he or she is maluwelu, or gentle, calm, and quiet. The term can be used to describe the lagoon or the wind when calm, as well as a personal style unrippled by offensive actions or emotions. The root of the word (*maliuw*) refers to looseness, such as that in a slack cord. The connections between this trait and the emotions are direct and multifaceted; the 'calm' person is not 'hot-tempered' and *is* 'fearful'. The following description of 'calm' children shows the trait's origin in the child's relationship with his mother:

> Children who are 'calm' stay with their parents and are 'afraid/anxious' among people. If one came here, she'd bend over in respect, talk slowly, and not make loud noises. They only go other places with their mothers. They are like this because they take after their mothers who also don't walk around. They are 'used to' their mother's way and so are 'afraid/anxious'. If there is a feast, and the mother tells the child to go get her some tobacco [from another person], he won't do it because he's 'afraid/anxious'. The child who is not 'afraid/anxious' will stand right up and do it.

The seeming contradiction between obedience and 'calmness' in the quote above is one that is also evident in daily life. Although obedience is absolutely expected of older children, noncompliance is both tolerated and even positively sanctioned if it arises out of the timidity associated with being 'calm'. In all other areas, however, the 'calm' person is obedient. Their 'kindly talk', respectfulness, and even temper are the basis for the judgment that calm persons are pleasant companions. Children are sometimes told that they should be 'calm' "so that others will like you."

The state of metagu, 'fear/anxiety' plays an important role in 'calmness', as it is seen as the most important response to the potential 'justifiable anger' of others at one's misbehavior. It is the potential for offending others (and provoking moral outrage or even violence) which leads to 'fear/anxiety' and from there to the trait of 'calmness'. I do not translate *metagu* as 'shame', however, even though both concepts entail the inhibition of behavior in public; *metagu* involves a balance of self-consciousness and other-consciousness that 'shame' does not. In addition, it is often the person who *has* misbehaved who is 'ashamed'; it is the person who is conscious of the danger involved in as-yet-not-occurring misbehavior who is 'fearful/anxious' and acts 'calmly'. The trait of 'calmness', then, arises not so much from an inner tranquility (although 'calm' people are not easily irritated) as from a sensitivity to and knowledge of cultural norms. The height of 'social intelligence', in fact, consists in large part of the thought, emotion, and behavior patterns characteristic of the 'calm' person.

'Calmness' is seen as antithetical to a number of traits which are characterized by 'show-off' behavior. There are many words to describe people who strut about, and "think they are number one." People who are *gaiseus* walk with their shoulders thrown back, and do not sit all the way down among a group of people. This manner of walking and sitting is seen as exemplifying a lack of respect and an attitude of superiority. People who are *gatinap* constantly talk about their skills or intelligence; a gatinap man brags about the number of fish he has caught and often thinks that many women like him. *Gabosbos* refers mainly to people who show off their material possessions and is often used for those who come from other islands with radios or new clothes and with knowledge of the outside world. The disvalue attached to this and other 'show-off' traits is due to the negative effects of such behaviors on others. Any behavior that stirs up jealousy or affronts another's rank is anathema. The number and constant use of terms descriptive of this constellation of traits is evidence of the high value placed on both egalitarianism and respect. In sum, the most highly valued trait on Ifaluk is 'calmness', as it results in harmonious, cooperative interaction. The opposed traits are those which involve 'hot temper', misbehavior, and immodesty. These traits are disvalued because they create social conflicts and bad feelings in others. Despite the presence of a hierarchy of clans and lineages, Ifaluk is an egalitarian society. Rank ideally should be nonobtrusive, and jealousy about differential fortunes, where such exist, should be minimized. Even, or perhaps particularly, the atoll chiefs should show humility and calmness. Their hereditary leadership is in fact spoken of as a service role; it is performed out of duty rather than because of any particular skill held by the incumbents and put forward as a rationale for their position.

Construing their labor as 'work' and as nurturance rather than as a personal achievement is consistent with other central Ifaluk values, including diligence and skill in work and generosity. Careful, diligent, and patient work is highly valued, and there are many words descriptive of traits related to it. *Tauyengang* 'one who is always working' is considered an ideal marriage partner; such a person likes to work as much as possible, either at gardening, weaving, fishing, or canoe building. *Laloolai* describes the patient, even-tempered person who enjoys work, and does not get upset by interruptions. *Sheowefish* are people who are industrious and take great care in their work. As with those who are laloolai, the secret to their success is in performing a task slowly and patiently, rather than doing it haphazardly or simply to finish. These traits, like 'calmness', are defined by the absence of irritability or 'hot temper'.

The opposite characteristic is gagu 'laziness'. Although this common epithet is used especially with children, it also describes any adult who shirks duties, whether familial or communal. This trait is related to the emotion of nguch 'sick and tired/bored', which occurs when one does not want to work. People will never say that they themselves are 'lazy' but rather that they feel nguch. While the former is very negatively sanctioned, the latter is not. A self-proclamation of nguch may, in fact, prevent the attribution of 'laziness'. "I am nguch" is a statement that one's failure to work is merely a temporary reaction rather than an enduring personal trait, and people are at pains to avoid being seen as a poor worker by disposition.

Another set of personal traits are those connected with the value of generosity. *Mweol* 'generous/friendly/obedient' describes a person who offers food, tobacco, and help freely, and who personifies the value placed on sharing. Opposed and commonly used epithets for those who will not share include *farog* 'stingy/selfish' and lalongaw 'bad-hearted'. A related accusation is involved if one is called a *mongolap* 'big eater'. Periodic food shortages on the atoll mean that one person's eating more will entail another's eating less. Here the unmarked trait, in Fajans's (chap. 10) terms, involves restraints in consumption such that an equal share of resources may be taken by all.

There are several trait terms that are specifically emotional types, that is, they describe a person in whom a particular emotion predominates. The two most common are sigsig 'hot-tempered/always angry' and garusrus 'nervous/excitable/always fearful'. A third and more general emotional type is tangiteng, which describes a tendency to cry often. Normal adults will only cry if someone has died or gone away or been lost at sea. It is said that all people cry sometimes: "It is not possible that someone would never cry." The person who is tangiteng is one who tends to experience a stronger than usual fago 'compassion/love/sadness' for others and/or who is sigsig. People who are tangiteng will also cry when they are *ker* 'happy/excited'. Children are tangiteng for many reasons, but the most serious among them is the emotional state of the mother as seen in the example given earlier. It is said that women, more often than men, are tangiteng. The person who was most often given as an example of a tangiteng person, however, was a man.

The types of virtues and vices to which trait terms refer are intimately related to Ifaluk values of cooperation, nonaggression, minimization of jealousies, and reciprocal sharing. Given these general values, it is not surprising that the ideal person is seen as calm, generous, hard-working, and modest, and that these traits are lexicalized and discussed. The relationship between these traits and 'thoughts/emotions' in ethnotheory is also evident, and involves (1) the absence of 'hot temper', which disrupts both interpersonal relationships, personal equanimity, and work habits, and (2) the presence of a good amount of 'fear/anxiety', which works to encourage obedience and 'calmness' and to discourage negatively valued behaviors, including aggression and 'showing off'. Both trait and state attributions on Ifaluk are not simply statements about the characteristics of sovereign individuals; they are not the private property of the self. Rather, they explicitly link characteristics of persons to situational and social-moral considerations. The traits of a 'good person' are those that create valued emotions in others and otherwise serve social ends.

CONCLUSION

The purpose of this chapter has been to describe the theories of self-in-interaction that are held on Ifaluk. In broad outline, the Ifaluk speak about themselves as relatively undivided persons, and as persons who are oriented primarily toward other people. The emotional mind with which the Ifaluk endow themselves ideally serves not simply to understand the world but to act in it. Thought and motivation, word and deed form relatively seamless units, in keeping with the idea that it is not presocial individuals who confront the community but rather persons who are profoundly influenced and defined by it. Finally, it has been seen that Ifaluk morality or cultural values are explicitly included in their views of persons, selves, and others. Although constraints of space have not allowed for a thorough examination of how this knowledge system is used in daily life, I have elsewhere (Lutz, in press, 1980, 1983) shown how these ethnopsychological beliefs provide criteria for the interpretation and evaluation of ongoing events, and for use in attempts to solve occasional problems in the functioning of self and others.

The descriptions in this chapter have been both explicitly and implicitly comparative, with the comparison point being other Oceanic and American ethnopsychologies. The claim has been made that no ethnopsychological system is ever explained "in its own terms"; to say that ethnotheory can be explored without reference to other theoretical systems is to claim that the anthropologist goes to the field as a tabula rasa, that is, without an ethnopsychological interpretive system of her or his own. In the translation of ethnopsychologies, we rely heavily on our own and others' understandings of concepts such as 'mind', 'self', and 'anger'. The invisibility of culture (the taking of belief for knowledge or of language for the object) has left opaque the extent to which attributions of 'anger' are cultural attributions. An elaborate and complex body of knowledge is involved in an American's identification and explanation of a case of 'anger' or 'emotionality'. This is not rivaled but paralleled by the knowledge involved in attributions of maluwelu 'calmness' or *song* 'justifiable anger' among the Ifaluk. If the terms of our description themselves are taken as nonproblematic (in a way in which the *choice* of terms in ethnography never is), we run the risk of reducing the emotional lives of others to the common denominator or intersection with our own.

This leads to another aim of this chapter, which has been to suggest a rethinking of the epistemological status of the academic psychology that is usually implicitly contrasted with ethnopsychologies. There are two senses in which the contrast between psychology and ethnopsychology is misleading. In the first instance, academic psychology has taken its research goals, terms, and metaphors from its cultural base, as has Ifaluk psychology taken its structure, uses, and ends from the institutional and belief system within which it is embedded. If psychology is, then, like anthropology, a culturally constituted enterprise, we cannot look to the former as a standard against which to judge the truth value of Oceanic psychologies. Rather, what is of primary concern is the articulation of particular psychologies with other aspects of culture and with environments. Thus, one important future goal for ethnopsychological study will be to explore what Wallace suggests is "an interesting question in the sociology of knowledge; what (if any) common sociocultural forces can be found to explain the existence of . . . similar psychological theories in two . . . different societies" (1958:234), or, conversely, to explain the existence of different psychological theories in two human populations. A central question to ask of Oceanic and American psychologies is why they want to know what they do about themselves and about the lives of members of other cultural groups. If the anthropological encounter is approached not simply as a view into another world but as an opportunity to throw into relief our own goals and beliefs as well, the ethnopsychology that is evident in academic psychology and elsewhere will hold a fascination and status equal to that of Oceanic psychologies.[25]

This is not to presuppose that there are no ethnopsychological tenets that are universally held (which is one sense in which a psychology may be termed 'true'). Ethnopsychologies are the result of reflections on experience and they are created to explain people to themselves. The human experience obviously has many pancultural aspects, some of which will be chosen for similar treatment and elaboration by most human groups. Two examples can be presented which suggest what such ethnopsychological regularities might look like. Through a search of the ethnographic record, Rogoff et al. (1975) have found that children in the great majority of societies are believed to undergo important changes at around the ages of five to seven.

As is the case on Ifaluk and in the United States, many groups see children as first acquiring substantial mental, behavioral, or social abilities at this time, and begin to assign them adult tasks and responsibilities. It has also been established that certain neurological maturational processes reach an important turning point at about the age of five (Milner 1967, cited in Rogoff et al. 1975). This suggests that most cultural groups elaborate on this aspect of change in the biological substrate of the species, thereby making that change a very significant one in the child's experience. Another interesting and apparently widespread aspect of ethnopsychologies is what might be called the natural pessimism of emotional perception. The vocabularies of temporary personal states of a number of cultures show more terms that members of the group would describe as negative (i.e., bad, unpleasant, or having disvalued antecedents or consequents) than positive.[26] This contrasts with the general cross-cultural tendency for people to much more often evaluate words positively than negatively (Osgood 1964) and to use positive words more frequently (Boucher and Osgood 1969). Although these examples obscure the richness of the meaning systems involved with such things as changes in children with age and the temporary states of persons, it is only from this level of generality that we may begin to explore commonalities in ethnopsychological understandings.

There is a second sense in which comparative ethnopsychology can be said to require more serious consideration as a mode of explanation for things 'psychological'. Involved is the premise that ethnopsychological language and knowledge have fundamental structuring effects on psychosocial experience and process. Ethnopsychologies are not simply ideological veneers that must be lifted in order to discover 'actual' psychological events (although there are obviously aspects of brain and social activity which ethnopsychologies do not address). Neither are they cultural meaning systems that, however rich, exist at a level apart from the psychological. To treat ethnopsychologies as 'cultural facts' is to organize our investigations of cross-cultural human experience around the Western bias toward splitting persons into presocial and social parts, a split that has its counterpart in the separation of psychological process from psychological content. A focus on ethnopsychologies can aid us in bridging that constructed gap and in reestablishing lived experience as the centerpiece of psychocultural investigation.

ACKNOWLEDGMENTS

Fieldwork on which this chapter is based was carried out in the West Caroline Islands from October 1977 to December 1978. Twelve of those months were spent on the atoll of Ifaluk. The financial support of the National Institute of Mental Health is gratefully acknowledged. I would like to thank Peter Black, Jane Fajans, John Kirkpatrick, and Geoffrey White for their helpful comments on an earlier draft of this chapter.

NOTES

1. The categorizing of an immense number of varied cultural groups under the rubric 'non-Western', both for heuristic purposes in this paper and explanatory purposes elsewhere, may arise in part from the fact that the less-acknowledged mission of anthropologizing has been to describe the Western self. For this purpose, any and all other cultures can serve as the other.

2. The method of introspection is held in varying degrees of repute (or disrepute) in academic psychology, but the notion itself is predicated on the belief that 'looking inward' accesses private material while 'looking outward' accesses the public world (Lutz 1982b). Different evaluations attach to the private and the public. The 'real me' is the private me, which is also the standard against which the public self is measured rather than vice versa; the high value placed on traits such as sincerity is one indication that this is the case. Via an analysis of attitudes toward the mask among the Iroquois and among Euro-Americans, Fogelson (1982:10) points out that the notion that the truest reality is that which is behind the mask (or otherwise at a depth and hidden from view) contrasts with the Iroquois feeling that "what is real and ultimately true . . . is what is outside and 'up front' in the faces and interfaces of these masked personages."

3. A notable exception here is the Japanese psychiatrist Takeo Doi's book, *The Anatomy of Dependence,* in which he asks why Americans do not appear to experience (or at least recognize) the emotion of *amae.* The work is unexceptional, however, insofar as it is Doi's status as a cultural outsider which provoked him to question the emotional otherness of Americans.

4. The last two points have overlapping implications in the context of the ethnographic interview. Strathern points out that ethnopsychological statements about gender differences made in interviews between himself and Melpa-speakers in New Guinea vary from those made in more public situations where rhetorical purposes may be at the forefront (1981:287–289).

5. Further ethnographic description of Ifaluk atoll is found in Burrows (1963), Burrows and Spiro (1953), and Lutz (1980).

6. In using the terms 'person' and 'self', I intend only to distinguish two contrast sets—in the case of 'person', between significant social actors (see n. 7) and nonsignificant ones (or nonpersons), and in the case of 'self', between particular perspectives that can be taken by persons. These appear to be categories and definitions that coincide reasonably with Ifaluk distinctions. I do not intend to distinguish between 'cultural' and 'psychological' levels of analysis as Fajans (this volume) has done. The term 'individual', with its connotations of the natural or precultural (Rorty 1976:315), seems unnecessary both from a theoretical perspective and from

the perspective of Ifaluk ethnopsychological ideas. Where 'individual' is used in this chapter, it is synonymous with 'particular person'.

7. I am restricting the term 'actor' here to those figures in the social environment whom the Ifaluk see as significant (i.e., as both salient and sufficiently complex) intentional agents. Animals are therefore excluded. An important exception is the porpoise, whose superanimal abilities have placed it in the category of 'spirits'.

8. These are my own terms, but they do appear to reflect implicit Ifaluk notions.

9. Not all person descriptions are, of course, individualized. Ethnic characterizations do occur, although these are almost invariably descriptions of distant peoples such as Yapese, Americans, Japanese, and New Guineans. The few statements I heard which stereotypically grouped island residents virtually all referred to one particular village. People of that village have traditionally been considered of low rank and interactions between them and members of other villages may have been less frequent, until quite recently. Thus, in both of these cases, *lumpen,* or group, representations occur when the other is more distant and unknown.

10. The root of this word—*feral*—is the center vein of a tree, through which sap rises. A synonym for niferash, in less common use, is *nifitigosh,* which is literally 'inside our flesh'.

11. The term translated here as 'think' is *mangimeng.* Although the dictionary (Sohn and Tawerilmang 1976) gives its meaning as "to think, remember, consider, ponder, expect," the term is not used in the same contexts as nunuwan. Mangimeng connotes somewhat aimless, confused, or ignorant thinking; as one woman told me, "socially intelligent (*repiy*) people don't mangimeng a lot."

12. The term *tip-* takes a direct possessive suffix, and will be used in its appropriate forms in the text including *tipei* (first person singular), *tipum* (second person singular), and *tipash* (first person plural, inclusive).

13. Both children and the mentally ill are labeled bush or 'incompetent'. The 'incompetent' have, according to some informants, "different insides." Depending on both the informant and the 'incompetent' individual in question, it is sometimes said that it is possible to be "socially intelligent inside" but unable to express that understanding in language.

14. There is a strong resemblance between this view of the role of expression and the theory behind the 'disentangling' sessions described by White (chap. 9) for the A'ara. In both cases, the goals of verbal expression are seen as psychologically and socially therapeutic. Similarly, the Marquesans (Kirkpatrick, chap. 3) see some mental events that do not lead to action as intrinsically disrupting or disorganizing for the person.

15. The English word "lovesick" is in common use by adolescents to describe the experience of loss or absence, particularly where an individual experiences unrequited love or separation from a boyfriend or girlfriend. It is relevant to the argument being advanced here that this, the only English emotion term that has been borrowed, includes an explicit association between emotion and illness.

16. The condition of gos is characterized by one or more of the following—a neck and joint rash, white spots on the skin, and a cough. Gos can occur, however, without the mother's mental/emotional state being seen as the root of the problem.

17. The Ifaluk do not distinguish emotions which are environmentally caused from those which are not. An elaborate set of propositions detail the situational causes of *all* of the emotions (Lutz n.d.).

18. There are a few special cases in which 'crazy' behavior occurs for what are seen as somewhat more understandable or elaborated reasons. Senility is the 'craziness of elders', while excessive grief, which in one observed case led to pushing and shoving to get near the corpse at a funeral, is the 'craziness of tears'. An intoxicated person who misbehaves usually has his actions explained simply by reference to his drunkenness. Occasionally, however, people speak of particularly misbehaving drunks as being 'crazy from toddy'.

19. Beliefs about innate sex differences are minimal. It is said that the only difference between male and female infants is in their cries; male cries are louder, stronger, and more constant, while female cries are softer, with more breathful pauses in between. Boy infants are also said to drink and eat more than girls; their crying is considered more problematic at later ages, and if a boy is labeled tangiteng he will be given medicine that should result in an end to this trait by the time he reaches adolescence. The position within the family of youngest and only children results in their being different from others. In infancy and early childhood, they are likely to be 'frequently crying' because there are no younger siblings competing for their mothers' attention. These children also frequently grow up to be somewhat 'bad-hearted' and 'hot-tempered'.

20. This and other poems collected on Ifaluk by Edwin Burrows (1963) are striking evidence both of the freedom with which feelings are expressed and of the centrality of other people in those feelings.

21. The belief in contact between individuals after death appears to predate the period of contact with missionaries, according to those with whom I spoke. Burrows and Spiro also report the belief at the pre-Catholic date of 1948, although they note that spirits in the afterworld lived not in the households they occupied at death, but at their clan lands (1953:214).

22. Most people assume they will become good ghosts. Accidental death, then, represents a reverse in expected fortunes.

23. Ward Goodenough, remarks to the symposium on Folk Psychology in Pacific Cultures, at the meetings of the Association for Social Anthropology in Oceania, Hilton Head, South Carolina, March 1982.

24. People are also distinguished on the basis of their gender, clan membership, chiefly status, and life experiences. Although important behavioral inferences about such categories of persons can be drawn by local observers, a consideration of these groups is beyond the scope of this paper. See Caughey (1980) for a lucid treatment of the relationship between social and personal identity.

25. The differences between academic psychologies and nonacademic psychologies (e.g., degree of elaboration) are obvious but, from my perspective, much overplayed.

26. Averill (1980) has demonstrated this in American English emotion vocabulary. An examination of four other state vocabularies shows the same feature. Among the Ifaluk, 25 out of 31 temporary-state terms are classed as 'bad'; among the Gidjingali of Australia, 5 of the 6 terms that Hiatt (1978) describes are translated

with negative English emotion words; in Briggs's (1970) glossary of Inuit Eskimo terms, 12 out of 19 unambiguously or unambivalently conceptualized emotion terms are seen as negative; and in Gerber's (1975) discussion of Samoan emotion terms, 21 out of 38 unambivalent terms are seen as unpleasant or socially undesirable.

GLOSSARY

bosu	excited/jealous
bush	crazy, socially incompetent
corason-	heart
fago	compassion/love/sadness
farog	stingy, selfish
folog	to preach, to lecture on proper behavior
gabosbos	show off; lit., causing excitement/jealousy
gachip	to calm down from emotional upset; to cure of an illness
gagu	lazy
gaiseus	arrogant, disrespectful
gatinap	braggart, show-off
gar	to want pain to end
garepiy	to teach, to cause to become socially intelligent
garusrus	easily and often frightened, nervous, excitable
gataulap	naughty, misbehaving
goli	to hide, to mask (e.g., laughter)
gos	medical condition of mother-infant pair often caused by emotional upset
got	the Catholic God
ker	happy/excited
lalongaw	bad-hearted, jealous, stingy
laloolai	patient and even-tempered
maluwelu	calm, gentle
mangimeng	to think confusing thoughts, to wonder somewhat aimlessly
metagi	pain

metagu	fear/anxiety
metau	playfully happy
mongolap	one who eats big
mwan	to want food (or a particular food)
mwegiligil	sexual sensation
mweol	generous/friendly/obedient
nguch	sick and tired/bored
niferash	our insides
nifitigosh	our insides; lit., inside our flesh
nunuwan	thought/emotion
pashu	horniness
pechaiy	hunger
repiy	social intelligence
rus	panic/fright/surprise
sag-	gut, stomach
sari	child
sheowefish	industrious and careful worker
sigsig	hot-tempered, easily irritated
song	justifiably angry
tangiteng	crying frequently; one who cries frequently
tauyengang	one who is always working
tip-	will/emotion/desire
ubw-	upper torso
waires	worry/conflict
yalus	spirit
yaremat	human person
yarofali	longing/missing

REFERENCES

Averill, J. R.
    1980   On the Paucity of Positive Emotions. *In* Assessment and Modification of Emotional Behavior. K. Blankstein, P. Pliner, and J. Polivy, eds.

Advances in the Study of Communication and Affect. Vol. 6. New York: Plenum.

Black, P. W.
1978   Crime and Culture: Tobian Response to Attempted Murder. Midwest Review 3:59–69.

Boucher, J., and C. E. Osgood
1969   The Pollyanna Hypothesis. Journal of Verbal Learning and Verbal Behavior 8:1–8.

Briggs, J. L.
1970   Never in Anger: Portrait of an Eskimo Family. Cambridge: Harvard University Press.

Buck-Morss, S.
1975   Socio-economic Bias in Piaget's Theory and Its Implications for Cross-culture Studies. Human Development 18:35–49.

Burrows, E. G.
1963   Flower in My Ear. Seattle: University of Washington Press.

Burrows, E. G., and M. E. Spiro
1953   An Atoll Culture: Ethnography of Ifaluk in the Central Carolines. New Haven: HRAF.

Caughey, J. L.
1980   Personal Identity and Social Organization. Ethos 8:173–203.

Crapanzano, V.
1980   Tuhami: Portrait of a Moroccan. Chicago: University of Chicago Press.

Csikszentmihalyi, M., and E. Rochberg-Halton
1981   The Meaning of Things: Domestic Symbols and the Self. Cambridge: Cambridge University Press.

D'Andrade, R. G.
1974   Memory and the Assessment of Behavior. In Measurement in the Social Sciences. T. Blalock, ed. Chicago: Aldine-Atherton.

Doi, T.
1973   The Anatomy of Dependence. Tokyo: Kodansha International Ltd.

Ekman, P.
1974   Universal Facial Expressions of Emotion. In Culture and Personality: Contemporary Readings. R. A. LeVine, ed. Chicago: Aldine.

Fogelson, R. D.
1982   Person, Self, and Identity: Some Anthropological Retrospects, Circumspects, and Prospects. In Psychosocial Theories of the Self. B. Lee, ed. New York: Plenum.

Gaines, A. D.
1982   Cultural Definitions, Behavior and the Person in American Psychiatry. In Cultural Conceptions of Mental Health and Therapy. A. J. Marsella and G. M. White, eds. Dordrecht: D. Reidel.

Geertz, C.
1973   Person, Time, and Conduct in Bali. In The Interpretation of Cultures. New York: Basic Books.
1976   "From the Native's Point of View": On the Nature of Anthropological

Understanding. *In* Meaning in Anthropology. K. H. Basso and H. A. Selby, eds. Albuquerque: University of New Mexico Press.

Gerber, E. R.
  1975   The Cultural Patterning of Emotions in Samoa. Ph.D. diss., University of California, San Diego.

Gergen, K. J.
  1973   Social Psychology as History. Journal of Personality and Social Psychology 26:309–320.
  1979   The Positivist Image in Social Psychological Theory. *In* Psychology in Social Context. A. R. Buss, ed. New York: Irvington Publishers.

Goodenough, W. H.
  1965   Personal Names and Modes of Address in Two Oceanic Societies. *In* Context and Meaning in Cultural Anthropology. M. E. Spiro, ed. New York: Free Press.

Goodnow, J. J.
  1976   Some Sources of Cultural Differences in Performance. *In* Aboriginal Cognition. G. Kearney and D. W. McElwain, eds. Atlantic Highlands, N.J: Humanities Press.

Hallowell, A. I.
  1955   The Self and Its Behavioral Environment. *In* Culture and Experience. Philadelphia: University of Pennsylvania Press.
  1960   Ojibwa Ontology, Behavior, and World View. *In* Culture in History. S. Diamond, ed. New York: Columbia University Press.

Hiatt, L. R.
  1978   Classification of the Emotions. *In* Australian Aboriginal Concepts. L. R. Hiatt, ed. Atlantic Highlands, N.J.: Humanities Press.

Hutchins, E.
  1980   Culture and Inference. Cambridge: Harvard University Press.

Jenkins, R.
  1981   Thinking and Doing: Towards a Model of Cognitive Practice. *In* The Structure of Folk Models. L. Holy and M. Stuchlik, eds. ASA Monograph no. 20. New York: Academic Press.

Kirk, L., and M. Burton
  1977   Meaning and Context: A Study of Contextual Shifts in Meaning of Maasai Personality Descriptors. American Ethnologist 4:734–761.

Lakoff, G., and M. Johnson
  1980   Metaphors We Live By. Chicago: University of Chicago Press.

LeVine, R. A.
  1980   Anthropology and Child Development. *In* Anthropological Perspectives on Child Development. C. Super and S. Harkness, eds. San Francisco: Jossey-Bass.
  1982   Gusii Funerals: Meanings of Life and Death in an African Community. Ethos 10:26–65.

Lutz, C.
  n.d.   Goals, Events, and Understanding in Ifaluk Emotion Theory. *In* Cultural Models in Language and Thought. N. Quinn and D. Holland, eds.

              New York: Cambridge University Press.
1980   Emotion Words and Emotional Development on Ifaluk Atoll. Ph.D.
              diss., Harvard University.
1982a   The Domain of Emotion Words on Ifaluk. American Ethnologist 9:113–
              128.
1982b   Introspection and Cultural Knowledge Systems. The Behavioral and
              Brain Sciences 5:439–440.
1983   Parental Goals, Ethnopsychology, and the Development of Emotional
              Meaning. Ethos 11:246–263.
Lutz, C., and R. A. LeVine
1983   Culture and Intelligence in Infancy: An Ethnopsychological View. In
              Origins of Intelligence: Infancy and Early Childhood. 2d. ed. M. Lewis,
              ed. New York: Plenum.
Mead, G. H.
1932   The Philosophy of the Present. Chicago: Open Court.
Milner, E.
1967   Human Neural and Behavioral Development: A Relational Inquiry, with
              Implications for Personality. Springfield, Ill.: Charles C. Thomas.
Osgood, C. E.
1964   Semantic Differential Technique in the Comparative Study of Cultures.
              American Anthropologist 66:171–200.
Osgood, C. E., W. H. May, and M. S. Miron
1975   Cross-Cultural Universals of Affective Meaning. Urbana: University of
              Illinois Press.
Quinn, N.
1982   "Commitment" in American Marriage: A Cultural Analysis. American
              Ethnologist 9:775–798.
Rogoff, B., M. J. Sellers, S. Pirotta, N. Fox, and S. H. White
1975   Age of Assignment of Roles and Responsibilities to Children: A Cross-
              cultural Survey. Human Development 18:353–369.
Rorty, A. O.
1976   A Literary Postscript: Characters, Persons, Selves, Individuals. In The
              Identities of Persons. A. Rorty, ed. Berkeley, Los Angeles, London:
              University of California Press.
Rosaldo, M. Z.
1980   Knowledge and Passion: Ilongot Notions of Self and Social Life. Cam-
              bridge: Cambridge University Press.
Sanjek, R.
1978   Who Are the 'Folk' in Folk Taxonomies? Cognitive Diversity and the
              State. Kroeber Anthropological Society Papers 53–54:32–43.
Sohn, H., and A. F. Tawerilmang
1976   Woleaian-English Dictionary. Honolulu: University Press of Hawaii.
Sorenson, E. R.
1976   Social Organization and the Facial Expression of Emotion. National
              Geographic Society Research Reports, 1968 Projects. Washington, D.C.

Strathern, A.
  1981   NOMAN: Representations of Identity in Mount Hagen. *In* The Structure of Folk Models. L. Holy and M. Stuchlik, eds. ASA Monograph no. 20. London: Academic Press.
Strathern, M.
  1968   Popokl: The Question of Morality. Mankind 6:553–562.
Straus, A. S.
  1977   Northern Cheyenne Ethnopsychology. Ethos 5:326–357.
Tyler, S. A.
  1978   The Said and the Unsaid: Mind, Meaning, and Culture. New York: Academic Press.
Wallace, A. F. C.
  1958   Dreams and Wishes of the Soul: A Type of Psychoanalytic Theory Among the Seventeenth Century Iroquois. American Anthropologist 60:234–248.
  1970   Culture and Personality. 2d ed. New York: Random House.
White, G. M.
  1978   Ambiguity and Ambivalence in A'ara Personality Descriptors. American Ethnologist 5:334–360.
  1980   Conceptual Universals in Interpersonal Language. American Anthropologist 82:759–781.
Whiting, B. B., and J. W. M. Whiting
  1975   Children of Six Cultures: A Psychocultural Analysis. Cambridge: Harvard University Press.

3

Some Marquesan Understandings of Action and Identity

John Kirkpatrick

INTRODUCTION

Marquesan ethnopsychology is viewed here as a field of cultural knowledge, with its own boundaries and forms of organization. Attention is paid to concepts of action, emotion, and identity because these appear central to Marquesans' accounts of human life. The approach chosen holds out the promise of learning from Marquesans a view of humanity, a perspective on action and identity organized in Marquesan culture. In striving for this goal, emphasis is placed on uncovering assumptions that provide a context of meaning for Marquesans' statements about persons.

Given this approach, terms such as "emotion" and "psychology" are used pretheoretically, to orient an inquiry that attempts to uncover the assumptions articulating Marquesan concepts. Similarly, distinctions such as those Rorty (1976) makes between "persons" and "selves" seem inappropriate at this point. The analytic separation of personal and social identity, which has proven fruitful in studies of Trukese life (Goodenough 1965; Caughey 1980), will also be held in abeyance. In this chapter, I am more interested in "shame" than in, say, craftsmanship or authority, but do not take these to be unrelated unless ethnographic grounds for that conclusion are reached.

The attempt to discover sets of underlying assumptions involves a risk: Marquesans' situated insights may be reduced to decontextualized props for an analytical edifice. The risk is a serious one, but it seems worth taking, if only because an attempt to study Marquesans' psychological concepts one by one quickly runs up against facts that are opaque unless Marquesan assumptions are known. A brief study of *hakā'ika* 'shame, embarrassment' will serve to illustrate the problem.

Shame

It is all too easy for a visitor to the Marquesas islands to see Marquesans as members of a shame culture.[1] Parents often rebuke children by asking, "Aren't you ashamed?" (*a'e koe hakā'ika?*)[2] Lists of potentially hakā'ika behaviors and presentations of self are easily gathered: 'it is shameful' (*mea hakā'ika*), for example, to be found naked, dirty, in the act of theft, or to learn that a person close to oneself was caught stealing. Again, Marquesans expect their consociates to make much of 'shameful' incidents. "People will chatter" (*e tekatekao te tau 'enana*), they say: unusual actions will be topics for extensive gossip and, in all probability, adverse judgments. In this environment, Marquesans prefer their actions to go undiscussed.

The issue of 'shame' may arise in a wide variety of situations, not just a few well-known ones. Thus one bridegroom seemed embarrassed by an offer of wedding photographs. He was 'ashamed' at the thought that he might seem to be showing off. In his embarrassment, his statement was nearly incoherent. Others recognized his predicament and restated it more fully. The 'shame' of this young man was an obvious and expectable matter to them. One linked this example to hakā'ika in other contexts:

> "It's hakā'ika because there are many people. People are hakā'ika at public Scripture recitals [*mātutu*] and drink two whiskeys to get up the energy to recite. They aren't skilled at that activity, so they are hakā'ika."

Hakā'ika seems a fairly predictable and recurrent part of Marquesan life, as 'shame' is in many Pacific societies (for examples, see Fajans, chap. 10; Lutz, chap. 2; and Schieffelin, chap. 5). Whether the term is glossed as 'shame', or 'embarrassment', or even 'stage fright', it points to a highly generalized sensitivity to others' opinions. (These glosses are taken from accounts of comparable concepts elsewhere. See Levy [1973], Geertz [1973], and Keeler's [1983] reanalysis of the 'stage fright' account.) What, then, to make of the following:

1. Informants who are willing to list many situations in which hakā'ika arises say, in a matter-of-fact way, that people who are observed in sexual intercourse are not hakā'ika.
2. While adult Marquesans come to public events, or even such

public places as stores, clean and well dressed, they may show no sign of hakā'ika if found dirty and sweating at their homes after a day's work. (And some of these people say that being seen to be dirty is hakā'ika.)

3. An old woman spends most of her time around her household. When she encounters the ethnographer, who has lived nearby for months, she is tongue-tied and apparently anxious. The ethnographer's guess is that she is extremely hakā'ika. An informant disagrees: perhaps some such people are 'thoroughly hakā'ika'; others, like the woman in question, simply weren't taught by their parents. These people may be a bit 'wild' and 'ignorant', but they are good people.

The last of these examples is consonant with a view of hakā'ika as a shame control, but it raises questions about 'teaching' (hakakō 'ia). The other examples suggest that the experience and expression of hakā'ika are limited in ways that cannot be predicted from informants' more general statements about hakā'ika or from the idea of a shame culture. They raise questions about why hakā'ika is possible and expected in some contexts but not others.

Marquesan informants are hardly articulate phenomenologists, but they do provide answers to these questions. The people engaging in intercourse are caught up in their 'lust' (hinena'o). Later, when it has ended, they may feel hakā'ika, but not in the act. The second example has a different sort of explanation, one suggested by those involved. When they have worked all day to support their families and themselves, their grime testifies to their industry, not just to an inattention to propriety. So what if someone comes to their house and finds them dirty—does anyone expect people to be immaculate when they have to make a living? Adults will feel the tug of hakā'ika in many contexts, but they expect others' judgments to be bounded by commonsense expectations of what people do and are.

While these answers hardly amount to a psychological or social theory, they show that an ethnography of 'shame' in the Marquesas is not simply a matter of contrasting shame and guilt as ways that social rules are internalized, or describing 'shame' as one of several emotions and sentiments. Something must be said about putatively uncontrolled actions, and about ideas of normal human action. Again, the *different* ways these shame-free situations are viewed needs explanation. The answers cited above are cogent only in relation to broader understandings of how people relate to the social world at different moments and at different points in the life cycle.

Indeed, the above examples are given in order to present a prima facie case for further study of Marquesans' ideas. Enough evidence has been presented to suggest that hakā'ika deserves a prominent place in an account of Marquesans' interactions and experience, and to argue that hakā'ika is only crudely understood apart from the matrix of cultural knowledge in which it is embedded.

Analytical Strategy

In this chapter, an attempt is made to convey the presuppositions that lie behind the sense that Marquesans make of the examples cited. The analytic strategy is to survey a range of concepts used to describe human action, to bring out commonalities among some of these concepts, and to show how sets of such concepts can be arranged in a model of types of human engagement in the world. Instead of surveying objects defined by my own native theories of internal experience or social control, I try to map some of the coherence Marquesans find in their accounts of human action. While the model covers a good deal of Marquesan ethnopsychology, I do not claim that it is exhaustive.

First, the social and linguistic contexts of Marquesans' normal use of psychological terms are sketched. Next, the problem of uncovering Marquesan ideas is approached by examining expectations of persons in general. One reason for taking this tack is that hakā'ika is one of several emotions or interactive attitudes that, Marquesans say, are typical of persons. These attitudes are then compared to look for similarities among them. I then ask whether other such sets of emotions or attitudes can be found. Four sets are identified. Since these sets are analytically discovered, I seek further grounds for establishing their ethnographic validity through a study of notions of human cognition and action. I show reasons for viewing the model as grounded in Marquesans' accounts of normal human behavior, and go on to describe recurrent situations and processes—friendships and the life cycle—that are discussed by Marquesans in terms mapped by the analysis.

Hence the first objectives of this chapter are to (a) show grounds for seeing Marquesans' ideas of action and emotion as orderly, as a cultural system and not a jumble of observations, values, and practices, and (b) describe that system. Next comes the issue of the relevance of the system for arranging and explicating social life in terms that seem correct, cogent, and informative to Marquesans. The question is whether the model simply arranges Marquesans' views of a few phenomena or whether it replicates criteria and means of organization that they use repeatedly in social life. I find the latter view more convincing, and hence I see Marquesan ethnopsychology as central to Marquesans' experience and knowledge of social life. This claim cannot be fully supported here, but I try to show that evidence for it is available and that the orderly properties of Marquesan ethnopsychology, not just a curious belief or two, are of general importance for recurrent social processes and structure.

ETHNOGRAPHIC CONTEXT

The Marquesas islands include six inhabited islands, with a total population of over five thousand. Nine hundred miles northeast of Tahiti, the Marquesas form a peripheral sector of French Polynesia. The local economy is based on a mix of subsistence horticulture, cash crop production of copra and coffee, and wage work, mainly for the government. Emigration has developed in recent years, and over a thousand Marquesan-born persons now live on Tahiti. Emigrants are scattered throughout the urban zone there, and do not form a tightly knit community.

The Marquesas are mountainous. People live in valleys between which communication may be difficult. Valley populations range from a hundred to nearly a thousand. In such valleys, the inhabitants come into contact with most of their fellows daily, and detailed biographic knowledge of consociates is widely shared.

Although formal organizations—islandwide communes, valley church congregations, sports associations—are found in the Marquesas, such organizations structure community events and roles relatively weakly. Marquesans view most organizations as composed of a few central members and an indistinct mass of those who may offer support. Whether that support is forthcoming on a particular occasion—at an election, for instance—is by no means certain. Marquesans discuss such matters in terms of apparently psychological constructs: the 'thought' of a populace, people's 'concern' and 'respect' for a leader, or their ingrained tendency to act contrarily out of 'envy'. Again, relationships that may be coded categorically, for example, by genealogy, are not seen by Marquesans as predictable on the basis of such codes. Ideally, kin should cooperate—but whether they fulfill this norm, find it a burden, resent it, or ignore it altogether is, for Marquesans, a matter that can only be judged given knowledge of personal qualities.

Marquesans do not speak of themselves as a society or even as a population upholding shared customs. They are *enana* 'folks', or 'people': a bunch of distinctive persons pursuing their own goals and making their own lives.[3] As is more thoroughly shown elsewhere (Kirkpatrick 1981*a*, 1981*b*, 1983), Marquesan ethnosociology is phrased as psychology, stressing persons, their goals and whims, not interpersonal groups, laws, or rights.

(Black [personal communication] suggests that a similar stress on persons, as opposed to institutions, is found among Tobians.)

Everyday production and consumption activities are mostly organized at the household level. Marquesans today view conjugal family households as sensible and proper, largely because fewer problems of cooperation among adults arise in them, compared to larger groupings. The establishment of such a household by a couple which has resided with the parents of one of the spouses is usually seen positively, as bringing independence: "it comes about that you [sing.] are your own boss" *(ua 'i'o na koe ta koe vivini)*. Similarly, older people who may depend on their children for daily sustenance are rarely willing to give up their own homes. They prefer having their children with them or nearby, rather than moving in with their children. Marquesans seem, then, to have strong allegiances to domestic units so long as they head them, or, more precisely, so long as they are recognized as maintaining them. This, I argue, has to do with their understanding of domestic commitment as an index of maturity. In becoming his own 'boss', a Marquesan not only escapes others' demands and criticism, but helps to reshape his identity in a way Marquesans value. Major aspects of domestic organization, then, can be seen as organized by Marquesans' self-understandings.

THE LANGUAGE OF ETHNOPSYCHOLOGY

The ethnopsychology discussed here is realized in everyday discourse, not in specialists' accounts of the world or strongly demarcated speech situations. The language of the ethnopsychology is Marquesan. Terms may be borrowed from other languages and nonlocal dialects of Marquesan, but usually with no transfer of meaning beyond that of a Marquesan term recognized as cognate to the foreign term. Thus, on 'Ua Pou island, 'envy' may be discussed as *keitani*, as *saru* (from French *jaloux*), or as *fina'i*, a term identified as southern Marquesan in origin. Imported terms may not be clearly identified with a single Marquesan cognate—the Tahitian word *feruri*, which for Tahitians bears a meaning much like that of the Marquesan *kaituto* 'reflective thinking', may be used as a synonym for *kaituto* or for the vaguer Marquesan term *ma'akau* 'think'.

Most Marquesans have some competence in two or three languages. They listen to Radio Tahiti broadcasts in Tahitian and understand some French. Many are so competent in Tahitian that they see no difficulty in communicating with Tahitians. Nowadays, young people are schooled in French.

Fluency in other languages does not seem to affect greatly a speaker's use of Marquesan psychological discourse. This is in part because of a tendency to treat foreign languages as appropriate to specialized subject matters. Political discussions are filled with Tahitian and French terms. For legal matters, a French vocabulary is integrated into Marquesan discussions. Liturgical Marquesan (southern dialect) is treated as carrying special theological senses. Only the last comes close to the vocabulary at issue here, for Catholic priests attempted to find, in ordinary speech, concepts close enough to their own to convey the meanings of the liturgy. Thus God's love (*ka'oha*) and glory (*kā'i'e*) are glossed by terms that Marquesans use daily to speak of more humble matters. The glory of God is one thing, however, and the 'arrogance' *(kā'i'e)* of men is another: when I asked, people told me that the kā'i'e of God is a mystery—and hence is not comparable to the attitudes of mortals.[4]

THE USE OF ETHNOPSYCHOLOGICAL TERMS IN MARQUESAN DISCOURSE

The terms at issue here, such as ka'oha and kā'i'e, occur frequently in discussions of human action and judgments about consociates. They are largely treated as mapping realities evident to people with any discernment, that is, they are offered with little or no overt backing. They may, however, be contested. When someone present in the speech situation is called 'brash' or 'arrogant', he is apt to disagree—but little discussion of the evidence ensues. The standard reply is not to *argue* that a claim is untrue but to refuse to grant the author of the claim any privileged position from which to make it, saying something on the order of "You're a fine one to talk!" or making a counteraccusation.

Ethnopsychological terms can, then, be employed as minor insults (*paha*) by Marquesans, although they rarely initiate a long exchange of insults. More often, they occur simply in descriptions of persons or summary statements that give focus to previous accounts of persons. In the latter case, the agreement of hearers with a conclusion may be sought. It comes in the form of statements that a description is 'fitting' (*hei*).[5] A description may 'fit' by being obviously true, situationally appropriate, or a rhetorically neat claim. Thus people occasionally find claims 'fitting' more because they are well phrased than because they compel agreement as veridical.

Marquesans' acceptance of ethnopsychological descriptions need not, then, testify to shared rules for applying them as true of particular persons. Acceptance may have much to do with the similarities of speaker and audience: it may be more an affirmation of their shared perspective than of the claim in question. When, for example, an adult terms a youth 'brash' (*va'avō*) and the youth disdains to reply, each may then seek out an audience which will affirm his or her low opinion of the other. The youth will find peers; the adult may do likewise or turn to his or her children as an audience that will approve, or at least not argue with, a parent's claims.

While the truth-value of particular claims may be hard to establish, the sense of the concepts involved is more clear-cut. The evidence here includes everyday acts of approval and disapproval, informants' explanations, and attempts to direct children. The last may involve explicit evaluations, for example, "You're brash, that's not nice," or simply efforts made to impress children with the salience of an ethnopsychological account of a situation. An example occurred when a friend was looking through some photographs I had taken. She came upon one of a person who had recently died. She immediately called this to the attention of her four-year-old child, crooning repeatedly that the person in the photo was an object of *ka'oha* 'concern'.

The present analysis draws on information from a wide range of informants. Explanations of particular terms, important for the first half of the chapter, are, however, largely drawn from work with adult informants. Adult views are perhaps overrepresented here, but then they are also predominant in public discourse in the Marquesas.

THE PERSON: GENERAL COMPETENCES

Marquesans have several stock expectations that they voice concerning normal human abilities. 'People' ('enana) differ above all from other beings by being resourceful actors able to adapt to the varied situations of a social world. "Mountains don't bump against each other; people do"—they meet, talk, and establish relationships. Again, I was told that, at the sight of a stranger, animals fight or flee—while people recognize the stranger as a person and try to chat with him. (When, in tales, a stranger is recognized as a nonhuman person, the human party is likely to flee. It must be stressed that this response follows on an act of recognition, not impulse or instinct.)

In speaking of themselves as prototypical 'people', Marquesans also stress adaptive relations to the material world. To *haka'enana* 'act as an 'enana' is to jury-rig or to make do with limited resources. One Marquesan spoke of his consociates as "*capable de tout*," capable of accomplishing nearly anything despite their isolation. In a related vein, while Marquesans value neighborly cooperation and reciprocity, they often strive for—and expect competent persons to strive for—a high degree of self-sufficiency as providers for their domestic units. Extensive interdependence might be fine in

theory, but Marquesans expect 'people' to be unwilling to submit to a rule
of continuing cooperation and to cherish a view of themselves as autonomous actors.

Effective activity in relation to the material world is only one side of
Marquesans' understanding of 'people'. 'People' have emotional capabilities
no less than physical ones. They expectably experience ka'oha, hakā'ika,
and keitani. All three of these involve complex attitudes toward life in a
social world. A close consideration of them helps to specify the attitudes
and processes of interaction that Marquesans find characteristic of 'persons'
in general.

1. *Ka'oha* 'concern'. This is mentioned in a wide range of contexts by
Marquesans. It is a greeting. The term is used in the phrase, *ka'oha nui tātou*
'great ka'oha (for/of) us all', that characteristically opens and closes speeches
to public audiences (Kirkpatrick 1981*b*). Gifts are termed ka'oha, in contrast
to payments or exchanges. However, for Marquesans ka'oha is above all a
matter of attitudes toward others. Accounts of ka'oha given by informants
share certain features: (a) ka'oha includes a recognition of the presence and
state of the other, (b) ka'oha normally includes or leads to action taken
toward the other, and (c) the proper and normal result of ka'oha is an
amelioration of the other's situation, making it more possible for both
participants to interact. Thus greeting activity is not simply a matter of
uttering a polite formula: to ka'oha a guest, one recognizes the other, says
"ka'oha," and makes him or her welcome.

Two more examples show how the sense of ka'oha as 'gift' and *mea
ka'oha* as 'object of concern, compassion' can be closely linked to a view of
ka'oha as a process integrating perception, emotion, and action:

"I'm poor. I don't come to your place. You recognize [this]; you come to my
place, bringing money [and] say, 'Take. You, your wife, your children will
eat'. You just give, I didn't ask. That's ka'oha."

"One man is going to Hakama'i'i [valley] on foot. It's hot. People think of
that man going along to that distant place. Ka'oha reaches him. [People] say
to him, 'Don't go away now. A boat will leave in the morning for Hakama'i'i.
You are a thing of great ka'oha, going on foot.'"

In both these cases, the informants' accounts make it clear that ka'oha
helps its object, although the upshot of ka'oha is not discussed in detail. It
is, however, clearly implied. The poor man no longer feels embarrassed,
and can interact with the other more easily. ("I don't come to your place"
implies both that the poor man does not beg and that he avoids interactions
because he is worried about his poverty.) The traveler's goal is made

realizable without great effort—and with the added benefit that he can spend the day where he is.

There is no suggestion in these examples that objects of 'concern' *need* charity. They labor under their burdens, but, at least in these cases, they can carry them. Ka'oha helps them to reach their goals with less effort, and to be available for interaction.

I gloss *ka'oha* as 'concern', not 'sympathy' or 'empathy', because it involves for Marquesans a respect for the other as goal oriented and a recognition that the actor can draw on his own resources to help the other, rather than an identification with the other's goals or feelings. What identification is visible in ka'oha is with a concept of humans as resourceful and adaptive, not with particular others. By experiencing and enacting ka'oha toward another, the actor draws on his own resources and sensitivity to a situation, while providing a basis for the other to act with similar competence.

2. *Hakā'ika* 'shame, embarrassment'. In the earlier discussion of hakā'ika, no attempt was made to convey Marquesan views of its components. An informant offered a detailed account: "The guts tremble; one fears; one doesn't want to go [i.e., to continue action]."[6] Another, who was willing to locate emotions in various bodily sites, situated 'shame' in others' eyes. He went on to characterize 'the head' as occupied with a statement of the 'shame'-inducing topic, "My friend stole that thing (so I hear from others)," while "the belly thinks" and turns the matter over.

Hakā'ika involves a recognition that others may disapprove of, mock, or be bothered by one's state or activity. It expectably impels a change in behavior, to minimize the offending quality or activity. Hakā'ika tends to inhibit action, especially when questions of skillful performance are at issue. Marquesans recognize a disvalued possibility, that hakā'ika may be 'fierce' (*hae*) and lead to withdrawal or an inability to interact. Children often find it impossible to interact with adult neighbors, when sent to do so by their parents. Adults find such behavior unsurprising, but in need of correction. One mother reports that she says to her child, "Don't be hakā'ika; get that thing from So-and-so. If you are very hakā'ika, we won't survive."[7]

Marquesans offer contradictory judgments as to whether it is good or bad to be hakā'ika, or good or bad to be va'avō.[8] The contradiction stems from the attempt to generalize across contexts, when both 'shame' and 'brashness' are recognized in the ways people respond to contextual cues and demands. The sensitivity to others that brings an actor to recognize impropriety or disapproval is seen as a needed interactive competence; persistent or extreme hakā'ika reactions threaten to make an actor incapable of interaction. Although the 'shame' of a normal Marquesan may leave him bereft of words in an encounter, its display shows him to be responsive to others and holds out the promise of interaction being easily possible in the future, if perhaps not immediately. Similarly, Fajans (chap. 10) notes that shame functions positively to "reassert the normative order" among the Baining.

3. *Keitani* 'envy'. Marquesans repeatedly speak of themselves as subject to 'envy'. They describe it as proceeding from a sense that another person is fundamentally the same as oneself, yet has gained an undeserved benefit or advantage. The action of 'envy' is expected to involve steps taken to bring the other to one's own level. Even when no steps are taken besides maligning the other, the 'envious' party awaits the other's comeuppance. Thus Marquesans speak of their richer consociates as only momentarily fortunate. One day, such people will need to depend on others—a likely occurrence given the uncertainty of supply of imported goods in the islands—and they may then go needy while those who now seem poor have enough for their wants.[9]

'Envy' is often noted at moments when expected cooperation fails to materialize. Thus, if a man fails to lend a hand to others unloading goods from a trade ship, his inaction may be ascribed to 'envy' of the owner of the goods. Conversely, a person's willingness to help at such moments might be seen as due to a hope for an exorbitant reward. Economic differences among Marquesans are fertile ground for suspicion and misunderstanding.

'Envy', then, involves evaluations of self and other, along with an understanding of how 'persons' expectably interact. Like the other examples discussed here, this process characteristic of 'persons' draws on broad expectations of them for both its internal representation—the envious party's sense that the other has 'raised himself up' (*hakatiketike*) over most people—and consequent action to rectify the situation.

EXTENDED AGENCY AS A PERSONAL PROCESS

Thus far, 'concern', 'shame', and 'envy' have been viewed together because they are predicated of 'enana ('persons, Marquesans') in general. Occasions on which persons are said to lack 'shame', or 'concern' have not been considered, for the immediate problem is to enunciate Marquesans' assumptions associated with these concepts. Similarities among the three cases surveyed are extensive. They can be treated heuristically as variant realizations of a general type of engagement in the world, as tokens of what here is termed a personal process. I here refer to the personal process, of which 'concern', 'shame', and 'envy' are taken to be exemplars, as "extended agency." [10] ("Agent" similarly refers to an actor viewed as enacting a personal process. These terms will be discussed later in detail.) In this section, some of the grounds for identifying extended agency as a model of Marquesan ideas are spelled out. In the next section, other personal processes will be described.

'Concern', 'shame', and 'envy', as Marquesans describe them, all depend on acts of recognition. All relate actors to general understandings of human competence. All ideally involve action consequent to recognition. That action changes an ongoing situation in the direction of a more normal or valued situation. These similarities make it plausible to suggest that the three cases are properly viewed as tokens of a type of engagement in the world.

The notion of general modes of engagement in the world, of personal processes, is useful for several reasons. An argument can be made that the Marquesan view of certain states as expectable of 'persons' follows from these being equally examples of a common type of process. It is, I submit, as tokens of a culturally formulated mode of action, not just as consequences of human social life or socialization, that they are expectable. Moreover, the notion of general modes of engagement suggests two further steps for the inquiry: (a) examination of other emotions and actions to see if they may be viewed as examples of this or another personal process, and (b) study of the varied activities mentioned as expected of 'persons' to see if they can all be understood as examples of or following from extended agency.

The second step can be quickly addressed. Clearly, the adaptive, resourceful competences of 'persons' depend on their ability to 'recognize' persons, situations, materials, and techniques. When someone jury-rigs an electrical system with chewing gum—'acts as a person'—she or he draws on a knowledge of electricity and of available materials, not an instruction book. [11] The combination of a detailed perception of the world, a clear understanding of one's abilities and resources, and effective action in the world typifies all the activities mentioned as typical of persons in general.

The question of whether extended agency accounts for expectations of 'enana will be raised again with regard to 'enana as mature adults, not persons in general. First, the variety of personal processes must be elucidated.

THE ARRAY OF PERSONAL PROCESSES

Extended agency can be seen as a single personal process, defined by the qualities shared by its tokens. (Those qualities include a reliance on general understandings of human competence, detailed recognition of the particular facts about self and other, and the integration of perception, judgment, and action in a single process.) Each of these qualities may be seen as a point on a dimension or as a value in an opposition. Such dimensions and oppositions are clearly at issue in many Marquesan accounts. For instance, the factor of detailed 'recognition' of the world, present in cases of extended agency, is said by Marquesans to be absent in some other activities and severely limited in others. (Examples will be given below.) By scanning Marquesan accounts of human attitudes and actions for cases that show similar patterning in relation to the dimensions noted above, two further personal processes, desire and self-absorption, can be discerned. After these are sketched, they will be defined more precisely in relation to extended agency and to each other.

1. *Desire.* Marquesans treat several sorts of desire as subtypes or synonyms of *makimaki* 'want, desire'.[12] 'Lust' (hinena'o) is usually distinguished from these, although it is discussed in much the same terms. Desires involve a need or demand stemming from a part of the person which can be satisfied only by taking in something from outside the person. When the object of desire is acquired, the desire ceases, along with the actions it has impelled.

Two further aspects of Marquesans' characterization of desires deserve note. First, desirous agents are treated as crudely single-minded. Rutting animals are seen as ignoring everything but their desire; 'lustful' persons are seen as much the same. Although I failed to investigate the point thoroughly, it is my impression that all agents are seen, when involved in desire, as having limited percepts, as scanning the world in search of the desired object and noting little else.

Next, the mention of body parts in descriptions of desires is unlike that found for examples of extended agency. Body parts may be mentioned in subject position in relation to common actions or experiences, for example, *ua oke te kōpū* 'the belly hungered'. Again, while Marquesans do not have an elaborated theory of bodily loci of emotions and processes, it makes sense to them to identify such loci in common expressions or in response to elicitation. Thus Marquesans may say, in ordinary speech, that someone 'reflected [on a matter] in the guts' (*u kaituto io he koekoe*). Informants can name loci for many emotions or processes, such as 'concern' and 'envy' in the 'guts' (*koekoe*) or in the 'belly' (*kōpū*).[13] 'Disgust' (*to'omanu*) is in the eyes: for "the belly is nauseous as the eyes see, [hence one is] disgusted" (*e ka'epu'epu te kōpū, na te mata e kite, e to'omanu*).

Marquesans' use of body metaphors singles out desires in three ways. First, terms for body parts are far more apt to be treated as sentential subjects of verbs of desire than of verbs of extended agency. Next, the bodily sites mentioned in relation to desires and to extended agency are involved with the actions in different ways. When 'the throat thirsts' or 'the belly hungers', the named site is a locus of initial sensation and, equally, of satiation. The loci named in relation to extended agency are points of initial impetus or mediation of a process that extends beyond them. 'Shame' is located in others' eyes, and 'disgust' in one's own eyes, but these processes unfold elsewhere. Finally, body parts may be discussed in such a way that speakers seem to be crediting them with a degree of autonomy, even a capacity to impel the actor. (This may be an artifact largely of the points noted above.) An informant's exegesis conveys this impression:

> You lust for a woman because there's action with that woman: there's your cock, her vagina. Your cock is the member and that's its friend, its proper place to act [*to ia vahi hei ai*].

2. *Self-absorption*. An apparently more diverse set of emotions and actions can be understood as tokens of a single personal process. They are discussed in similar terms, as involving planning or percepts of the agent which lead to action that has little or no relationship to the ongoing social situation. Some examples of self-absorption are 'craziness', drunken behavior, and 'arrogance'.

Marquesans may use the term *koea* 'crazy' in a limited sense, in reference to madmen, or in a broad one, with regard to actions of ordinary people. Their accounts of either case underline the disjuncture between 'craziness' and the ordinary flow of social interaction. "Crazy people don't look at the person in front of them." One informant characterized those people whom he knows to have had something much like psychotic breaks as "people who don't think about their work." 'Crazy' people do think, but they are involved in their own, offstage reality. Again, the behavior of ordinary people that is deemed 'crazy' is to interrupt: "I'm doing my work and you come and play. I'll say, 'Go, what's your craziness?' You're not really crazy, that's just [what's] said."

The last informant quoted treated extreme drunken states as a form of 'craziness': "When drunk, you may get angry or say things that you don't understand. . . . That's crazy, you no longer [have/are] human nature; drunkenness takes control." [14]

The preceding cases of self-absorption involve extreme states. The process is not only found in such abnormal cases, however. 'Arrogance' (kā'i'e) is more widespread, for it is attributed regularly to many people, especially the young. 'Arrogance' involves a concentration on one's own resources, usually one's beauty and grace. 'Arrogant' youths spend much time primping in front of the mirror. Their elders may find other reasons for self-absorption. An informant reports that 'arrogance' "doesn't disappear in adults, even old people. One old man told me that it's still there. The old get money and are arrogant about having a lot. That's surely true."

'Arrogance', like other types of self-absorption, involves a concentration by the agent on himself to the exclusion of others and situational details. Parents complain that young people 'do not think' of others when busy with their own concerns. Yet 'arrogance' may result, in Marquesan tales at least, in more than narcissistic pleasure and reproofs from others. The beauty of young protagonists, male or female, may shine out and compel others' admiration. (See Handy 1930:45–51 and 118 for examples; Lavondès 1968 has commented on the central place given to beauty in these tales.) There is no hint in the tales that beauty is used by a protagonist to attract or seduce others, that he or she has an interpersonal end in view. Instead, others are overwhelmed by beauty, much as persons' resistance to a demand may 'snap' under the impact of persistent desire.

Agents engaged in either self-absorption or desire pass through the social world oblivious to most of its details. Yet these processes are not merely lapses from social life, or lacking social consequences: they are expectably part of both personal experience and social interaction.

Distinctive Features

The three types of personal process considered differ in many ways. A few distinctions seem especially prominent, however, in accounts of the most salient examples of these processes. The possibility arises that these distinctions participate in a model in which the different processes are aligned, that is, that they are features distinguishing elements in a system. The possibility can be investigated, although it cannot be shown that Marquesans have such a model in their heads.

In cases of both extended agency and desire, action mediates between the agent and the world. With self-absorption this is not so: the agent is caught up in his or her own thoughts, and any interaction is of others' making.

The next point may be approached by noting that 'thinking' and similar activities are mentioned in talk of some, but not all, of the processes discussed so far: in desire, the agent's activity is discussed as springing from a felt need, not a thought or percept. In contrast, the agent engaged in extended agency or self-absorption may 'think', 'recognize', or 'plan'— indeed, some cognitive activity seems a necessary component of these processes. 'Cognition', however, cannot be treated simply as a distinctive feature of these processes, for it does not map a Marquesan domain. (Since *kite* may be glossed as 'see' as well as 'know' or 'recognize', serious questions arise when it is treated in terms of an analytic domain that gives much weight to one possible gloss, and less to others.)

Rather than claim that extended agency and self-absorption are both cognitive, we can point to the sort of construct that must be cognized or recognized for the processes to unfold. In both cases, the agent's sense of his or her own being and constituents is detailed. The self-absorbed agent relates to his or her own beauty or the like as something that can be perceived and appreciated as one's own. In extended agency, the agent scans personal resources, viewing them in relation to the needs of self and others and to a model of self-sufficient competence. In both processes, then, the agent takes a stance in relation to his or her constituents, drawing on or erecting a self-concept, while the only comparable construct in processes of desire is a sense of need, a demand for something outside the agent.

This point clears up a potential misunderstanding. Statements that a body part impels action in desire might be read as pleas of diminished responsibility. Although the desiring agent is held to be hardly aware of the proprieties of social action, these statements cannot be viewed as excuses. They cannot succeed as pleas: a 'shameless' act of desire may not arouse immediate recognition of irresponsibility in an agent, but it still counts against his repute in others' eyes. Also, when Marquesans say, for example, 'the throat thirsted', they are not abdicating responsibility—responsibility is hardly at issue.[15] Instead, they are describing an action as immediately responsive to a bodily state and, by implication, as unmediated by the agent's self-concept.

These two distinctions, in terms of the mediation of self/world boundaries and the presence or absence of a mediating self-concept, suffice to separate the personal processes studied thus far. Moreover, the distinctions, taken together, suggest the possibility of a fourth member of the set of processes, for they suffice to distinguish four, not three, types of process. This fourth case corresponds to the activities Marquesans term 'groundless'. Using + and 0 to indicate the presence or absence of a distinctive feature, we thus have:

	Boundary	*Self-concept*
Extended agency	+	+
Desire	+	0
Self-absorption	0	+
'Groundless' activity	0	0

'Groundless' Activity

Two major sorts of action are termed 'groundless': adult responses to interaction which follow on a constant personal predisposition, not the details of the situation, and certain tantrums expected only of children.

If persons are 'constantly irritable' (*ha'o ananu*), so that they show anger or displeasure in any interaction, their responses are held to be 'groundless' (*a'e he pi'o* or *a'e he tumu*).[16] The responses can be explained in terms of the person's character. This, however, is not an adequate 'ground', in Marquesan eyes, for such undifferentiated responses. (According to the definition offered above, a willingness to be kindly or generous in any situation might equally be viewed as 'groundless'. Marquesans do not say this, but do find such conduct so puzzling that they doubt whether it exists. When extremely nice people are considered in this light, others suggest personal interest as a ground or point to situations in which the agent is less than kindly. They hence argue that his or her behavior is really motivated, and predicated on, situational details.)

Kaipipi'o 'childish rage' is the more salient and more common activity termed 'groundless'. Marquesans can identify a scenario leading to kaipipi'o. Two children play, and perhaps begin to quarrel over a toy. One passes from argument to a tantrum, and soon the other joins in. Informants deny that the quarrel was a 'ground' for the tantrum, and describe the tantrum as going beyond the bounds of one child or the other. When kaipipi'o erupts, play and the ongoing definition of situation dissolve: a contrast between a continuing, developing interaction of play—or of quarreling, for that matter—and a sudden shift when 'it went bad' is emphasized. Kaipipi'o is dissociated from the normal flow of events. Informants agree that children must be forcibly distracted from their tantrums, or the squalling would continue on and on. When the children meet again, however, the earlier tantrum does not affect their interaction: they expectably play as if nothing had happened.

In these cases, although interaction of a sort occurs, it is not predicated on the details of the situation or on self-concepts—it is 'groundless', I believe, for the former reason or for both. (Were irritability dependent on a self-concept, it might be absent in situations where that self-concept is fostered or supported; the hallmark of 'groundless' irritation, however, is its application to *all* situations.) The interaction cannot progress from 'groundless' activity to a more fruitful interchange—it is simply broken off.

PROCESS AND AGENCY

With the model of personal processes sketched, closer attention can be given to its terms and implications. Terms such as "personal process," "agent," and "agency" have served as labels for Marquesan views, but their use has not been justified. They were chosen to point toward what I take to be a Marquesan perspective. Their utility is most obvious with regard to extended agency, but not limited to it.

In cases of extended agency, a series of events, involving perception, cognition, action toward the outside world, and a change in the world, are concatenated. In speaking of ka'oha ('concern'), for instance, Marquesans may emphasize one or another event, speaking of 'concern growing' in someone or 'concern arriving' at its object, but it is clear that the entire series of events is implicated. The notion of ka'oha, then, does not refer to an action or emotion but a process in which these are interrelated. The processual character of other examples of extended agency or of desire is also fairly obvious. As for self-absorption, it involves repetitive experiences and, usually, sequences of perception, cognition, and self-directed action. The only mode of engagement in the world which lacks a processual dimension is 'groundless' activity. The common themes in Marquesan accounts of cases of 'groundless' activity are that it is not responsive to situation, it does not change or develop in response to either internal or external events, and it does not seem to have any interactive upshot beyond a cessation of interaction. We might conclude that this is no process at all, but I submit that the 'groundless' activity is notable for Marquesans as an image of the absence or negation of processual engagement. It is the negation of the other processes, rather than something unrelated to them. (A further implication can be drawn from the argument: to map Marquesan understandings, the + and 0 symbols used above should be *reversed*. Extended agency is taken as matter-of-fact, and not distinctive, while at the other extreme 'groundless activity' is highly distinctive.)

Why call these *personal* processes? The obvious answer is that persons enact them. Not just persons but 'enana enact them: the contrasts Marquesans make between 'beasts' as instinctual actors and 'persons' as capable of construing an interactive situation and acting so as to facilitate interpersonal communication links the idea of personhood with processual extension. Moreover, all but desires are processes that are enacted only by 'enana. A 'person' or 'persons' may feel 'concern' or 'shame'; 'beasts' do not.[17]

In talking of desire, Marquesans both note similarities between human and animal urges and, like many peoples, feel that humans should act unlike animals. This is most obvious in the case of 'lust'. The term *heko*—a common, but impolite, term for sexual arousal and intercourse—is explained as having been extended semantically from its sense as 'boar'. Sexually voracious and promiscuous persons are termed *mako* 'sharks'. Incest is said to be 'beastlike' behavior, for 'beasts do not recognize kinship'. The last example suggests that while humans and animals can have much the same 'lust', humans are expected to socialize it by combining desire with a major component of extended agency, 'recognition' or 'knowledge'. Similarly, parents may scold demanding children for 'not recognizing' their parents, that is, not moderating their demands out of a wish not to burden the parents or from knowledge that the parents cannot or will not supply every want. Desire may be indifferently human or animalistic, but humans should be able to temper it, given their personal capacities.[18]

"Agency," in contrast to "action" and "behavior," is used to underline the difference between Marquesan and Western views of events. Weber's (1978:4) well-known definition of action as behavior to which subjective meaning is attached focuses on internal events problematic for social scientists. What seems of basic interest to Marquesans is the extent of linkage among situation, perception, cognition, personal abilities and resources, and action—not a typology of subjective meanings. Furthermore, we typically treat status as an attribute of an actor separable from action, if informing it. I will submit in a later section that Marquesans view certain social statuses as both products of agency and identities realized in agency. An agent, then, does not simply act: he is expected to experience and act in a single process and, I will argue, to realize thereby major aspects of his social identity.

FURTHER APPLICATIONS OF THE MODEL

So far, an examination of Marquesan accounts of certain named emotions and attitudes has yielded a model of four personal processes. The analysis might suffice to show that the model maps the assumptions Marquesans draw on to define 'concern', 'lust', and the like. It remains to be seen (a) whether the distinctions stressed are important ones for Marquesans; (b) whether the model applies to Marquesans' discussions of a wider range of actions and attitudes; and (c) whether it applies to views of ongoing actions, not just to explanations of concepts. The first issue can be addressed by noting Marquesans' evaluations of the various actions and emotions discussed above. Validation is found for the model in that Marquesans evaluate extended agency positively and cases of self-absorption and desire negatively, in terms similar to the distinctions identified above. The remaining issues will be addressed by looking for similar evaluations and similar distinctions among much-used ideas in other contexts.

The claim that Marquesans stress agentive process does not mean that distinctions between inner and outer, impulse and action, demand and satisfaction are invisible to Marquesans. Rather, they are understood as expectably interrelated in human activity. When such connections are not made, Marquesans treat the activity in question as limited or flawed.

Self-absorption, with its disjuncture from the world, is seen as extremely limited. Desire, for all its inevitability and the pleasures it brings, may be seen as 'worthless' (*mea pao*) because it is not productive. While it is pleasant to fill the belly or enjoy orgasm, these ends are of limited value. Marquesans see food production, for instance, as properly culminating in the feeding of a family, not just oneself, and sexuality as ordained by God for procreation, not just pleasure.[19] For Marquesans, the begetting and nurturance of others offers, in the long run, deeper gratification than do momentary pleasures.

Similar attitudes are expressed with regard to other cases. When cognition and feeling are dissociated from action or from a complex social world, Marquesans see an incomplete process, not pure cognition or feeling. For example, Marquesans view opinions—'thinking' expressed but not acted on—dubiously, treating them as 'worthless' or suspecting they do not reflect an agent's convictions. Again, when effective action is impossible, Marquesans see agents as vulnerable. *Vivi'io* 'loneliness' is a matter of frustrated attachment for Marquesans, and dangerous in that the agent, unable to establish contact with loved ones or his homeland, may pine. The 'lonely' person searches for remembered others where they can no longer be found and breaks off other social ties.

Marquesans attempt to minimize states of dislocation by engaging the mournful agent with his surroundings. Thus one man explained that should his brother's wife die, he would feel great 'concern'. It would come to focus on his brother. Seeing the latter mourn, he would find a woman to be the brother's new wife, so that the latter's grief would end. Here both the informant and his brother have feelings directed to another, the dead woman, toward whom effective action is impossible. Both men's grief is resolved by the substitution of other persons with whom they can be engaged. (Similar practices of deflecting attention from a source of anxiety or grief are reported for Samoa by Clement [1982].)

Although three of the four personal processes clearly have emergent qualities, they differ in their complexity and their temporal extension. Desire is clearly bounded: it endures from the inception of a demand to its satiation, and brings together a demanding part of the agent, its object, and the agent as searching for and obtaining that object. Self-absorption may last for shorter or longer periods, but it is equally lacking in an outcome beyond its particular focus. As with desire, it engaged only some of the abilities and resources of the person.

Extended agency, in contrast to these processes, involves the coordination of all major aspects of the agent. Moreover, it differs greatly in outcome, for it results in a state of interactive readiness or engagement, not merely a cessation of action. This is most obvious with redressive activities such as 'concern' or 'shame' which bring agents to involvement with each other in an ongoing situation as competent and reciprocally aware. This also holds for other cases, such as the everyday tasks of maintaining a domestic unit. When a person works to support a household, his work—planning, planting, caring for crops, harvesting, and preparing food—results in well-being for both the agent and others. Such work is treated as a product of 'thinking', ability, and perseverance, as part of a personal commitment to the domestic unit, rather than simply as necessary drudgery or the outcome of a desire.

The distinctive outcome of extended agency will be shown to be central to Marquesan understandings of the life cycle. It is helpful to turn first to Marquesan accounts of mature friendships, in order to show (a) that both extended agency and desire contribute to the definition of relationships, not just actions; (b) that these processes can coexist intelligibly; and (c) that the difference in their outcome is of importance for Marquesans.

Personal Processes in Mature Friendships

Marquesans expect friendships to involve people similar in age, sex, circumstances, and interactive style. An informant, asked if a girl and an old woman might befriend each other, expressed doubt:

> "Girls and old women think differently, [they] don't fit. The old woman recognizes ka'oha, while the *taure'are'a* ['errant youth'] woman has no ka'oha in her thinking, has different thinking. Mature adults, even if they are not friends, talk to one another; they have mature thought [unlike the young]."

Adults' friendships are seen as different from those of the young, even though most develop from youthful ties. Those that begin among previously unacquainted adults are described as involving an exchange of help, food, or talk—yet, it is not a balanced exchange but a demonstration of commitment that is crucial. One man, for example, counts a paramedic on another island as a 'friend' (*hoa*). When the man first came to the hospital he was sick and disoriented. While convalescing there, he would sit at the edge of conversational groups. Slowly, he came to join in the talk. The paramedic enjoyed jokes, and often made fun of people, including the informant. The informant was not offended. When the informant finally returned the favor, making fun of the paramedic, and both knew that the other accepted these jokes in good spirits, not as intrusions or slights, then a friendship existed. Other examples, involving different bases of collaboration, make the same point: friends have a commitment to each other which is established when they show that they accept the other's demands and quirks and can arrange their other commitments to make themselves available for the friend.

Mature friendships do not need to be enacted in any one particular way, although friends expectably chat, lend and borrow, and help each other in time of need. The absence of a ritualized scenario of friendship follows from Marquesans' view of the relationship as a matter of recognized interpersonal 'fit' (*hei 'ia*) or 'accustomedness' (*hani 'ia*), and as based on 'concern', 'faith', and 'remembrance' (*hakama'akau*, equated with the Tahitian *ti'aturi*). Friendships exist between persons, not in standard enactments. Talkative persons chat a good deal with their friends; others do not. Poor people get help from their friends; those who do not need such help tend not to expect it.

Marquesans' talk of 'concern' and the like highlights the role of extended agency in friendships. Yet this also discloses a problem when the self-sufficient competence of 'persons' associated with extended agency is kept in mind. If friends are capable of providing for themselves, what remains to be done in their interactions? Part of the answer is that relaxed, friendly interactions are pleasant in themselves. Part of the answer is that people are not expected to be self-sufficient in all ways at all times: sooner or later, anyone will need a little help from his friends. Thus, when friends meet, one or another is often needy or desirous—less than self-sufficient and perhaps not manifesting the extended agency that characterizes a mature friendship. The other helps the friend, if possible, and hence helps him or her regain self-sufficiency. Strictly speaking, while the friendship of the mature follows from a detailed perception of 'fit' between persons, from exchanges of kindness and demonstrated commitment—from the extended agency of both parties, in short—it is often enacted in scenes in which extended agency is not manifest on both sides, only one party having the resources or the processual organization at issue. This is not to say that people fail to live up to ideals, only that friends need not enact their full personal capacities at all times. Instead of a needy friend being less than a friend, it seems that a helpful friend can encompass the other's need, allowing the other to return to the form of agency that characterizes him or her as a partner in the friendship as well as the relationship itself.

Extended agency, then, is more than a form of engagement of an agent with his or her world while he or she acts in it. It can be called on to build relationships and to arrange matters so that other processes can reach their fulfillment. It can provide organization for an agent, his or her surroundings, and others. Its value does not lie simply in its complexity, but in its role in making a world in which the various personal processes are enacted, a world that is orderly yet allows fulfillment of people's diverse aims. This becomes even more evident when Marquesan views of life stages are examined.

THE LIFE STAGES

Marquesans can view the life cycle in several ways. The most notable of these is a model of life stages which sets out a career that persons expectably follow. This career is not inevitable, for some people do not progress through all the stages. The stages, as Marquesans understand them, differ from each other along many dimensions. Taure'are'a, for example, differ from *tō'iki* 'kids' in their physical development, their mobility, their domestic relations, their friendships, their consumption preferences, their forms of play, and their 'thinking'.

The distinctions among the life stages are not of equal weight, for some have explanatory value in relation to the others. The life stages are best understood as syntheses of personal resources and situation achieved through characteristic patterns of thought and action. Those patterns are distinguished from each other in ways that recall the differences among personal processes: the set of life stage patterns includes one example of effective and enduring activity based on extended agency, and other cases of less effective, less situationally nuanced, more immediate action. Hence, while the life stages cannot be identified in a one-to-one match with the personal processes, the set of life stages is organized in the same sort of array by similar distinctions with a similar stress on the efficacy of processually complex action.

The stages correlate only roughly with age differences; other categories specify age more precisely than do these. The term taure'are'a is the clearest case. Graceful, vivacious young people are exemplary taure'are'a, but the term can be applied to persons from fifteen to fifty years old. Specific terms for 'young people' (*te po'i hou* and gender-specific terms) focus more clearly on people of fifteen to twenty. The independence of taure'are'a, as a life stage category, from age is evident when Marquesan adults talk of 'going to taure'are'a' (*he'e i te taure'are'a*) at feasts. They do not claim to act like or resemble youths but to 'go to' a setting in which their activity is that of taure'are'a. Conversely, young people may go to great lengths to show that they are not idle taure'are'a but hardworking and moral persons—although this does not stop others from expecting them to act as taure'are'a sooner or later.

'Infants' (*kaiū* or *pēpē*) have few competences, but they have a will of their own. Although infants a month or two old are seen as 'not knowing how to play' (or do much else), their movements are interpreted as intentional and responsive to circumstances. During the first year, much of the work of socialization amounts to an attempt to engage the infant with the social world and to develop the motor and perceptual skills necessary for the infant to take a place as a separate agent in that world. (See Martini and Kirkpatrick [1981] for more detail.)

'Kids' (tō'iki) are dependent on adults for their care and feeding, if less so than are 'infants'.[20] They wander away from domestic sites while engaged in 'play'. Adults claim that 'kids' are incapable of work without adult direction: their attention wanders, and even when they do work, they 'play' at it. Again, while 'kids' may practice 'concern' or 'shame', these are not 'firm' in them: they do not arise regularly, or may not arise at all without adult supervision. 'Kids' have 'friends' (hoa), but adults claim that 'kids' befriend anyone available for play. These relationships are therefore things of the moment. Similarly, 'kids' do not hold grudges, and those who indulge in kaipipi'o, tantrums, or angry bickering one day will expectably play together happily the next.

'Infants' become 'kids' as they become increasingly mobile; 'kids' become taure'are'a when their interest in play turns from innocent to 'bad' forms, above all, to sexuality. One does not become a taure'are'a at a set age or after a rite of passage, but only when taure'are'a thought 'grows'. Then one engages in typical taure'are'a activities: close same-sex friendships spiced with singing, gossip, the sharing and divulging of secrets, and occasional tricks played on elders or members of the other sex, as well as attempts at cross-sex liaisons.

While 'kids' wander away from their homes, taure'are'a are seen as having their own socially liminal loci: 'on the road' or, when engaged in clandestine sexual encounters, 'in the bush'. Taure'are'a are expected to 'wander' from valley to valley when they can, seeking new experiences. Such travels are the basis for memorable friendships between residents and travelers, who may even become name-giving partners.[21] These friendships may be more intimate than those of the mature, for taure'are'a may share their adventures and secrets. They are less secure relationships, however, if only because secrets can be retold to other associates.

I was told that 'taure'are'a thought' and 'mature adult thought' come to people at the same time. It is impossible to predict from the actions of a 'kid' what sort of adult he will become. The 'kid' acts according to his or her version of 'kid's thought', and his or her later behavior will be conditioned by both enthusiasm for taure'are'a life and his or her 'mature adult thought'.

Taure'are'a life has its joys. In youth, physical skills reach their high point, and young taure'are'a have a grace and beauty that will soon diminish with age. Although particular graceful actions, such as skillful play in a soccer match, may not be impelled by taure'are'a 'thought', the grace and beauty of youth are often discussed as part of a person's *tai taure'are'a* 'period of errant youth'. This is because young people are regularly treated as though they are devoted to taure'are'a values, and hence as though developing their skills for taure'are'a ends, above all, enjoyment of self-display, active involvement in 'merriment' (*'eka'eka*), and 'orgasmic pleasure' (*mānini*).

Taure'are'a life has drawbacks, for taure'are'a are viewed as participants in a part-society with few goals and interactants. Many religious young people deny being taure'are'a; other unmarried youths may find taure'are'a life increasingly ill-fitting. Thus one man returned to his home island to find his age-mates married, and took up life as a taure'are'a with younger social peers. Soon, however, he 'was not accustomed' to these associates and wanted a domestic life of his own: he found 'a woman to mother' him, and quickly married her.

The transition between the taure'are'a and 'mature adult' (*'enana mōtua*, literally 'parent person') stages is a lengthy and uncertain one. With marriage, a couple takes on a new social identity, but Marquesans do not expect newlyweds to learn to live together quickly. They bicker about work to be done, about money, about each spouse's time spent with old friends, about suspicions of adultery. Such bickering is ample evidence for Marquesans that the spouses are not 'mature adults'. (They may still be called taure'are'a even if they no longer participate in taure'are'a groups.) In time, as children are born and the couple establishes a home and domestic routines suited to personal temperaments, the spouses 'do not persist in opposing' each other. They find a modus vivendi. Informants estimate that people settle down and 'mature thought' usually emerges about the time a second child is born to a couple.

This emergence of 'mature thought' deserves some comment. First, it is clear that the activity most closely identified with 'mature adulthood' is work to support a household. The mature "recognize the work to be done, and do it"; when "the day ends, the work is done." Their work is oriented to domestic maintenance, and evinces their commitment to a continuing project of domestic production and reproduction—in short, of 'life' (*pohu'e*) as Marquesans understand it. Second, this emergence of 'mature thought' may seem unnecessary given its prior existence in the agent. If 'mature thought' is present in the agent at his entry into taure'are'a life, or, as Marquesans may also say, at the time of first Communion, is anything new occurring later? The answer is that 'mature thought' becomes a recognized central constituent of the mature agent, not an occasional practice unsupported by internal predispositions or social circumstances.

Certain factors impel a transition toward 'mature adult' life. Taure'are'a life, if continued when grace disappears, is apt to be 'disgusting', and middle-aged drunks may find few associates for revelry. More important, taure'are'a ends can only be achieved regularly with forethought of a sort not ascribed to taure'are'a. Continuing sexual liaisons must be maintained by gifts, pledges of love, and secrecy. If they become publicly known, they end or are transformed into recognized marital unions.[22] And they do become known, whether because one member tells his friends or because others deduce the existence of the liaison. If one is to remain a taure'are'a, one is condemned to an endless search for new sexual partners and to dealing with new, younger, same-sex peers. Marriage is nearly inevitable, and while it does not bring maturity, it makes the pleasures of taure'are'a life possible only as occasional binges at feasts.

The 'mature adult' has as a locus the home maintained by his or her efforts. The householder does not simply stay at home, but neither does he or she 'wander': the mobility of the 'mature adult' is found in purposeful action, in getting food and supplies for the household.[23] The domestic relations of householders are characterized by productive efficacy, based on their personal resources and the ability of spouses (and other housemates) to work out ways to combine their skills and labor. In contrast to the consumption preferences of the immature (milk for 'infants', candy for 'kids', sexual partners for taure'are'a), the 'mature' feed a household. The friendships of the mature may derive from earlier ties, as was noted, but they are based on proven commitments and endure over time, unlike the stormy relations of taure'are'a.

People may speak of themselves as 'old' while still under forty. As their physical abilities decline, skills and planning are of increasing importance in accomplishing tasks. As physical decline continues, three distinct styles of being 'old' are visible. Many strive to maintain their domestic units, by supervising others' work if not so much by laboring themselves. They find work to do and, if need be, dependents to support. In the terms used here, they are prolonging their identity as 'mature adult' householders in the face of old age. A few find themselves reduced to dependence on their children and to near immobility in their children's households. No longer 'fit' in this world—they ache, their efforts are no longer adequate to support themselves, and their knowledge is of little value in a changing world—they prepare themselves for the next world by means of prayer and worship. Finally, some few elders are *ko'oua oko* 'strongly old', that is, senile. They no longer have 'mature thought' but are "as kids once again."

Strictly speaking, then, old age is not a life stage fully comparable to the others discussed here. Instead, with age comes a series of problems to be surmounted the best people can. The preferred solution is to hold on to the direction of a household, and thus to an activity and a material context that stand as visible evidence of 'maturity'. If that is not possible, the old can still try to match their personal resources with a world, heaven, in which they can hope to find a place and in which their limitations are irrelevant. 'Old persons' draw on personal constituents quite unlike those of the 'mature' only when reduced to senility, an outcome feared by Marquesans.

The preceding sketch should suffice to establish certain points and suggest others. The life stage concepts integrate multiple distinctions into coherent identities. Those identities make sense to Marquesans in part because types of 'thinking' are seen as underlying diverse actions. Immature identities are treated as based on limited forms of 'thinking'. The activities characteristic of such identities are coded as disjointed and without cumulative results, even though the intermittent quality of particular young people's activity may not be so apparent to an outside observer. Maturity, while it involves continuing efforts to maintain dependents, a home, and relationships beyond the home, is seen as having long-lived consequences. Dependents live, thanks to their elders, and a site of domestic order is erected and maintained.

A point needs clarification: why should such notions as 'mature adult thought' have explanatory force for Marquesans? When 'thought' is not enacted, Marquesans take it to be unknowable. Thus they claim ignorance of others' opinions without detailed evidence in past events as a basis for inference. In speaking of life stages, Marquesans treat 'thought' as more evident and seem to grant it the status of a cause of behavior. I think the latter impression is incorrect, for 'mature adult thought' is a matter of capacity and general orientation, not a specific content. It therefore does not cause specific behaviors. Also, such 'thought' is found in numerous empirical indices. A 'mature adult' has a home and dependents, and a history of devoting his particular skills and energies to their support. Marquesans do not argue that a particular 'thought' impels action; instead, they sum up evidence of past action, present ability, and continuing concerns in terms of 'mature adult thought'.

A person becomes a 'mature adult', in others' eyes, by acting as one, and is a 'mature adult' by continuing to do so. 'Thought' contributes to a person's maturity, but so does the evidence of past productive work—neat, well-fed children, a sturdy home kept clean and in good repair—and the demands of dependents for continuing care.

THE LIFE STAGES AND LIVED IDENTITIES

The life stage categories inform Marquesans' views of self and others. They provide a model of the life course in which actions, phases of life, and modes of relationship make detailed sense. This does not mean, however, that identifying particular persons with one state or another is a simple matter. This is obvious in referentially problematic situations, as with young married adults who are neither committed to taure'are'a pleasures nor granted respect as capable, mature householders. Also, shifting ascriptions may be made by a speaker about another. One man would often praise his wage-earning son as an industrious 'youth' (*maha'i hou*), viewing his activity as more productive than that of taure'are'a. He would also occasionally speak of the son as a taure'are'a in relation to such contexts as festivals. Next, I was surprised by his response to my question of whether this skilled and hardworking young man could organize his own wedding feast. He could never manage this, the father said, "[he is] a kid." Here, incompetence rather than the urges of taure'are'a is at issue, as, probably, are the informant's own ability to oversee his household and organize complex events. His son is therefore labeled as a less than competent dependent, despite his age and extensive work for the household.

Speakers do use the life stage categories to pinpoint persons' identities, but their claims are often challenged. It is not so much in dividing a social universe into sets of actors whom all see to be similar, as it is in motivating action that confirms or invalidates such identifications, that the life stage categories play a part in Marquesan life.

The 'kid' identity usually poses little problem. Children of ten or so do not describe themselves as stochastic agents, but they accept being designated as 'kids'. With this label they often have to accept a devaluation of their labor as 'play' or as depending on adult instruction for its efficacy. Assumptions about the agency of 'kids' appear to be self-validating when we note that a parent may tell a child, "Don't play," in reaction to any behavior—obstructive, cooperative, or otherwise—the child produces without prompting.

The expectations associated with taure'are'a identity can hardly be realized by a person continuously.[24] At the other end of life, the decrepitude of 'old people' is abhorrent to Marquesans. Young people and elders are apt to claim, by word or deed, that they are responsible producers. The value of 'mature adult' identity is amply shown by Marquesans' efforts to disavow alternative life stage interpretations of their existences.

'Mature adult' identity cannot be ascribed simply on the basis of momentary activities. The immature may enact extended agency, but such action is taken to be poorly rooted in the agent's 'thinking'. Conversely, those who maintain a domestic space may feel free to relinquish their serious concerns for a moment, to carouse and 'go to taure'are'a', so long as this does not endanger their ongoing commitments. The life stage categories, then, do not encode ways to evaluate particular actions so much as contexts in which actions can be seen as evidence of a dominant personal organization, of momentary aberrations that are possible given the stochastic nature of immature agency, or of nondominant impulses encompassed by mature organization.

Finally, it should be noted that 'mature adulthood' is not easily claimed. The 'mature' are committed to work and a supple interactive stance, not self-praise. Moreover, their efforts can easily be found inadequate should the question arise. While a peaceful home and well-fed children testify to mature agency, such factors as the children's misbehavior can always be ascribed to a failure of the parents to teach proper behavior instead of to the children's willfulness. Again, what may seem momentary relaxation at a feast may be construed by others as a sign of recurrent insobriety and limited commitment to domestic production. Even if a positive identity as a 'mature adult' is obvious to a person's consociates, it cannot be defended and validated against all suspicions.

The life stages provide a set of judgments about persons which synthesize varied data, but which hardly portray in detail how persons actually live. Nonetheless, the categories are credible ones for Marquesans, for they dovetail with expectations of (a) the interrelations of internality and action; (b) the superiority of extended agency as a productive form of life and action; and (c) the superiority of such agency as organizing both the agent and his world as enduring phenomena, not just intermittent gestures.

CONSTRUING PERSONS

Much of the previous discussion shows ways Marquesans view their consociates. Persons may be seen to engage in recognized sorts of agency. More generally, they may be variously construed as stochastic beings involved in 'play' or the like, but not in providing thereby an enduring organization for themselves; as effective, 'mature adult' agents who organize both themselves and others; or, if self-absorbed or continually 'irritated', as involved in a private world that detracts from their humanity as it separates them from realistic engagement in interaction.

The analysis can advance another step by noting how one Marquesan reaches an understanding of a person as a unique being. Marquesans expect persons to have 'distinctiveness' (*hakatu*), and they expect the distinctive qualities of adults, at least, to be part of a recurrently visible personal organization. (This is not equivalent to saying that they believe in and value a cultural construct of individuality, as Dumont [1970] stresses.) 'Distinctiveness' is an expected aspect of persons, but hardly a valued one.

One informant was sickly and to support his household, he depended on his children's work and his own exchanges, with the French, of local produce for imported goods. When he said that he did not 'know the distinctiveness' of a French newcomer, I was surprised. His daughter worked next door to the new arrival's home, and had surely described him. He had attended feasts at which the newcomer was present. He had no doubt heard much talk from others about him. All this was indeed the case—but he did not yet have the right sort of information. He had not yet interacted face-to-face with the newcomer. Should the Frenchman have dealings with him, then he would know the other's 'distinctiveness'. The informant did *not* say that extremely close relationships are necessary for people to know one another. A few exchanges of greetings, news, and food would suffice to specify who the Frenchman was. A few days later, the Frenchman came to get produce; the informant dealt with him for a few minutes and thus 'knew his distinctiveness'.

One point of this story is that ethnic labels, occupation, and observed traits do not tell Marquesans much about a person—but interactive style does. What is more, the informant trusts his own feelings and skills at negotiation in complex interactive settings (the Frenchman knowing no Marquesan, the informant little French) to give a true and adequate picture of the other. Persons are known in and through interaction. Extended agency is not only sought in the other to be known but is also deployed as a process of knowing. It is precisely the ability of the Frenchman and the informant to come to terms with each other, to find their common ground, that is at issue.

CONCLUSION

In the introduction, two challenges were raised: learning from Marquesans a perspective on human action and identity and, more specifically, identifying the sense made, for Marquesans, in various limits on 'shame'. Those limits can now be understood in terms of the capabilities ascribed to agents engaged in different processes and of the value placed on the productive extended agency of mature householders. 'Shame' and 'lust' are incommensurate, being exemplars of distinct processes. The grime of the mature might be a matter of 'shame', but the mature welcome others' recognition of signs of their hard work.

The first challenge is more difficult. Certainly, some of the knowledge of humanity Marquesans convey in talk of 'concern' and in interpreting actors as engaged in complex processes of situated agency has been covered. I have also tried to depict the ways Marquesan ethnopsychology can help people to find value and self-esteem in their daily activities and domestic careers. In so doing, I have underlined the point that cultural knowledge of psychology can be applied to much more than the job of distinguishing among persons. It can provide keys to understanding careers, relationships, and even larger social groups. The informant discussed in the last section, for example, described the commune administration in terms of a field of extended agency, not an organizational chart. For him, projects "in the head" of the mayor are crucial to the commune's experience. The mayor conceives them and plans their execution. He gives orders and explanations to foremen, who then tell work crews what jobs are to be done. The result is that the 'thought' of the mayor is realized, and the people enjoy salaried work and the benefits of the accomplished project.

A full account of the uses of Marquesan ethnopsychology is beyond the scope of this chapter. Also, it should be noted that many pertinent questions have not been raised. For one, little attention has been given to variations in the incidence and expression of 'shame' through the life cycle. As Rosaldo (1980) has shown, the cultural recognition of quite disparate experiences and reactions through the life cycle under a single rubric such as 'shame' both delineates an expected developmental course and helps socialize actors to it. (Poole [chap. 6] and Lutz [chap. 2] develop this insight in accounts of developments much like the one at issue here.) As both the model developed here and these comparable studies suggest, 'shame' emerges in childhood, for Marquesans, out of a less valued and less differentiated 'fear' (ha'ameta'u). The 'shame' of the young may paralyze action when they are subjected to disapproval. With adults, 'shame' is expected to function more as a guidepost to situations to be minimized or avoided, as it did for the bridegroom whose sense of 'shame' stopped him from making a request.

Moreover, the structures delineated here do not suffice to predict many Marquesan interpretations of particular events. The model of personal processes and the life stage account of human careers do affect both the interpretation of action and Marquesans' self-presentation as observers commenting on others. This is not, however, a sufficient basis for detailed and reliable predictions of Marquesans' situated interpretations, only a starting point adequate to account for many events and to highlight unexplained features of other interactions Marquesans may find puzzling.

As a study of ethnopsychological structures, I have aimed more at delineating recurrent practices of interpretation than at dealing with all the specifics—social context, personal biography, the pragmatics of interpersonal negotiation—that may be involved in a particular situated account. (See Black's analysis [chap. 7] for a study dealing with such specifics.) Many of the inferences Marquesans can draw from ordinary events have been identified, and shown to be rooted in an organized perspective. In conclusion, I wish to highlight a few of the potentials of that perspective for making sense of actors and actions. In doing so, I do not deny that, as Marquesans draw on it, they often make vague, inaccurate, and highly motivated judgments.

Marquesans manage to convey complex information about situated qualities of action in their comments. They code actions, in terms of continuity with ongoing activity and fit with others' expectations, as 'crazy' or 'shameful', and the like. They can and do identify action as proceeding from complex intentional and cognitive schemata, and as contributing to personal careers.

At one level, these points are not novel. It is difficult, perhaps impossible, to devise a language for describing action which does not carry some such information, at least by implication. Folk reasoners elsewhere draw complex inferences from minimal evidence (see Garfinkel [1967] and McHugh [1968] for examples). What seems worth noting is Marquesans' evaluation of persons in terms of activity and interactive potentials, not fixed innate character traits. (See White, chap. 9, for a related, but slightly different, assessment of A'ara evaluations.)

Marquesans can 'know' persons' 'distinctiveness' and recognize each other as friends in terms of abilities and willingness to engage in extensive interaction. Maxims used by English speakers, such as "Birds of a feather flock together" or "Opposites attract," point toward broad notions of personality to explain why people get along with each other.[25] Marquesans note, instead, the capacities of agents to interact in particular ways, in 'play', conversation, or reciprocal aid. Friendship can be erected by agents on the basis of similar capacities and enacted in similar or complementary processes.

This view does not rely on a static notion of personal predilections or traits, at least with regard to adults. The immature are treated as developing relationships based on a limited set of shared interests. But adults are taken to be far more complex; they can find ways to interact with a wide range of others. Both similarities between persons and complementary needs can help relationships develop, but Marquesans stress neither. They point instead to the achievement of interpersonal trust and tolerance as the hallmark of 'mature adult' friendships.

One Marquesan shared a hospital room with me when I lacked the energy and linguistic skills needed to do or say much. Nonetheless, he found enough evidence to feel 'accustomed' to me, and we later became close. Others saw me more as an object of 'concern' around that time; the kind and patient help they gave in response to my plight did much to advance my fieldwork. Marquesans can draw on their notion of interpersonal 'fitness' and 'concern' to create quite novel relationships, as well as relationships involving less exotic partners.

I should add that 'concern' and a confidence that one can be 'accustomed' even to an ethnographer do not blind Marquesans to interpersonal differences. I suspect that many saw my questions about opinions and practices as 'crazy', an interruption in the normal give and take of conversation. Even I managed to hear a few hints to this effect. Marquesans can see others as 'stingy' or 'sneaky', yet still find ways to live amicably with them.

The perspective outlined in this chapter contributes doubly to this tolerance: in allocating value to skills of interpersonal accommodation and in limiting the force of notions of personal differentiation. So long as persons are seen in life stage terms, their goals and interactive competences are varied but recognizable. Moreover, their more unusual traits may be seen as limited to the enactment of particular processes or to particular interactive routines, not as endemic to an agent's character. The ethnographer may be 'crazy' in many situations, and another man may 'twist' (*kāvi'i*, glossed above as 'sneaky') at times, but other people can determine when these propensities emerge, can find ways to make them tolerable in interaction, and can explore other interactive capacities of these persons. After all, a defining feature of 'persons' is the ability to find ways to communicate and cooperate with other 'persons', no matter how strange they may be.

The assumptions Marquesans deploy in making sense of their world thus qualify their recognition of human differences. Other ethnopsychologies may involve similar implicit subtleties, but these have received little recognition. Unless, as students of human practical reasoning, we attend to the detailed expectations people employ in interpreting actions and traits, we risk reducing the complex judgments and heuristics of everyday life to lifeless stereotypes.

ACKNOWLEDGMENTS

The research on which this paper is based was conducted in French Polynesia from August 1975 to August 1977. I am grateful to the National Institutes of Health and the National Science Foundation for financial support, through a fellowship (PHS 1-F31-MHO5154) and grant (SOC 75-13983), to the administration of the Territory of French Polynesia for permission to do the research and for extensive cooperation, to the Centre O.R.S.T.O.M. on Tahiti for many kindnesses, and to the officials and people of 'Ua Pou for their patient and hospitable reception. Mary I. Martini did fieldwork with me in 1976–77; she has helped in many ways. Comments and work by others in the ASAO Folk Psychology group,

particularly Jane Fajans, Catherine Lutz, and Geoffrey White, have helped
me to clarify much of my analysis.

NOTES

1. Benedict (1946) offers the classic statement of the shame culture concept.
Singer (in Piers and Singer 1953) has a detailed critique of the theoretical and
empirical application of the concept. Levy (1974) has developed a new argument,
based on data similar to those considered here, for distinguishing shame and guilt
as behavioral controls found in different mixes in different sorts of society. His
model is not considered in this chapter, as hakā'ika and the like are studied as cultural
constructs, not as behavioral controls.

2. Marquesan forms are presented here so as to follow standard usage on the
island of 'Ua Pou. Most residents of the island speak a variant of the northern
Marquesan dialect, one notable for its retention of /k/ in some slots where /'/ is
found elsewhere, for example, *koe* 'you (sing.)'. The apostrophe is used to represent
glottal stops. The macron indicates a long vowel. Vowel length in Marquesan may
be minimally enunciated, or not enunciated at all in many contexts. For some
indications of vowel length I am indebted to the prior work of Henri Lavondès and
his Marquesan collaborators. However, I cannot guarantee that all long vowels are
indicated here. For more information on the Marquesan language and the linguistic
situation in the Marquesas, see Dordillon (1931–32) and Lavondès (1972).

3. 'Enana need not be restricted to the meanings discussed here. The term may
embrace nonhumans and may separate unmarked sorts of persons from marked
classes of foreigners, women, or children. In this chapter, most of these complexities
and the interesting problems associated with an ethnopsychology potentially applicable to God, ghosts, and humans alike are ignored. For a much more detailed
account of 'enana, see Kirkpatrick (1983).

4. A more interesting separation was noted among Marquesan Protestants.
Tahitian is their language of worship, and church members read the Tahitian Bible.
This may affect their Marquesan usage. One Protestant informant discussed *mana*
with me as a general concept, drawing on biblical examples (Kirkpatrick 1983).
Were Tahitian used as a language for understanding everyday life in the light of
God's revelations, as is done in *tuaro'i* discussions of Scripture by Tahitian Protes-
tants, a more pervasive effect of the religious language might be expected. Such
meetings rarely occur in the Marquesas, however. When a Marquesan emigrant on
Tahiti tried to show me how tuaro'i speeches worked, he found that he could not
reproduce in Marquesan the processes of textual criticism that he managed in
Tahitian. Unless such meetings become far more frequent among Marquesan Protestants, I do not expect Tahitian religious language to affect Marquesan usage much.

5. I believe that Henri Lavondès pointed out to me that *hei* is best translated
thus, in line with his informants' view of the term as related to the way a floral
garland (*hei*) fits on a person.

6. 'Fear' in this text translates as *hōpū* (*hopo* in the southern dialect, of which

Dordillon [1931:172] gives a detailed description). This term seems to cover a range of feelings, from fear to respect, that restrain action.

7. The phrase *a'e tō tātou pohu'e*, glossed as 'we won't survive', might be more literally phrased 'our (pl.) life will not be'. The speaker is stressing a notion of shared domestic 'life' or 'livelihood'.

8. Similarly, I was given contradictory advice by Marquesans on how to do fieldwork. Some told me to be 'brash' and demand anything of people; others emphasized interpersonal sensitivity, urging me to 'go gently'.

9. A similar insistence on the fundamental equality of 'persons' is visible in accounts of why claims to chiefly rank are rare nowadays. After the demographic crisis of the last century, I suspect that any Marquesans might claim some chiefly descent—but informants do not mention this point often. Instead, they see claims to chiefly status as invalid without the support of the populace. To paraphrase one informant: "That's worthless. If you say you're chief, others will reply, 'Sure, but who gets the work done?'"

10. Elsewhere (Kirkpatrick 1983), the phrase "mental activity" is used for what here is called extended agency. Unless a Marquesan account of mental process is stressed, the earlier phrase may be misleading, so I no longer use it. Also, in that analysis, I emphasized cognitive components of extended agency in a way that now seems inadvisable for two reasons: it gave priority to one part of extended agency over others without extensive ethnographic justification, and it imputed existence to a domain of "cognition" which seems to have little ethnographic reality.

11. 'Recognize', 'see', and 'know' are all glosses for the Marquesan term *kite*. Marquesans may distinguish technical know-how (*have 'ia*) from 'knowledge' in general (*kite 'ia*), but treat this as a special case of 'knowledge' in general. What is 'known' is strongly distinguished both from ignorance and/or incompetence and from uncertain knowledge based on what one has 'heard' (*oko 'ia*) but not experienced directly.

12. Not all instances in which makimaki is mentioned map unambiguously the personal process of desire discussed here. The discussion deals with Marquesan accounts of agency and the large part of everyday discourse illuminated by them, on the assumption that if Marquesans do not count ambiguous cases against their accounts of agency, they need to be so counted here.

13. Except when standardized expressions militate for identifying an experience with a single bodily locus (e.g., *makoekoe* 'rumination' in the koekoe), Marquesans need not agree on one locus or another. The matter is complicated by such factors as part-whole relations, as between the 'guts' and 'belly', and Marquesans' knowledge of the European imagery of the heart.

14. 'Human nature' glosses *natura 'enana*. This phrase is borrowed from mission teachings. Here the informant is developing a concept not widely used by Marquesans.

15. Here I am arguing against a facile application of the notion of depersonalization to studies of discourse in other languages without careful study of the various ways agentive roles may be represented in such languages. I believe that this criticism counts, for instance, against specific readings of Tahitian statements by

Levy (1973:497). It does not necessarily count against his delineation of Tahitian behavioral strategies, which he sees as cases of depersonalization.

16. Dordillon (1931:326, 414) translates *pi'o* as "motive, subject, cause" and *tumu* as "principle, cause, source, head, capital, subject, beginning, foundation." The latter term's major objective referent is the trunk or stalk of plants. Both these terms are commonly used in talk of causation. Tumu, however, is semantically richer, as a few collocational examples show: *ka'avai tumu* 'home valley' (of a person who has lived in several places), *tumu hāmani* 'schoolteacher' (*hāmani*: 'paper').

17. This statement is based on general impressions, not extensive interviewing on the specific point. Does a sow ka'oha her piglets? I think not—or, rather, I think that Marquesans would answer the question in the negative, but might speak jokingly of particular pigs as enacting ka'oha. It is notable that a term for self-abasement, *ha'anuhenuhe*, is seen as properly applying to dogs, and to people only by loose analogy. It refers to dogs' fawning before their masters. It is not treated as a variant of 'shame'.

In addition to desire, animals are capable of 'fear' (*ha'ameta'u*) and 'anger' (*ha'aha'a* or pekē). These do not fit neatly into the model developed in this chapter. 'Persons' should, in Marquesans' opinion, 'fear' little and banish 'anger' from their hearts. Hence the problematic status of these two at least does not affect the presentation of the model as an account of how Marquesans feel persons should act in social life.

18. The neologisms I have introduced apply well to most of the Marquesan notions discussed here. With not-so-personal desire, or not-so-processual 'ground-less' activity, we might wish to abandon these usages. To do so, however, is to treat these as isolates, not elements in a structure. An analogy may make the point clear. In many societies, persons have extensive, well-defined legal rights, but children's rights are highly qualified. Indeed, children's rights might be more limited than the range of rights that legal experts would deem inherent in persons. This hardly means that children are nonpersons; rather, they are viewed as persons who merit special treatment. Their rights are derived from a consideration of them as persons, although subsequent considerations greatly affect their legal status. Similarly, I submit that Marquesans treat human action as processual and personal, and treat cases that fit these descriptions poorly as problematic cases, not as nonprocessual or nonpersonal.

19. This distinction is most visible when the definition of 'cannibalism' and 'incest' (both *kaikaiā*) in terms of 'eating', that is, pure consumption, is noted. In contrast, 'feeding' (*hākai*) is criterial of several conjugal and ascendant domestic statuses for Marquesans (Kirkpatrick 1979). Again, for Marquesans a household in which a couple subsists alone is hardly a home: only with dependents to be 'fed' are adults productive, valuable beings.

20. I gloss *tō'iki* as 'kid', not 'child', in order to reserve the latter term, with its clear relational component, as a gloss for *tama*. Marquesans may speak of someone as "my kid" (*ta'u tō'iki*), but the term *tō'iki* does not necessarily indicate an intergenerational relation, as *tama* or *pō'iti* (masc.) and *pāho'e* (fem.) 'beloved child' do.

21. The giving of names after baptism is intermittently practiced in several con-

texts in the Marquesas. The giving of one's name to a non-kin friend, usually termed *hakahoa*, literally 'making friend', seems to happen rarely nowadays except among young people from different areas. The practice usually has few social consequences except as a way of enacting friendship convincingly; the fact that a name is given may be quickly forgotten by everyone except the name giver and name receiver.

22. The phrase "recognized marital unions" is used to cover marriages and a few cases in which people live together publicly without benefit of marriage, usually because the spouses are of different churches and refuse to convert to each other's faith. The children of such unions are legitimated by civil acts.

23. Contrasts between gender ideals are ignored here, to bring out the basic themes on which gender variations are elaborated. Marquesans speak as if men leave and return to their households with food and fish, while women stay, cleaning and cooking. This claim suffices to show men as outside and women as inside producers of domestic life, but it obscures the fact that mature persons of either gender are known to be able to support households by their own efforts. Also, it should be noted that Marquesans do not treat the inside/outside complementarity as a rule that must be followed. Variant organizations of domestic task routines are evaluated in terms of their efficacy. So long as a household is maintained, it is appropriate for householders to allocate tasks according to their predispositions and situation. It may, for instance, be very unusual for a man to stay home cooking while his wife works for a salary, but Marquesans would find a couple somewhat bizarre if they could only earn money in this way and chose not to do so.

24. Much more could be said about both the limitations ascribed to people labeled as taure'are'a and the varied ways people act so as to challenge their being identified in this way. In another paper (Kirkpatrick 1982), I suggest that the inaccuracy of the taure'are'a stereotype as a portrait of young persons' complex lives functions to mobilize processes of self-discovery, and hence the development of differentiated personal identities.

25. These examples are in O'Hare and Duck (1981). Their paper stimulated some of these remarks.

GLOSSARY

'enana	person, Marquesan, adult human, mature adult (see Kirkpatrick 1980 for further senses)
'enana mōtua	mature adult
feruri	reflective thought (Tahitian)
fina'i	jealousy, malice (southern Marquesan)
ha'aha'a	anger
ha'anuhenuhe	self-abasement, groveling (as a dog before its master)

haka'enana	to act as a person; to jury-rig; to work out interpersonal arrangements, not legal ones
hakā'ika	shame, embarrassment
hakama'akau	remember, have confidence in
hakatiketike	put oneself above others
hakatu	distinctiveness, characteristic
hani	accustomed, at ease with
ha'o	irritable
have	know (of a skill or technique)
hei	fitting, appropriate, also wreath
heko	in rut; boar
hinena'o	lust
hoa	friend, other person
hōpū	fear
hou	young, new
ka'epu'epu	nauseous
kā'i'e	arrogance, self-love, glory (of God)
kaikaiā	cannibal, incestuous
kaipipi'o	childish rage
kaituto	reflective thought
kaiū	baby, small
ka'oha	concern, compassion, fellow feeling
keitani	jealousy, envy
kite	see, know, recognize
koea	crazy
koekoe	guts, intestines
ko'oua	old man, old person
kōpū	belly, stomach
maha'i	young man, boy
makimaki	desire, wish
mako	shark
oke	hunger

oko	hear; learn by hearing, not seeing or practicing
paha	insult
pao	consumed, worthless
pekē	anger
pēpē	baby
pi'o	ground, cause, reason, fault
pohu'e	live, livelihood
saru	jealous
tama	child
taure'are'a	errant youth
tō'iki	kid, child
to'omanu	disgust
tuaro'i	(Tahitian) group recitations and discussions of Bible texts
tumu	trunk, cause, source, reason
va'avō	brash, intrusive
vahi	place
vivi'io	longing for an absent person, loneliness
vivini	boss, understand, command

REFERENCES

Benedict, R.
   1946   The Chrysanthemum and the Sword. New York: World.
Caughey, J. L.
   1980   Personal Identity and Social Organization. Ethos 8:173–203.
Clement, D. C.
   1982   Samoan Folk Knowledge of Mental Disorders. *In* Cultural Conceptions
           of Mental Health and Therapy. A. J. Marsella and G. M. White, eds.
           Pp. 193–213. Dordrecht: D. Reidel.
Dordillon, R. I.
   1931   Grammaire et dictionnaire de la langue des Iles Marquises. Travaux et
           Mémoires de L'Institut d'Ethnologie, nos. 17 and 18. Paris: Institut
           d'Ethnologie.
Dumont, L.
   1970   Homo Hierarchicus. Mark Sainsbury, transl. Chicago: University of
           Chicago Press. (Original French edition published in 1966).

Garfinkel, H.
    1967   Studies in Ethnomethodology. Englewood Cliffs, N.J.: Prentice-Hall.
Geertz, C.
    1973   Person, Time, and Conduct in Bali. *In* The Interpretation of Cultures.
            Pp. 360–411. New York: Basic Books.
Goodenough, W. H.
    1965   Rethinking 'Status' and 'Role': Toward a General Model of the Cultural
            Organization of Social Relationships. *In* The Relevance of Models for
            Social Anthropology. Michael Banton, ed. ASA Monograph Series,
            no. 1. Pp. 1–24. London: Tavistock.
Handy, E. S. C.
    1930   Marquesan Legends. Bernice P. Bishop Museum Bulletin 69. Honolulu:
            Bishop Museum.
Keller, W.
    1983   Shame and Stagefright in Java. Ethos 11:152–165.
Kirkpatrick, J.
    1979   Famine, Cannibalism, and the Domestic Mode of Production. Paper
            presented at the 78th annual meeting of the American Anthropological
            Association. Cincinnati, Ohio.
    1981*a* Meanings of Siblingship in Marquesan Society. *In* Siblingship in
            Oceania: Studies in the Meaning of Kin Relations. Mac Marshall, ed.
            ASAO Monograph no. 8. Pp. 17–51. Ann Arbor: University of Michi-
            gan Press.
    1981*b* Appeals for 'Unity' in Marquesan Local Politics. Journal of the Polyne-
            sian Society 90:439–464.
    1982   Adolescent Identities in the Marquesas Islands. MS.
    1983   The Marquesan Notion of the Person. Ann Arbor: UMI Research Press.
Lavondès, H.
    1968   Le Vocabulaire des valeurs culturelles dans la littérature orale des Iles
            Marquises. *In* Proceedings of the Eighth Congress of Anthropological
            and Ethnological Sciences. Vol. 2. Pp. 49–61. Tokyo: Science Council
            of Japan.
    1972   Problèmes sociolinguistiques et alphabétisation en Polynésie Française.
            Cahiers O.R.S.T.O.M.: Série Sciences Humaines 9:49–61.
Levy, R. I.
    1973   Tahitians: Mind and Experience in the Society Islands. Chicago: Univer-
            sity of Chicago Press.
    1974   Tahiti, Sin, and the Question of Integration between Personality and
            Sociocultural Systems. *In* Culture and Personality: Contemporary Read-
            ings. Robert A. LeVine, ed. Pp. 287–306. Chicago: Aldine.
Martini, M. I., and J. Kirkpatrick
    1981   Early Interactions in the Marquesas Islands. *In* Culture and Early Inter-
            actions. T. Field, A. Sostek, P. Vietze, and P. H. Leiderman, eds.
            Pp. 189–213. Hillsdale, N.J.: Lawrence Erlbaum.
McHugh, P.
    1968   Defining the Situation. Indianapolis: Bobbs-Merrill.

O'Hare, D., and S. Duck
   1981   Implicit Psychology and Ordinary Explanation. *In* Indigenous Psy-
             chologies: The Anthropology of the Self. Paul Heelas and Andrew Lock,
             eds. Pp. 285–302. London: Academic Press.
Piers, G., and M. B. Singer
   1953   Shame and Guilt. Springfield, Ill.: Charles C. Thomas.
Rorty, A. O.
   1976   A Literary Postscript: Characters, Persons, Selves, Individuals. *In* The
             Identities of Persons. Amelie O. Rorty, ed. Pp. 301–323. Berkeley,
             Los Angeles, London: University of California Press.
Rosaldo, M. Z.
   1980   Knowledge and Passion: Ilongot Notions of Self and Social Life. Cam-
             bridge Studies in Cultural Systems. Cambridge: Cambridge University
             Press.
Weber, M.
   1978   Economy and Society. Guenther Roth and Claus Wittich, eds. Berkeley,
             Los Angeles, London: University of California Press.

4

Rage and Obligation: Samoan Emotion in Conflict

Eleanor Ruth Gerber

INTRODUCTION

Emotions, perhaps more than any other element of ethnopsychology, lead us directly into the phenomenology of the experience of other selves. It may be for this reason that emotions are among the elements that Geertz (1976) has suggested might bear on the concept of the person. This chapter discusses the role concepts of emotion play in Samoan ethnopsychology, examined in the light of ethnographic data and recent research on affect. I shall argue that the intrapsychic importance of emotions lies in the fact that they derive meaning from two vitally important sources: the social world and innate affective patterns.

Anthropologists have long recognized that emotions are culturally constituted concepts, defined and classified in much the same way as any other conceptual system (Geertz 1959; Doi 1962; Gerber 1975; Myers 1979; Lutz 1981, 1982, chap. 2; White, chap. 9). However, if one accepts an assumption common in psychology that emotions arise at least in part from a biological substrate, then emotions present a rather special case of cultural classification. The existence of a biological basis means that cultures are less than entirely free in their ability to define the emotional world arbitrarily. If we accept the hypothesis that this biological patterning is panhuman, a tendency exists which limits the range of emotional variation across cultures. Recognizing this can be of great assistance in making comparisons between one emotional system and another.

The biological substrate of emotional patterning does not, however, act exclusively as a limitation on human mental possibilities. It partially controls the subjective experience of emotion, although this innate patterning is always culturally redefined and is probably never directly experienced. I argue in this chapter that two levels of patterning exist which shape the subjective experiences that we recognize as emotional. We can call the first of these the culturally constituted emotion system, and the second, "basic affect."[1] The culturally constituted emotion system is an organized, verbally expressed set of feeling concepts; and it is readily available for ethnographic analysis. These emotion concepts "express" patterns of feeling and behavior arising from basic affect; that is to say, concepts of emotions derive motivating force from affective patterns that also shape the phenomenology of emotional experience. But not all of an individual's basic affect need be effectively channeled into these culturally prepared tracks. People continue to experience affective arousal that is neither expressed nor controlled in their cultural systems. Basic affects and the culturally constituted emotion system therefore interact in complex ways, and from this interaction may arise personal conflicts that are characteristic of the members of a particular culture.[2]

This chapter is concerned with the interrelationships of two sets of emotions with each other and with their affective substrates. I argue that the available cultural expressions of anger do not permit Samoans to channel effectively all their hostile feelings, particularly when the objects of these feelings are social superiors. The second group of emotions with which I am concerned represent culturally approved feelings toward social superiors. These emotions are defined in such a way as to permit only the feeling tone of docile submissiveness. Submissive feelings toward authority figures are highly elaborated in Samoan culture and function to attach Samoans to an important set of social obligations. Periodically, however, unexpressed rage occasioned by these obligations, and the superiors who enforce them, emerges. Since this anger comes into conflict with the social requirements to remain submissive behaviorally, and to feel docile and willing internally, both personal and social difficulties are created.

The interaction between basic affects and the culturally constituted emotion system may help to explain the rather contradictory public image of Samoans. Popular accounts of Samoans in urban environments frequently depict them as highly aggressive, renowned for their large size and propensity to employ it as a means of intimidation (see, e.g., Wolfe's essay "Mau-mauing the Flak Catchers" [1970], or Thompson's *Fear and Loathing in Las Vegas* [1971]). However, Margaret Mead (1928, 1930, 1973) depicted Samoans as gentle, unaggressive people, rather retiring and essentially uncomplicated. This image was perpetuated in the ethnography of Lowell Holmes (1957). Other studies have presented a picture of much greater complexity (Freeman 1964, 1973, 1983; Shore 1976, 1980, 1982), resembling in some ways the folk wisdom about Samoans. These divergent views, underscored most forcefully by Derek Freeman's (1983) recent challenge to Mead's earlier descriptions, provide a strong clue that certain potentials of the Samoan self have been overlooked, oversimplified, or misjudged. In what follows, I argue that such unrecognized potentials may arise from the interaction of basic affects and the culturally constituted emotion system.

After a brief examination of theories of affect, I discuss their implications for the study of cultural formulations of emotion. A number of methodological questions are raised, especially issues of translation connected with the use of linguistic data and forms of direct questioning in describing emotion concepts and emotional experience. This methodological discussion is followed by the presentation of ethnographic data on the Samoan domain of emotion. My approach to translation begins with informants' own explications and judgments of word meanings, but goes beyond this to interpret cultural data in light of research on affect. Interpretation of the Samoan data poses certain epistemological questions about the limits of awareness in the articulation of affective experience. As might be suspected from insights into the psychodynamic functions of emotion, lack of awareness may not be simply a product of arbitrary limitations, but of culturally patterned processes that have adaptive value in the overall ordering of personal and social experience (see Black, chap. 7). I conclude by suggesting that just this type of systematic shaping in Samoans' articulation of emotion and self may underlie the recent controversy about Samoan behavior raised in Freeman's challenge to Mead's early work.

THE QUESTION OF AFFECT

Since most anthropologists do not share a standard theory of affect, it is necessary to be explicit about working assumptions that underlie my use of the concept. For reasons I will discuss below, I regard basic affect as the panhuman, biologically based component of human emotions. "Affect" refers to an inborn psychophysiological program, which is activated by cultural evaluations of external situations, defined and modified by cultural concepts, and expressed in culturally appropriate behaviors. Since human beings construct all experience using cultural understandings of the world, the subjective experience of pure affect probably does not occur.[3]

The existence of a biological component in emotions is very generally recognized in psychology. Most theories include a notion of dual causality, including some evaluation of an environmental event and a change in bodily activity in response to it (Strongman 1973, chap. 1, passim). In a recent philosophical discussion of emotions, Lyons (1980) has reviewed four "theoretical streams." All of them recognize a biological component in emotions, and view it as a pan-specific trait. Lyon's review demonstrates that each of these theoretical streams uses basically the same elements to explain the emotional process. Thought, attitude, judgment, or another aspect of mentation is combined with a biological component: instinct, drive, or patterned somatic disturbance. Various arrangements of these elements are used, different notions of causality are applied, and factors are given different degrees of emphasis. But there is nevertheless considerable similarity between physiologically oriented theories and those which stress the mental aspects of emotion. One concludes, with Rorty (1980), that the differences between those theorists who concentrate on the somatic and those who stress cognition may be more apparent than real:

> They appear to be at odds only when both theories get reductionally ambitious: when denying overdetermination, each tries to explain all phenomena at all levels. . . . [This results in] an unilluminating struggle whose sterility will be masked by the parties, goading each other into dazzling displays of ingenuity. (P. 118)

It is worthwhile to look more closely at Lyons's four theoretical streams to examine their treatment of affect, and to discuss how the ethnography of emotions can benefit by taking these views into account. (This may be particularly important in certain anthropological circles, where suggestions that human biology is an important factor in human experience frequently create controversy. I hope to remind ethnographers of emotion that it is both time-honored and commonsensical to use the idea of basic affect as a primary working assumption.)

Affect as a Panhuman Trait

Although all the theoretical streams that Lyons discusses recognize a biological element in emotion, the term "affect" is primarily associated with psychoanalytic theory. Affect plays a role in Freud's elaborate theoretical apparatus of psychic energy and its discharge. It was seen as a safety valve in this system, permitting the escape of pent-up energy through various physiological disturbances. It was thought to occur only when the appropriate behavior to gratify an instinctive drive was blocked (Lyons 1980:27). These views are shared by no other theory of emotion, and need not concern us further here.

I find the term "affect" to be of use for two reasons. First, it does not leave us with the impression that the "patterned physiological disturbances," as this component of emotion is sometimes called, is somehow abnormal, a kind of disease of the central nervous system. Second, and most important, I find that this term concentrates our attention on the subjective experience of emotion, rather than on peripheral or visceral reactions. These internal sensations are only one aspect of the internal sensations that make up a subjective emotional state.

The Freudian view of affect also explicitly recognizes that emotions may have an adaptive significance for species survival. This was suggested by Darwin in his study *The Expression of Emotions in Man and Animals* (1873). The adaptive perspective occurs even in the work of those who are most zealously sociocultural in their orientation.[4] Recognizing the panhuman nature of the emotional substrate will be very useful to ethnographers. Assuming the commonality of basic affect will enhance ethnographic comparison of one emotional system with another. Basic affects supply a means of comparing feelings in different cultures which are partially similar, but which have been differently defined and elaborated.

Physiological Activation in Emotion

A second important theoretical approach in the psychology of emotions holds that the essence of an emotional experience is the inner perception of metabolic and muscular disturbances. Lyons (1980:4) traces this idea back to Descartes, who postulated that the passions (phenomena occurring in the soul) were transferred to the brain, heart, and limbs through an intermediate causal agent called "animal spirits." In modern psychology, the Cartesian view became the basis of the extremely influential James-Lange theory of emotions.

James (1884) changed the Cartesian doctrine by identifying the physiological changes that occur in the emotional process as the cause of the characteristic subjective feelings associated with it. This made the essence of emotion clearly physiological. It stimulated a vast body of psychophysiological research aimed at distinguishing one affective pattern from another in terms of muscle tension, visceral changes, galvanic skin response, and the like. Most of these studies concentrate on what James called the "coarser" emotions, like rage, fear, and grief. These affects, which were assumed to have strong, clearly identifiable somatic patterns, stimulated much research. Other emotions that were considered "subtler" by James (i.e., love, indignation, and pride) were relatively ignored (Lyons 1980:13).

It would be convenient for theorists of emotion if indisputable physiological evidence existed by which basic affects could be distinguished from one another. Unfortunately, the evidence, though massive, is far from

clear. An excellent recent review of psychophysiological research is provided by Grings and Dawson (1978). The authors recognize that the evidence does not coalesce into a meaningful pattern:

> Although our personal experience may lead us to believe that different emo-
> tions are associated with different bodily reactions, the research results do not
> strongly support this hypothesis.(P. 6)

Lyons (1980:19) agrees:

> the claim that there are patterns of physiological changes peculiar to each
> emotion is at best supported by conflicting evidence and at worst should be
> considered falsified.

It is interesting that neither of these sources rejects the possibility of
physiological differentiation among emotions. Grings and Dawson attribute
the unimpressive results to severe methodological problems. They maintain
that it is difficult to create and manipulate "true" emotions under laboratory
conditions. In addition, they point out the difficulty of measuring all indicators of emotion simultaneously (1978:6). Lyons similarly is not distressed
by the possible falsification of the physiological hypothesis. He suggests
that the problem lies in the concentration of most psychophysiological
research on the wrong somatic phenomena. The differentiation among
basic affects may not lie in metabolic activity and its visceral and muscular
consequences; instead, we should perhaps look at electrochemical states of
the brain (1980:67). The suggestion that brain states may eventually provide
differentiating patterns for various affects is not an unreasonable one, and
there has already been considerable research on this subject. (I refer the
reader to the bibliography in MacLean 1980.) Certain brain research indicates the differentiation between pleasant and unpleasant affects (MacLean
1980:20). It is possible that brain states may be capable of even finer distinctions. MacLean discusses the experience of certain patients with temporal
lobe epilepsy who have sensations of déjà vu, which may represent "*only
the feeling* that accompanies the act of remembering." Other seizures produce
"eureka-type feelings," a sensation of complete conviction and total understanding (ibid., 20–21). These innovative classes of affect, whether or not
they are substantiated by further research, remind us that the basic affects
defined by brain states may be somewhat different from the traditional
categories.

Behaviorist and cognitivist approaches to the study of emotion in
psychology illustrate certain methodological problems also encountered by
ethnographers of subjective states. According to Watson, an emotion was
an inborn "pattern reaction" primarily of the visceral and glandular systems.

"By pattern reaction, we mean that the separate details of response appear with some constancy, with some regularity and in approximately the same sequential order, each time the exciting stimulus is presented" (Watson 1919:195, quoted in Lyons 1980:18). Watson recognized that this formulation becomes problematic if complex social behavior is assumed to be part of the pattern response. Lyons suggests that these difficulties led Watson to concentrate on patterns of physiological change, which he hoped would prove more stable than behavioral responses. He regarded these as hereditary, and argued that they were found in pure form only in newborn infants. In later life, these hereditary patterns become "broken up" and difficult to identify, but experiments with infants led Watson to believe that fear, rage, and something like libido were "original and fundamental affects" (Watson 1919:195). But this approach involved contradictions in its own logic of investigation. These contradictions are also discussed by Lyons.[5]

Cognitive theories of emotion are those in which some aspect of thought or judgment plays an important role in differentiating one emotion from another. Lyons (1980:34) traces this theoretical stream back to Aristotle, who held that the cause of an emotional reaction lies in the views and state of mind of a person experiencing the emotion. This emphasis was carried into European philosophy through Aquinas and Spinoza, and into modern psychology through the seminal work of Alexander Shand (1914). In more recent psychology, one of the most complete cognitive accounts of emotion was presented by Arnold (1960, 1970).

Cognitive approaches to emotions are relatively compatible with an anthropological interest in the cultural component of emotions. Theories such as Arnold's include a stage of "appraisal" or "evaluation" of an external event which initiates an emotional process (Lyons 1980:45). This stage is easily modified by social learning and influenced by cultural systems of interpretation.

Rorty (1980) suggests that certain emotions in a complex system of feelings are primarily cognitive or "intentional," while others are primarily affective:

> The physiological and the intentional aspects of our emotions do not enter into all emotions in the same way. The difference between a distaste for malicious gossip in departmental politics and the terror of waking after a nightmare whose drama one has already forgotten, the difference between nostalgia-for-the-lilacs-of-yesteryear and fear in the face of a powerful danger are differences in kind. (P. 118)

Rorty apparently means these intentional emotions to be understood as highly cultural in nature, specific to particular social circumstances, and relatively low in activation. She regards these as being "different in kind" from the basic affects of raw terror and sorrow.

THE ETHNOGRAPHY OF SUBJECTIVE STATES

An essential methodological problem implicit in behaviorism has not been entirely solved by taking a more cognitive approach. Behaviorists avoid the description of internal subjective states and identify the phenomenon under study with readily available reactions. Although cognitivists do not wish to avoid discussing subjective states, they are nevertheless forced to use some sort of external evidence as an indicator of covert internal phenomena. The best indicators we have are often the manifest verbal behaviors of our informants. In the case of emotions, however, I think it is unwise to identify these verbal expressions too completely with subjective inner experience. Where complex subjective or psychological states are concerned, the relationship between a term and the mental phenomena it expresses is not necessarily one of complete representation.

In the Samoan data, it is apparent that emotion vocabulary does not perfectly express subjective experience in at least two respects. First, the verbal concept may not include every element of complex inner events. Most Samoans say, for example, that they are aware of no particular bodily feeling that accompanies emotions, yet it is apparent that they undergo many of the same physiological disturbances that have been investigated by psychologists. They laugh, cry, flush, shout, and so on, in situations that are interculturally recognizable as affectively stimulating. I argue below that this indicates Samoans experience these physiological aspects of affective arousal on some level, but their explicit verbal emotion system does not define them as particularly relevant or memorable.

The second factor that leads me to expect an imperfect verbal mapping of covert subjective emotional states arises from the investment of moral significance in certain emotions. Especially where feelings are disapproved, it may be difficult for an individual to acknowledge the direction or strength of these feelings, or to admit experiencing them at all. Certain verbalizable cultural constructions function to preserve the individual's lack of awareness of the nature, intensity, or object of these affects.

One Samoan emotion provides a good example of how a concept can function in this way. According to Samoan values, it is very bad to express anger toward parents, and the performance of work and service for one's kin is considered a primary expression of love. Nevertheless, a certain amount of resistance is expressed to the more onerous demands of authority. One possible label for this resistance is the term *musu,* which expresses a person's reluctance to do what is required of him or her.[6] The internal state is not described as an angry one, but the close association of the term with a group of other strongly negative, anger-like feelings in a test of semantic similarity (see below) indicates that the basic affect of anger plays some role in the inner experience of musu.

One's musu is a sufficient explanation; it is never questioned by others or justified by the person who experiences it. The self-attribution of musu serves, then, as a mechanism by which a person can avoid a burdensome situation while at the same time not having to admit to the existence of unacceptable feelings. Variation no doubt occurs among individuals in the degree to which they consciously experience their own covert anger at burdensome responsibilities. However, the existence of the cultural definition of musu can assist Samoans in remaining unaware of their own conflicts, or at least in masking them. The term seems to function as much to conceal the nature of a particular inner experience as it serves to express it.

We may therefore expect an incomplete identity between the patterning of basic affects and the verbally expressed concepts of emotion. As I attempt to demonstrate below, this discontinuity is a source of patterned conflicts that are typical aspects of personal experience in Samoan society, even though they are not generally culturally recognized.

The Samoan data also suggest that certain emotion terms are closer to expressing the inborn affective program than are others. However, I do not regard them as phenomena essentially different from emotions in which the affective bases are less evident. My view is that the subjective experience of all but a few emotions is shaped both by basic affective patterns and by complex cultural influences. Some emotions, however, have relatively specific cultural scenarios to which they are considered relevant. Perhaps it is clearer to say that they arise to express the specific feelings associated with certain narrowly stereotyped events. Because of this specificity, terms that express such feelings cover relatively narrow ranges of meaning. Other terms are more global, and are therefore available to be used to express something closer to a basic affective pattern. "Nostalgia-for-the-lilacs-of-yesteryear" is an example of the former sort of emotion, while "sadness," to which it is clearly allied, is an example of the latter. "Sadness" is broader in that it is relevant to many experiences, many levels of intensity, and is associated with a wider range of expressive behaviors than is nostalgia. Both of these concepts are given force by the same basic affect; to the extent that nostalgia is capable of moving us, it is because we are innately programmed to respond to loss. Equally, every experience of loss, whether described by a specific or more global term, is culturally defined and conditioned. We are taught which experiences appropriately trigger the loss program, what behavioral reactions to it are expectable, and what the

appropriate subjective tone of the experience ought to be. This places the
basic affect into a particular cultural milieu and makes it socially useful.[7]

In the Samoan system of emotions, the distinction between more
global and more specific terms is also evident. The word *ita* 'anger', for
example, is a relatively general term, applicable to a wide variety of circumstances. I have already discussed musu ('reluctance'), a more specific
term related to anger. Several other closely related terms are similar low-
level expressions of pique: *fiu* 'fed up', *'augatā* 'lazy', *'o'ono* 'suppressed
anger', *fa'a'ū'ū* 'sulky'. They are all connected with stereotyped scenarios
having to do with work.

It is not always evident which basic affect empowers a feeling. This
chapter discusses a group of related feelings which are not especially "good"
in the hedonic sense, but which are very much the feelings of a "good
person." These feelings are designated by a group of terms which all
indicate a proper response to hierarchical contexts. Because these terms are
seen as highly similar in meaning (see lexical data below), I believe that
they share an affective basis, even though I do not know what to call the
affect that underlies them. The complicated issues surrounding the use of
semantic data to infer underlying affects are taken up further below.

I do not, however, think that every concept classed with emotions is
necessarily the reflection of some basic affect. It seems quite possible that
cultures can define categories of feeling which do not stimulate any inborn
pattern. It may be very difficult to distinguish such affectless emotions from
others, especially when they are constructed according to the analogy of
more highly affective feelings. Certainly on an individual level, the
phenomenon of the affectless emotion is very common. Some individuals
may not experience the affects others do in connection with certain feelings;
having no direct access to the subjective worlds of other people, they would
by very unlikely to be aware of the difference.[8]

The Samoan concept of respect, *fa'aaloalo,* may be an emotion that a
number of informants do not experience in an affective manner. For some,
it is a definite though undefinable "feeling inside," but other people specifically reject this suggestion. For them, respect consists entirely of the ritual
behaviors by which persons in high positions are honored. They seem to
have no sense that others feel (or claim to feel) anything internal when these
actions are performed.

Another possibility exists. It seems reasonable to assume that some
affects may be left completely undefined and unclassified by a culture. This
may explain some of the differences among the emotional arrays presented
by various cultural systems. It remains problematic how these "emotionless
affects" are experienced. Since appropriate cultural concepts are lacking, it
is likely that people would have some difficulty in expressing these feelings,

if indeed they are conscious of them at all. Such culturally ignored feelings would not be easily recoverable by ordinary verbally oriented techniques, which often rely on the explication of recognized meanings. It might be that other kinds of textual or symbolic analyses are more appropriate to accomplish this task. Whatever the difficulties, such inchoate feelings are legitimally part of the ethnography of emotions. My data, however, do not allow me to discuss them, and they are therefore beyond the compass of this chapter.

THE ROLE OF EMOTIONS IN CONCEPTS OF THE SELF

Before beginning an investigation of the Samoan system of emotion concepts, let us examine the role this system plays in the organization of the larger self-system. I would like to suggest that Samoan concepts of the person are not organized into one tightly integrated domain. Rather, personal concepts are drawn from a wide variety of domains, and are linked together by a loose network of associations which cut across domains. Materials from the entire cultural repertoire can be brought together in meaningful ways, making use of informants' generative capacity for creative thought. The domain of emotions therefore serves as one source of raw material for constructing ideas of personhood.

Perhaps an example of the blending of cross-domain ideas might be useful here. When I asked Samoan informants about the feeling of *alofa* 'love' which exists between parents and children, I was surprised to learn that many of them believed a father's beating was an appropriate sign of his love. This was explained to me in the following way: fathers and children are closely identified, and the behavior of children reflects almost directly on the reputation of the parent. They are socially and legally responsible for any of their offsprings' wrongdoings, and are entitled to take credit for their achievements. Because of this close identification, fathers stand to be shamed if their children misbehave. They must therefore teach them right from wrong, but children, especially young children, learn only with the incentive of pain. Concerned fathers, who worry about their children's capacity to shame them and wish to make their children good people, therefore beat them. This logic is so compelling that several informants told me that if their fathers failed to beat them, they would be sad, since it would be a proof of paternal indifference. Presumably, where the strength of the tie is diminished, so is the father's sensitivity to being shamed by his child.

This set of ideas seems to take concepts from several different domains. It uses concepts of emotion (e.g., notions of love, the obligations it entails, and reasonable causes of shame and sadness), of kinship (the role of fathers and what they owe their children), and of child development (a particular theory of learning). The domains used may be mutually relevant at a number of points. Emotions and kinship, for example, are closely inter-locked. As I shall describe later, elements of intimate kin relationships are important in describing certain emotions. Less intimate kin relationships, such as the wider structure of Samoan extended families or the hierarchy of chiefship, are very seldom mentioned by informants in connection with emotions.

Undoubtedly, many other domains would deserve mention in a com-plete representation of Samoan folk psychology. Certain religious beliefs (e.g., the nature of the soul and the behavior of entities such as ghosts and witches) are important. Folk medical beliefs are undoubtedly relevant (see Clement 1982). For example, some informants believe that infants who cry a great deal when they are young are in life-threatening danger (see Lutz, chap. 2). One young woman who had been such an infant reported that native doctors had advised her parents to indulge her in everything, or risk her early death or possible possession by a ghost. This was obviously a very great exception to ordinary child-rearing practices, and in fact this informant was regarded by others as rather spoiled and arrogant.

Methodological Quandaries

The organization of these beliefs bears on our selection of methods with which to represent and analyze them. First of all, different field techniques are applicable to coherent lexical domains and to sets of beliefs which are assembled from many domains. In the former case, the discovery techniques of cognitive anthropology and linguistics will frequently be appropriate. It is doubtful if these techniques will be effective in investigat-ing variously assembled cultural materials. For example, coherent lexical domains are often analyzed in terms of "features" or "dimensions." If the concepts under study are drawn from many cultural sources, there is no reason to expect that they will all be explicable in terms of the same set of underlying features. One of the features which distinguishes between emo-tion terms is what is frequently called "hedonic tone," that is, how pleasant or unpleasant the feeling in question is. This is clearly not a feature that defines kin relationships, which are frequently conceptually linked with emotions. Informants might be able to apply hedonic criteria to kin terms, but this would certainly not be definitional, and might prove to be an artificial way of thinking.

Second, when a researcher assumes that the informant's domain is isomorphic with a similar domain in his or her own culture, ethnographic questions may misfire. The resulting confusion may lead to missing the more natural ways knowledge is usually assembled into an account of experience. Something of this sort appears to have happened to Margaret Mead. In an appendix to *Coming of Age in Samoa* (1973:141–142), Mead reported a series of interviews in which she asked her informants to give "character sketches" of members of their households. She found it almost impossible to get beyond her informants' automatic response, "Search me, I don't know." She found, in this pattern, evidence of lack of interest in persons or unwillingness to explain them, and elsewhere refers to a "lack of curiosity about motivation" (ibid., p. 68). From this Mead concluded that Samoans had only a rudimentary interest in, or understanding of, the behavior of others. This conclusion formed part of the basis for her assessment of Samoans as simple, personally undifferentiated individuals.

I myself asked many similar questions of informants, and unerringly got the same reply, "I don't know." But I was investigating emotions, and knew from other data that there existed a complicated framework by which explanations of other people's behavior could be, and were, constructed. After a period of confusion, I discovered a way into my informant's interpersonal assessments. If I brushed aside their initial plea of ignorance, saying, "Yes, I know—but why do *you* think, in your own mind, that he did this?" suddenly my informants' eyes would light up. "Well," they would say, "in my *own* mind . . ." and then would follow an explanation that (to my disappointment) frequently had nothing whatever to do with emotions.[9]

What prevented my informants from answering the first question was not lack of interest in motivation, but a belief about knowledge. Samoans frequently say, with the full force of self-evident conventional wisdom, "we cannot know what is in another person's depths," or "we cannot tell what another person is thinking." Given this idea, it becomes very difficult to state with assurance what another person's motives in fact *are,* especially since the question "why" is apparently interpreted as calling for nothing but the truth. As a consequence, the only possible answer to this question about matters internal to another person is "I don't know."

It is interesting that even after I learned this, I was not able to stop asking "why," and had to go through the whole routine of doubt and reassurance almost every time I asked a similar question. I attribute this to the strength of my own folk psychology, where "why" is a legitimate question, and where it is acceptable to believe firmly one's own account of another person's behavior. The imposition of even a few key beliefs can lead to serious distortions of the way in which informants assemble their knowledge of persons.

The temptation exists for the ethnographer to strain for a coherence in the description of a domain which is in fact not called for. It is easy, for example, to require informants to close the gaps in logic; being cooperative, they may generate relevancy for the ethnographer on the spot. This will result in the creation of formulations according to cultural principle, but not part of the informants' normal cognitive operations.

I am referring here to the distinction between clearly institutionalized ideas and the sort of concept which can easily be generated from them. The former may exist as bits of conventional wisdom, such as "Jewish mothers want their daughters to marry doctors." This is a typical cross-domain relational formula, which links ethnicity, kinship, and status in a culturally appropriate manner. Other connections between these domains may be created by informants from their understanding of the underlying principles, as, for example, "Jewish mothers will settle for computer systems analysts." There may be a temptation for the ethnographer to regard the second formulation as having the same degree of cultural salience as the first, but this is clearly a distortion.

Let us turn to a Samoan example: when I asked my adolescent informants about the connection between fathers' beatings and love, they responded readily. But when I reversed the proposition, and inquired about unbeaten children, it seemed that more calculation was required. The informants showed classic ethological signs of puzzlement—creased brows, nervous twitches, hesitation in speech. I had clearly set them a problem, which they were attempting to solve. I doubt that the proposition "children are sad if their fathers don't beat them" has the same level of cultural fixity as "fathers beat their children if they love them." In fact, I am not even certain that the former proposition is true, except in logic: I never observed a child asking to be beaten. Hypothetical questions that require the informant to create new formulations can be useful in checking the ethnographer's understanding of the basic principles by which informants process their understandings. But it seems wise to distinguish these responses from ones with a traditional place in conventional wisdom.

In dealing with domains assembled from a wide range of cultural materials, analytic choices are necessary in deciding which associations to pursue and how far to pursue them. For example, it seems reasonable that intimate kin relationships might have a bearing on emotions; but what about more distant kin? Fathers are certainly always relevant, chiefs occasionally relevant; if that is true, why not systematically inquire about patterned feelings toward every formal status in Samoan village life? And if, for example, *taupous,* traditional ritual princesses, are included, then why not investigate feelings toward such recently acquired statuses as "bus driver" or "nurse"? My informants probably could have generated answers to such questions as "When do you feel love for the bus driver?" but I am not sure it would have been worth their effort, and I suspect they would have rebelled.

Since informants can generate these connections so readily, it becomes difficult to recognize the "natural boundaries" of an assembled domain. It appears, then, that the examination of domains structured in this way depends on analytical choices that control the extent and direction of the investigation.

THE SAMOAN DOMAIN OF EMOTIONS

Having outlined some of the methodological difficulties in the study of emotion and emotion concepts in the context of culturally constructed selves, I would now like to turn to consideration of the Samoan domain of emotions. My approach draws on ethnographic observation of emotional behavior as well as on the things that Samoans say about emotions. I made use of several forms of direct questioning, including interviews and more formal elicitation of judgments about the meanings of emotion words. In what follows, I briefly discuss the cultural basis for the Samoan domain of emotion, and describe some of its general characteristics, such as the orientation toward social or situational referents rather than internal sensations. I then present data collected from informants asked to make judgments about the meanings of a set of salient emotion words, represented with a hierarchical clustering technique. The resultant clustering of emotion words is used to interpret cultural and affective bases for Samoan emotion concepts, and to address a number of issues related to the translation and interpretation of emotion words as expressions of basic affect. This discussion draws on a number of constructs derived from affect research, including dimensions of arousal such as hedonic tone or level of activation (see, e.g., Schlosberg 1952; Russell 1980), specific basic affects such as anger, and ethological notions such as aggression, withdrawal, and social bonding.

The Loto

The Samoan theory of the origin of emotions involves the operations of what is called the *loto*. In other contexts, this word simply means depth, as for example in the phrase *i loto o le sami* 'in the depths of the sea'. In a personal context, however, the loto is thought to be the repository of some of a person's thoughts and feelings. The feelings that occur here, *lagona i le loto* 'feelings in one's depths', are roughly equivalent to "emotions" in English. Other feelings (lagona), such as physical pain, are thought to have nothing to do with the loto, but occur exclusively in the body. The kind of thoughts most closely associated with the loto are thoughts that arise spontaneously. A person may, for example, suddenly think of going to visit a friend: the desire, the thought, and the plan of action are all believed to arise in the loto.

The loto is understood to be physically located in a person's body, but its precise site is ambiguous. Most informants put it somewhere in the chest, often somewhere near the heart. The physical heart, however, is understood to be quite different, and there is another word for it: *fatu*.

Adjectives may be appended to the word *loto,* and certain of these modifications create emotion terms. The Samoan language uses a positional metaphor for feeling in a way somewhat different from English. High and low refer not to degrees of activation or to the purity of a person's moral intentions, as they do for us; rather, they refer to an individual's self-placement in a social hierarchy. The person with a 'high loto' (*lotomaualuga*) is arrogant, rejecting appropriate authority. A person whose loto is low (*lotomaualalo*) is correspondingly humble.

A metaphor of purity is also used. *Lotomamā* 'clean loto' implies the absence of angry feelings. The loto may also be *leaga,* an adjective that means both 'bad' and 'dirty'. *Lotoleaga* implies the presence of bad thoughts, particularly jealous or envious ones. The loto may also be strong or weak. *Lotovāivai* (a weak or tired loto) implies timidity, and sometimes sadness. To be *lototele* (having a lot of loto) implies bravery. Lotos may also be 'sweet' (*lotomalie*). This refers to general cooperativeness and willingness to do as other people require.

Sometimes these modifications of the loto seem to refer as much to cognitive operations as to feelings. Two of these terms were included in my investigation for the sake of completeness, although they were not as common as some of the other terms. These were *fa'alotolotolua* (having two lotos, being in a state of indecision) and *lotofuatiaifo*. The latter is primarily associated with formal church contexts and is used to express the voluntary quality of choice. If one freely chooses to give, and what or how much to give, this action indicates one's lotofuatiaifo. The term is translated in Pratt's Samoan Dictionary (1911) as "conscience," but this has connotations of guilt and repentance which were completely unfamiliar to my informants.

These terms are usual cultural and linguistic formations. The concept of the loto can also be used productively, to create other expressions. I asked informants whether it was acceptable to say, for example, *lotoita* (an angry loto). They agreed that there was nothing ungrammatical about the expression, and that it might be useful at times. They were split, however, about what it meant. To some it implied a habit of feeling, and would be used to refer to a person who was perpetually angry, or who became angry over small things. In this sense, the loto may be used to express personal dispositions, something similar to the English notion of character. To other informants, the term only indicated a momentary state or feeling. An angry person, by the logic of emotions, has an "angry loto." *Lotoita* was to them essentially synonymous with unmodified *ita*. Such formulations did not seem to be very common, and were not spontaneously introduced by informants. It seems, therefore, that this is an area in which Samoans use the domain of emotions in a generative way to create responses to ethnographic questions.

Externalization of Associations

Americans frequently associate emotion terms with internal sensations (Davitz 1969). They seem to be highly interested in describing the exact state of their internal proprioceptions, frequently using metaphorical language to aid them. Thus, happiness might be described as "a bubbly feeling; makes you feel warm all over." Judging from Davitz's interviews, his informants exerted a great deal of effort in preparing accounts of these sensations.

In contrast to Americans, Samoan informants offer very few descriptions of internal sensation. They direct their attention externally, into the social world (similar to what Lutz [chap. 2; 1981] describes for Ifaluk). In the course of interviewing informants about the meanings of selected emotion terms, I found people readily able to describe the typical situations and relationships that give rise to certain emotions as well as the consequent actions usually associated with them. My informants tended to describe emotions in terms of the actions the feelings called forth, the stereotyped scenarios in which the feelings would be an appropriate response, and the specific relationships with close associates (e.g., parents, siblings, and friends) common to those scenarios. The context of these relationships had a strong effect on the perceived outcome of an emotional interaction. A father's anger was seen as calling for a humble response; anger in a friend was the occasion for reciprocal anger. In sum, Samoans were primarily concerned with social interactions and important relationships in which emotion played a role.

My informants almost never mentioned proprioception of bodily sensation spontaneously. Nor did they tend to describe the subjective quality of affective experience. Since this behavior was so different from that described for Americans, I specifically inquired if "there was any special feeling in the body" that was associated with the emotion under discussion.

In all but a few instances, the informants denied that there was. I did find some informants, however, who were particularly able to supply descriptions of proprioceptions. These informants' responses were not atypical in other respects: the social scenarios they offered were similar to those of other informants. This suggests that the external orientation of the responses was culturally standardized, and only certain informants had a greater sensitivity to, or articulateness about, the subjective aspect of emotional experience.

I believe, however, that Samoans experience internal sensation in association with emotions, although they are generally unable to express it verbally. Two kinds of evidence lead to this conclusion. First, as I have mentioned previously, Samoans exhibit ethological signs of affective arousal in situations that are interculturally recognizable as affectively stimulating. Such ethological signs, particularly facial expressions, are often regarded as being universal and are associated with inborn affective patterns (Ekman 1972). In this instance, I am not concerned with the precise meaning assigned to various expressive behaviors in different cultures, or in their distribution across particular situations. My point is that a wide range of external signs of affective activation occur among Samoans, and that these readily observable manifestations are systematically linked with covert, internal aspects of affective activation. It is more reasonable to argue that an entire affective pattern occurs as a unit than to hold that physiological mechanisms are variously arranged in different cultures. Therefore, where we witness external signs of affect—such as changes in facial expression, laughter, shouting, crying—we may assume that somatic changes—such as fluctuations in blood pressure or muscle tension—are likely to occur at the same time. These internal changes are the manifestations of emotion about which Samoans have so little to say. Granting that Samoan bodies are essentially like those of informants who report somatic changes in emotion, we may conclude that Samoan unawareness of physiological activation in emotion is a matter of relative attention.

LEXICON OF EMOTION: WORDS AND AFFECTS

My study of the Samoan domain of emotions includes several kinds of direct questioning aimed at exploring the meanings of terms for emotion (see Gerber 1975 for a fuller discussion of methodology). This work is based on forty-four key terms selected with the help of informants as a representative corpus of salient Samoan words for emotion. Interviews were particularly useful as a way of examining the extent to which informants could verbalize their knowledge about the emotions represented by these terms.

Questions about situational antecedents and consequent actions proved particularly fruitful in evoking articulate responses. In addition, however, I used an elicitation procedure of asking informants to judge similarity in meaning among the terms. These data are complementary to interviews and observations since they are based on informants' understandings about emotions but do not require verbal articulation. This information is presented here in order to discuss problems in the interpretation of emotion words, particularly on the basis of their relation to basic affects. Issues of translation are taken up with particular attention to the Samoan word *alofa,* in anticipation of the later discussion of ways in which affect and emotions such as alofa reinforce socially valued behavior.

I asked a sample of informants to make similarity judgments among the forty-four terms by indicating, for each, which other terms were the most like it in meaning. This task produced a matrix of judgments showing relative similarities among all the terms in the corpus. Analysis of data such as these is facilitated by the use of multivariate techniques (in this case, hierarchical clustering) to transform the matrix of similarities into a visual form that is more readily interpretable. The Samoan data are represented in a hierarchical diagram (fig. 1), produced by a clustering program developed by D'Andrade (1978). The diagram depicts those words judged most similar to one another by grouping them within the same cluster, indicated by the merging of branches in the tree structure. Successively larger clusters are formed as one scans the diagram from left to right, until all forty-four terms are merged in a single, overarching cluster.

There are many aspects of the structure represented in the clustering diagram which have heuristic value in drawing attention to Samoan concepts of emotion, and which have been discussed elsewhere (Gerber 1975). For the purposes of this discussion, I have indicated the largest groupings represented by the clustering by labeling the four major clusters as well as the two major subclusters (1a and 1b) that make up the first of these.

Interpretation of Samoan Emotion Clusters: The Role of Affect

A brief inspection of figure 1 will show that similarities in basic affect seem to underlie many of the similarity judgments made by informants. For example, in Cluster 4, a variety of terms that have a common tone of withdrawal and lack of activity have been placed together. These include terms for 'fear' (*fefe*), 'sadness' (*fa'anoanoa*), 'hurt' (*māfatia*), 'shyness' (*matamuli*), 'shame' (*māsiasi*) and 'timidity' (*lotovāivai*). In Cluster 3, terms with a basis in hostility and/or aggression have been selected as similar. Among them are *ita* and *fa'ali'i* (nearly synonymous terms for 'anger');

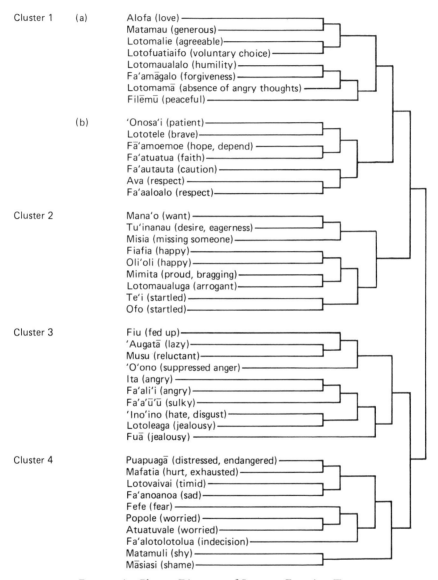

FIGURE 1. Cluster Diagram of Samoan Emotion Terms

'ino'ino 'hate, disgust'; and *lotoleaga* 'jealousy'. The co–occurrence of these terms does not necessarily indicate, however, that the informants were sorting on the basis of similarity of hedonic tone. They might have been reacting to other similarities in meaning, particularly in terms of social

context or consequences for a relationship. We therefore cannot argue directly from the clustering that informants were aware of any physiological component in the subjective experience of emotion.

Certain aspects of the hierarchical clustering may indicate, however, that despite their inarticulateness on the subject, Samoans do experience physiological activation on some level. This can be seen where the terms clustered together do not share a close similarity in denotative meaning. For example, in Cluster 2, a series of terms has been linked together whose social significances are very different. *Fiafia* 'happiness', *lotomaualuga* 'arrogance', and *te'i* 'startle' have been judged to be relatively similar to one other. Fiafia is highly positive in terms of the level of pleasure it indicates. It is also a socially approved emotion. Lotomaualuga (literally, a 'high' loto) is emphatically disapproved, as it implies placing oneself above the normal controls of authority. While fiafia is normally associated with pleasant social encounters like dancing, lotomaualuga is usually described as occurring as part of scenarios in which conflict is generated. Te'i, unlike both of the other terms, is often associated with noninteractional events, such as sudden loud noises. It is always a suddenly emergent feeling; it does not connote a personal disposition, as lotomaualuga may.

The terms clearly are very different. Why, then, do informants place them so close together? I argue that informants were responding to a basic similarity in the high level of activation each term represents. The hedonic qualities of each emotion are quite different, but all connote a high degree of active stimulation. In this instance, the level of activation seems to have been enough to override strong contexual similarities between lotomaualuga and the aggressive feelings in Cluster 3 which the term resembles in many ways. Samoans do not talk about level of activation as a dimension of meaning when they discuss emotions. They do not, for example, create metaphors expressing the strength or size of an emotion, or its ability to "carry you away." Activation, then, is not part of the set of concepts Samoan culture provides to make sense of emotional experiences. Nevertheless, a partial, nonverbal awareness of gross somatic activation allowed informants to generate the similarity judgments by which the terms in Cluster 2 were put together. (It should be pointed out that nothing in the method forced the placement of these terms in larger clusters. They could have formed isolates or small clusters of their own.)

The perceived similarity of these high-activation terms suggests to me that other kinds of eliciting techniques might uncover linguistic evidence that physiological activation does, in fact, form part of the subjective experience of Samoan emotions. If this is true, Samoans' concentration on the social pole of emotion might be regarded as a matter of culturally directed relative attention. We might think of body cues as available for notice, but generally ignored, while social and external cues have been highly elaborated.[10]

This distinction might help to explain the impression Western ethnographers sometimes give of Polynesian shallowness and superficiality of feelings. If a researcher expects reports of internal process, their absence may seem to indicate something is greatly lacking. It is perhaps also true that a high level of interest in psychological process is more consonant with a mode of thinking in which internal cues and sensations are of overriding importance.

The Relation of Affect to Categories of Emotion

Emotions may be viewed as social constructions from several different points of view. First, the definitions of feelings themselves may be considered as socially constructed understandings. If social processes are the only factors taken into account, emotions will be regarded as much more culturally arbitrary. In this view, there are no biological factors constraining cultural creativity. We might therefore be led to expect an extremely wide range of variation in emotional experience among cultures. Emotions could be regarded as culturally specific experiences whose conceptual content and hedonic qualities are unique to a particular group. Precise counterparts to such culturally specific emotions might occasionally occur in other cultures, but we would not expect to see a pattern of similarity replicated almost universally, across many kinds of social systems.

If, however, we accept that complex culturally defined emotions rest on biologically based patterns of basic affect, the freedom and arbitrariness with which emotional experiences are defined can be seen to be somewhat limited. As Rosch points out, many categories do not merely segment "a kaleidoscopic flux of impressions which has to be organized . . . by the linguistic system in our minds" (Carroll 1956:213, quoted in Rosch 1975:178). Rather, such categories are formed around a "core meaning" or "prototype" that exemplifies qualities that are regarded as central to the category in question, and are "natural" and "biologically given."

> In domains in which prototypes are biologically "given," categories can be expected to form around the salient prototypes and, thus, to have elements of content as well as principles of formation which are universal. (Ibid., p. 196)

And, specifically, Rosch regards "facial expressions of emotion" as "a surprising addition to the class of natural categories" (Ibid., p. 186). The prototype emotions that Rosch accepts as underlying these universal facial expressions are the six defined by Ekman (1972): happiness, sadness, anger, fear, surprise, and disgust. She suggests (1972:186) that when blends of emotion and ambiguous and nonemotional expressions are eliminated from consideration, the facial expressions representing these emotions are recognizable in a wide variety of cultures.

It seems possible, then, that basic affects serve as prototypes for the development of a series of more culturally specific categories. I do not, however, think that these emotional prototypes can best be defined by facial expressions, which are only one expressive channel out of many and do not reflect the complexity of emotional processes. Certainly, the clusters of emotions in figure 1 do not correspond one-to-one with Ekman's basic emotions. Some culturally important groups of Samoan feelings, particularly those in Clusters 1a and 1b, do not reflect any of Ekman's prototype feelings. Are we then to conclude that they are ambiguous blends or nonemotional phenomena? Further research is necessary to define the basic affects in a nonethnocentric way. Linguistic evidence must be taken into account to ensure that affects with no clear facial responses are adequately represented. I think it likely that such research will show that emotional systems in various cultures do tend to cluster around a series of universal centers of meaning. Recognizing this will greatly facilitate intercultural comparison of emotion systems.

However, the relationship between a basic affect and its culturally standardized verbal expressions is more complicated than the simple prototype structures Rosch uses as illustrations. The complexity arises from the duality of patterning of basic affects and the terms that express them. As all affects undergo the social process of definition and refinement, no term directly expresses a basic affect. Rather, all the emotions in a set of related concepts should be regarded as forming around an underlying psychological pattern that is probably never directly experienced or expressed.

Translation Issues

In the case of emotions, the linguistic and cultural codes that structure categories and category use are highly elaborated, to the degree that some emotions may appear to be completely arbitrary, socially constructed understandings. This is most evident when feelings unfamiliar to us are examined. Among Samoan emotions are several that seem to be feelings we do not have, and therefore are extremely difficult to translate into English. For example, there is no direct equivalent in our culture to lotomamā, which has been translated as 'innocent'. It refers, as mentioned previously, to a loto that possesses no angry feelings. Situationally, informants always associate it with averted conflict: either there had been a quarrel and it was resolved, or the potential for a quarrel existed and was not taken up. Occasionally false accusations were mentioned, but the emphasis was always placed on the accused's lack of resentment. Once again, the defining characteristic of the situation is that a person who might be angry is not.

From the above description it appears that lotomamā is defined by the lack of something, rather than by a particular cognitive or hedonic state. Yet my informants were quite clear that lotomamā was a specific, identifiable feeling. Because of their general inarticulateness about internal cues, I am not certain what the experiential quality of this feeling is, and cannot be sure that speakers of English do not experience it in some covert way. But it strikes me as genuinely unfamiliar, a truly specifically Samoan way of feeling. The translation of 'innocent' given by Pratt's Dictionary (1911) is inexact, carrying only some of the same connotations.

Other terms similar to this one exist within the domain. Lotomalie, for example, is situationally connected with willingness to agree with the desires and requests of others, no matter what they are or how burdensome they may seem. It is clear from informants' descriptions that the agreement is freely given, and that the person who has a 'sweet' loto remains cheerful about it. In this case the feeling seems quite clear: it could be described in English as a kind of flexible dependency, or a happy passivity. I think we can recognize this turn of mind in our own culture, but it has not been conceptually crystallized or raised to the formal status of a named emotion. Our evaluation of the feeling is also somewhat different. American adults who display this attitude are suspected of being insufficiently self-directed. The English terms "easy-going" and "happy-go-lucky" carry some of the same meaning as lotomalie, but people who exhibit these characteristics are suspected of irresponsibility. By contrast, social yielding is an approved characteristic even in a mature Samoan. (Americans do seem to require this feeling from children; it is probably part of what makes a "good" or "cooperative" child.)

Most of the other feelings that differ conceptually from those with which we are familiar have a similar status. The experiences they represent are perhaps not totally foreign, but they have been defined in different ways, have different connotations, and are applied and evaluated differently in social context. The problem in understanding them is not real incomprehensibility but the kind of general mismatching that has always made translation so treacherous. I should also note that it is impossible to give complete descriptions of each of these terms without indulging in more words than available space allows. More extensive discussions of each of these terms have been presented elsewhere (Gerber 1975).

Because of its importance in Samoan thought, it will be worthwhile to present one further example of this kind of variability. This is the concept of alofa, which I have translated as 'love'. My reason for choosing this translation is explained below.

This feeling is a major way in which Samoan values about mutual help and giving are expressed. The idea of giving is the concept most commonly associated with the feeling: this is true both in situations where there is a great deal of obligation and in situations where there is relatively little obligation. In fact, the feeling of alofa is viewed as being owed to everyone. Informants frequently claim that "Samoans love all our people."

The scenario frequently invoked to illustrate this sense of alofa as a minimal behavioral requirement is as follows: an old person, often portrayed as a stranger, is seen walking along the road, carrying a heavy burden. It is hot, and perhaps the elder seems ill or tired. The appropriate response in this instance is a feeling of alofa, which implies helpful or giving actions such as taking over the burden or providing a cool drink and a place to rest.

In these stories the feeling of alofa approaches the sense of compassion, empathy, or pity. These latter concepts have figured prominently in the translation of terms cognate to *alofa* elsewhere in the Pacific (Kirkpatrick, chap. 3; Levy 1973). I am unsure if the Ifaluk term *fago,* which Lutz describes in this volume (chap. 2), is a linguistic cognate to *alofa*. It is clearly a similar concept, but it is more definitely sad in tone than is alofa. In a hierarchical clustering diagram of Ifaluk emotion terms (Lutz 1982:116), fago appears in a group of terms which stress loss as a typical situational scenario. It apparently refers primarily to "one's relationship with a more unfortunate other" (ibid., p. 117). Such compassion is only one part of the meaning of the Samoan term. When Samoans see someone unfortunate, a cripple or someone particularly vulnerable like an orphan or a very small child, they may remark on it with the expression *tālofa'i*. This is a contraction meaning "I love him." But I have never had the impression that it was a particularly powerful feeling. This contrasts strongly with Levy's (1973:340–346) description of how the feeling *arofa* can overwhelm Tahitians.

The connection with giving and helping is much more important, and appears to be universal in all descriptions of alofa. This is true in intimate relationships as well as more casual ones. The alofa between parents and children, between siblings, and even husbands and wives, is described in terms of giving and helping. The emphasis, even in these close relationships, is on mutual obligation rather than intimacy. Samoan adolescent informants associate the term primarily with working for their parents. Cooking and serving food to their parents are particularly strong symbols of what young people must do to express alofa. Parents' alofa is thought to be expressed by giving to their children. In other relationships, various combinations of giving, helping, and working appear as major associations of the term.

There are significant conceptual differences between the Samoan *alofa* and the English term that has been chosen to translate it. Based on several informal interviews with Americans, one important connotation of the term "love" is the physical demonstration of affection, embraces and smiles being particularly salient. "Caring" is also mentioned, which implies, among other things, the mutual exchange of confidences. Even "sharing," which sometimes expresses aspects of appropriate exchange relationships, is usually interpreted as an exchange of intimacies. These associations never appear in Samoan descriptions of the term *alofa*. Smiling (a minor Samoan category) appears only in association with fiafia, 'happiness'. Embraces, even between husbands and wives, are not mentioned as expressing alofa; sexual love is glossed by other terms, such as *mana'o* 'want' and *tu'inanau* 'desire' or 'eagerness'.

'Love' is therefore not a perfect English rendering of the Samoan. These connotative differences are inherent in all translation, of course; a perfect equivalent should not be expected. It is necessary to make some sacrifices if the word is to be rendered into English at all. One could perhaps argue that it should not be so rendered, and discussion should rely entirely on italicized repetitions of the native term. The inconvenience to readers caused by this approach is considerable, requiring them to keep in mind long and frequently insufficiently remembered explications. When a number of such terms must be remembered, the reader may easily lose track of the argument. It is for these pragmatic reasons that I favor cautious translation into English.

'Love' is a good translation for *alofa* for several reasons. First, some of the meanings inherent in the Samoan term are in fact relevant to the English term, although perhaps they are less culturally salient for us. For example, various religious and philosophical analyses of "love" imply both the universality and the compassion inherent in the Samoan concept. The sense of obligation so important in Samoan thought is evident in American thoughts about love, as expressed by a corollary concept, "commitment" (Quinn 1982).

Second, the term 'love' is an appropriate rendering of *alofa* because both concepts are primary ways, within their systems of emotions, to express positive social ties between people. The two concepts thus have extensively similar functions in their respective cultures. My position here is that the exact matching between emotion concepts in different languages is less important in arriving at a translation than a general evaluation of the role the emotion plays in people's lives. As ways of expressing interpersonal bonding, love and alofa have an important functional similarity.

The study of such functional equivalencies would be put on a firmer basis if it rested on a systematic framework of comparison. Perhaps such a framework of comparison can be found in an analysis of basic affects. Because they are rooted in human adaptive mechanisms, a general functional significance is already part of the structure of basic affects. In addition, if functional comparisons between emotion terms rest on a similarity of basic affects, it is likely that there will be additional correspondences between the experiential qualities of the two concepts thought to be equivalent.

CRITERIA FOR THE IDENTIFICATION OF TERMS EXPRESSING BASIC AFFECTS

The task of distinguishing which basic affects underlie a set of emotion concepts is an important one. It may involve two main approaches. First, we might be able to distinguish terms that are more and less like the kinds of prototypes suggested by Rosch. In the discussion below, I suggest that some emotion terms are more global, that is, express a wider range of phenomena, than others, and are therefore likely to express more aspects of the basic affective pattern than narrowly defined terms. Some criteria by which global and culturally specific terms may be distinguished are offered as tentative hypotheses, with the hope of stimulating discussion. But, as we have seen, all of the terms in some important groups of emotion may be of the narrowly defined variety, and the basic affect on which they are based may not be apparent from a study of a single culture. Perhaps basic affects that are difficult to identify in one system will be more distinguishable in another.

The second approach to discovering basic affects therefore involves intercultural comparison. Specific methods for such comparisons will be developed through further research. We should be cautious, however, about drawing hasty conclusions from areal characteristics, largely because of issues surrounding Galton's problem (Naroll 1973) which are implicit in all comparative research: it is difficult to know if one is dealing with many cases, or a single coordinated case. If one concentrates comparison in a single area, it is likely to produce strong clusters of meaning around feelings that have an areal importance. If we do not take a wide range of societies into consideration, we run the risk of defining basic affects in a way ethnocentric to the area under study rather than to the society from which we come. Anthropological students of Polynesian societies might, for example, elevate *alofa* and *mā* and their areal cognates and functional equivalents into basic affects, which is no real improvement on defining basic affects in terms of "love" or "shame." An adequate definition of basic affects will therefore have to wait until the evidence of many different systems can be compared.

I have nevertheless introduced an occasional informal comparison with American English emotion terms in the course of this chapter. I hope that these are recognized for what they are: first attempts to begin clarifying the methods of comparison. The criteria I would like to suggest for distinguishing terms on the basis of their closeness to basic affects are discussed below.

Range of Applicability

Certain emotion terms have highly specific social referents and, consequently, exhibit a limited range of situational associations. For example, *lotomamā,* the term discussed earlier which refers to an un-angry loto, is restricted to a very narrow range of situations. It is only relevant to incidents that have an outcome of averted conflict. By contrast, the term *fa'anoanoa,* 'sad', presents a much wider range of social applicability. When informants describe this term, many different causative events are called upon, drawn from a wide range of interactional possibilities. Fa'anoanoa may result from any number of untoward situations: deaths, disappointments, nostalgia for missing relatives, quarrels with certain categories of persons, missing possessions, illnesses, and the like.

The same sort of contrast may be observed even between terms that are closer to each other in meaning than the above. For example, the term *ita,* 'anger', is quite closely related in meaning to the term *fa'a'u'ū,* which means something like 'sulky' and can be expressed by a recognizable sour facial expression. Both terms are associated with situations of conflict, but fa'a'u'ū is associated primarily with conflict over work. Fa'a'u'ū is a feeling that may accompany being assigned an unwelcome task by a person in authority. The authorities mentioned by my informants were nearly always a parent or an older sibling. By contrast, a variety of actors—teachers, strangers, friends, younger siblings, and social superiors—may be actors in situations involving ita. A wider range of events may bring ita about, and a wide range of behaviors such as hitting, sharp words, suicide, and gossip (to name only a few) are thought to express anger. The social specificity of *fa'a'ū'ū* and its narrow range of expressive signs indicate a term that is more narrowly socially defined than *ita.* Since both terms appear to be hedonically similar, it is reasonable to conclude that *ita* expresses more aspects of the basic affect that enlivens both feelings.

Degree of Stereotypy

The terms that reflect more of a basic affective pattern may have less stereotyped associations. This effect is very noticeable with Samoan informants because, as Torrance (1962) and Johnson (1963) have demonstrated, they exhibit generally high levels of cultural stereotypy. An example of a fairly unstereotyped term is *popole* 'worry'. When asked about popole, informants tended to describe one or two situations that in some way involved uncertainty, but there was relatively less overlap between their responses than between responses to other terms. The entire range of meaning, taken together, is very broad, which suggests that *popole* may be a relatively global term.

Exclusivity of Social Association

A third possible criterion that may distinguish narrowly defined terms from more global ones is the extent to which they are absorbed into the social interaction system. I would like to suggest that feelings that have exclusively interpersonal referents are unlikely to reflect basic affective patterns very closely. I base this suggestion on a hypothesis about the way in which such terms function. It seems to me that we may regard such narrowly defined emotion terms as having arisen to serve particular social ends. They express (or serve to crystallize and influence) the feelings that arise from certain typical interactional contexts in the lives of people who use the system of emotion terms. They seem to gloss the feelings engendered in particularly important or problematic points in the flow of social interaction. (See Black, chap. 7, about the nature of problematic events.) As such, their associations are likely to be heavily drawn from the interpersonal world. All emotion terms seem to have important interpersonal contexts, but only the most narrowly defined will have these contexts exclusively. Reactions to the nonsocial world must be glossed by some term; I suggest they are glossed by the most broadly defined terms because they do not fit in anywhere else.

The clearest problematic situation in the Samoan emotion system is the obligation of working for one's kinsmen. A number of emotions seem to be centered on this event. Alofa, 'love', and lotomalie, 'agreeable', in Cluster 1a, have already been discussed. In Cluster 1b, *'onosa'i* 'patient' is often described as an emotion appropriate to enduring such demands. *Fa'amoemoe* 'hope, dependence', expresses the faith Samoans place in their kinsmen that they will meet their obligations. In Cluster 2, lotomaualuga, 'arrogance', relates to the rejection of such obligations, and is usually explained in terms of refusing orders to do certain work. The entire first subcluster in Cluster 3 is related to this work situation. Fiu, 'fed up', is usually connected with dislike of persistent day-to-day drudgery. *'Augatā* 'lazy', expresses a low level of resistance to these work demands, as does musu, 'reluctance'. 'O'ono, 'suppressed anger', is specifically connected by my informants with obligations that are experienced as excessive and burdensome. Informants described scenarios in which foster parents exploited children by treating them as servants as typical of the situations to which this emotion is appropriate. In Cluster 4, māfatia, 'hurt' or 'exhausted', and *puapuagā* 'distressed' are sometimes described as resulting from strenuous physical labor. The work situation, and its complex set of obligations to kin, is thus very important in defining Samoan emotions. Some of them, particularly the subgroup of terms in Cluster 3, have meanings that are almost exclusively relevant to this problematic set of interpersonal interactions.

Other terms are associated with other important interpersonal situations. Fa'aaloalo and *āva* 'respect', for example, are always associated with interpersonal contexts in which social superiors are honored. (I am including various spiritual actors as social superiors.) We might contrast this with a term like fefe, 'fear'. In this case there are two distinct kinds of associations: some drawn from the social world and some drawn from the natural world.

When fear is projected into the natural world, informants picture a situation of physical danger, such as fishing in a canoe in a sudden windstorm. This sort of association has a simplicity of form and an obvious relationship to personal welfare. The *social* associations to the term *fefe* are much more complex and require an understanding of Samoan social structure. The most common social association to fear, in these data, was a situation in which the informants imagined doing something wrong and knew that their fathers would find out about it. The fear was specifically related to the beating they believed would inevitably result.

Range of Intensity Levels

The fourth possible criterion that might indicate a term's relation to basic affect is the range of intensity levels it can express. Basic affects can be experienced at many levels of intensity, and the global terms reflect this versatility. Ita, 'anger', and fa'anoanoa, 'sadness', are capable of expressing many states of activation, from the most minor irritation and disappointment to severe rage and grief. By contrast, some of the more narrowly defined terms seem to express only a very narrow range of intensity. *Fa'a'ū'ū*, 'sulky', is related to anger, but expresses only a controlled and small amount of negative feeling. But narrowly defined terms need not always express the low end of the scale of activation. Puapuagā, 'distressed', reflects only the upper end of the scale.

These criteria are neither definitive nor exhaustive, and are offered primarily as bases for further research. I would also like to point out that the distinctions I have discussed above probably do not generate clusters of characteristics which will define mutually exclusive types of emotion terms. I think it more likely that emotion terms might be placed on a continuum by which highly specific and more general terms can be seen to intergrade. We might look at one end of this continuum (the more globally defined terms) as providing a relatively complete mapping of a basic affect, covering a wide range of its experiential characteristics. The narrowly defined terms, by contrast, map only a narrow segment of some affect; they contain within their meanings a relatively complete map of a particular social or interpersonal situation.

EMOTION AND OBLIGATION: THE ACCEPTANCE OF SOCIAL VALUES

I have argued that certain emotions function to express the feelings that arise in interactional contexts of some special cultural importance. Once defined, these socially specific emotions serve as models that influence and guide an individual's feelings. Action is also guided by emotion: certain behaviors are defined as flowing "naturally" from a state of feeling and are regarded as proper expressions of it. From these processes another very important function of emotions arises. If the feeling itself is defined as the proper reaction of a "good" person, and if the behaviors consequent upon it are socially valuable, an emotional disposition toward socially correct action is created. "Good" people tend to have socially approved feelings the individual expresses by selecting from a range of socially valuable behaviors. The emotion therefore reinforces important social values. If the feelings in question rest on a basic affect, the emotional force of that powerful underlying psychological pattern is therefore put to the service of society.

Let us examine an example from the Samoan data. In the hierarchical clustering diagram (fig. 1), Clusters 1a and 1b contain a number of terms that appear to serve the functions described above. Perhaps the most culturally salient emotion is alofa, 'love'. Informants primarily associate this term, and others closely connected with it (*matamau* 'generous'; *lotofuatiaifo* 'free choice in giving'; and *lotomalie* 'agreeable'), with giving and helping. These feelings are considered proper in certain interactional and relational contexts. Alofa, for example, is the normal state of feeling toward most kin. The behaviors that "express" the feeling are also morally correct and socially obligatory. Generally, the social demands for both the feeling and the actions blend. A "good" child therefore works for his parents both to gain a reputation for moral behavior and as an outward sign of inwardly experienced alofa. The desire to express and experience the sense of bondedness is channeled into the performance of particular social obligations.

There are times when the obligation and the feelings do not coincide. As I have mentioned before, informants described cases in which a young person was sent to live with adoptive parents who had no particular alofa for him. Without the element of emotional bondedness, the obligations were experienced as burdensome, but they remained in place. Thus, such unfortunate young people continued to work for the parent-surrogates, but the work was not a sign of reciprocal alofa and was resented. The feelings thought to arise in the situation were described as 'onosa'i, 'patience'; 'o'ono, 'suppressed anger'; or even occasionally puapuagā, 'distress'. The evaluation of the social obligation therefore depends on the perceived emotional state of an important relationship. If the alofa exists, working for a parent is experienced as a validation of one's social identity. It marks one as a good kin relation, a loving child, and even perhaps as a favorite offspring. (One informant told me that she knew her father loved her best of all her siblings because he always chose her to do his laundry.) The work is also an expressive gesture: if a child feels a particularly overwhelming sense of alofa, the work is always waiting there for her or him to do. Alofa, then, serves to guide behavior toward particular moral aims, and reinforces the important Samoan value of mutual assistance and support between kin.

Other terms in the first cluster seem more connected with the values of hierarchy and of assuming one's appropriate place in it. Fa'aaloalo, 'respect', is the most obvious of these. The feeling is associated exclusively with socially sanctioned attitudes and behaviors toward people who are regarded as "higher" than oneself. Primarily, this involves elders, parents in particular, and people with high formal statuses, either in the traditional or modern American systems.

Several other terms in the first cluster also support this value. Lotomaualalo, 'humility', is the feeling one properly has in dealing with authority. If one is given an order, it should be accepted with a soft voice and downcast eyes, with a feeling of smallness and accepted inferiority. This tone is required in dealing with formal authorities, but the truly "good" individual may be seen to extend this attitude into all his dealings. It is as though the "good" person assumes a low position in the hierarchy with respect to everybody.

This marked lowness, and consequent willingness to be told what to do, is characteristic of the term *'onosa'i,* 'patience'. This is what makes it relevant to the experiences of foster children, who, if they cannot be loving, can at least be properly humble. As my informants use the term, it implies a consciousness of having been put upon. The properly low and respectful individual may sense a grievance, but will 'onosa'i and endure it without any comment.

Taken together, the terms in Clusters 1a and 1b represent many of the emotional dispositions of good persons: social bondedness, respect, faithfulness, bravery in adversity, not becoming angry, a peaceful or quiet heart, and so on. Good people are also thought to experience some hedonically negative emotions as well. 'Shame' (mā or māsiasi) and 'shyness' (matamuli) are approved inner experiences in reasonable amounts. Too much shame is thought to result in aggressive reactions (see Black, chap. 7, for a Tobian example of the dangers of a "shame script"), and too much shyness is considered a handicap in normal social interaction.

The behavioral dispositions consonant with these feelings may be seen as a connecting link between the upper-level values of a society and their day-to-day expression in people's behavior. By defining "right" feelings in a consonant manner, adherence to the values of mutual aid and hierarchy is not only made surer; it is rendered less painful. A Samoan gives, therefore, not only because he or she has been trained to view giving as morally correct but also because his or her training has created a disposition to feel such an act as "natural," seeming to arise out of the very depths of his or her being. Similarly, acceptance of hierarchical relations is given an emotional underpinning that is likely to reduce tendencies to chafe under associated societal strictures.

The functions of emotions which I have been describing might be observed whether or not the feelings under consideration express a basic affective pattern. But I suspect it will prove to be the case that emotions which serve these moral functions often do rest on some powerful underlying feeling. The stronger the feelings involved, I believe, the more closely the individual can be bound into social relationships that involve him in the performance of his obligations.

I am of the opinion that the emotions in Cluster 1 do engage basic affective patterns. *Alofa* and the terms that are most closely related to it in meaning probably code a basic affect involved with social bonding. The terms that express respect may, it seems to me, rest on different affective bases. The emotions that reinforce social hierarchy may be related to an affect of submissiveness; perhaps this will prove to be an etiolated form of fear.

It is interesting to note that, although social bonding is an important element of these emotions, they are not particularly hedonically pleasant.

This is true even of alofa, love, which was judged to be minimally pleasant, almost neutral, by most informants. A few even rated it as slightly unpleasant. In fact there is a general lack of terms expressing the more expansive joyous feeling in the Samoan emotion vocabulary. Americans, by contrast, devote more attention to elaborating ways to feel good than do Samoans.

ANGER IN SAMOAN ETHNOPSYCHOLOGY

I have argued that emotions are an important element of folk psychology in at least two important ways. First, culturally constituted emotions are used to classify and define physiologically based patterns, giving them social significance. Second, because certain emotions create dispositions to act in socially appropriate ways, they play a role in creating an appropriate social self. An individual's self-image will reflect his or her ability to feel in culturally appropriate ways, and to act on the basis of these specific motivations. In reporting on their feelings, however, it is likely that people will overestimate the extent to which they and others are motivated by these highly moral feelings. This arises primarily from the fact that people like to think well of themselves. But this does not prevent emotions from running counter to the primary trends a culture has established as appropriate. I would like to examine these general processes on the basis of an example drawn from the Samoan data presented above, and the divergent descriptions of Samoan behavior given by Freeman (1983) and Mead (1973).

We have seen how important taking an appropriate position in the social hierarchy is in defining Samoan emotions, such that there is literally no socially acceptable way of directly expressing anger against one's parents. Several terms exist which indicate covert angry responses to parental demands. These are 'augatā, 'laziness', 'o'ono, 'suppressed anger', fiu, 'fed up', and musu, 'reluctance'. They have in common not only semantic similarity but also the fact that they express resistance to parentally assigned work. But they do not represent high levels of intensity: in no instance is a vehement expression of anger toward parents permissible. Situations may occur, however, in which parental demands are experienced as excessive. To the extent they can, people will channel their anger into these mild, less disruptive feelings. To the extent they are successful, they may be unaware of how deep their anger is. It is likely, however, that they will continue to experience residues of socially unacceptable rage which they are unable to express, and of which they may not be aware.

This can lead to a familiar psychological process: an unacceptable feeling is suppressed and subsequently reemerges to intrude on the positive image of the well-socialized self. The point here is that the existence of these suppressed "immoral" feelings creates an inherent difference between people's cultural description of themselves and the way in which an observer would describe them. Accounting for feelings people do not recognize in themselves may therefore be an important part of ethnopsychology.

In the Samoan case, these suppressed immoral feelings are primarily concerned with anger toward social superiors and the demands that they are in a position to enforce. Unawareness of these feelings may have had an important effect on ethnographic descriptions of Samoan people. Several possible explanations for the contradictory reporting of Samoan character are opened up by this line of thinking. First, it is possible that Samoans cyclically lose control of this pool of unexpressed anger, and from time to time violence erupts. Judging from the episodic nature of Samoan drinking and the episodic violence it induces, this is reasonable. However, such violence is in fact not very frequent, and may not be directed against social superiors at all but against peers. This misdirection, which no doubt has the effect of helping to maintain an individual's mask of peaceful submission, also makes it more difficult for observers to understand the systematic nature of this violence. An observer may not be present when it occurs, or may regard it as a nonstandard event, not important enough to influence his or her judgment of the whole. This would leave him or her primarily with a picture of rather flat and uncomplex Polynesian emotion. This image would be reinforced by the public statements of Samoans, who like to see themselves as "good" in the typically Samoan ways.

This discussion leads me to comment briefly on the controversy about Samoan psychology engendered by the publication of Derek Freeman's book, *Margaret Mead and Samoa* (1983). Without becoming involved in epiphenomenal issues about the forgivable inferiority of first field research or the improprieties of calling attention to it after fifty years, I think it is possible for all students of Samoan culture to agree that Mead's presentation of Samoan character lacked a certain depth and complexity. In the course of this chapter, I have pointed out several ways I think such a flattened picture of Samoan intrapsychic process might have developed; I would like to add an additional comment. The peaceful, undemanding, rather gentle and submissive character that Mead described might have been taken almost entirely from the description of certain Samoan emotions which reinforce the Samoan values of mutual assistance and hierarchy. As we have seen, these emotions form a significant part of the socially approved emotional self. Mead's description, perhaps biased in favor of informants' self-reports, accurately captures the surface ideology about the way that persons ought to be. And, in fact, Samoans behave in accordance with these values. They are deeply motivated by the emotions involving mutuality, agreeableness, and submissiveness. The inner experiences they represent are both real and socially important. The behaviors that flow from them are genuine pro-social expressions of the Samoan's involvement in his or her society.

Mead's mistake was therefore not a complete misreading of Samoan psychological process, but an overconcentration on only one aspect of it. In particular, her picture of Samoan character ignores the potential anger that develops vis-à-vis authority and the obligations it enforces. This anger bursts out only episodically, is not part of the usual flow of social interaction, but instead contrasts markedly with it. It is therefore possible that Mead witnessed few acts of violence during her stay in Manu'a, which may help to explain how her oversights came about. Nevertheless, she seems to have taken Samoans too much at their word about who they were, not only in reports of sexual adventuring but in accepting an ideological version of the self as the whole truth.

Freeman (1983) recognizes the existence of a countertrend in Samoan personality, and indeed, most of the book is devoted to citing examples of angry and otherwise passionate behavior. He regards Samoan character as having a dual nature, which results from the use of severe punishment in child rearing. This discipline is imposed

> with such dominance as to produce a profound ambivalence toward those in authority, with love and respect alternating with resentment and fear. Because of this system of childrearing and the stringent demands that those in authority make upon the growing individual, Samoan character . . . has two marked sides to it, with an outer affability and respectfulness masking an inner susceptibility to choler and violence. (P. 276)

Freeman is so impressed with the existence of this anger that he regards the "outer affability and respectfulness" as a "mask." In fact he frequently interprets Samoan compliance with the demands of those in authority as extracted under duress, and not stemming from genuine feelings at all. For example:

> The child learns early to comply overtly with parental and chiefly dictates while concealing its true feelings and intentions. As a result, Samoans, whatever may be their real feelings about a social situation, soon become adept at assuming an outward demeanor pleasing to those in authority. . . . it is usual, especially in demanding social situations, for Samoans to display an affable demeanor which is, in reality, a defensive cover for their true feelings. (Ibid., p. 216)

Even though Freeman recognizes the existence of this ambivalence, he gives more weight to the feelings of anger than to the feelings of love and respect. In fact, the latter are not regarded as genuine feelings at all, but are only a duplicitous means of coping with hated authorities. It seems, then, that Freeman not only thinks that Samoans lied to Margaret Mead (ibid., p.108), he believes that they lie continually to their parents and other authorities about themselves. The only emotions Freeman appears willing to credit as "real" or "true" feelings are the hidden hostile ones, while he gives little credence to the subjective reality of the generous, agreeable, and submissive ones. But, as we have seen, parental demands are usually interpreted as an integral part of a mutual relationship of love; the obligations are interpreted as onerous primarily in situations where love is no longer thought to apply. For the most part, the performance of obligatory work and service is genuinely expressive of the feelings that Freeman does not regard as "real." Rejecting the importance of these feelings is a mistake equally as great as, and directly opposite to, Mead's inability to see the potential for anger in the Samoan character.

Both errors are essentially alike in that both stem from oversimplifications of immensely complex cultural and psychological processes. Freeman seems, for example, to have assumed that emotional reactions, particularly violent ones, are evidences of genetically controlled behavior, "nature" as opposed to "culture." Thus, when Samoan chiefs become more polite as they get angrier in difficult meetings, until they lose control, it indicates to Freeman

> an extremely rapid regression from conventional to impulsive behavior. For our present purposes the significance of such incidents is that when the cultural conventions that ordinarily operate with chiefly assemblies fail, activity does *not* suddenly come to an end, but rather the conventional behavior is replaced in an instant, by highly emotional and impulsive behavior that is animal-like in its ferocity. . . . impulses and emotions underlie cultural convention to make up the dual inheritance that is to be found among all Samoans, as in all populations. (Ibid., pp. 300–301)

In the distinction Freeman draws between the genetic and the exogenetic, emotions are clearly assigned to the former. This ignores the complex processes of social definition of emotions which I have described in this chapter, and does not permit the possibility of emotions serving the sort of social functions I have described. Thus, despite Freeman's call for "a synthesis in which there will be, in the study of human behavior, recognition of the radical importance of both the genetic and the exogenetic and their interaction" (ibid., p. 302), he does not seem to have been aware of how these factors are complexly blended and mutually conditioned in human experience. My discussion of the role of basic affects in the patterning of the conceptual system of emotions is a demonstration of the way in which one specific "genetic" factor is absorbed into enormously complex human social and psychological experiences.

A second point I would like to make regarding underlying anger against authority is that it may help to explain Samoan violence in situations where authority is removed. We have seen how a young person's father is viewed as being responsible for his conduct, and how paternal beatings are expected and viewed as evidences of parental concern. We have also seen that the primary social association with the word *fefe* 'fear', is cast in terms of these parental beatings. The fear occurs when the child has misbehaved and knows the father will discover it. My informants universally rejected the possibility that a father would not learn of a misdeed. "But he will find out," they insisted. "Someone will see me; someone always sees, and they will tell him." This worry about being observed in wrongdoing and the certainty of being seen are associated with the emotion of shame both in these data (fig. 1) and in the Polynesian literature. It appears, then, that for Samoans the fear of parental beatings must rank along with shame as a source of intrapsychic pain connected with bad behavior. I believe that Samoans rely as much on the fear of the father to control their behavior as they do on the avoidance of shame. The beatings may therefore play a dual role—both in the creation of resentment and hostility and in its subsequent control.

What happens, then, if the father is removed from the situation either in actuality or in emotional terms? The individual's self-control might be expected to correspondingly weaken, and hostility toward social superiors (no doubt given an extra sharpness by the resentment stemming from all those beatings) is likely to emerge.

Perhaps this is the reason for the occurrence of violence primarily in a peer context, where parental authority may be experienced as emotionally most distant. However, in Samoa itself, it is impossible to completely escape the authority of social superiors. Even if one's own father dies, a host of other family chiefs and village functionaries are present to supply the emotional weight of the parent.

This authority may be vitiated when Samoans migrate to cities in the United States. The superstructure of chiefs becomes weakened or disappears, and contact with American attitudes toward parents may erode the authority of even present, living fathers. To the extent that the individual has relied on parental authority to maintain self-control and social submission, the channeling of unexpressed anger may fail. Samoans seem to recognize this possibility when they send young people who get into trouble in the United States to relatives in Samoa, where, it is said, "everything is stricter." This process may account for different levels of Samoan violence at home and in the United States.

CONCLUSION

The study of emotions is important to ethnopsychology not only because they are interesting and powerful subjective experiences in themselves but also because they provide a means by which important social values are linked with behavior. In addition, emotions help to define the image of the socially approved self. In this chapter, I have argued that the study of emotions should take into account the distinction between the inner experience of subjective emotional states and the conceptual systems by which emotions are defined and classified. These two levels of patterning are highly interconnected, but not entirely isomorphic. The cultural conceptual system may not express all phenomenological aspects of complex inner events, or may even serve to mask them. Nevertheless, the conceptual system serves as a model for proper feeling, shaping an emotional basis for the development of morally valued action. Emotions therefore serve to reinforce important social values.

In this analysis, I have assumed the existence of inborn patterns of affective arousal. This is useful in several important ways. First, it allows us to approach the experiential nature of inner experiences which a particular conceptual system leaves implicit and uncodified. In cultures like the Samoan, where attention is turned outward to social and interactional cues, informants may not be able to express inner experience directly. An understanding of basic affect, drawn from comparative material, may be the only clue to important areas of inner experience in this situation.

Second, basic affects pattern the conceptual system of emotion, and serve as centers around which clusters of meaning develop. This is similar to the "natural prototype" structures suggested by Rosch (1975). I have argued that some emotion concepts are more globally defined and express more of the phenomenological aspects of a basic affective pattern than do others, which are more narrowly defined as applicable to particular social situations. Understanding basic affects is therefore vital in describing the structure of the important and complex domain of emotion.

Third, because these basic affects are panhuman, they will provide a basis for comparison and translation between systems of emotion in different societies.

Fourth, and most important, understanding basic affect permits us to examine the way in which a society constructs or fails to construct a basic affect in cultural terms. In the Samoan case, intense anger toward social superiors is culturally impermissible, but individuals are partially unsuccessful in channeling this anger into more acceptable low-level expressions of the same basic affect. This is the source of subsequent personal and interpersonal disruption.

Perhaps a clearer, ethnopsychological understanding of these processes might have aided Mead and Freeman in avoiding the kinds of oversimplification to which both Samoans and ethnographers must object. The fact that they could have reached such symmetrical and mutually exclusive oversimplifications is an indication of the depth and internal intricacies of Samoan culture and Samoan lives.

ACKNOWLEDGMENTS

The fieldwork on which this chapter is based was carried out in American Samoa, from September 1972 to December 1973. It was funded by NIMH predoctoral Fellowship No. 1F01 MH53627. I would like to thank the editors of this volume and Roy G. D'Andrade for their useful comments, and Peter Black and Kevin Avruch for their invaluable theoretical and moral support.

NOTES

1. Lutz (1982:125–126) points out the importance of distinguishing between the public, verbal aspects of emotion and emotion as a subjective experience.

2. The concept of affect is widely and variably used in psychology (as discussed below). I employ it here without commitment to any particular theoretical school.

3. Possibly it might occur in dreams.

4. For example, Averill (1980) takes as his major point that "*emotions are social constructions.* That is, emotions are responses that have been institutionalized by society as a means of resolving conflicts which exist within the social system" (p. 37). Nevertheless, in evaluating the biological determinants of emotion, he relies on concepts from ethology, in which patterns of external behavior are explained with reference to their adaptive significance for the species.

5. Primary among these is the following: "So Watson's behaviorist account becomes self-refuting. Watson has told us that an emotion is a 'pattern reaction', chiefly of physiological changes, which is found in its unadulterated form only in the newborn child, though it is difficult to get evidence of this. Since he admits that this pattern reaction is adulterated or becomes etiolated, or both, soon after infancy, he is admitting in effect that with adults we cannot distinguish one emotion from another, or emotional reactions from other sorts of reactions, by means of a behaviorist account" (Lyons, p. 18).

6. Resistance toward parental demands is most often expressed indirectly, by grimacing silently when orders are given, by carrying them out slowly, or quite commonly by simply disappearing when orders are likely to be given. Young

Samoans do verbalize resentment toward other social authorities, such as chiefs and teachers, but it is usually to sympathetic peers.

Freeman (1983) also relates musu to inexpressible anger against authority, but he concentrates only on rare states of extreme social resistance, the upper end of the intensity scale. When an individual is "seriously *musu*," according to Freeman, he is "in a disaffected and emotionally disturbed state. . . . On occasion the demands of this stringent system generate such internal resentment and stress that an individual can take no more and becomes intractable, or *musu,* sullenly refusing all commands and admonitions. A person in this state is very near the breaking point, and if harried further may become violent or even commit suicide; therefore when an individual does become seriously *musu* he is usually left to his own devices until his dangerous mood has subsided" (pp. 218–219).

Some of my informants mentioned this extreme sense of musu, usually in the context of parental pressure to marry an unacceptable spouse. But it was appended as an afterthought to discussions of the more usual low-level experience of musu, in which the angry element very nearly disappears. Although it is far less dramatic than the desperate cases Freeman cites (ibid., pp. 220–222), I would like to offer the following incident as an example of musu. An eight-year-old girl was sitting in the back room of a house with an older woman who visited seldom and whom the child liked. Laughter could be heard; the little girl was observed through the window batting a large blue balloon in the air. Suddenly her mother called her from one of the outbuildings, ordering her to go on an errand. The girl dropped down out of sight below the window, and there was silence. After calling two or three more times, the mother sent an older sister to the window to see what was happening. "She doesn't want to go, she's musu," was the report. The mother looked cross briefly and said, "Then you'll have to go."

This incident is more in accordance with my informants' description of the feeling of musu than are Freeman's cases. I cannot find an "emotionally disturbed state" in it. Further, the mother's acceptance of her daughter's musu seems more like collaboration in the avoidance of a closer examination of the child's resistance than an attempt to avert violence. Instead of being dangerous adversaries, they collude to keep the level of conflict low. In this sense, they perhaps act more like Mead's Samoans than Freeman's. On the basis of the description of such incidents, I remain convinced that musu is more properly regarded as a low-intensity expression, and that it serves more as a safety valve for social resistance than as a symptom of incipient loss of control.

7. The relationship between the more specific and more global terms is reminiscent of relationships of inclusion between lexical items. I think informants might respond that one emotion was a "kind" of another in some cases; but in others, the relationships might not be that clear.

8. This phenomenon is probably related to the psychiatric concept of flattened affect.

9. Samoans frequently rely on the principle of personal or social gain (cui bono) in constructing explanations of motives.

10. The distinction between reliance on bodily vs. external cues is reminiscent

of the psychological phenomenon of field dependence and independence. In the rod and frame experiment, for example, a subject is placed in a darkened room and told to watch a dimly lighted figure in front of him. Gradually the subject's chair is tilted, making the figure appear askew. Those who are considered "field independent" rely on the evidence of proprioception, and correctly report that it is the chair that has changed position. Those who are classically "field dependent," by contrast, ignore proprioception and report that the external cue (the lighted figure) has changed in orientation (Price-Williams 1975:6–8). I would like to suggest as a tentative hypothesis that where emotion terms are described almost exclusively by external social cues, as in Samoa or in Ifaluk (Lutz, chap. 2), this performance may form part of a general cognitive style of field dependence. A valuable topic for further research would be to establish if Samoans and others with a similar approach to emotions are in fact cognitively field dependent.

Levy (1972) has suggested that these general orientations correspond to different kinds of sociocultural integration. Where the individual faces rapidly changing social parameters, the locus of social control must become internal because there is nothing else to rely on. Other systems exhibit a homeostatic balance, and are characterized by the individual's smooth fit into the social world (pp. 297–300). These modes of sociocultural integration may provide an underlying causal explanation for the cognitive and emotional styles discussed here.

GLOSSARY

alofa	love, stresses social bonding and obligation
atuatuvale	worried
'augatā	lazy
āva	respect, in respect language
fa'aaloalo	respect, common language
fa'ali'i	angry, synonymous with *ita*
fa'alotolotolua	indecision
fa'amāgalo	forgive
fa'amoemoe	hope, depend on
fa'anoanoa	sad
fa'atuatua	have faith
fa'autauta	be cautious
fa'a'ū'ū	sulky; also refers to sour facial expression that accompanies this feeling
fatu	the physical heart

fefe	fear
fiafia	happiness; may also refer to parties
filēmū	peaceful
fiu	fed up
fuā	jealousy, in respect language
'ino'ino	hatred, disgust
ita	angry
lagona	feelings, sensations
loto	the quasi-organ in which emotion and some thought takes place
lotofuatiaifo	voluntariness in choices; translated by Pratt (1911) as "conscience"
lotoleaga	jealousy, bad thoughts; lit., a 'dirty' loto
lotomalie	agreeable; lit., a 'sweet' loto
lotomamā	absence of angry thoughts; lit., a 'clean' loto
lotomaualalo	humility; lit., a 'low' loto
lotomaualuga	arrogance; lit., a 'high' loto
lototele	brave; lit., 'a lot of' loto
lotovāivai	timid, sorrowful; lit., a 'soft' loto
mā	shame
māfatia	hurt, exhausted
mana'o	want
māsiasi	shame, ashamed
matamau	generous
matamuli	shy
mimita	proud, bragging
misia	missing someone; from the English, "to miss"
musu	reluctant
ofo	startled
'oli'oli	happy; syn. fiafia
'onosa'i	patient
'o'ono	suppress; as an emotion term, always suppressed anger

popole   worried

puapuagā   distressed, endangered

taupou   traditional ritual princess

te'i   startled

tu'inanau   desire, eagerness

REFERENCES

Arnold, M. B.
  1960   Emotions and Personality. 2 vols. New York: Columbia University
          Press.
  1970   Feelings and Emotions: The Loyola Symposium. New York: Academic
          Press.
Averill, J. R.
  1980   Emotion and Anxiety: Sociocultural, Biological and Psychological De-
          terminants. *In* Explaining Emotions. A. Rorty, ed. Pp. 37–72. Berkeley,
          Los Angeles, London: University of California Press.
Carroll, J. B. (ed.)
  1956   Language, Thought and Reality: Selected Writings of Benjamin Lee
          Whorf. Cambridge: MIT Press.
Clement, D. C.
  1982   Samoan Folk Knowledge of Mental Disorder. *In* Cultural Conceptions
          of Mental Health and Therapy. A. Marsella and G. White, eds. Dor-
          drecht: D. Reidel.
D'Andrade, R. G.
  1978   U-Statistic Hierarchical Clustering. Psychometrica 43:59–67.
Darwin, C.
  1873   The Expression of Emotions in Man and Animals. London: Murray.
Davitz, J. R.
  1969   The Language of Emotion. New York: Academic Press.
Doi, L. T.
  1962   *Amae:* A Key Concept for Understanding Japanese Personality Structure.
          In Japanese Culture: Its Development and Characteristics. R. J. Smith
          and R. K. Beardsley, eds. Pp. 132–139. Chicago: Aldine.
Ekman, P.
  1972   Universals and Cultural Differences in Facial Expressions of Emotion.
          In Nebraska Symposium on Motivation. J. K. Cole, ed. Lincoln: Uni-
          versity of Nebraska Press.
Freeman, D.
  1964   Some Observations on Kinship and Political Authority in Samoa. Amer-
          ican Anthropologist 66:553–568.

1973   Kinship, Attachment Behaviour and the Primary Bond. *In* The Charac-
          ter of Kinship. J. Goody, ed. Pp. 109–120. Cambridge: Cambridge
          University Press.
1983   Margaret Mead and Samoa: The Making and Unmaking of an An-
          thropological Myth. Cambridge, Mass.: Harvard University Press.
Geertz, C.
1976   "From the Native's Point of View": On the Nature of Anthropological
          Understanding. *In* Meaning in Anthropology. K. H. Basso and H. A.
          Selby, eds. Albuquerque: University of New Mexico Press.
Geertz, H.
1959   The Vocabulary of Emotion: A Study of Javanese Socialization Pro-
          cesses. Psychiatry 22:225–237.
Gerber, E.
1975   The Cultural Patterning of Emotion in Samoa. Ph.D. diss., University
          of California, San Diego. Ann Arbor, Mich.: University Microfilms.
Grings, W., and M. Dawson
1978   Emotions and Bodily Responses: A Psychophysiological Approach.
          New York: Academic Press.
Holmes, L.
1957   Ta'u: Stability and Change in a Samoan Village. Journal of the Polyne-
          sian Society 66:301–335.
James, W.
1884   What is an Emotion? Mind 9:188–205.
Johnson, R. T.
1963   The Growth of Creative Thinking Abilities in Western Samoa. Ph.D.
          diss., University of Minnesota.
Levy, R. I.
1972   Tahiti, Sin and the Question of Integration Between Personality and
          Sociocultural Systems. *In* Culture and Personality: Contemporary Read-
          ings. R. LeVine, ed. Pp. 287–306. Chicago: Aldine.
1973   Tahitians: Mind and Experience in the Society Islands. Chicago: Univer-
          sity of Chicago Press.
Lutz, C.
1981   Situation Based Emotion Frames and the Cultural Construction of Emo-
          tions. *In* Proceedings of the Third Annual Conference of the Cognitive
          Science Society. Pp. 84–89. Berkeley.
1982   The Domain of Emotion Words on Ifaluk. American Ethnologist 9:113–
          128.
Lyons, W.
1980   Emotions. Cambridge: Cambridge University Press.
MacLean, P.
1980   Sensory and Perceptive Factors in Emotional Functions of the Triune
          Brain. *In* Explaining Emotions. A. Rorty, ed. Pp. 9–36. Berkeley, Los
          Angeles, London: University of California Press.

Mead, M.
1928   The Role of the Individual in Samoan Culture. Journal of the Royal
        Anthropological Institute 58:481–495.
1930   Social Organization of Manu'a. Bishop Museum Bulletin 76. Honolulu:
        Bishop Museum.
1973   Coming of Age in Samoa. New York: American Museum of Natural
        History. Originally published in 1928.

Myers, F.
1979   Emotions and the Self: A Theory of Personhood and Political Order
        Among Pintupi Aborigines. Ethos 7:343–370.

Naroll, R.
1973   Galton's Problem. *In* A Handbook of Method in Cultural Anthropology.
        R. Naroll and R. Cohen, eds. New York: Columbia University Press.

Pratt, G.
1911   Pratt's Grammar and Dictionary of the Samoan Language. Western
        Samoa: Malua.

Price-Williams, D.
1975   Explorations in Cross-Cultural Psychology. San Francisco: Chandler
        and Sharpe.

Quinn, N.
1982   "Commitment" in American Marriage: A Cultural Analysis. American
        Ethnologist 9:775–798.

Rorty, A. O.
1980   Explaining Emotions. *In* Explaining Emotions. A. Rorty, ed. Pp. 103–
        126. Berkeley, Los Angeles, London: University of California Press.

Rosch, E.
1975   Universals and Cultural Specifics in Human Categorization. *In* Cross-
        cultural Research Methods. R. Brislin, S. Bochner, and W. J. Lonner,
        eds. New York: Wiley.

Russell, J. A.
1980   A Circumplex Model of Affect. Journal of Personality and Social
        Psychology 39:1161–1178.

Schlosberg, H.
1952   The Description of Facial Expressions in Terms of Two Dimensions.
        Journal of Experimental Psychology 44:229–237.

Shand, A.
1914   The Foundations of Character. New York: Macmillan.

Shore, B.
1976   Ghosts and Government: A Structural Analysis of Alternative Institu-
        tions for Conflict Management in Samoa. Paper presented at the meeting
        of the Association for Social Anthropology in Oceania, Charleston,
        S.C., February 1976.
1980   Speech Styles and Social Context: A Samoan Case Study. Paper pre-
        sented at the meeting of the Association for Social Anthropology in
        Oceania, Galveston, February 1980.
1982   *Sala'ilua:* A Samoan Mystery. New York: Columbia University Press.

Strongman, K. T.
  1973   The Psychology of Emotion. London: Wiley.
Thompson, H.
  1971   Fear and Loathing in Las Vegas. New York: Random House.
Torrance, E. P.
  1962   Cultural Discontinuities and the Development of Originality of Think-
            ing. The Exceptional Child 29:2–13.
Watson, J. B.
  1919   Psychology From the Standpoint of a Behaviorist. New York: Lippin-
            cott.
Wolfe, T.
  1970   Radical Chic and Mau-mauing the Flak Catchers. New York: Farrar,
            Straus, Giroux.

5

Anger, Grief, and Shame: Toward a Kaluli Ethnopsychology

Edward L. Schieffelin

INTRODUCTION

The study of human personality in relation to culture has usually been the domain of psychological anthropologists. Until recently, their major focus has been the attempt to determine the effect of particular social or cultural variables on particular personality configurations, relying primarily on the idea that particular aspects of culture exert a determinate influence on the personality during its development in childhood. Shweder, in a recent series of articles (1979–80), has criticized the ethnocentrism of much of this work, pointing out that there is a widespread failure in these approaches to differentiate between behavior that derives from personality variables, and that which is part of the normal culturally patterned behavioral and expressive order. Consequently, patterned social behavior is treated as if it derived from personality functioning. There are two ways to approach this dilemma. One is to redouble efforts to distinguish aspects of psychological behavior from social behavior through various methodological refinements. The other is to consider that they are indistinguishable and examine the social construction of many aspects of the person normally thought of as traditional personality variables. What is needed to begin with is what Shelly Rosaldo (1984) called an ethnography of the self.

Until very recently, few anthropologists attempted to determine what the people they study themselves assume about human personality, how

they model it, on what grounds they assess it, and how they interpret what
we would term features of psychological functioning within the normal
course of cultural life.

Ethnopsychology is a major movement in this direction: the attempt
to determine a people's own cultural perspective on that aspect of the person
which corresponds roughly to what we would term personality. This is
not always a straightforward undertaking. The people in question may not
have an articulate "theory of personality" or human psychology, and what
they think about human nature and personality may become clear only by
examining the assumptions about human nature which seem to underlie
their discourse and behavior in relation to others. I will undertake here this
kind of exploration of the relationship of anger, grief, and shame among
the Kaluli people of Papua New Guinea, to discover what these emotions
reveal about Kaluli assumptions regarding human personality and behavior.
Of course, anger, grief, and shame do not exhaust the inventory of affect
among the Kaluli (which also includes fear, desire, compassion, etc.), but
they do form a particularly important nuclear group whose central importance is recognized by Kaluli and is presented prominently in their ceremonial performances (Schieffelin 1976; Feld 1982). I will be particularly
interested in these affects in their cultural rather than psychological dimensions, that is, how they are related to one another as a cultural and expressive
system. In the absence of a systematic and articulate Kaluli theory of personality, this is a reasonable way to explore and encompass Kaluli assumptions
and perspectives on human nature. The underlying claim here is that the
experience, justification, and meaning of emotions are not separable from
the role they play in the expressive order of interaction, or from the implications of the cultural scenarios in which they participate. In this I follow
Durkheim's notion that how people feel in a particular situation is not only
supposed to be "natural," given the situation, but it is also socially expected,
or even socially required. Not only the individual but also the situation has
its emotional dimensions, and what the individual feels is to a significant
extent a function of the emotional requirements of the situation. Affect,
I argue, cannot be divorced from its expression and the setting of its
expression.

I begin by considering the vocabulary of emotion terms used by the
Kaluli to speak of their feelings, and show that it is necessary to look at the
context of expressive interaction to understand what Kaluli mean when
they feel. I then move to the social context, broadly conceived, and discuss
the implications of the egalitarian Kaluli social structure for their dominant
modes of interaction and the two sides of their cultural ethos, which, it will
be shown, facilitate a particular emotional style. I then discuss Kaluli social
reciprocity to show the implications it has for the way Kaluli understand

social events and thus the way it affects the shaping of emotional attitudes and expectations within the expressive order of interaction. Finally, I discuss shame in relation to the expression of these emotions as part of the rhetoric of power and influence.

KALULI EMOTION TERMS

A conventional point of departure for investigating a domain of experience as a cultural system is to examine the terms that people use to talk about it. Thus, we should perhaps begin by examining Kaluli terms for emotions. The assumption underlying this approach is that the distinctive features and systematic relationships that delineate the meaning of the lexical items reflect the manner in which the domain they refer to is actually thought about by the people who use them. This assumption works well for botanical classifications and some nosological systems (Frake 1961), where the major conceptual aim of the array of terms is to enable people to make fine discriminations within a set of relatively concrete items. More often, however, such a taxonomic aim is not the central concern of human discourse, and the ways in which the terms are used to make sense of the world go far beyond the simple schemata by which they may be discriminated from each other as a lexical set. This is particularly true for emotion terms. It seems doubtful, for example, that terms for emotions or feelings can readily be mapped onto a set of discrete and unambiguous internal states. Certainly it is difficult to do so with English terms. Moreover, there is the problem that emotion labels from other cultures may not really be translatable into English either because they are not conceptually equivalent to the nearest English term or because they refer to states of feeling which are not available, or at least not discriminated, in Western experience (see Lutz, chap. 2). With this in mind we should approach Kaluli linguistic expressions for emotions with due caution and skepticism.

Kaluli words for affects are not nouns describing types of feeling, but verbs describing states of the individual. They correspond to English usages such as 'to be angry' or 'to be desiring'. These expressions are as follows.

For anger:

gadiab	he/she is moderately to strongly angry
kulufeyab	he/she is very angry
imolab	he/she flies into a furious rage

kegab	he/she talks angrily to spouse (a spat)
kanolab	he/she is angry over a long time
migi hedab	he/she appears gloweringly angry (lit., face hangs)
ilib negalab	he/she is angry inside (lit., chest hurts)

For grief or sadness:

| *nofolab* | he/she feels compassion, sorry for, feels sad |
| *kuwayab* | he/she grieves (implies weeping) for death or misfortune |

For shame:

| *sindilowab* | he/she feels ashamed |
| *wanalowab* | he/she feels ashamed (implies cringing or turning away) |

The question is, what does this list really tell us? The most obvious feature is that the terms for anger receive the most lexical elaboration. This in itself, however, does not necessarily tell us very much about how Kaluli think about anger. As Levy (1984) has pointed out, the complexity and availability of terms for anger do not necessarily indicate that anger is frequently encountered or even much discussed in everyday life in a given culture. Nor are the semantic dimensions that differentiate the lexicon, such as intensity (*gadiab* vs. *imolab*) or mode of expression (*migi hedab* vs. *ilib nagalab*), consistent or necessarily the salient ones for discourse. The saliency of the lexicon can only be arrived at by examining how it is used in discourse. The Kaluli do, as a matter of fact, find anger a fascinating and problematic emotion. But this is not a finding that could be established by examining the semantic field of the emotion terminology alone. Without denying that this semantic field may be of intrinsic interest, it is apparent that the significance of emotions to the Kaluli is more likely to be revealed from an examination of the ways they talk about or express their feelings in various contexts rather than from examination of the lexicon of emotion words by itself. To learn that significance, we need to know about the contexts in which emotions are expressed and the general structure of emotional behavior in the expressive order. Accordingly, we turn now to examine Kaluli ethnography and social organization and the implications they have for Kaluli emotional style.

KALULI SOCIETY

The Kaluli people (population about 1,200) live in twenty longhouse communities scattered about an hour's walk from each other in the tropical forest region north of Mount Bosavi in the Southern Highlands Province. Like most Papua New Guinea societies, the social ties among longhouse communities are primarily based on marriages between people in different longhouses. These ties, however, are maintained through the offering of support and hospitality, and the exchange of prestations of meat in a system of balanced reciprocity with delayed exchange.

Kaluli society is egalitarian. There are no big men or traditional positions of authority among the various longhouse communities. A man is customarily expected to take initiative in making his way in Kaluli society and gaining the support of others. He achieves what influence he has through his ability to give vigorous support to his friends, play conspicuous roles in important events, initiate projects in which he can inspire the cooperation of others, and maneuver situations to his own advantage. This puts a premium on the individual's own initiative and force of character, and Kaluli men tend to adopt a posture of energetic assertiveness in any undertaking where their interests are at stake.

Culturally, this posture of assertive energy is articulated in an ideology that emphasizes the productive vitality of male essence and supports the favored Kaluli ethos of exuberant vigor and personal dynamism (Schieffelin 1976, chaps. 6, 7). This ethos infuses much of Kaluli male public activity: the giving of an oration, the grabbing of weapons in response to a threat, the splendor of decorated bodies entering a compound on a ceremonial occasion to the accompaniment of drums. It expresses a man's energy, strength, health, pride, and personal force (see Poole, chap. 6). The assertive behavior it shows is meant to be provocative, intimidating, and beautiful, arousing fear, excitement, admiration, and desire. Traditionally, a man who failed to show a certain amount of personal assertiveness was considered a weakling and of no account, or was thought to be ill.

A point must be made here about the concept of ethos. Bateson (1958:118) formulated its original usage for anthropology as "the expression of a culturally standardized system of organization of the instincts and emotions of individuals." Or, more briefly, ethos refers to the dominant emotional emphases, attitudes, and modes of expression of the culture as a whole. The problem is how these broad cultural emphases are to be related to the details of cultural behavior and individual experience. The concept of ethos has generally been used as a descriptive ethnographic characterization. However, to the extent that individuals regularly exhibit attitudes and moods characterized by the ethos, that ethos can be considered expressively normative. That is, it is culturally expected that a person feel a certain way and adopt a certain affective posture and expressive style in relation to particular events. One may even be evaluated as a person in part according to the manner and to the degree that he or she does so. A culture's ethos is thus not only a characterization of a style of feeling and behavior but also a model for it.

In the Kaluli case, there are two dimensions to the dominant ethos: personal dynamism and assertiveness (especially emphasized in male style, though women embody it too), and vulnerability, dependency, and appeal. We will discuss later how these two sides of Kaluli ethos are joined in the scenario of reciprocity where grief may be resolved in retaliation.

THE POSTURE OF ASSERTION

Within the assertive modality, Kaluli sometimes appear to an outsider as somewhat pushy or intrusive in everyday interactions. They are insistent, while avoiding direct confrontation. At the same time, however, it is in this assertive modality that anger is an important emotion and expressive form.

A man's temper, or 'tendency to get angry', is a major feature by which Kaluli judge his character and assess the degree to which he is a force to be reckoned with. It represents the vigor with which he will stand up for or pursue his interest vis-à-vis others, and the likelihood that he will retaliate for wrong or injury. Anger is an affect that is both feared and admired.

The vigor or personal energy a person is expected to have is broadly exemplified in an emotional style that I have characterized elsewhere as volatile (1976:119). It might be more accurately described as expressively passionate. When Kaluli feel strongly about something, they are not likely to hide their feelings. Rage, grief, dismay, embarrassment, fear, and compassion may be openly and often dramatically expressed. Frequently, the intent is to influence others, whether by intimidation (e.g., with anger) or by evoking their compassion (e.g., with grief). A man whose expectations have been frustrated or who has suffered wrong or injury at the hands of another does not usually suppress his outrage. Rather, he is likely to orchestrate his anger into a splendid frightening rage, projecting himself with threats and recriminations against his (often equally angry) opponent in a volatile exercise of social brinkmanship that occasionally leads to violence. Dismay or grief similarly may be openly expressed, often evoking others' sympathy and support. These displays of affect have to be seen more as declarations of mind, motivation, and/or intention than mere cathartic expressions of feeling.

EXPRESSED FEELINGS AS DECLARATIONS
OF MOTIVATION AND INTENTION

Given this apparent openness of affect, it comes as some surprise to an outsider who asks an informant how another person feels about something when she or he receives the reply, "I don't know. How is one to know how another man feels?" Even if the informant observed the event in question, if the protagonists were less than completely explicit about their thoughts and feelings, he is likely to report that they "acted as if they were angry (or happy or dismayed, etc.)." This does not mean, of course, that unless a man tells others explicitly what he feels or thinks they have no idea of his emotions.

As B. B. Schieffelin has pointed out (Schieffelin and Ochs 1983), Kaluli, like most other people in the world, are usually able to assess how others are likely to feel and respond to particular situations. But they avoid making statements that attribute feelings, motivations, or intentions to people (even if they have a pretty good idea what they are) unless these feelings have been in some way publicly expressed or made explicit.

This reluctance to talk about the feelings and motivations of others is part of a more general reluctance to paraphrase or present interpretively another's statements of claim or purpose. When reporting a conversation or event, Kaluli are usually careful to make clear whether they observed the situation themselves or only heard about it. Indeed, Kaluli never paraphrase or summarize the substance of a conversation, but quote it verbatim so that the narrator of the report may not be accused of telling lies or gossiping. The point to be made here is that to impute feelings, motivations, or intentions to a person which have not been made publicly clear by that person is, in effect, to put words into his or her mouth and to misrepresent him or her. Insofar as feelings expressed are a public expression of thought and attitude, they can have significant and troublesome social implications. Making speculative attributions about other people's feelings, like spreading misinformation, amounts to spreading mischievous and trouble-making gossip (*sadedab*), and risks provoking suspicion and hostility.

Of course, like most other people, Kaluli do gossip. But it is significant that the feelings they most avoid making comments about are those that are most likely to arouse socially problematic situations and conflict: desire for the opposite sex, anger, envy, and avarice. Messages about these, when they are passed, have to be based on statements the original speaker can be held accountable for, or they amount to trouble-making gossip. A person who learns that such attributions have been made about him or her may take them as provocative.

SOCIAL RECIPROCITY: A SENSE OF PROPORTION

While Kaluli ethos casts Kaluli expressions of feeling in an explicit and declarative mode, it does not provide the sense of proportion that limits that expression. Nor does the display of anger derive its justification from ethos alone. The framework that gives anger its justification and social implications, and that also provides the sense of proportion that constrains it, is social reciprocity. Social reciprocity also frames the order of events that anger sets in motion. I have already spoken of how social ties between different longhouse communities are maintained through exchange of prestations in a system of balanced reciprocity with delayed exchange. In this system, one person makes a gift or prestation to another with the understanding that the recipient will, at a later date, make an equivalent return gift. Such a return gift, conceived of as an exact equivalent, is known as *wel*. For our purposes, what is important is that this pattern of balanced reciprocity is not restricted to exchange of prestations, it also represents a fundamental pattern of behavior and a model for managing situations of many kinds beyond that of exchange in material objects or food. For example, just as in a prestation where a gift of pork requires that an equivalent gift of pork be made in return (called wel), so in the case of the theft of a pig, the enraged owner may appropriately resolve it by a return, countertheft of one of the thief's pigs (also called wel). (Alternatively, he may settle for compensation [*su*] in objects of wealth.) Similarly, if a man has lost a relative to death by witchcraft, traditionally he might raid and attempt to kill the witch in return (once again, wel). Similar reciprocal resolutions are attained in fights, ceremonial performances, the curing of illness, and relations with the spirit world (see Schieffelin 1976, chap. 5). For the Kaluli, what we would call exchange or reciprocity broadly represents a system of social facilitation (prestation for prestation), dispute settlement (wrong and retaliation, or redress), a form of drama (Schieffelin 1976), and a general mode of action which returns situations to proper proportion by, in some sense, evening the score.

This kind of balanced reciprocity outlines a scenario that provides the Kaluli with a model for dealing with many types of situations. If one can interpret a set of events as involving a loss and an opposition between protagonists, there is a shared understanding about the appropriate course of action to take. Implicit in this is a sense of proportion (reflected in the notion of wel) and a legitimate set of expectations and appropriate attitudes oriented toward the outcome of this well-understood type of resolution.

Returning to Kaluli anger, nearly every reason to be angry—any loss, wrong, injury, insult, or disappointment—is interpreted in terms of the scheme of reciprocity (Schieffelin 1980). The height of a man's rage is partly measured by the amount of loss he has suffered, and redress is sought in proportion through the notion of wel (or equivalent compensation, su). For our purpose, this has two important implications. First, for the Kaluli, anger almost always bears the implication that the angry person has suffered a loss of some kind, even if only in the form of a frustrated desire or disappointed hope. Second, because loss in a scheme of reciprocity implies that one is entitled to return, the person who is angry is in some sense owed something; he or she has a legitimate, if often hopeless, expectation that redress is due.

When a man has suffered wrong or loss, he may stamp furiously up and down the hall of the longhouse, or the yard outside, yelling the particulars of his injury for everyone to hear in order to arouse their sympathetic attention and inspire their backing for redress. Such an angry person is not only intimidating but also a figure of pathos for the Kaluli, and the display of anger is frequently meant to be a forceful plea for support.[1] Thus anger gains a particular rhetorical force, a certain measure of legitimacy, and a set of social implications from the way it is situated in the scenario of reciprocity. At the same time, the two sides of Kaluli ethos begin to converge as anger becomes a form of appeal.

THE POSTURE OF APPEAL

Although the assertive posture, of which anger is a part, represents the dominant and favored expression of ethos for the Kaluli, it is not the only mode of experiencing events, pursuing one's ends, and influencing others. The other posture Kaluli tend to adopt is the contrasting one of appeal, which represents the ethos of intimate sentimentality and nostalgia which obtains between people who are close friends or relatives. If assertion exerts its influence by provoking, intimidating, exciting, and inspiring, and represents the stimulating application of productive energy, appeal exerts its force through the evocation of a sentimental intimacy, pathos, and compassion. Adopting this posture, a person projects an attitude of need, vulnerability, and dependence, using a soft intimate tone or even a begging, whining intonation, inviting others to feel sorry for him or her and do something. In contrast to the posture of vigor and energy, it projects dependency and misfortune.

As anger is the extreme expression of the posture of assertion, grief is the extreme posture of vulnerability and appeal. Grief is given meaning, like anger, within the Kaluli sense of reciprocity. It represents a person as reduced to powerlessness and vulnerability by devastating loss, a figure of pathos, one who is entitled to redress. Powerful in rage, men are reduced to particular helplessness in grief, weeping in a hysterical and uncontrolled manner (*ganayelab*; Feld 1982:90). Women, who are more subdued in anger, are not so expressively devastated by grief. They turn their weeping into a form of wept song.[2]

Loss is the point of contact between anger and grief. It also forms the point at which, through the scenario of reciprocity, grief may be transmuted into anger and effective action. A raid to kill a witch responsible for a death is the satisfying result of the transformation of grief into anger, and the movement of grief to anger is the theme of most Kaluli ceremonial performances (Schieffelin 1976, chap. 11). For our purposes, it is important to point out that though anger and grief show the greatest possible contrast in the projection of power versus vulnerability in the projection of self in a situation, they are alike in the context of reciprocity in that both are the result of loss, and both contain the implication that one is entitled to redress. Anger claims it with a demand for compensation or a move toward vengeance, while grief waits upon the compassion of others to provide it (or becomes transmuted into anger).

SOCIAL INTERACTION AS THE BASIS OF SHAME

While reciprocity provides a sense of proportion for assertive moves and a means of redress for anger, in normal circumstances Kaluli prefer to control unwanted assertive actions before they get to the point of provocation at which the scheme of reciprocity becomes irrevocably engaged. The problem boils down to one of managing the importunate assertive (or appealing) moves of others in everyday contexts without provoking grounds for retaliation. The major tactic for countering such moves is shaming.

Shaming is visible in its most elementary form in the domestic family. In a typical situation, a child will take (or beg) some food or other object that another person doesn't want him or her to have. Rather than refuse the request or tell the child to put the object down, the parent (or sibling) will ask, "Is it yours?" or some similar rhetorical question that throws the legitimacy of the child's claim into doubt. The phrasing of the challenge as a rhetorical question aims to avoid a confrontation or clash of wills and risk of anger, and throws the one to whom it is directed on the defensive.[3] Moreover, the rhetorical question "Is it yours?" implies that the request for the object amounts to a kind óf potential theft, and hence suggests a threat of retaliation in line with the Kaluli sense of reciprocity. It is in the context of this set of implications that the child is rhetorically called to account for the legitimacy of his or her move.

To examine more closely what is going on in this situation of shaming, it is useful to consider Goffman's concept of interactional face. Goffman (1967:5) defines "face" as "the positive social value a person claims for himself by the line he takes in a particular situation." The "line" a person takes is the way he expresses his view of the situation and his evaluation of the participants, particularly himself. A person is said to be "in face" when the line he effectively takes presents an image of him that is consistent and supported by the judgment of the other participants in the interaction. A person's face is thus not located on the person himself but is diffusely located in the flow of events in the encounter, since it depends to some extent on the other participants. If other participants withhold judgmental support of a person's line, it collapses, and the person loses face and is shamed.

In terms of our concerns here, the modalities or postures of assertion and appeal are the basis for the line that supports the particular face that the individual wears for an interaction. Whether a person presents himself as good-humored but demanding, or whining and dependent, in a given interaction, these postures are at least legitimate in principle. However, they also may represent moves that are not welcome to other participants in the interaction.

Consider the following interaction, taken from Schieffelin's (1979) study of Kaluli child socialization. A mother has just finished cooking some pandanus and is preparing to offer it to two young children. Her older daughter Binalia has already eaten more than her share of pandanus that morning, and her mother does not intend to give her more. Nevertheless, Binalia, hungrily watching the others, begins to make an appeal for food. She says to the other children: "Can you eat that large amount of pandanus by yourself?" Her mother counters on behalf of the younger children: "What was left of yours [from this morning]?" The mother then turns to her son and says: "Say to her: 'where did you put it?'; [say:] 'Is this [the freshly cooked pandanus] yours?'" The mother then continues teasing and provoking Binalia by offering more pandanus to the other children, and as Binalia continues to whine for it, challenges her again: "Is it yours?! Did you pick it?!" (p. 97). In effect, these rhetorical questions place in doubt Binalia's claims to the food and so undermine the legitimacy of her appeal, shaming her.

Shame is revealed here as a situation as much as a private emotion. Its existence and meaning are both products of interaction. Like grief, shame involves a sense of vulnerability, but unlike grief, which has a claim to social support, shame has none. It represents a situation, or state, of powerlessness and rejection, in which the legitimacy of one's basic posture or claim has been removed by others.

ANGER AND SHAME

The Kaluli are well aware that this kind of rhetorical question is a shaming move and have a word for it (*sasindiab*). The person being shamed may respond by not answering the question but withdrawing the move. Or, one may challenge the attempt to shame one by answering the rhetorical question with one of one's own. For example, if asked "Is it yours?!" one may retort, "Is it YOURS?!" or some similar question in the attempt to undermine the legitimacy of the other's challenge. Binalia did not do this because she would have risked enraging her mother. This brings us to another counter to shame, namely, once again, anger. One does not attempt to shame another person if one does not think one can dominate the situation. If one tries to shame a stronger opponent without proper social support, one's opponent may become provoked, override shame, and dominate one by intimidation. In this way an assertive response may sometimes thrust a shaming move aside and retain control of the situation. For this reason, Kaluli rarely attempt to discredit a person by reference to his past reputation, an act that could be interpreted as an insult or as gossip and hence could give the individual an opening for legitimate anger. They prefer, instead, to challenge the other's immediate posture and claims in the situation.

The most dramatic situations of public shame occur after a dispute over a wrong done to someone in which the aggrieved gains the advantage and bawls out the culprit with an angry self-righteous oration. Even here, past reputation is not so much at issue as are the implications of the present moves seen through the forms of reciprocity. The culprit is rhetorically cast in the role of debtor toward the person he has wronged and the oration takes the tack: "You did such-and-such [a provocative or illegitimate move], and I didn't say anything [read: so you owe me]. . . . Now you are doing this [another illegitimate move]. Who are you to do that? You are like a dog that steals the food another person has laid down for himself." In the circumstances the culprit can do little but attempt to divert the argument with excuses or weeping in shamefaced anger and self-pity, which draws little sympathy.

CONCLUSION

I have shown that the emotions of shame, anger, and grief are closely interrelated within the larger expressive system in which Kaluli social experience and action are ordered. Understood in relation to the cultural ideas of loss and reciprocity, they participate in a single cultural system. Insofar as they represent the cultural organization of psychological attitudes, they form part of a culturally shared ethos and set of attitudes supported by a world view. But, in their expressive aspects, they represent interactional postures with rhetorical force, and gain their particular significance, proportions, and social implications (among the Kaluli) from the resolutely social process of reciprocity. Thus Kaluli emotions, however privately experienced (though Kaluli try to make anger, shame, and grief as public as possible), are socially located and have a social aim. To this degree they are located not only in the person but also in the social situation and interaction that, indeed, they help construct.

One important message to come out of this analysis is that anthropologists interested in affect and culture may legitimately look outside the private interior of the individual to the processes of social interaction, not just for the sources that provoke feeling but for a substantial part of the form and significance of emotion as well. Geertz (1973) has remarked that one does not have to look to the privacy of the individual to understand significant cultural symbols and beliefs: their meaning may be found in the marketplace. To a great extent, the same may be true of human feelings. Not only do socially shared meanings supply much of the significance and implications of feelings for individuals, the feelings are in part a social construction of the situation in which they participate.

NOTES

1. This sense of being owed something when angry gets its start early in childhood (especially for little boys) in the strategies mothers adopt in dealing with their children's anger. Schieffelin (1979) has shown that mothers attempt to allay anger either by distracting their children's attention to something else or by buying it off by offering some compensatory food or object—which is sometimes explicitly labeled as wel. This develops a diffuse sense of entitlement to redress, or to having something done for one when angry over a frustration or loss. The significance of this practice in my view is not mainly to be found in the implications of such parental indulgence for the development of dependency needs or similar constructs that are taken to describe aspects of personality manifest in cultural behavior. As Shweder (1979:281–282) has pointed out, it is important to distinguish between behavior that

derives from personality variables and behavior that represents "what any rational person would have done under the circumstances"—or, I would amend, what is socially expected or expressively normative. Here the expectation of redress for anger is a matter of learning what is "rational" and legitimate (as well as strategic) in the situation by Kaluli lights. The feeling of entitlement to recompense for anger, which to a Westerner looks a bit like the attitude of a spoiled child, is an entirely legitimate social posture (especially for men) among Kaluli even if it is not an expectation that is always fulfilled.

2. Steven Feld's (1982:90) phrase is more precise: "Sung texted weeping" (*sayelab*).

3. For a more detailed account of the use of rhetorical questions for shaming, see Schieffelin 1982.

GLOSSARY

gadiab	he/she is moderately to strongly angry
ganayelab	he/she weeps in an uncontrolled, hysterical way (Feld 1982)
ilib nagalab	he/she is angry inside (lit., chest hurts)
imolab	he/she flies into a sudden furious rage
kanolab	he/she is angry over a long time; long-standing anger
kegab	he/she talks angrily to spouse or children; a spat
kulufeyab	he/she is very angry
kuwayab	he/she grieves (implies weeping) for death or misfortune
nofolab	he/she feels compassion, sorry for someone; feels sad
sadedab	mischievous and trouble-making gossip
sayelab	she engages in sung texted weeping (women only) (Feld 1982)
sasindiab	he/she shames (someone)
sindilowab	he/she feels ashamed
su	compensation payment
wanalowab	he/she feels ashamed (implies cringing or turning away)
wel	equivalent returned in prestation or extracted in retribution

REFERENCES

Bateson, G.
    1958   Naven. Stanford: Stanford University Press. Rev. ed.

Durkheim, E.
   1965   The Elementary Structures of the Religious Life. New York: Free Press.
            (Original French edition published in 1912.)
Feld, S.
   1982   Sound and Sentiment: Birds, Weeping, Poetics and Song in Kaluli
            Expression. Philadelphia: University of Pennsylvania Press.
Frake, C.
   1961   The Diagnosis of Disease among the Subanun of Mindanao. American
            Anthropologist 63:113–132.
Geertz, C.
   1973   Ethos, World View, and the Analysis of Sacred Symbols. *In* The Inter-
            pretation of Cultures. Pp. 126–141. New York: Basic Books.
Goffman, E.
   1967   Interaction Ritual. Garden City, N.Y.: Anchor Books.
Levy, R. I.
   1984   Emotion, Knowing and Culture. *In* Culture Theory: Essays on Mind,
            Self, and Emotion. R. A. Shweder and R. A. LeVine, eds. Cambridge:
            Cambridge University Press.
Rosaldo, M. Z.
   1984   Towards an Anthropology of Self and Feeling. *In* Culture Theory:
            Essays on Mind, Self, and Emotion. R. A. Shweder and R. A. LeVine,
            eds. Cambridge: Cambridge University Press.
Schieffelin, B. B.
   1979   Getting It Together: An Ethnographic Approach to the Study of the
            Development of Communicative Competence. *In* Developmental Prag-
            matics. E. Ochs and B. B. Schieffelin, eds. Pp. 73–108. New York:
            Academic Press.
   1982   Teasing and Shaming in Kaluli Children's Interactions. Paper presented
            at the annual meeting of the American Anthropological Association,
            Washington, D.C.
Schieffelin, B. B., and E. Ochs
   1983   A Cross-cultural Perspective on the Transition from Prelinguistic to
            Linguistic Communication. *In* The Transition from Prelinguistic to Lin-
            guistic Communication. Robert M. Golinkaff, ed. Pp. 115–132. Hills-
            dale, N.J.: Lawrence Erlbaum Associates.
Schieffelin, E. L.
   1976   The Sorrow of the Lonely and the Burning of the Dancers. New York:
            St. Martin's Press.
   1980   Reciprocity and the Construction of Reality. Man 15:502–517.
Shweder, R.
   1979-80 Rethinking Culture and Personality Theory. Ethos 7:255–311; 8:60–94.

6

Coming Into Social Being: Cultural Images of Infants in Bimin-Kuskusmin Folk Psychology

Fitz John Porter Poole

When infants are very small, their *finiik* ('type of spirit or life-force') is tiny and weak and 'crooked' (*wernaam*). The finiik 'flows' (*guuriguuraaniin*) like twisting rivulets of rainwater on a smooth rock, and small things 'block' (*duugamiin*) its path. The finiik is soft and stringy and flutters like the tatters of a rotten pandanus frond in a strong wind. Pieces of the infant's finiik may fly about or become 'twisted together' (*fuugamiin*) when the infant cries or laughs or sighs or hiccups or struggles, when it is ill or hungry or afraid, when it is weary or becomes 'confused' (*iruum-kiim khaamiin-kha*). The finiik has no 'roots' (*kiimkiim*), no 'path' (*daib*), no 'kernel of meaning' (*dop aiyem*) . . . no 'source in life' (*kwan ker tabiin*), no 'strong support or foundation' (*miit kitiir*). . . . The infant has no 'strong attachment' (*adetera'fefebaanam duur-kha*) to its agnatic kin and ancestral clan land. Its 'shadow' (*ataan takhaak*) and 'reflection' (*ok takhaak*) are not clear. Its 'footprint' (*yan tem*) is faint and twisted. . . . Also, the infant's *khaapkhabuurien* ('type of spirit or life-force') knows only the womb and the breast and the netbag. It has no 'skin' (*kaar*) of its own [i.e., no experience of life, no 'shame' (*fiitom*)]. . . . Only their mothers understand their 'baby talk' (*uurfeng aur-weeng*), but there is no 'sense or truth' (*daam*) in it [i.e., for others]. . . . Until the soft skin of the fontanelle becomes strong and ceases to throb and the temples no longer vibrate to the touch, their eyes flit over everything and often close in sleep, or return to the breast and the mother's eyes. . . . They do not 'understand truly' (*kiinangkhaamiin fen-*

kha). . . . They cannot 'control' (*faatebeemiin*) the 'body' (*fom*) or the 'heart'
(*iboorop*) [i.e., the central locus of emotion, intellect, judgment agency, and
consciousness]. They cannot see clearly. . . . They are filled with 'anxiety'
(*sakhiik*) and with 'fear' (*finganiinaan*) of everything but the mother. . . . Until
they have 'strength' (*kitiirnam*) of eyes and heart and body and finiik, they
wander in a place unknown to them. . . . They may fall ill or die before we
can 'really know' (*tuurun taamamiin*) them.[1]

INTRODUCTION

In this chapter, I explore selected features, contours, and constellations of
some ethnopsychological constructs which are brought to bear on making
sense of the underlying nature and particular circumstances of infants as
persons among the Bimin-Kuskusmin of the West Sepik hinterland of
Papua New Guinea. These folk constructs are deployed to conceptualize,
analyze, and evaluate those dispositions, motivations, activities, and experiences that are attributed to infants as a consequence of their nature as
incipient persons and of their behavior in particular settings.[2] The Bimin-
Kuskusmin model of infancy is focused on aspects of both interpersonal
and intrapersonal variation and normal and abnormal development with
respect to a particular category of person and to more general considerations
of personhood, the life cycle, and "human nature."

Geertz (1976:225) suggests a useful focus of analysis in maintaining that
"the concept of person is, in fact, an excellent vehicle by means of which
to examine . . . how to go about poking into another people's turn of
mind." Indeed, concepts of the person and ideas of folk psychology are
mutually implicated in descriptions and explanations of the culturally significant lineaments of human thought, feeling, and action. Thus, this
analysis is informed by considerations of fundamental notions of personhood as a set of cultural premises with respect to which particular formulations of indigenous psychology are constructed among Bimin-Kuskusmin.
In important ways Bimin-Kuskusmin ideas of personhood provide the
nexus between more or less abstract knowledge of "human nature" and of
the "individual-in-society" and particular knowledge of actor and situation
which lends structure to "the network of concepts pertaining to psychological phenomena, imbedded in ordinary language" (Smedslund 1978:10).

For purposes of this analysis, personhood refers to those critical attributes, capacities, and signs of "proper" social persons that mark a moral
career (and its jural entitlements) in a particular society (see Fortes 1973;
Harris 1980; Mauss 1938, 1969). The concept of the person involves some
attribution of culturally delimited powers to the person which are linked

to notions of control and intentional agency in a sociomoral order and to related ideas of responsibility for choice and action (see Harré 1981; Harris 1980; Rorty 1976). Although such powers may also be linked to particular conceptualizations of the components, structures, processes, states, boundaries, and interconnections (with other human and nonhuman entities) of the body, these corporeal limits neither encompass nor define the person (see Lévy-Bruhl 1916). Indeed, persons are essentially social beings who develop over time and to differing degrees in a "culturally constituted behavioral environment" (Hallowell 1955:87).

The various endowments of power, control, agency, and responsibility which are associated with the person are often predicated on some notion of an experiential self which is the foundation of judgmental capacity and which is generated by some combination of inherited or innate propensities, personality characteristics, life experiences, socialization and enculturation processes, acquired knowledge, and reflexivity. Among Bimin-Kuskusmin, ideas of the 'person' (*kunum*)[3] and of the 'self' (*kaar kiimkiim*; lit., 'skin root')[4] are almost invariably bound up together in the fabric of ethnopsychological constructions. It should be noted, however, that the attributes, capacities, and signs of personhood (with the implication of reflexive selfhood) may be imposed upon (or denied to), in whole or in part, not only particular human actors but also categories or collectivities of human actors or nonhuman entities.[5] Indeed, the personhood (and selfhood) of infants among the Bimin-Kuskusmin is notably unstable and incomplete in many consequential ways. It is this general characteristic of instability and incompleteness, and consequent fragility and proneness to misfortune, in infants which appears to promote the extraordinary elaboration of ethnopsychological attention to infancy among Bimin-Kuskusmin.

The analysis examines the implications of Bimin-Kuskusmin constructions of personhood (and selfhood) in a variety of ethnopsychological appraisals of infants which focus on thought, feeling, and behavior. Although many aspects of personhood and folk psychology among Bimin-Kuskusmin may take the form of covert categories, tacit understandings, and intricate metaphors in ordinary discourse, attention to some of the semantic contours, foci, and ranges of certain "key words" (Quinn 1982) may reveal significant dimensions of the underlying folk model, which is often particularly explicit and elaborated in ritual or divinatory discourse (e.g., the opening quotation).[6]

I probe some of the implicit and explicit formulations and semantic connections of the highly condensed and polysemic ideas of finiik and khaapkhabuurien—types of "spirit" or "life-force"—as they are used in different ways in diverse social contexts with respect to infants and older persons (cf. Strathern 1981 on the Melpa concept of *noman*). Many features of the social person are founded and shaped with respect to the idea of the finiik, and the khaapkhabuurien implicates certain cultural recognitions of the experiential self and of the problem of the individual-in-society. The various particular balances, strengths, and anatomical distributions of these forces are invariably central to the portrayals of finiik and khaapkhabuurien—either implicitly or explicitly—in most ethnopsychological accounts. By unpacking some of the complex significance of these notions for Bimin-Kuskusmin, I am able to show how they tend to interconnect various foci of folk psychological reckonings and how they provide a structure of inference that bridges between observable behavior in certain contexts and attributions of underlying perceptions, thoughts, feelings, wishes, motivations, or intentions.

These analytic concerns are focused on infants from birth to the ritual bestowal of 'female names' (*waneng win*) at about two years of age for several reasons. First, this culturally elaborated phase of the life cycle has special ethnopsychological significance among Bimin-Kuskusmin and is marked as the period of the 'new child' (*men kikiis*), 'helpless, sucking newborn baby' (*aur maamuruup muut*), 'mother's infant' (*aurfaat*), or 'umbilical path child' (*daib abinaam men*). Second, this period is a critical developmental stage during which rudimentary facets of personhood (and selfhood) are first manifested and recognized as being significantly 'human' (*fiitep*), and an essential development of the finiik and khaapkhabuurien becomes especially prominent during this phase. Third, this stage is marked by special ethnopsychological characteristics that are set in explicit contrast with features of more mature development, which, it is important to note, are attained through "natural" growth, food, social experience, cultural understanding, and the ordeals of subsequent rites of passage (see Poole 1977, 1981*b*, 1982*b*, n.d.).[7] Fourth, explicit discussions concerning the infant contrast with the usual reticence to comment unambiguously in public discourse on the ethnopsychological significance of particular behaviors of known older actors. To probe explicitly the psychological flaws of adults outside of certain divinatory contexts is considered to be not only a severe breach of etiquette but also a verbal assault upon the person, which infants have not yet become in any developed sense. Fifth, beyond extensive informal interpretation of infant behavior, ethnopsychological exegesis is particularly explicit, detailed, and elaborate in those formal rites of passage, divinations of health and misfortune, "clinical" assessments of maturational processes, and diagnoses of death that focus on infancy. The high mortality and feared fragility of infants is believed to demand constant attention to subtle features of behavior as delicate indices of the normal or aberrant development of the personhood and "proper" ethnopsychological traits of the infant.

In addition to these privileged contexts and conditions of the ethnographic focus of inquiry, the acknowledged vulnerability and the incipient, partial personhood of infants in many or most societies may provide special illumination of some basic assumptions of ethnopsychologies which often remain more tacit or obscure in cases of primary attention to other categories of persons. LeVine (1977) has proposed that universal foci of parental concerns and goals include attention to physical survival and health, development of behavioral capacities for ensuring later modes of "economic self-maintenance," and enhancement of behavioral capacities for the maximizing of other cultural values. Parental priorities are focused on those concerns and goals that are seen to be most seriously threatened. Coherent cultural beliefs that recognize the critical problems and offer meaningful solutions to them tend to reduce overt anxiety. Thus, in societies with high infant morbidity and mortality, there tends to be a more or less nonanxious indulgence of immediate "needs" of the infant, but "there is no place for an organized concern about the development of the child's behavioral characteristics and social and emotional relationships" (ibid., p. 25). Indeed, affective, behavioral, and cognitive aspects of development tend to be deferred to later years in parental priorities.

The Bimin-Kuskusmin, however, are extremely anxious about the perceived high fragility and mortality of infants despite elaborate cultural beliefs that recognize the conditions of infants at risk and provide intricate solutions (see Poole 1982a).[8] In turn, these solutions extend well beyond immediate "needs" (in LeVine's sense) to focal concerns about the development of a range of affective, behavioral, and cognitive capacities. For Bimin-Kuskusmin, infants must be not only protected, fed, calmed, and nurtured in the ways that LeVine suggests but also strengthened in terms of their affective, behavioral, and cognitive capacities. Attention to the detail of the personhood and folk psychology of infancy and to the structure of their connections demonstrates why Bimin-Kuskusmin parental goals do not conform in important ways with respect to LeVine's model.

With reference to the partial personhood (and imputed selfhood) of infants, therefore, I am concerned with exploring two facets of Bimin-Kuskusmin ideas of folk psychology. On the one hand, I trace some of the general symbolic coherences and ambiguities of these ideas as part of a complex corpus of culturally constituted, more or less organized knowledge about human behavior, feeling, and thought. On the other hand, I note some instances of the situational deployment of these ideas in both recurrent and unusual contexts in order to render particular behaviors of identifiable actors (and categories of actors) under recognizable circumstances somewhat comprehensible and available to the scrutiny and judgment of public discourse. Of course, what is represented as a model of Bimin-Kuskusmin psychology is based on a delicate weaving together of explicit discourse and implicit assumptions across a selected range of situationally embedded formulations. Although this model is only partially representative of the complexity of some basic ideas of Bimin-Kuskusmin commonsense psychology, it is an ethnographer's model that is based on an interpretive assemblage of linguistic and other cultural data.[9] It seeks to capture some of the subtle discriminations and other nuances of folk psychological reckonings among Bimin-Kuskusmin through attention to how general, abstract cultural understandings about persons and selves are given shape in particular contexts and with respect to particular categories of persons. It also attempts to show how the model of folk psychology is both representational and operational (see Caws 1974),[10] although, for most Bimin-Kuskusmin, the model is often largely operational, depending on procedural knowledge involved in diagnosis and action (see D'Andrade n.d.).[11]

Probably all folk models possess an important tacit dimension. Thus, Heider (1958:4) observes that commonsense psychology is "the unformulated or half-formulated knowledge of interpersonal relations as it is expressed in . . . everyday language and experience" (cf. Hallowell 1955:91). Indeed, his view of the "naive scientist" analogy extends only to "that part [of interpersonal relations] which . . . inclines toward the side of 'intellectualism'" (Heider 1958:298). As indicated in the opening quotation, explicit ethnopsychological "theorizing" by Bimin-Kuskusmin ritual specialists in formal contexts may be quite elaborate, but many assumptions on which these esoteric formulations are founded also remain tacit.

Any analytic attempt to demonstrate the patterns of symbols, idioms, and lenses and the structures of inference that Bimin-Kuskusmin bring to bear on making sense of human behavior in diverse contexts is fraught with difficulty. Natural discourse on matters of folk psychology is typically unelaborated, highly condensed, often fragmented, and notably context-sensitive. Yet, the abstract exegesis of ritual experts and diviners, community involvement in extended discussions of infant development, and gradually learned modes of elicitation that more or less adhere to indigenous scripts enhance comprehension of these general, but tacit, understandings that emerge from analysis of a range of contextually embedded ethnopsychological "diagnoses" of persons. Frequent challenges to particular folk psychological constructions as they are applied to particular configurations of actor, behavior, and situation also bring into focus otherwise tacit assumptions and suggest that disagreements tend to concentrate more on the appropriateness of the *application* of general principles to particular circumstances than on the general principles themselves (cf. Lutz, chap. 2).[12]

Formal contexts of divination and other rites that demand delicate and detailed probing of ethnopsychological states and processes provide yet another range of closely related data which further interpretation. Nevertheless, Bimin-Kuskusmin ritual elders often speak of the 'meaning' (*aiyem khaa*), 'root speech' (*weeng magaam*), or implicit concepts that lurk 'inside' (*mutuuk ker*) or 'beneath' (*afaak ker*) the 'covering or wrapping' (*khymin*) of 'ordinary speech' (*weeng ken*). It is the 'kernel meaning' (*dop aiyem*) that must be 'brought to the eye' (*yom kiin daakhamin ker*) and is 'hidden' (*niimteywa*) in the heart from which only 'fragments' (*giitakhaa*) enter the mouth in 'speech' (*weeng*) (see Poole 1976). Thus, the ethnographer is perhaps finally faced with accepting that the nuances and contours of ethnopsychological reckoning are learned slowly, painstakingly, and subtly through acquired sensitivity to field experiences, as well as through more formal techniques of elicitation (see n. 9).

An analytic rendering of Bimin-Kuskusmin psychological discourse in terms that are more or less faithful to the shape, scope, and force of indigenous constructs and comprehensible to an anthropological audience demands a hermeneutic approach of some delicacy. It is conventional to conceptualize ethnopsychology in terms of an analogy between ordinary, commonsense descriptions, interpretations, and explanations of (inter)personal behavior and experience, and essentially Western psychological theories that also bound an apparently similar "domain" of interest (cf. Antaki and Fielding 1981; Heider 1958). Such an analogy, however, provides the potential of both illumination and distortion in analysis (see D'Andrade n.d.; cf. Lutz, chap. 2, and White, chap. 9).

Indeed, notions of folk psychology among Bimin-Kuskusmin are not readily encompassed by any simple view of a bounded semantic domain, but are better represented as an open set of concepts (susceptible to contextual transformations) related more in accordance with Frake's (1969:132) idea of "paths of interlinkage" or Wittgenstein's (1958:32*e*) view of "the overlapping of many fibers" in "family resemblances." These contours, linkages, and resemblances should not be expected to conform simplistically, a priori, or phenomenologically to any Western genre of bounding a psychological "domain," but must be explored ethnographically. In turn, ethnopsychological concepts among Bimin-Kuskusmin are "opentextured" (Waismann 1965)—as are any psychological concepts—and require translation that goes beyond any simple, monolexemic glosses that ignore the special values and presuppositions embedded in the more or less peculiar orientations of an English "psychological lexicon." Furthermore, the structure and logic of inference that bind together the elements of an ethnopsychological construct in a particular way must be carefully explored, not merely assumed to be analogous to particular modes of Western psychological analysis. Thus, the sensitive use of analogy in the interpretation of folk psychological discourse among Bimin-Kuskusmin perhaps requires some approximation of Geertz's (1976) endeavor to unpack layers of signification through a "dialectical tacking" back and forth between the "particular" and the "general," the "experience-near" and the "experience-distant."[13]

Following a brief introduction to general features of Bimin-Kuskusmin society and culture and views of infancy, I turn to an analytic unraveling of a few of the complexities of the folk psychology of infants. First, I present some key aspects of the procreative formation of the infant on which notions of personhood and folk psychology are founded. Second, I explore some selected patterns of folk psychological reckonings that are particularly characteristic of assessments of the significance of the behavior of infants.

BIMIN-KUSKUSMIN SOCIETY, CULTURE, AND INFANCY

About one thousand Bimin-Kuskusmin dwell in a rugged, ecologically diverse, mountainous area in the southeast Telefomin District of the West Sepik Province of Papua New Guinea. Speaking a Mountain-Ok language, they note with pride the distinctiveness and enduring strength of their cultural traditions and emphasize the splendor of the legacy of myth and ritual that is the foundation of these traditions and that will be bestowed upon and passed on by their children. Yet, important networks of trade, alliance, warfare, intermarriage, and ritual relations bring them into more or less sustained contact with other groups of the Mountain-Ok region and beyond. They have known of the existence of Europeans at least since the Kaiserin-Augusta-Fluss expedition (1912–1914) reached the Telefomin plateau to the west, but first direct contact with a European patrol was experienced by a very few individuals in 1957. The coming of the Europeans brought new and frightening illness, which markedly increased an already high rate of infant mortality.[14] On the eve of fieldwork (1971), however, both government and mission still had little regular contact with or influence over Bimin-Kuskusmin, who often feared and avoided the small European stations to the north. Indeed, in matters of pregnancy, birth, and infant health, they continue to avoid Western clinical facilities (see Poole 1982a).

Bimin-Kuskusmin social structure is marked by complex arrangements of kindreds, lineages, clans, ritual moieties, and initiation age groups. Folk models of agnatic descent reveal significant cognatic complications. These folk models, which are cast in the form of bodily substances laid down in procreation and reinforced in ritual, sharing of food, and social action, are central to constructions of personhood (see Poole 1977, 1981b). Indeed, the couvade performances that link father, mother, and infant to a protective and supportive sphere of kindred, lineage, and clan are structured with respect to substantial connections of bodily elements and foods which are said to encompass the infant both psychologically and socially (see Poole 1982*b*). The hamlet and parish settlements are ideologically associated with particular lineages and clans, respectively, and these communities exhibit an elaborate segregation of men and women in most social activities and spaces. Women and young children largely inhabit a realm of house, hearth, sweet potato garden, pig tending, foraging in nearby forest and stream, and child care. Men hunt, trap, tend taro gardens and stands of food trees, and devote much time and energy to ritual and political undertakings. They tend to stand aloof from the hamlet-centered domain of women and infants (see Poole n.d.). Gender difference is highly elaborated in myriad ways and is a central feature of the reckoning of personhood (see Poole 1981*b*, 1982*b*). Although most ethnopsychological appraisals of infants do not emphasize gender difference, little girls, who by Bimin-Kuskusmin reckonings are already polluting and who are more unstable cognitively and emotionally than their brothers, are adorned with tiny skirts within the first month of life. Male infants, who are considered to be more vulnerable to harm, are the focus of more frequent and elaborate divinations and are often handled more roughly, spoken to more intensely, and fed more often than their sisters, for they are said to require more activity, nurturance, and strength to survive and develop properly than female infants.

Although both men and women often express a preference that the firstborn be male, the birth of a normal infant of either sex is an occasion of much joy and also considerable anxiety.[15] One of twins (usually the firstborn) and any infant marked by congenital deformities of the head or genitalia (except the male pseudohermaphrodite)[16] are killed at birth, for they are not believed to be properly human or to be endowed with the essential foundation of personhood. The normal newborn infant, however, is extremely fragile and prone to many serious illnesses. Such maladies may often be caused by attacks of witches or sorcerers, by a variety of ancestral and other spirits, by excessive motor activity and emotional outbursts, and by the mother's neglect, erratic behavior, or emotional outburst. As a consequence, elaborate rites of couvade begin in the second trimester of pregnancy to protect the unborn child from all manner of harm (see Poole 1982*a*). This protective ritual envelopment of the infant is distinctly social in that members of the patrilineal lineages and clans and of the cognatic kindreds of each parent participate in a complex pattern of food taboos designed to reinforce their substantial links to the not-yet-born or newborn child (see Poole 1977, 1982*a*). Some participation in couvade rites is also acknowledged by members of the parents' hamlet and parish and of the father's ritual moiety and initiation age group. Thus, even before birth, the

infant is symbolically embedded in a critical set of social categories on which
it may depend for personal support of many kinds throughout its lifetime.

Once a ritual midwife of the father's clan has overseen a normal birth,
the father emerges from his couvade ritual seclusion in the forest and eats
large quantities of finiik-bearing 'male foods' (*kunum yemen*) to ensure the
growth, strength, and protection of the newborn.[17] He takes the infant to
a nearby stream of mythic significance for his clan to wash the extreme
pollution of birth from its body and to anoint its face with white *bukhuum*
pigment taken from his own body in order to protect the newborn from
illness and to ensure a finely shaped nose, mouth, and forehead, which
are signs of future forcefulness and 'strength of character' (*kaar kitiir*; lit.,
'strong skin'). He also rubs the child's skin with pig fat to make the skin
glisten as a sign of promising development and to guard the newborn
against the cold of wind and rain and the wandering forest spirits that may
capriciously attack it. For a firstborn child, who is especially vulnerable to
harm and requires special ritual protection, he adorns himself with either
cassowary plumes (for a son) or a band of red *giik* pigment on his forehead
(for a daughter). These amulets enhance the efficacy of preventive rites he
may perform to avoid serious illness in the infant. Finally, he bestows on
the infant four names. Two are teknonyms that link the newborn to both
mother and father, although only the mother-infant teknonym is used
publicly in infancy; the infant is the 'mother's child' (aurfaat).[18] The father-
child teknonym is uttered only in times of extreme crisis for the infant when
elaborate ritual procedures are undertaken in clan cult houses. On occasion,
in the case of an acutely or chronically ill infant thought to be near death,
other teknonyms may be ritually created to link the child with important
agnatic, cognatic, or uterine kin. More rarely, special teknonyms may be
devised to link the infant to powerful ancestors of the recent past.

Another type of name is usually constructed from special circumstances
surrounding the event of the infant's birth, but it is a kind of nickname that
may change to reflect even more auspicious omens that are recognized in
the infant's early development. If the nickname is used by the mother as a
sign of endearment, the first sign that the infant is responding to this name
is taken as an indication that the omen associated with the name is being
fulfilled. In addition, the father bestows on his child a 'secret name' (*win
boroorep aur*), which he will utter in private at his lineage shrine or in his
clan cult house during extreme crises in the infant's development. In the
case of a son, however, the father may also whisper the secret name in
certain contexts of ritual, hunting, trapping, gardening, warfare, and ceremonial exchange to promote his son's future success in these male pursuits
and to enliven his finiik by embedding his secret name in these masculine
activities.

As couvade restrictions are gradually lifted from the father, the infant is returned to the exclusive care of the mother and the clan midwife in the seclusion of the birth hut for several days. If the newborn is one of twins, a breech birth or born with a caul, or marked by a prominent birthmark or congenital defect, some couvade restrictions may be reinstituted on a variable range of cognatic kin. Couvade restrictions may also be resumed in the event of illness or some inauspicious sign in divinations of impending illness, misfortune, or death. Indeed, the father may continue such taboos for a prolonged period in the case of a fragile firstborn child. Normally, however, the ritual midwife imposes or lifts these restrictions during infancy, and she preserves the child's umbilical cord for preventive or curing rites that are focused on the infant. On the bestowal of a 'female name' (*waneng win*) at the end of this period of infancy, the umbilical cord will be buried in a ritual taro garden (for a son) or sweet potato garden (for a daughter) on clan land to ensure the future fertility and the proper ancestral 'attachment' (*adetera'fefebaanam*) of the child. Until the occurrence of that critical rite of passage, the infant will be nursed and tended exclusively by the mother and will be subjected to a variety of ritual assessments of its proper development by both clan ritual experts and a range of close kin. Both formal and informal divinations of infant development are cast in the idioms of the procreative formation of the newborn.[19]

PROCREATION, SUBSTANCE, AND ETHNOPSYCHOLOGICAL DEVELOPMENT

In matters of procreation, Bimin-Kuskusmin maintain that males and females transmit to their progeny separate, distinctive, and complementary substances. Proper development requires the uncomplicated acquisition of the entire set of these substances. Each substance is believed to have a particular function in the formation of the body, of sexual characteristics, and of more subtle aspects of the person which are of special ethnopsychological importance. The last are related to such phenomena as 'spirit' (*kusem,* including both khaapkhabuurien and finiik), 'personality' (*iraap kukaar*), 'judgmental capacity' (*yegaar*), 'emotional stability' (*biriir saaninam*), 'intellectual acuity' (*utuung-khraan*), 'social identity' (*ugaam-kaar*), 'moral character' (*kugaar kemataak*), 'responsibility' (*ogookaarem*), 'loyalty' (*tiibaanam*), 'stoicism' (*araang*), 'trustworthiness' (*duugamaan*), and so on.[20]

For purposes of interpreting the idioms of ethnopsychological discourse, the key elements that are forged in procreative process include the following basic discriminations. First, 'male blood' (*kunum khaim*) is transmitted in its strongest and most enduring form through males. Once transmitted through a female, it remains viable for only three descending generations. Female substance, especially menstrual blood and other vaginal discharges, weakens it. Its transmission is central to the reckoning of lineage and kindred categories. Indeed, it is the logic of the male and female transmission of male blood that defines the infant's cognatic kindred, which links it to its own patrilineage and the lineage categories of its mother, father's mother, mother's mother, father's father's mother, father's mother's mother, mother's father's mother, and mother's mother's mother. These substantial connections symbolize a pervasive kind of both mystical and social control which cognatic kin may exert over one another, and these links also enable those persons who share male blood to 'see inside' (*mutuuk kiin dugaamiin*) or understand one another with special sensitivity.[21] It is on the basis of this heightened interpersonal sensitivity that cognatic kin provide special social, ritual, mystical, and also psychological support for the developing child. In the newborn infant, however, the bonds of male blood that extend to such kin are extremely weak due to the polluting effect of proximity to women, birth events, menstrual blood, and breast milk. Thus, members of the infant's kindred must take responsibility for strengthening these bonds of substance through their consumption of finiik-bearing male foods, which are believed to strengthen the connection of male blood.

On occasion of crisis, the infant's father may transfuse his own 'strong' (*kitiir*) male blood into his offspring, either by mouth or through a hornbill-bone tube connecting their forearms. Indeed, for all male children such "transfusions" normally occur during the ritual bestowal of 'female names' at approximately two years of age (see Poole 1976).[22] If an infant is not protected by the enveloping bonds of kindred male blood, its physical growth will be stunted in both general stature and physique and particular internal organs and structures. Also, the cognitive and emotional components of its judgmental capacity will not develop.[23] Its finiik will not be properly strengthened by male blood and will not be properly embedded in male parts of its anatomy (notably the heart). Furthermore, infantile male blood that is not strongly connected to the child's kindred in any mystically significant way opens a 'path' (daib) for the onslaughts of certain dangerous 'spirits of the unavenged dead' (*aiyepnon*), wandering khaapkhabuurien and forest spirits, and malevolent magic and sorcery. The diagnostic signs of such attacks on the infant typically are high fever (producing apparent disorientation or hallucination), lack of coordination, vomiting, convulsions, and 'mindless anger' (*tiibisaak guur*), which is indicated by persistently clenched fists, curled toes, throbbing temples, pulsating fontanelle, thrashing, and incessant howling (cf. Lutz, chap. 2). The mother is usually advised to calm the child and to restrain most physical movement.

Second, 'menstrual blood' (*mem khaim*) has a highly ambiguous nature, and is transmitted only through female or uterine links. It may carry the potential for *tamam* witchcraft capacity (see Poole 1981*a*), other kinds of mystical malevolence, and certain dangerous 'black blood' (*khaim mighiir*) illnesses. It is the most polluting of all female substances and is highly destructive to all male substances. Infants of either sex are believed to be extensively contaminated by menstrual blood as a consequence of their experience of the womb and birth and their proximity to the mother in the menstrual huts. It is commonly said that the development of the male elements of the infant will not progress properly unless male ritual intervention thwarts the influences of menstrual pollution, which especially damages the male blood, semen, and finiik of male infants. As a consequence, the father of the child must perform rites of purification at regular intervals and during moments of crisis. Constant divinations monitor the results of these ritual acts. If the delicate balance of normal menstrual contamination in the infant should be much exceeded, a generalized kind of 'infantile madness' (*foguraar*) may follow and lead to uncontrollable shrieking, thrashing, convulsions, bloating, and eventual death. Yet the inevitable and normal imbalance of menstrual blood in the infant leaves it particularly vulnerable to the attacks of witches, especially when the protective bonds of male blood are too weak to offset such attacks.[24] Typically, the ravages of malevolent witches, magicians, sorcerers, or forest spirits, which are usually female in this instance, are said to follow the 'path' of menstrual blood, either directly by attacks through the blood and pus of open sores or through saliva, sweat, urine, feces, breast milk, or even footprints. Thus, the bodily wastes of infants are carefully guarded and secretly discarded, and open wounds are quickly tended and covered with ritually protective leaves. Infants are rarely allowed to touch the ground when they are newborn, and any footprints are rapidly obliterated. Only breast milk is more difficult to protect, and it is the most common 'path' of mystical attacks that are linked to the menstrual pollution of the infant.

Third, 'semen' (*maiyoob gom*) is transmitted only by males. It produces those anatomical parts of persons which are strong, hard, 'internal' to the body, and ritually most significant.[25] It also creates the reproductive fluids (except menstrual blood) of both sexes and bears the finiik. It forms the forehead, through which sacred male knowledge passes. It is manifested as fertile fluids and breast milk in females, as semen and genitalia in males, and as pus in both sexes. It also forms those critical sites of ethnopsychological significance which are associated with the heart, lungs, liver, kidneys, brain, eyes, ears, and fontanelle. Although semen (and the attributes that it forms) is a strengthening influence in the development of male elements in the constitution of the infant, it can destroy the flow and nutritive value of breast milk and cause the newborn to weaken and die. Consequently, there is a very strict taboo on sexual intercourse for the mother of an infant at this critical stage of early development.[26] Inappropriate transmissions of semen to the infant, either too little or too much, through procreation, ritual acts involving semen-coated taro,[27] or parental sexual intercourse will severely weaken its already fragile finiik. Thus, the substantial strength of its attachment—in the idiom of finiik—to the living and dead of its clan and, subsequently, for males, of its ritual moiety and initiation age group is threatened. Too much or too little semen (and finiik abnormalities) may cause a severe weakening of the critical sense organs (eyes, ears, nose, mouth, tongue, fingers, fontanelle, and heart), all of which are male organs. The disability of any of the senses associated with these organs implicates an imbalance of semen (and finiik) in the infant, and the imbalance must be corrected by the mother through her consumption of particular male and female foods that will alter the composition of her breast milk. Divinations that focus on the senses will yield recommendations for the ritual remedy of the imbalance by the father as well.

Fourth, 'fertile fluids' (mem gom) are female transformations of the male procreative contributions of semen. They form those anatomical parts of persons which are weak, soft, 'external' to the body, and ritually least important.[28] They also produce the genitalia of females. In infants, an excess of fertile fluids may result in a daughter developing the traits of a witch or a wanton, or a son exhibiting signs of monorchidism or subtler characteristics of a lack of masculinity.[29] In either case, this condition will weaken the finiik, to the detriment of masculine development. Furthermore, an excess of fertile fluids may cause the infant to exhibit rapid, uncontrollable, and otherwise inexplicable oscillations between extremes of being 'happy' (kakaat) or 'anxious' (sakhiikuur), for example.[30] Yet, a deficit of fertile fluids may result in permanent 'stupidity' (khaabomnaam), which is a consequence of too much semen in relation to too little of the fertile fluids. Once again, the mother must adjust her diet of female and male foods in accordance with divinations of the case. Fertile fluids, however, also form loci of ethnopsychological importance associated with the spleen, gallbladder, and stomach, as well as feces, urine, saliva, sweat, and mucus.

Fifth, the 'forehead' or 'fontanelle' (kok abinaam or yabaar abinaam) and the 'navel' (kumun abinaam) are male and female procreative contributions, respectively. The former permits the transmission of powerful male knowledge that is the foundation of ritual understanding, 'mystical power' (kuun aiyem), oratorical prowess, political control, and social competence. The latter is associated with 'antisocial' (tingiip gooran) or 'mundane' (ken kuup) female knowledge that focuses on either the secrets of malevolent female mystical powers such as witchcraft or everyday matters of sweet potato gardening, tadpole hunting, pig tending, nursing infants, or cooking food.

Both forms of knowledge are necessary for the proper maturation of the infant as a social being, but male knowledge is perhaps the most critical for the necessary scope and force of appropriate socialization and enculturation, especially for boys. During the period of infancy, however, the mother covers the baby's forehead with the yellow mud of funerary mourning and cleanses the navel to enhance the influence of female knowledge (see Poole 1981*b*). If divinations indicate that the child is not learning what is expected during the first two years of life, its navel will be sealed with funerary mud to block the influence of female knowledge, and its forehead will be shaved and cleaned with ritually powerful leaves to promote the passage of male knowledge.[31] When the fontanelle and temples are seen to throb or pulsate vigorously, however, it is believed that female influences 'block' (duugamiin) the passage of male knowledge and that little socially significant learning is taking place.

Sixth, the male (upper body) and female (lower body) 'joints' (*miing*) are distinct procreative contributions. The former permit the passage of various ritual powers that are believed to strengthen the finiik and enhance masculinity. The latter, however, admit various kinds of female malevolence in children of both sexes (e.g., "black blood" illnesses, witchcraft, and other forms of female mystical attacks associated with menstrual pollution). Although gender development is not emphasized during the period of infancy, the fingers, wrists, elbows, shoulders, and necks of baby boys are sometimes covered with protective white bukhuum pigment not only to ward off illness and mystical attack but also to lay the foundation for the subsequent maturation of distinctively masculine attributes of the person. The 'male joints' of baby girls, however, are left unadorned, for female development is seen to require far less ritual intervention in the normal course of maturation. But within the first year of life, often within the first month, infant girls are dressed in tiny grass skirts, for their genitalia are already sexually significant and polluting. Boys remain naked, with their genitalia exposed. In infants of both sexes, nevertheless, the toes, ankles, knees, groin, and waist are often covered with black *mighiir* pigment to seal them, especially when children are ill or have been divined as being highly vulnerable to harm. If the 'female joints' are left exposed, there is always the danger of some form of inadvertent or deliberate pollution or mystical attack, especially of the male elements of the infant. Open sores on or near the 'female joints' are particularly worrisome, for the possible contact of menstrual blood with these sites would damage underlying male organs and the finiik permanently.

Seventh, the 'body shadow/reflection' (*fom takhaak*) is a combined male and female procreative contribution. It is the only major aspect of the folk model of procreation which is not implicated in gender development or in later characterizations of contrasts between man and woman, male and female, and masculine and feminine.[32] This image persists after death in the form of a dangerous wraith, and the wraiths of dead infants, who do not become ancestral spirits, often attack their mothers through an 'infantile revenge' (*aur-abaarang*) that may bring about suicidal depression. During life, this image may appear in dreams, shadows, reflections, the smoke of sacrificial fires, pools of blood or water used in divinations, or in the eyes of a diviner. In infant divinations, the appearance of the 'body shadow/re-flection' is usually an omen of impending misfortune for the child. It is a generalized human image, possessing neither distinct gender nor clearly individual characteristics. In many ways, it is the image par excellence of the normal, newborn infant. But in infant divinations, it is generally blurred or fragmented in a manner that is said to indicate that the child has been encompassed by the 'control' (*tuurakhaamiin*) of some nonhuman entity, usually a forest spirit.[33] Because the young infant is not believed to be able to control itself, it can easily be possessed or otherwise taken over by various spirits; it must be protected through the mother's care and the father's rituals. When controlled by a spirit in this way, the infant suddenly becomes 'dull' (*khaakhuut*) and 'passive' (*tiinabiin*), showing neither interest in nor response to the breast, physical stimulation, discomfort, pleasure, or any stimulus available to its underdeveloped senses. Sometimes this control by a spirit may be broken by loud chanting or drumming, by immersion in cold water, by rubbing the belly with mild stinging-nettle leaves, or, in extreme cases, by touching a firebrand to the sole of the infant's foot. This state may also be brought about by mystical attack, abuse or neglect, or some innate propensity toward 'depression' (*duur sakhiik mutuuk*), 'fear' (finganiinaan), or some form of 'anger' (*guuraan*) that has been produced by certain prenatal experiences in the womb, the circumstances of birth, or an aspect of 'fate' (*kwan werkhaak*) produced by the prenatal influences of ancestral spirits. The condition is recognized to be one of a 'weak' (*tuuk-menaam*) finiik and a 'weak' (*baruut*) heart.[34] It is often indicative of a more or less total loss of bodily, spiritual, and psychological 'control' (*faate-beemkha*) which may foreshadow permanent madness or death. The condition may be remedied and the 'body shadow/reflection' restored through a balance of the father's ritual acts and the mother's increased nurturance.

Finally, the 'spirit' (kusem) constitution of the person, including both the finiik and the khaapkhabuurien, is the primary focus of folk models of procreation, personhood, and psychological phenomena among Bimin-Kuskusmin. The finiik, strengthened by male blood, semen, male food (for the infant, infused in breast milk), ritual activities, and social concern and nurturance, is a male procreative contribution transmitted through semen. The concept of finiik is highly polysemic and acquires somewhat different significance in different contexts. In general, the finiik represents the critical social dimensions of personhood—the ordered, controlled, careful, thoughtful, socially proper aspects of personality and self. It is the foundation of learning, it stores socially significant knowledge and experience, and it becomes the Durkheimian *conscience* and valued intellect of the person. It encompasses the notions of 'will' (*faaran*), 'desire' (*kaaragaam*), 'intention' (*diikhraa*), 'consciousness' (*yuguurgaamiin*), 'understanding' (*fuugunaamiin*), 'motivation' (*tabiin-khraa duur*), 'concentration' (*kiim-fuugaar*), and 'social competence' (*buurgaang*), all of which have a distinctively social force and scope in this context and possess more or less masculine connotations. One thinks and feels in and with the finiik, which is the basis of judgmental capacity. The state, process, scope, force, and focus of the finiik instigate and guide thought, feeling, and action. It involves the capacity to understand, to evaluate, to plan, and to translate or transform 'thinking/feeling' into socially comprehensible and sensible action. It organizes experience, and the very capacity to learn is finiik. It fuses desire and social propriety. It affects bodily growth and dexterity, intellectual acuity, and emotional stability. It gains sustenance from interpersonal relations in which it demands appropriate reciprocity for the person, and, when thwarted, it produces 'justifiable anger' (*kuurdaam ken*), which elicits 'shame' (fiitom) (cf. Lutz, chap. 2).

The finiik is present in the fetus from conception, and is drawn from an undifferentiated corpus of clan ancestral spirits. These ancestral spirits guide its developments, shapes, directions, and movements, bringing illness when 'self-centeredness' (*kaar dugaamkhaa*) goes too far or when 'social encompassment' (*taak faraak*) becomes too oppressive. Ancestrally imposed 'fate' limits its capacity, but it must be 'planted' (*duurgaamiin*) in a social community where it is nurtured and socialized, grows, and acquires shape and strength through learning and experience. Tales of isolated, feral beings in ancestral times and at the periphery of human habitation clearly suggest that the finiik cannot develop outside of an essentially social context. Flagrant parental violations of important moral or jural understandings (in the form of incest or rape) may produce a fetus in which the endowment of finiik is blocked by ancestral wrath and community anger.

The social communities of the living and the dead together give shape and vitality to the finiik in its passage through the life cycle. At death, it departs from the body to enter the corpus of ancestral spirits from which it originated and to return to the living in the form of a new baby, of its own volition or when summoned by ritual activity. The weak finiik of the infant, however, does not at all or altogether return to the ancestral underworld, but tends to disappear. Among the living, the finiik is a medium or channel of communication with the ancestors, especially when it is condensed and invigorated in the heart during ritual acts. During dreams, illnesses, trances, and other forms of mystical experience, the finiik may temporarily depart from the body to wander abroad and even to visit the ancestral underworld. But when the finiik departs, the critical attributes, capacities, and signs of Bimin-Kuskusmin personhood are no longer present—the body is primarily the external symbol of and vehicle for personhood. On occasion, the finiik of one person may come to resemble that of another when the relationship is one of long-term and special importance and is strengthened by a sharing of male blood, semen, male foods, and clan myths, secrets, rituals, and social support. Thus, the son of an important elder may be seen to share his father's qualities in a way that suggests shared qualities of finiik. More generally, all social interactions have the potential of affecting the growth of the finiik.

The finiik represents many critical features of the person, although it is not synonymous with the 'person' (kunum). It is associated with many central aspects of masculinity, but it is a focus of development in both males and females. It is ambiguously transmitted through semen and strengthened by proximity to or consumption of male substance and through the experience of male rites. It contrasts with the more 'unruly' (*kutaang*) khaapkhabuurien 'spirit', which gains vigor from female substance and ritual and represents the more idiosyncratic, unmodulated aspects of personality and self. Indeed, unmodulated behavior, as exemplified in the 'man of perpetual anger' (*atuur kunum*), 'promiscuous woman' (*waasop waneng*), or 'witch' (tamam), is held to be a sign that the finiik has become weakened and the khaapkhabuurien is becoming dominant. The erratic behavior of the infirm, entranced, insane, or very young, however, may be viewed as a temporary imbalance of these two aspects of 'spirit' (kusem)—an imbalance that sometimes can be remedied by ritual means and social and psychological support. This notion of relative 'balance' (kuurkuuraak) is highly elaborated in contexts of divination. Male ideological assertions suggest, nevertheless, that women, with the sole exception of female ritual elders (see Poole 1981b), are forever dominated by the unpredictable khaapkhabuurien. Ordinary women, of course, have not experienced the strengthening force of male rites and ritual male foods. Thus, infants, in the exclusive care of women, often are said to possess a highly dominant khaapkhabuurien.

The khaapkhabuurien is created de novo in each human being at conception. It is formed from 'vapors' *(uunaan)* that swirl in the warm womb and is activated by the first heartbeat. From that time onward it is entirely the product of individual experience. Overstimulation from the mother's angry 'thoughts/feelings', exertions, accidents, improper diet, anxieties, and lack of desire to give birth or to be pregnant may produce persisting flaws of character which can never be overcome by the developing finiik. During life, the khaapkhabuurien affects others only through the individual in whose body it remains more or less contained. It may sometimes become detached from the body in dreams, shadows, reflections, spirit possessions, trances, and illnesses, but it rarely causes harm independently as long as the individual lives. In any state or condition, it is indelibly marked by the peculiar personality traits by which the person is recognized as an individual actor. At death, the khaapkhabuurien emerges from the corpse to become a wandering, capricious ghost that lingers near the lifetime haunts of the deceased. It may appear in the form of mist or smoke or a bird suddenly taking flight. Sometimes it is recognized as a wizened, red-skinned figure crouching in semidarkness near gardens or settlements. Almost always, it possesses recognizable individual characteristics of the deceased. It may attack passersby at whim, but more often it attacks those who have inherited from, or are known to have injured, angered, or maligned, the deceased. It often attacks mourners. Eventually it wanders into the deep forest where it preys on unwary travelers or frightens away the game. On occasion, it may return to garden or settlement areas, but there are ritual techniques for driving it away. The khaapkhabuurien of the infant, having little content or structure from limited life experiences, is said to attack only the mother and father before soon disappearing forever.

In life or after death, the behavior of the khaapkhabuurien is entirely the product of the life experiences of the individual. Indeed, this 'spirit' represents perhaps the closest Bimin-Kuskusmin analog of an "inner self" and of a sense of individuality. The behavior attributed to the khaapkhabuurien is more or less predictable only to those who have known the individual intimately for a long time and are privy to many important, but highly personal experiences. In contrast, the behavior attributed to the finiik is believed to be largely predictable from the known social identity of the person and the more or less publicly recognized expectations and experiences that social identity entails. Because the finiik and the khaapkhabuurien always exist in relationship and in an ever-shifting balance (or imbalance), however, neither aspect of behavior is ever entirely comprehensible or predictable. There is always a dimension of individual behavior, thought, and feeling that Bimin-Kuskusmin acknowledge to be unfathomable by any person or by any divinatory means. Indeed, the actor himself may be surprised by an unexpected insight, change of mood, or disruption of social harmony in which he has been instrumental.[35]

In important ways, the complex concepts of finiik and khaapkhabuurien and their delicate and changing relationships and balances are central

to Bimin-Kuskusmin reckonings of personhood and of their folk psychology. The states, processes, balances, and interrelationships of these 'spirits'
give shape to particular constellations of ethnophysiological notions and
linked concepts of emotion, cognition, judgmental capacity, and intentional
agency which are forged in particular ethnopsychological assessments of
behavior. Through an indigenous lens, they confront the general analytic
(and folk) problem of the individual-in-society by linking human agency
in a sociomoral order to supernatural forces, to anatomical constraints, to
social learning, competence, and performance, and to personal life experiences. While the idea of khaapkhabuurien brings into focus the individual
actor's particular experience of his or her life cycle history,[36] the notion of
finiik emphasizes categories of persons in terms of their essentially social
and ritual development. The folk psychological construction of the special
nature, interrelationship, and balance of the finiik and khaapkhabuurien
during infancy sets certain limits to the acceptable shape of more context-
sensitive ethnopsychological formulations that interpret particular infant
behaviors. Indeed, these two concepts occupy a central and privileged
position in the Bimin-Kuskusmin folk model insofar as they are the primary
mediators and transformers of other elements.

     In the infant, the khaapkhabuurien is believed to dominate the finiik
in all instances, but the finiik is gradually strengthened as the infant is
increasingly embedded in a moral, social, and ritual community. The infant's experiences in an exclusively female domain, however, constrain the
development of finiik due to constant proximity to noxious female influences that partially prevent its growth and integration. During the months
of prenatal development, the finiik remains dispersed throughout the fetal
body in a highly fragmented state and is essentially dormant. As a consequence of the origin of the finiik in a clan corpus of ancestral spirits,
ancestral 'fate' has already set limits on its future development, which may
ultimately prove to be insufficient for the attainment of full personhood.
This 'fate' is believed to be intentional but unfathomable, and it may result
in a flaw in some critical aspect of personhood, which often remains unde-
tected for many years. Some further ancestral influences may temporarily
activate some movement of the finiik, as indicated by fetal hiccups, kicking,
turning, and so forth. The prenatal phase of couvade ritual may also enliven
and strengthen the finiik (see Poole 1982a). But such influences largely
expand the finiik and do not give it form, focus, direction, stable location,
or agency. Ritual acts and other mystical influences that ultimately determine the sex of the unborn child may also set some limits to the future
development of the finiik, for the course of the development of personhood
is always marked in some way by gender difference. Yet whatever social,
ritual, mystical, or ancestral legacy may be embedded in the fetal finiik

remains no more than a set of limitations on development and a potential for subsequent maturation. No socially significant learning takes place during prenatal development. Thus, although the infant is weakly linked, at the moment of conception, to its lineage and kindred by virtue of bonds of male blood, it is not embedded in its clan in any significant way. Clan affiliation is reckoned in terms of the sharing of strong ancestral finiik. Although encompassed by the moral, social, and ritual protection of its clan, the infant is not firmly or irrevocably attached to it.[37]

In contrast, the khaapkhabuurien does take on rudimentary shape during prenatal experience. The mother's diet, rituals, activities, and attitudes form many of the initial characteristics of the infant's general disposition. Any accidents, spirit possessions, illnesses, mystical attacks, or other significant events that she experiences will be impressed on the fetal khaapkhabuurien. Most important, her attitudes toward the unborn child will be incorporated into the khaapkhabuurien. As a consequence, it is said that the mother alone best understands the temperament of her newborn child. Indeed, the 'mother's child' or mother-infant dyad is often treated as a single person, for the mother encompasses the newborn in significant ways.

At birth, the infant is in a highly polluted state, and fragments of the finiik temporarily escape during, for example, sleep, fever-producing illnesses, and rapid expulsions of 'breath' (*mem*) in hiccups, sighs, coughs, burps, and shrieks. Because the finiik is not strong and integrated and its ideal abode in the heart is not secure, it is the mother's responsibility to 'calm' (*buur saaniin*) the infant with gentle fondling, cradling, warming, and nursing, and by speaking to it frequently and with 'affection' (*kuiraak*).[38] These 'calming' actions and attitudes are believed to reduce the 'thinking/ feeling' and motor activity of the child in all respects to prevent the finiik from escaping and leaving the child more vulnerable to misfortune. Often the infant is firmly restrained from moving. Expectably, such restraint may produce struggling, which requires further and firmer restraint. In effect, the elaborate maternal nurturance and control of the infant is believed to be what more or less attracts and holds the finiik within its body during the first month or so of life.

If momentarily departed aspects of the finiik should fail to return, it is said that a permanent and diffuse form of 'retardation' (*iboorkuun*) would result, in which critical features of psychomotor, sensory, intellectual, emotional, and social development would not proceed normally. The prescribed rites performed by the father to implant the infant's finiik firmly in its body (and more or less in its heart) complement the mother's nurturant activities. But an abusive or neglectful mother severely threatens her newborn child's development and, thus, is subject to a range of moral, social, and ritual sanctions. She must control her own recognized fear and anger when an infant is unruly. Until the still formless finiik is firmly implanted, she must especially try to guard the infant against extreme emotional displays that persist beyond the immediate circumstances of their perceived cause, and against being startled or frightened. All babies are expected to show signs of 'infantile rage' (*atuur aur kaar*), 'irritability' (*duubakha*), and 'frustration' (*babuuraan*), but these normal reactions must be controlled by the mother so that they do not fuse together and then persist in a dangerous state of 'mindless anger' (*tiibisaak guur*). This state is particularly dangerous to the constellation of male blood and semen in the heart which invigorates the finiik and readies it for the strength, integration, and focus that comes from social interaction and learning. Once the infant begins to react to the mother's face and movement in its immediate environment, to manipulate the breast, or to struggle in the netbag in a normal fashion, the initial crisis of the newborn has passed. The finiik can now begin that slow development which will continue for a lifetime.

If the mother has harbored malevolent 'thinking/feeling' about her unborn child, has experienced birth complications, or has abused or neglected her newborn infant, however, 'innate anger' (guuraan) may indelibly mark the khaapkhabuurien in a manner that permanently or enduringly damages the finiik. As a consequence, fragments of this 'spirit' become 'matted together' (*duunduun*) in a twisted mass that prevents proper socialization and enculturation. In such cases, the infant is said often to remain 'passive' (tiinabiin) and 'dull' (khaakhuut) and unresponsive to social and other environmental stimuli beyond the expectations of normal development. The mother's failure to contain her menstrual pollution may reinforce this unfortunate state, and then 'innate anger' may become a permanent condition, producing an erratic and irascible khaapkhabuurien and impoverishing the development of the finiik and the concomitant attributes, capacities, and signs of complete personhood.

The fitful, raging, sleepless, anorexic infant is dominated by an uncontrollable khaapkhabuurien, is vulnerable to a vast range of illnesses and mystical attacks, may exhibit an 'innate anger' in all behaviors, thwarts the intended efficacy of the father's rites and the mother's nurturance and control, and often approaches death. The baby, with no manner of self-defense against this misfortune, is smeared with protected pigments, adorned with several kinds of powerful amulets, tightly swaddled in bark cloth in a netbag, forcefully fed premasticated bits of finiik-bearing male foods, and subjected to various divinations and rites to strengthen the finiik. The most feared omen is a divinatory sign of possession by a forest spirit or of having been 'pierced' (*bugumiin*) by a wrathful ancestral spirit. Either of these attacks may cause severe respiratory disorders, further loss of finiik, and almost inevitably death for the infant. As a preventive measure, excessively morose or irritable infants are often washed with solutions of water from ancestral springs, wild boar or marsupial blood, and male blood from the father in an effort both to strengthen the finiik and to weaken the 'innate anger' condition of khaapkhabuurien.

When the infant begins to show signs of 'consciousness' (yuguurgaa-miin), 'will' (faaran), and 'intention' (diikhraa) through early coordinated movement and later 'baby talk' (uurfeng aur-weeng), which the mother alone can understand, then the finiik is considered to be ready for the beginnings of the social interaction and learning that will give it definite shape and solidarity. Before the middle of the second year, this process is believed to have begun in a significant way, although Bimin-Kuskusmin recognize that it has already begun in a rudimentary fashion at seven to nine months. Gradually and delicately, the finiik must be given 'direction' (*unannkuur*), 'solidity' (*kaasaknaam*), and a 'straight path' (*daib kiyoorkuup*) by significant social others in intimate interaction with the infant, the mother being the primary agent of this development, or the finiik will remain 'crooked' (wernaam) and unable to incorporate knowledge. The mother is therefore expected to interact with the infant through speech, play, physical stimulation, and so on, as actively as possible without provoking some form of anger and rage.

The infant is now believed to be susceptible to the beginnings of rudimentary social control that includes verbal as well as physical manipulation. It is also recognized now as attempting to control others, notably the mother, through more or less understandable verbal signals, physical movements, and more elaborate strategies to gain attention, engage interaction, and prolong interesting sights (e.g., through smiling, cooing, looking, peekaboo "games," and other turn-taking activities). Later, in the second year of infancy, much attention will be paid to the development of language beyond 'baby talk' (especially in interactions between mother and child), of increasingly complex forms of play, of recognition of socially disapproved wrongdoing, as well as of abilities to imitate simple tasks, to coordinate movements, to control emotional displays, and to 'remember' (*abuurkhamiin*) previous experiences in a manner that affects present action. Yet most of these developments are considered to be quite rudimentary until after the ritual bestowal of female names at two years of age. Indeed, despite a sizable and comprehensible vocabulary before the age of two, the infant is still believed to utter 'baby talk', for other capacities of comprehension and proper social use of speech are considered to be hallmarks of 'children's language' (*weeng taan-kem*).

Folk notions about infant characteristics and development among Bimin-Kuskusmin, often cast in the idiom of finiik and khaapkhabuurien, are remarkably complex (see Poole 1981*b*, 1982*a*, 1982*b*, n.d.), and only a sketch of selected features has been presented here. Indeed, the period of infancy is a "hypercognized" aspect of the ethnopsychology of Bimin-Kuskusmin, that is, "there are a large number of culturally provided schemata for interpreting and dealing with" infants (Levy 1984). The course of infant development is monitored at regular intervals by formal divinations associated with pandanus and taro harvests, clan cult house and lineage shrine activities, and pig and marsupial hunts, and at times of recognized crisis. Much informal public attention is focused on the maturation of infants, and inauspicious signs of deviant development are quickly noted and conveyed to the infant's parents and close agnatic and cognatic kin. Fathers tend to observe mothers' child care and to note interactive problems of the aurfaat dyad, for mothers are generally held responsible for much that may go wrong with infants.

Minor rites of passage between the couvade rituals of birth and the ritual bestowals of female names take place in the hamlet or adjacent forest or at nearby lineage shrines. Kith and kin join together in recognizing and celebrating the expected kinds and degrees of maturation in the infant, and take immediate and concerned action with respect to perceived developmental problems. The support of ancestral spirits is invoked by the father in these rites to strengthen and stabilize the ever-changing finiik of the child and to invigorate the male elements of the infant's anatomy which will nurture and anchor the finiik. Throughout the course of the two years of infancy and the succession of rites of passage, divinations, and informal monitorings that mark its passage, attention is focused on the delicate balance and structure of particular folk psychological constellations. Both these constellations and their elements exhibit varying degrees of elaboration (see Levy 1984). I shall now examine some of the contours of selected formulations of folk psychology in the context of the evolving personhood of the Bimin-Kuskusmin infant.

ETHNOPSYCHOLOGICAL CONSTRUCTIONS AND PERSONHOOD OF INFANTS

The particular ethnopsychological constructions that are explored below develop some of the intertwined meanings of sets or clusters of terms for 'thinking/feeling' states and processes that have significant social ramifications. They form "natural" clusters because, in both the contextual usage of everyday and ritual discourse and more formally elicited judgments, the members of a set or cluster are seen to implicate one another in some more or less logical and coherent manner, to pertain to the same or similar situations or circumstances, or to be associated with the same or related anatomical sites or physiological process (cf. Lutz, chap. 2). Most important, by some or all of these criteria, these sets or clusters are meaningful to Bimin-Kuskusmin. In all cases, the relationship and balance between finiik and khaapkhabuurien are explicit and central features of the ethnopsychological construction. In all cases, some actual or imagined social interaction or category of social interaction form important dimensions of the context of the formulation of the infant's thought, feeling, and behavior. For the period of infancy, the focal interactive unit is unquestionably the aurfaat mother-infant dyad, and the mother is the responsible agent for certain normalities and many misfortunes in infant development. Indeed, the Bimin-Kuskusmin have elaborated a *mal de mère* syndrome that enters into many aspects of child (especially male child) development, and that is a cornerstone of the complex symbolism of gender (see Poole 1981*a*, 1981*b*, 1982*b*).

Fear, Anxiety, and Boldness

Fear (finganiinaan) is held to be a characteristic trait of infancy that may be expressed in a variety of ways, and, in infancy, has special features and modes of expression. Displays of fear may range from sullen, cowering 'withdrawal' (*bubuuniinaam*) to a protected place or person to 'tantrums' (*yagaak*) that may be accompanied by urination, defecation, and vomiting. Withdrawal and tantrums implicate the passive and active aspects of 'infantile rage' (atuur aur kaar). The former is often allowed to persist, although mild coaxing and cuddling may be used to induce the infant to engage in some new activity. Tantrums are dealt with by restraining the child, and there is no public attempt to punish the infants physically. On occasion, however, women are reported to abuse infants physically in private, a most serious action that is never considered to be legitimate.

The key behavioral signs of infantile fear tend to be some apparent reaction of one or more sense organs (such as widening, blinking, or averting the eyes) as a kind of startle response, some sudden movement of avoidance or aggression, and a rapid increase in breathing and in the visible throbbing of the temples or fontanelle. Elaborate clinging to the mother, seeking the breast, turning the head, and thrashing and howling are also frequently noted indices of fear in infants. Indeed, fear among infants importantly involves 'surprise' (*agetaanok*) and 'diffuse panic' (*kaardaak*), which implies an extension of initial fear to all sounds, movements, temperature, changes, light alterations, and so on, in the immediate vicinity. Such fear is not predicated on past experience and memory of some specific misfortune that is again recognized by environmental cues of some kind, but rather on a lack of familiarity and experience with some entity nearby.

Mature fear more often involves a considered appraisal of the potential danger of some specific entity in a recognized context. Infants, however, are lacking in the knowledge and judgment to make such assessments. A sudden breeze, a startled pig, a bird taking wing, a loud noise, or myriad other everyday occurrences may provoke fear in the infant. But, in the second half of the first year, reactions to persons other than the mother or frequent caretakers are often cited as the most common causes of infant fear. For the young infant, almost everyone is more or less a stranger at first.

It is said that infantile fear reactions typically result in a rapid and forceful expulsion of breath followed by a sudden and deep inhalation. This initial breathing shift leads to a state of 'infantile confusion' (*aur-kiireng*), which reinforces the fear and extends it as diffuse panic to many or most of its most immediate surroundings. This form of confusion is believed to be a kind of 'thinking/feeling' disorientation which is indicated by rapid attention shifts, mood swings, and signs of generalized agitation. The rapidity of exhalation and inhalation produces confusion by disrupting the fragmented infantile finiik and temporarily expelling shreds of it, only some of which are recaptured through inhalation. The heart beats rapidly and becomes momentarily 'spongy' (*kimerok*), and noxious fluids from the gallbladder are absorbed by the heart. This bile weakens the male blood and semen in the spongy heart and, therefore, further weakens and fragments the finiik. Fear thus expands, as the finiik can only be brought under control by the mother's nurturance, which both calms the infant's agitation and removes the child from the threatening situation as quickly as possible (cf. Lutz, chap. 2).

The fear itself is believed to be lodged in the spleen, which then produces black fluids that are akin to menstrual blood, and that may stimulate urination, defecation, and vomiting. Because the infantile khaapkhabuurien also becomes concentrated in the spleen during moments of fear and is strengthened by splenic fluids, this 'spirit' is said to absorb and envelop the fear and, consequently, to prolong and complicate it in various ways. Without the counterbalance of a strong finiik, the khaapkhabuurien may increase the fear to such an extent that the infant is driven to a frenzied state of uncontrollable tremors that require immediate ritual intervention by the father. Therefore, it is only late in infancy that the mother will remain with the child in the threatening situation and will seek to calm it by offering comfort with respect to the specific object of fear. If that object is a person, an increasing familiarity with kith and kin already will have begun to reduce the fear of strangers.

Infantile fear is commonly contrasted with the 'infantile boldness' (*fuugamkha*) of infants, but the latter typically occurs only after the most diffuse and dangerous forms of fear and panic have begun to abate. 'Boldness' is interpreted from behavioral signs that the infant has begun to explore its environment by crawling, but 'infantile boldness' never extends beyond the clear view and earshot of the protective mother, except by apparent accident. Then it is accompanied by a return of fear. Moving away from the mother, protective persons, or protected and familiar places to explore new objects, persons, and environments is strongly encouraged in the infant by hamlet kith and kin, and the child is fondled, patted, and praised for its daring exploits. Other infants are often placed in its path in a deliberate effort to establish its interest in future hamlet playmates, and young infants do seem to take a special interest in vocalizing at and touching one another. Adults and older children actively encourage the infant to extend the sphere of its explorations through various endearments and enticements, and there is much touching and guiding of the infant when, at around the beginning of the second year or slightly earlier, it crawls about the interior, safe spaces within the hamlet. Indeed, physical contact with other persons, no longer tempered by earlier signs of fear, is a central characteristic of infantile boldness toward the middle or end of the second year.

The 'bravery' (*atuur fagamiin*) and occasional 'arrogance' (*kaar giisuup*) that are associated with the boldness of older youths, however, are not applicable to the case of infant boldness. Early infantile exploration is severely restricted in scope and does not imply any specific, planned goal of action or any special pride of accomplishment. Furthermore, the 'boldness' of infancy, unlike the brashness of youth, cannot give rise to insult. An act that would be a grave insult later in childhood is usually only cause for merriment when performed by an infant because the requisite 'understanding' (fuugunaamiin) and 'intention' (diikhraa) of 'insult' (*buukhrok*) are not present. The infant cannot be provoked to embarrassment and more developed shame until he is older and possesses greater social competence. The inability to give insult is a characteristic among Bimin-Kuskusmin only of the period of infancy.

Infantile 'boldness' is seen as a positive advance over diffuse and disabling fear, and signals that the finiik is beginning to direct action and seek social praise in a rudimentary fashion, which will soon become more developed. Boldness also indicates that the finiik is now more centrally located in the heart, that the gallbladder is quiescent, and that the khaapkhabuurien has shifted from the spleen to the diaphragm, which is a less turbulent suborgan of the spleen and does not secrete black fluids. It is the khaapkhabuurien, however, that limits the extent of infant boldness by producing fleeting 'impulses' (*mamaak*) of fear when prior experience is being markedly exceeded in the course of cautious new explorations or when the sight and sound of the mother have been lost. When the boldness of an infant propels it toward a particular object or person in a more or less straight path and without constant searching for the mother, it is said that the finiik is 'smooth' or 'tight' (*terotero*) and has fashioned a 'bridge' (*turuum*) between the heart and liver, which is usually considered to be the site of a panoply of aggressive tendencies. In some obscure way, the finiik, which has temporarily become strong in the heart, has harnessed 'infantile aggression' (*aur-orsaak*) to its strength in order to stimulate boldness. One of the characteristics of infancy, however, is that the finiik is not anatomically stable, and it is recognized that the important connections it makes among anatomical sites of special ethnopsychological significance may be only weak and temporary.

Boldness in the infant is typically tempered by 'anxiety' (sakhiik). Anxiety keeps the infant from extending the range of its explorations to a point where vague, generalized fear reemerges. Anxiety has both 'internal' (*mutuuk*) and 'external' (*bangep*) aspects, distinctions not commonly noted in the folk model of infancy. The former are diffuse, inchoate kinds of sensations that may connote a particular form of depression, irrational fear, inexplicable worry, an approximation of guilt, and other related types of 'thinking/feeling' that are given no clear form, etiology, or outward expression. These states are associated with the khaapkhabuurien, especially when it is concentrated in the stomach. Thus, divinatory signs of 'internal anxiety' (*sakhiik mutuuk*) are gluttony, anorexia, stomach disorders and pain or bloating, and nervousness about and withdrawal from social situations. The latter, however, are specific, identifiable, and socially acquired assessments of situations that typically involve interpersonal relations or relations with supernatural entities. These assessments produce understandings that connote caution, rational fear, concern, a different form of depression, and other related forms of 'thinking/feeling' that are given shape, etiology, and expression in regard to shared social knowledge about risk, threat, misfortune, and so forth. These states are associated with the finiik, especially when it is primarily located in the heart. Therefore, the indices of 'external anxiety' (*sakhiik bangep*) are overt complaints and expressed assessments of recognized, worrisome phenomena in the "behavioral environment" (Hallowell 1955). These verbal signs of legitimate concern are often accompanied by the nonverbal, vague indices of internal anxiety. To the extent that the two aspects of anxiety are related in a particular situation, however, the sufferer is more able to construct a contextual rationalization for apparently diffuse, internal states than if the internal anxiety alone appeared. Divinations recognize these complications.

In the infant, early fear is associated only with internal anxiety, for the anxious fear cannot be articulated and is produced by the excessive dominance of the force of the khaapkhabuurien. In this regard, fearful internal anxiety in the infant has some affinity with 'innate anger' (guuraan) and 'mindless anger' (tiibisaak guur); it, too, may be associated with prenatal influences, as are these forms of anger. Some older adolescent and adult persons, who show a persistent disposition toward chronic depression, asocial tendencies, and suicide, are forever driven by an unfathomable internal anxiety that is the consequence of an often dominant and enduring trait of the khaapkhabuurien. Most persons show in their behavior and expressions of complaint a delicate balance between internal and external anxieties, which are inevitably bound up together in different manners under different circumstances. The first signs of boldness in an infant are believed to indicate that a rudimentary form of this balance is being momentarily achieved and that the finiik and khaapkhabuurien are related in a particular, but unstable way. Both diffuse fear and panic (internal anxiety) and 'caution' (*tiinkaar*) (external anxiety) limit the explorations of the child. Proper caution is slowly being learned from other persons who guide its crawling expeditions and guard it from harm. In time, when the finiik is stronger and the rationality and judgment of external anxiety are more developed, boldness will be tempered by 'recognition' (*agaat fugooriinaam*) of hazards that have been previously encountered and can be publicly explained.

Thus, fear, boldness, and anxiety are states that take on peculiar characteristics in infancy, but they are also processes insofar as they are seen to exhibit developmental continuities and discontinuities. They are bound together by virtue of mutual implication, of linked etiologies and contexts of expression, of association with differing relationships and balances of finiik and khaapkhabuurien, and of location in male and female anatomical sites or physiological processes. Internal anxiety and diffuse fear and panic, in their association with the khaapkhabuurien, are enhanced by contact with female substances and influences, particularly female foods, menstrual blood, and witchcraft. The mother's nurturant indulgence and forceful restraint of the infant seem to both reduce and aggravate these linked states in the child and also to complicate development beyond them. External anxiety and boldness, in their linkage with the finiik, draw sustenance from male substances and influences, especially male foods (infused in breast milk), male blood and semen, and male ritual endeavors focused on the aurfaat mother–infant dyad. These constructions of fear, boldness, and anxiety, both separately and together, form a set of common understandings in folk psychology among Bimin-Kuskusmin which may be used more or less as a standard against which to evaluate normal and deviant behaviors in the scheme of infant development.

Desire, Will, Impulse, and Intent

'Desire' (*kaaragaam*) is a notable characteristic of all Bimin-Kuskusmin persons, but it possesses an extensive array of connotations, only some of which are applicable to infant behavior and experience. Most obviously, the infant is incessantly driven by 'bodily desires' (*oorkhraan*) to eat, sleep, defecate, urinate, seek warmth, and so on. Interestingly, 'lust' (*isaar*), related to but not a kind of bodily desire, is a recognized attribute of the aurfaat bond, as indicated by the erect penis of baby boys when rubbed by their mothers and the hardened nipples of mothers when fondled by their infants.[39]

More generally, desires involve some sense of wanting something in a way that is often more or less self-centered and asocial, or is more or less morally, socially, and ritually appropriate. All desires of older persons are usually seen to have both tendencies in some balance. Infantile desires, however, tend toward the extreme of being 'self-centered' (*kaar dugaamiin-khaaraak*) (cf. Kirkpatrick, chap. 3). These self-centered desires will gradually be altered to take account of community expectations and the expected desires of others. But, in the infant, these wants are associated with the weakness of the finiik and the dominance of the khaapkhabuurien. They are differentiated in terms of their loci in various female organs, processes, and substances in which the khaapkhabuurien is concentrated and, consequently, from which particular desires spring. Thus, for example, the desires to eat or fast, to cause misfortune, discomfort, and mischief, and to frighten, threaten, anger, or make anxious are associated, respectively, with the stomach, gallbladder, and spleen, each of which gives a particular shape, force, and scope to the khaapkhabuurien. Of particular importance, the more defiling infantile desires of excretion are linked to feces, urine, saliva, sweat, mucus, and other secretions, all of which emanate from female organs that the infant cannot control. Similarly, the infant cannot 'control' (faateebeemiin) its desires in any orderly or socially proper manner; however, the resulting behaviors do not give rise to insult.

Only toward the end of infancy do the first glimpses of the controlled and socially appropriate desires associated with the finiik appear, for the finiik is bound up with the development of both 'external' (bangep) and 'internal' (mutuuk) forms of 'control' (tuurakhaamiin and faateebeemkha, respectively). These desires are linked to different male elements of the anatomy, which become temporarily invigorated by the finiik, and to male blood and semen, which, in turn, invigorate the finiik. Thus, wishes for esoteric knowledge and ritual understandings of different kinds, as well as for the knowledge required for everyday practical skills, are linked in different constellations to the heart, fontanelle, eyes, and ears. Desires for oratorical power and physical force are situated, respectively, in the lungs and kidneys. Wishes for dreams, trances, spirit possessions, and other dissociated states of ritual value are generated in the connective "tissue" of male blood, semen, and finiik 'spirit' which links the heart and brain. Desires for both positive reciprocity and legitimate revenge flow from the liver. Lust sensibly emanates from the genitalia. The desires of the khaapkhabuurien are often attributed to the linked agency of particular female organs, processes, and so on, which are not readily brought under the control of the person. But the wishes associated with the finiik are guided by moral, social, and ritual understandings and, consequently, result in more controlled and appropriate behavior. All of the more or less developed desires of the finiik, however, appear only in most rudimentary and subtle form in late infancy; unless the infant is unusually precocious, their first manifestations are rarely noted, interpreted, or acted on because of their presumed instability. They are therefore largely a matter of attention in formal divinatory interpretation.

All desires require 'will' (faaran) for their implementation. Will seems to provide a mechanism in the folk model for making the 'thinking/feeling' aspects of desire more or less clear and for transforming desire into behavior. Will has quite different consequences when it is linked primarily to the forces of the finiik or the khaapkhabuurien. In desires of the finiik, will must be accompanied and shaped by social competences and cultural values, which the infant almost entirely lacks. In its primary association with the khaapkhabuurien, the infantile will is very vigorous, but it is also unfocused, uncontrolled, and unsocialized. Thus, the attempts of older infants to implement many desires, especially those that have begun to be associated weakly with the finiik, are often clumsy, ineffective, calamitous, and futile. The infant is most successful in fulfilling the desires associated with the khaapkhabuurien, where will is coupled with primitive and altogether unsocialized 'impulses' (yaamyaam) located in the spleen and diaphragm. These two female organs are linked by a delicate tubular network of mesentery through which courses splenic black fluids, which are akin to menstrual blood and engorge and heat the khaapkhabuurien. The 'hot' (kaarkaar) state of the khaapkhabuurien produces a frenzied effort by the infant to fulfill its wishes, but the frenzy precludes the steadfast 'concentration' (kiim-fuugaar), associated with powers of the finiik, that is a prerequisite of organized intention and judgment. The infant does not yet possess the capacity to 'think/feel' certain desires in an organized manner. But the more primitive desires associated with the khaapkhabuurien are said not to require organized 'thinking/feeling' and behavioral expression for their fulfillment in most instances.

In contrast, the infant rarely succeeds in implementing the wishes associated with the finiik, where will is inevitably linked to the judgmental quality of 'intention' (diikhraa) situated in the heart. This male organ is believed to be engorged with male blood and semen, which strengthen and heat the finiik and also reinforce the linkage between a personal manifestation of the finiik, a community of kin, living and dead, and cultural values. In the infant, the finiik, male blood, semen, and heart remain too weak and the judgmental capacity of intention too impoverished to fulfill more than the most rudimentary social desires, and then in an often awkward manner. But the complex of desires associated with the khaapkhabuurien, linked only to will and impulse, enables the infant to engage in a diffuse and largely uncontrollable self-centeredness and to bend others to its wishes through behavioral displays of 'thinking/feeling' such as tantrums.

Envy, Embarrassment, and Shame

'Infantile envy' (suuniin) is intimately bound up with the fulfillment of desires and is driven by the powers of will, impulse, and self-centeredness. But infantile envy implicates the desire, will, and impulse of another person. It implies either ignoring the possibility that the other recognized person must be taken into account in any social manner, or some rudimentary recognition of a social relationship (by sharing or negotiating the desired entity) or a denial of relationship (by opposing or refusing sharing or negotiation). At the very least, infantile envy presupposes that the infant perceives another person (or, perhaps, even an animal) as seeking what it wants, attaining the desired entity, and thus denying it to the infant.

The most primitive upshot of infantile envy is expected to be forceful grabbing, shoving the other person away, and often some form of tantrum that may bring assistance in the fulfillment of the desire. Such early envious behavior is considered to be a product of the khaapkhabuurien, which, as was mentioned above, is engorged with menstrual blood and splenic fluids and is concentrated in the gallbladder, spleen, and whatever other female organs and substances are associated with the particular desires that are revealed in behavior. The force and scope of infantile envy at this stage are entirely self-centered; the other person is said to be perceived as though he or she was an inanimate object. Indeed, Bimin-Kuskusmin often note that very young infants treat some other people as they treat sticks, stones, and leaves. I have heard infantile envy attributed to a child who raged against a rock in its path or a netbag slung over the mother's breast. In this respect, infantile envy is closely coupled with 'infantile frustration' (babuuraan), which is also associated with the khaapkhabuurien when it is located in the gallbladder, spleen, and other female organs of particular desires. But infantile envy is most commonly focused on a person, and, consequently, may be loosely linked to a weak finiik, while infantile frustration does not distinguish other persons from inanimate objects and is exclusively associated with the khaapkhabuurien.

Although envy is expected of infants, it is socially disapproved in its earliest stages as an impulse of the khaapkhabuurien which must come to be dominated by the growing finiik. Its developmental importance for Bimin-Kuskusmin resides in the envious infant's apparent recognition that another person may lay claim to a desired entity. In this regard, the development of envy focused on other persons is an important transformation of the behavior usually associated with those desires linked to the khaapkhabuurien. Yet infantile envy remains largely a product of will and impulse. Only the rudiments of intention and concentration are perceived in the infant's efforts to remove by primitive coercion the other person's claim to the desired entity.

Concentration never becomes well developed during this stage of maturation. When envy and intention are more clearly linked later in infancy, however, there is the beginning of a gradual developmental movement from 'embarrassment' (*kaar kuureng-mamiin*) to 'shame' (fiitom). Once the infant has been reprimanded repeatedly for its jealous tantrums and has been denied the desired entity as a consequence of such behavior, Bimin-Kuskusmin presume that it begins to 'see' (*kutem-gamiin*), if not quite 'understand' (*kiinangkhaamiin*), the connection of reprimand, denial, and certain states of 'thinking/feeling' which are characteristic of infantile envy.[40] Envy will then increasingly become bound with embarrassment, a product of the finiik, which, still in fragmented form, courses through the male blood and has not yet stabilized in the heart. The idea of embarrassment is crucial in Bimin-Kuskusmin views of proper infant development, for its appearance signals an infantile recognition of wrongdoing or impropriety that involves both the self and others in relationship. For Bimin-Kuskusmin, embarrassment requires a real or imagined audience, and infants require an immediate and tangible audience for its first expressions.[41] Indeed, the infant must 'see' the impropriety of acts in relation to unambiguous and direct audience disapproval.

Most important, infantile embarrassment begins to temper the expression of desire, will, and impulse through some form first of immediate and then of retrospective self-monitoring or reflexivity in the infant. As the infant learns to 'see' its acts in the light of audience judgments, it is said that its 'thinking/feeling' becomes more developed and more focused. This development connotes an increase in the strength and coherence of the finiik. Embarrassment is a sign that the relationship of opposition and balance between the finiik and the khaapkhabuurien is now becoming integrated in a more stable fashion, and that the khaapkhabuurien is no longer as clearly or as strongly dominant in infant behaviors. In older youths, embarrassment is believed to be a relatively superficial expression of some underlying condition of the finiik, for 'shame' (fiitom), which is firmly linked to a strong finiik, becomes the key sign of proper development. In early infancy, however, the significance of embarrassment is less ambiguous; it cannot yet be confused with 'shame', which infants in their first twenty months or more are not yet capable of. Although infantile embarrassment involves growth, integration, and stability of the finiik, it has no strong, stable 'roots' in the finiik (from which it emanates). The connection between the finiik and infantile embarrassment is fragile and momentary, and must be reinforced by an immediate and clearly judgmental audience. The solitary infant is believed not to exhibit signs of embarrassment without that critical audience.

Indeed, infantile embarrassment is no more coherent or organized than the infantile finiik. Such embarrassment appears in 'fragments' (giitakhaa) as more or less immediate reactions to the disapproval of an audience with respect to a particular act and does not extend to similar acts when there is no audience or no audience reaction of disapproval. The still dominant and powerful khaapkhabuurien prevents the full integration of embarrassment by blocking any clear 'comprehension' (khaim-khraakkhaan) of the more general significance and rationale of audience disapproval.[42] The expression of infantile embarrassment remains embedded in very particular kinds of contexts and is not extended beyond them, for there is no recognition among Bimin-Kuskusmin that the young infant comprehends what makes a particular act wrong or improper from the perspective of the audience.

In the last months of infancy, however, the contours of embarrassment begin to change in very subtle ways. A variety of particular behaviors, such as expressions of envy, become more restricted in scope, force, and context. When they occur, they are often coupled with expressions of embarrassment even when the audience shows little interest or disapproval. Embarrassment now begins to be extended to an ever-widening sphere of socially discouraged acts and, especially, to inappropriate bodily displays. As language competence increases, embarrassment often accompanies the child's peculiar, insulting, or obscene verbal constructions. Indeed, this form of embarrassment is now recognized as a feature of the infant's emerging ability to act in a manner that requires at least rudimentary capacities of concentration and intention, memory and recognition, appreciation of social context, control of impulses and desires, more advanced 'thinking/feeling' organization, physical dexterity, and social competence. Although these capacities remain limited, as does the development of the finiik, it is no longer entirely clear that infantile embarrassment is present in all respects. As with other children, embarrassment is now considered to be only a superficial expression of more complex underlying development. Most significant, audience ridicule, insult, and milder forms of disapproval are no longer necessary to provoke the infant's embarrassment, for the child has now begun to 'understand' (kiinangkhaamiin) in a rudimentary way something of the social propriety of its acts.

With these marked changes in the scope, force, context, and 'motivation' (tabiin-khraa duur) of embarrassment and the decline in public expressions of envy, which have been brought under the partial control of the finiik, the first signs of 'shame' begin to appear. (Cf. Fajans, chap. 10, Kirkpatrick, chap. 3, and Schieffelin, chap. 5, on notions of shame. See also Lutz, chap. 2, on Ifaluk fear.) In some ways, shame is an extension of embarrassment in the Bimin-Kuskusmin scheme of development; in other ways, it is distinct. One key feature of contrast between embarrassment and shame is that only the latter is linked to motivation, which in some ways is complementary to intention and is also linked to will. In the view of Bimin-Kuskusmin, intention gives will a 'path' (daib), direction, or perhaps goals, whereas motivation gives will a 'force' (araar-taan) that propels it along the path of intention. In a more developed form, strong motivation is associated with a kind of 'single-mindedness' (agetaam-kuraa) of which infants are incapable, for their general 'thinking/feeling' states and processes still are prone to 'wander' (iruum kamiin) (cf. Kirkpatrick, chap. 3).

More generally, shame is associated with a stronger, more stable, and more integrated finiik, which is now more or less concentrated in the heart. Shame almost always involves social interaction that focuses on the legitimacy of some claim made by one person on another. And that claim, in the form of a forceful assertion or a more subtle appeal (cf. Schieffelin, chap. 5), is recognized to be illegitimate and unworthy of social support, leaving the shamed person vulnerable to a public erosion of "face" (Goffman 1955). In turn, the act that produces shame in the actor elicits 'justifiable anger' (kuur-daam ken) in the person toward whom the act was directed (cf. Lutz, chap. 2).

Infantile shame among Bimin-Kuskusmin often involves any sign of an incipient recognition that social relationships require a sense of 'reciprocity' (abuusaarkha). The beginnings of infant shame are the first clear indication that the more or less exclusive self-centeredness of early infancy is being altered in a significant and presumably enduring way. Shame is an encompassing index of a generalized 'social competence' (buurgaang) that is beginning to be 'planted' (kiimraakhiin) in the finiik and the heart.[43] It permits the infant to establish rudimentary friendships that endure beyond the moment of interaction and can be extended to older and more sophisticated children. As a consequence, the appearance of shame alters both the character and the social sphere of infant play. Indeed, shame is perhaps the pinnacle of infant development, and significantly foreshadows the more complex social world of early childhood after the ritual bestowal of 'female names'. Even the rudimentary shame of infants shows signs of possessing both internal and external aspects—a distinction more common in the folk psychological models of early childhood and beyond. In often subtle ways, the advanced infant is said to not only make amends when reciprocity (especially with the mother) has been ignored or denied but to also 'feel/ think badly' (*fudiim-duurkhanii*) about such events. In this context, to make amends is an external behavior that suggests a rudimentary social competence and understanding of reciprocity. To 'feel/think badly' is an internal process that almost approximates implicitly a sense of guilt. For Bimin-Kuskusmin, however, both aspects are encompassed by 'shame' and are unambiguously within 'consciousness' (yuguurgaamiin) or awareness. The external, behavioral aspects of shame are 'on' (*aar-ker*) the skin, and the internal aspects that connote 'feeling/thinking badly' are 'beneath' (*afaak-ker*) the skin (cf. Strathern 1977, 1981). It is this latter sense that is significantly bound up with the Bimin-Kuskusmin notion of self or 'skin root' (kaar kiimkiim) (see n. 4). Thus, unlike embarrassment, shame has strong roots in the finiik, which has both public and private manifestations that are closely aligned.

Anger

The most powerful and feared state of the infant is often one of 'anger' (*guur*), for most kinds of infantile anger invigorate the khaapkhabuurien and weaken the finiik, thus inhibiting proper infant development. Indeed, anger may exert highly significant influences on all the 'thinking/feeling' states and processes that have been previously discussed. Both embarrassment and shame, for example, may give way to primitive desire, will, and impulse in the context of anger. Perhaps the most feared form is 'innate anger' (guuraan). It is fashioned by ancestral 'fate' and prenatal experiences, strengthened by postnatal trauma and proximity to polluting female substances and influences, and may become associated with a lifelong condition of submission of the finiik to the khaapkhabuurien. Innate anger indicates that the khaapkhabuurien is regularly located in the heart, from which it displaces the finiik. In turn, the dislodged finiik becomes twisted and damaged, leaving the infant passive, dull, and unresponsive to its environment. Innate anger may markedly shape the course of an unfortunate lifetime and lead eventually to suicide; in the infant, if innate anger is severe, it is often lethal. It may utterly block all significant dimensions of infant development recognized by Bimin-Kuskusmin. The uncontrolled and often uncontrollable fury of the child is not only directed outward, primarily toward the mother, but also disrupts all of the developing and critical balances on which maturation depends. Even the aurfaat mother-infant dyad is said to be disrupted, and the mother has no understanding of her own child. Only the most powerful of ancestors can intervene in the course of innate anger, although the behavior of the mother must also be modified in ways prescribed by divinations.

Innate anger is said to be similar in appearance to 'mindless anger' (tiibisaak guur), but the latter is provoked by postnatal experiences, notably the mother's abuse and neglect and the resulting illnesses with high fevers. Indeed, mindless anger focuses most forcefully on the mother, but quickly extends to almost everything in the infant's behavioral environment. It has no clear rationale and blocks proper infant development in a manner similar to that of innate anger, but it has a recognized etiology in the mother's behavior. The mother's prenatal resentment of the unborn child is said to produce a special vulnerability in the fetus to harsh postnatal experiences, but her postnatal treatment of the infant is the critical factor in the formation of mindless anger.[44] Nevertheless, fetal aggression in the womb against the hostile mother is said to be an indication that an incipient mindless anger is already forming during the prenatal development. During the trauma of postnatal experience of the mother's hostility, aggression, and pollution, the vital male substances of male blood, semen, and the heart are damaged, and the finiik is weakened. With the consequent dominance of the khaapkhabuurien and the appearance of early infantile fear and internal anxiety, the infant becomes especially vulnerable to attacks by various spirits and malevolent magic and sorcery. An aggressive, hostile mother is sometimes suspected of being a witch. She may attack the infant. But even if she does not, her virulent witchcraft capacity could seriously pollute it. Infant boys are particularly vulnerable to maternal hostility, and all of these maternal influences may contribute to the formation of mindless anger. This state can be remedied, however, by a combination of the father's ritual acts and severe modifications of the mother's behavior toward her child. The rites to correct a state of infantile mindless anger are said to entice the khaapkhabuurien from its temporary locus in the lungs (male organs close to and linked with the heart) to the stomach (a female organ). Vomiting in the infant, often induced by noxious fluids, is taken to be an auspicious sign that the khaapkhabuurien has been relocated to a less significant site in the body.

Less serious are more or less expectable 'irritability' (duubakha) and 'infantile rage' (atuur aur kaar), but both states are diffuse in their behavioral expressions and may shape many different kinds of 'thinking/feeling' states and processes. If these states are not carefully controlled by the mother, however, they may become fused together with 'frustration' (babuuraan) to form mindless anger. Infantile rage is a characteristic only of the period of infancy. It is a consequence of both diffuse fear and panic and internal anxiety, before signs of boldness appear, and, most important, of frustrations provoked by the mother's control of infant behavior. Infantile rage is often said to be a consequence of the ways in which the infant is restricted in the netbag, isolated in a woman's house, constrained in its explorations, and forced to breast-feed beyond its desires. Such rage is a part of as well as a reaction to fear in its earliest and most generalized form, but it is also a form of hostility and aggression which may be expressed in sullen withdrawal or violent tantrums. Infantile rage is produced by the khaapkhabuurien and attacks the unstable fragments of the dispersed infantile finiik. On the basis of divinatory or informal advice, the mother is solely responsible for controlling and remedying infantile rage.

In contrast, irritability is believed to almost always have a specific etiology located in environmental causes, which include its interaction with the mother. A minor illness, a slight sore, a cool breeze, or a warm fire may bring about discomfort in the infant which is expressed in the characteristic whimpering, twisting, and grimacing of a state of irritability. Such a state implies that the khaapkhabuurien has been stimulated in any number of ways and is moving among several female organs. This movement is believed to be responsible for particular erratic behavioral shifts of many kinds. The condition is temporary and in most cases far less serious than infantile rage, for when the khaapkhabuurien ceases its wandering activity, irritability wanes. However, when irritability persists and expands despite the removal of its apparent cause, it may be transformed into the more permanent and dangerous state of being 'short-tempered' (*atuur ket*). It is the mother's responsibility to ensure, through her immediate responses to the apparent causes of irritability, that this transformation does not occur.

In the condition of short-temperedness, the infant will continue to express some rage in a restricted but ever-changing set of situations. Short-temperedness indicates that the khaapkhabuurien has continued to move among a number of female organs, as in the case of irritability, but is now itself fragmented. Indeed, fragments are said to course through menstrual residues in the infant's body which randomly take root in different male organs, notably the organs of the senses. The short-tempered infant will oscillate between states of calm and rage in a highly unpredictable manner, and some modified version of this trait will probably persist as a recognizable part of the character of the individual throughout a lifetime. In the infant, however, the more pronounced form of short-temperedness will impede the proper development of social competence and the forging of enduring social relationships. There is no remedy for this condition, although the mother's nurturance and indulgence of infantile whims may reduce its force.

Once the infant begins to exhibit the rudimentary signs of shame, Bimin-Kuskusmin recognize the appearance of 'justifiable anger' (kuurdaam ken). This form of anger is intimately bound up with shame and is associated with more advanced development of the finiik and social understanding (cf. Lutz, chap. 2). In adult men, this kind of anger, coupled with the threat of violence, is the most pronounced expression of an assertive ethos among Bimin-Kuskusmin which is considered to be socially legitimate. (See Schieffelin, chap. 5, on the assertive ethos among Kaluli.) 'Justifiable anger' is both motivated and constrained by an increasingly subtle sense of appropriate social reciprocity. If 'shame' indicates the recognition that one has wronged another by not granting reciprocity, 'justifiable anger' suggests that one has been wronged by another in a failure of expectable reciprocity. Thus, this type of anger is associated with the finiik in the same manner as is shame, and its first and rudimentary expression is expected to parallel the first appearance of shame in infant development. With shame and with justifiable anger, the infant is believed to be ready to enter an increasingly complex social realm of kin, kith, friends, strangers, and enemies in which important social relationships can and will be forged with other persons. Shame and justifiable anger indicate that the finiik, the most important attributes, capacities, and signs of incipient personhood, and the judgmental qualities and social competences that personhood entails are developing normally. These critical aspects of development are believed to be the signs that the infant must now acquire a 'female name' and enter the new realm of early childhood.

CONCLUSION

In this chapter, I have attended to an analytic construction of some aspects of a highly elaborated folk model of Bimin-Kuskusmin ideas about personhood, infancy, and developmental states and processes concerning 'thinking/feeling', behavior, and context. Although I have constructed an ethnographer's model of features of the folk psychology of infants from various orders of convergent data, it is apparent that Bimin-Kuskusmin exegesis on such matters is very complex. I have suggested that cultural perceptions of, and anxieties about, the extreme fragility of infants are bound up with the hypercognized (Levy 1984), that is, highly elaborated, cultural category or developmental phase of infancy (cf. LeVine 1977). Indeed, I have explored only certain selected complexes of the folk psychology of infants. Yet this exploration complicates LeVine's (1977) hypothesis about such folk models of infancy. Thus, for example, I have ignored a complicated ethnopsychological cluster that focuses on infantile 'distress' (*iimtaar*), 'dejection' (*ungi-maan*), 'sorrow' (*fuukhaap*), and 'desolation' (*busaat*), which become the foundation of 'sadness' (*aget-buurnam*) and 'compassion' (*kuguurnam*) in later childhood (see n. 30). I have only alluded to complex matters of infantile hostility and aggression. Despite brief mention of 'seeing', 'comprehension', and more advanced 'understanding', I have discussed neither related elaborations of 'recognizing', 'observing', 'knowing', 'thinking/feeling about', and more esoteric 'analyzing', nor notions about heart and brain as centers of 'thinking/feeling' processing and storage, respectively. In an already long essay, I have only hinted at aspects of the situational deployment of folk psychological constructs in assessments of individual infants. Yet the exploration of some of the complexities of a folk psychological model of infancy among Bimin-Kuskusmin has illuminated several matters of general interest in the study of ethnopsychology.

The folk model implicates a developmental scheme that more or less bounds and situates the stage of infancy, which is bracketed by rites of couvade and female naming. Development within this stage is marked by intertwined complexes and sequences of 'thinking/feeling' states and processes and their manifestations in behavior and is punctuated by minor rites of passage and by divinations that are aligned with diagnostic and prognostic features of the model. Both explicitly and implicitly, the model compares aspects of infancy to earlier, prenatal, and later, childhood, phases of development to suggest a cultural recognition of both continuity and discontinuity in processes of maturation. Prenatal influences may impinge on the structure and process of infant development not at all or weakly or strongly, and only within infancy or beyond infancy into childhood. Infantile characteristics are variously cast as unique features of that stage of development with no discernible further consequences, as positive or negative precursors of later development which are nonetheless bounded and distinctive, and as aspects of longer or shorter developmental gradients or sequences which portray differences as more a matter of degree than of kind. Some developmental facets of infancy shape or extend into early childhood or even later stages of maturation. Many developmental problems that arise within infancy may preclude or hinder aspects of subsequent maturation in various ways.

The developing infant is conceptually linked, through notions of procreative process, to a highly differentiated set of bodily and mystical substances, structures, states, and processes which are marked by gender differences and provide a kind of anatomical and physiological map of sites of vulnerability and of 'thinking/feeling' states and processes that are in normal or abnormal developmental flux. Through these discriminations, the folk model situates the infant with respect to social categories of persons extending from the mother to parents, kindred, lineage, and, somewhat more implicitly and indirectly, higher-level categories of clan, ritual moiety, and tribe. The model also embeds the infant in a cosmological cycle of regenerated ancestral finiik which links a mythic past to the present and interconnects bodily and mystical phenomena in the infant to the social categories of persons that envelop the infant.

Indeed, infant development as a process depends on the supportive and directive force of these interconnections, for the very notion of infant development among Bimin-Kuskusmin seems to presume the probability of deviation from normal developmental lines, of consequent and often severe abnormality, and of the necessity of social, ritual, and ancestral intervention. Perceived failures or weaknesses in any of the linkages that both constitute and situate the infant provide identifiable loci of recognized damaging forces that disrupt aspects of maturation, and both divinatory and therapeutic efforts focus on these vulnerable features and structures of infant developmental process which are predicted in the folk map of the territory of infancy. The most hypercognized (Levy 1984) aspects of the developmental scheme of infancy emphasize negatively valued states and processes in an implicit comparison of normal and abnormal lines of development. Yet, the protective, supportive, and nurturant dimensions of those essential social interactions, notably with the mother, which set infant development on a proper 'path', are also recognized to produce trauma. The mother's proper attempts to reduce the force of behavioral expressions of extreme 'thinking/feeling' states and processes (either active or passive) through restraint thus often lead to an exacerbation of the problem. The folk model gives recognition not only to this inherent dilemma of infant development but also to the conflict generated by hostility and aggression on the part of both mother and infant. The mother-infant dyad is characterized by both centripetal and centrifugal forces in the model, but concern with the former brings the most emphasized and explicit recognition of this bond.

The folk model also implicates more general considerations of personhood in positing connections and balances between the 'person' (kunum) and the 'self' (kaar kiimkiim) and in formulating a particular cultural construction of the general problem of the individual-in-society. Through an often implicit comparison with later stages of development, the attributes, capacities, and signs of personhood are both assigned and denied to normal and abnormal infants in a limited manner in order to construct the category of infancy as one of incipient and fragile personhood. Particular aspects of socialization and enculturation are marked in these various attributions, and they are founded on the limited bodily constitutions, the 'thinking/feeling' and behavioral capacities of infants as they develop in a "culturally constituted behavioral environment" and in accordance with the expectations of fragility, deficit, deviance, stability, progress, and so on, in maturation. In this regard, one explicitly hypocognized focus of the folk model—the constellation of persons, self, and individual-in-society—illuminates in a limited way some structures, balances, and interconnections of internal and external states and processes in the infant which are still relatively undifferentiated and will be elaborated more extensively in folk models of later development. As notions of person, self, and individual-in-society become more intricate in childhood and beyond, however, the connotations of internal and external dimensions of personhood become not only more complex but also more central to the explicit focus of the model of subsequent maturation. Throughout the course of infancy, social interdependence and competence, albeit in rudimentary form, are granted increasing prominence as central features of developing personhood. Internal and external states and processes are gradually merged, although never quite fused, in a limited fashion through a growing awareness of the self as an agent and a recognized person in a particular behavioral environment. With respect to more tacit dimensions of the folk model of infancy, however, internal and external aspects of the infant are highly significant in the formal structure of both the representational and the operational aspects of the model (see Caws 1974).

The Bimin-Kuskusmin model of infant development has an elaborate structure of both hypercognized and hypocognized (Levy 1984) schemata that connect observable, external behavioral events to internal states and processes by constructing the former as signs of the latter and by establishing modes of inference that posit a more or less complex (folk) theoretical relationship between external signifier and internal signified. Modes of inference are intimately linked to notions of causation, for those selected and patterned infantile behaviors that are significant in folk model as signs of underlying states and processes are believed to be significant because they are generated in a patterned way by those same underlying states and processes. Indeed, the emphasis of the focus of the model implies that particular infantile behaviors are selected and seen to have diagnostic pattern as a consequence of notions of internal causation. This emphasis of the model, however, is complicated in at least three apparent ways. First, certain internal states and processes tend to undergo alterations as a consequence of normal processes of infant development, and these alterations produce changes in the external behavioral signs of the underlying states and processes. Second, certain external, mystical forces may cause a change directly in internal states and processes, which alters their behavioral signs.

Third, certain external, social forces may bring about a change directly in particular behaviors, which produces changes in their underlying states and processes, which, in turn, modify the particular behaviors that brought about those internal changes and that are signs of those states and processes. Each of these modes of reckoning causation locates cause(s) differently. Like many structural aspects of Bimin-Kuskusmin folk models, these constructions of causation and inference with respect to infancy may be simple or complex, may exhibit both tacit and explicit features in varying patterns, may possess coherence and also contradiction or compartmentalization in various ways, and may be deployed both representationally and operationally in different ways that suggest particular and partial selections from the model, which then tends to remain tacit in all other respects.

The schemata of particular ethnopsychological complexes within the folk model of infancy not only are given structural shape by the general framework of the model, they also have particular internal elements and structures and external interlinkages with other schemata of other complexes of the model. In demonstrating how these complexes are more or less coherent, bounded, and also linked to aspects of other complexes and more general features of the model, I have adopted a strategy of interpretation that is implicitly comparative. On the one hand, I have provided simple, often monolexemic English glosses of Bimin-Kuskusmin terms for particular 'thinking/feeling' states and processes. These glosses have been selected, however, with some care and attention to what I imagine to be the more or less expectable range of connotations in English. On the other hand, I have embedded these simple translations in relatively thick ethnographic descriptions of their focus, structure, context of usage, and range of Bimin-Kuskusmin connotations in order to qualify and shape them in accordance with Bimin-Kuskusmin understandings. Whenever possible, I have tried to compare the Bimin-Kuskusmin terms themselves, both directly and in terms of how they are embedded in the model, in order to locate them structurally and semantically in particular complexes as well as more generally in the model. In accordance with Bimin-Kuskusmin explications of the folk psychological model of infancy, I have paid particular analytic attention to unraveling the extraordinary polysemy of the notions of finiik and khaapkhabuurien, both in general and in the context of the model of infant development, the ethnopsychological complexes within that model, and the particular terms, elements, and structures within those complexes. Indeed, the concepts of finiik and khaapkhabuurien and various constructions of their interrelationships and balances provide an apt ethnographic focus for exploring the semantic contours and foci and the structural shapes and interlinkages of almost all parts of the model. Thus, for example, although both Lutz (chap. 2) and I have translated particular Ifaluk and

Bimin-Kuskusmin terms as 'justifiable anger', these terms are embedded in ethnographic context in such a way that comparison is possible.

Although this essay and most other chapters in this volume are not explicitly comparative, I would suggest that comparison is the next step in expanding our understanding of folk psychologies. One approach to comparison is through the analytic refinement of the concept of personhood, with which most of these essays deal in different ways. In the present chapter, as I have argued, infancy may provide a privileged focus of the exploration of personhood. Another comparative approach is to attend to structural similarities and differences of the folk models in a comparative framework that does not grant a privileged position to particular Western psychologies, as D'Andrade (n.d.) has demonstrated (cf. Harré 1981). I have shown here, sometimes implicitly and sometimes explicitly, how these two approaches may be integrated in a way that permits comparison to focus on similarities and differences in the cultural constructions of persons, selves, and individuals-in-society in relation to structural configurations of states and processes of thought, feeling, and behavior. I have concentrated in this essay primarily on the representational dimensions of the Bimin-Kuskusmin model of infant "psychology" and only briefly alluded to how that folk model also is operational in important respects. Yet, how ethnopsychological models are selectively put to use in sociocultural contexts in which assessments of particular actors are made, the ways in which significant contexts are structured and recognized, and the characteristics that inform the structure and process of folk psychological decision making must come to be an explicit and integral part of the comparative endeavor. Only then may we begin to explore the problematic relationship between representational and operational aspects of ethnopsychological models (cf. Caws 1974).

ACKNOWLEDGMENTS

Field research among the Bimin-Kuskusmin (1971–1973) was generously supported by the National Institutes of Health, the Cornell University-Ford Foundation Humanities and Social Sciences Program, and the Center for South Pacific Studies of the University of California, Santa Cruz. The New Guinea Research Unit of the Australian National University provided valuable assistance. I wish to thank Peter Black, John Kirkpatrick, Michael Lieber, Catherine Lutz, Marc Swartz, Donald Tuzin, and Geoffrey White for thoughtful and insightful criticisms of an earlier draft of this essay. To those Bimin-Kuskusmin who shared their joys and fears about the wonders and vulnerabilities of their cherished, fragile infants, however, is owed the primary debt of gratitude.

NOTES

1. The quotation is from a discussion, during formal divination, of an eight-month-old infant's illness, by Bosuurok, a curer-diviner and ritual expert. This highly elaborate, formal exegesis follows a typical pattern of commenting on the general character of infancy before examining the suspected pathologies of a particular case. In this quotation, only the general commentary is presented. The pervasive emphasis on the underdevelopment or negation of more developed qualities of the person is characteristic of the construction of the folk psychology of infants among Bimin-Kuskusmin, especially in contexts of formal divinations or rites of passage.

2. Settings, situations, or contexts are more or less culturally and socially bounded arenas that are given particular recognition, shape, and significance by individual experience in everyday activities. Such settings provide a cultural means of framing what is considered to be most immediately relevant to most ethno-psychological considerations. For infants, the most obvious settings include the arenas of woman's house, hamlet, and nearby path, forest, or garden with respect to the diurnal and nocturnal cycles of community life.

3. In its marked form, *kunum* denotes 'man' or 'male person'. The unmarked form, however, includes all persons, male and female, who are endowed with some minimum of recognizable and valued features of personhood. The designation *kunum fen* 'true person' refers only to Bimin-Kuskusmin persons, living and dead, who are linked by shared traditions to a known ethnic community. With the qualification of *fiitep* 'human', 'mortal', the focus is further restricted to living persons and those immediate ancestors known personally to living persons within the Bimin-Kuskusmin community. Indeed, the Bimin-Kuskusmin notion of person may be shaped contextually and qualified lexically in an extraordinary variety of ways. Because of the nature of infants as incipient persons, the term *kunum* is rarely applied to them and then only with elaborate qualification.

4. The association of an experiential self with the 'skin root' notion of Bimin-Kuskusmin is based on the indigenous view that the public presentation of self is related in some way to a more personal, unseen sense of self. Hence, what other people can see or discover is more or less on the skin, but what is discernible is linked (by 'roots') to a more or less 'interior' *mutuuk* set of perceptions, thoughts, feelings, wishes, motivations, or intentions. That 'interior' set, associated with the khaapkhabuurien in many contexts, may be more or less aligned with discernible evidence of the self, which is linked with the finiik generally. To the extent that guilt and shame can be distinguished among Bimin-Kuskusmin, guilt is related to the interior aspect, and shame is on the skin, although ideally both shame and guilt should be roughly aligned in the mature (male) person when the finiik is dominant (cf. Strathern 1977 and Strathern 1968 on the Melpa ideas of *pipil* and *popokl*). With an underdeveloped and unstable finiik, however, the young infant is identified with

the dominance of the khaapkhabuurien and its most immediate experiences and is believed to be utterly without a sense of shame, which is dependent on a more developed finiik.

5. For example, certain flora and fauna of ritual or mythic significance, sacred crystals and other stones of power, ritual artifacts, celestial bodies and events, and other specially marked features of the Bimin-Kuskusmin behavioral environment are endowed with at least some facets of personhood.

6. Although ritual and divinatory forms of discourse are highly elaborated, they too are inevitably predicated on tacit understandings that are not explicitly unraveled or explored. Some of these tacit dimensions are held to be esoteric male ritual knowledge, which accounts for why some abstract aspects of personhood and folk psychology are most highly developed among adult men (especially male ritual elders).

7. Although infantile characteristics are sometimes attributed (largely in divinatory contexts) to adults who are ill, deranged, defective, or otherwise deviant, the analogy between normal infant and abnormal adult traits is severely limited. The ethnopsychological characteristics of infancy are the more or less linked traits of a culturally bounded developmental stage, and there is no elaborated notion of regression, in any usual sense, among Bimin-Kuskusmin.

8. It should be noted, however, that, with the appearance of European epidemic diseases over the last few decades, the incidence of infant mortality has risen dramatically—both statistically (insofar as data are available) and in the perceptions of Bimin-Kuskusmin. On the basis of admittedly slim ethnohistorical data, I suspect that Bimin-Kuskusmin may have elaborated their folk model of infancy and infant risk in some ways during this period of high infant mortality. See n. 14.

9. More formal analysis of Bimin-Kuskusmin terms and concepts in the "domains" of emotion, cognition, and personality descriptors is not central to this analytic endeavor, for such analysis has not been much focused on matters of infant behavior and development.

10. Caws (1974:3) notes that "the representational model corresponds to the way the individual thinks things are, the operational model is the way he practically responds or acts."

11. With respect to procedural knowledge, D'Andrade (n.d.:3) observes that "most informants do not have an organized view of the entire model. They *use* the model but they cannot produce a reasonable description of the model."

12. Apparent inconsistencies or contradictions among the basic tenets of Bimin-Kuskusmin folk psychology are typically attributed to ignorance, incomplete understanding, or loss of ancestral knowledge, which is believed to have eroded over "historical" time. Apparent logical entailments of the folk model sometimes are denied as being irrelevant, suggesting a compartmentalization of some aspects of the model and a suppression of some logically expected linkages within it.

13. Geertz is not optimistic about the possibilities of comparative analysis, and my present concerns are not explicitly comparative. Nevertheless, I reject the view that folk models or cultural meanings with respect to ethnopsychology are, in principle, unique and incommensurable, although any comparison may reveal some

culturally special features of particular folk models. I believe that a comparative analysis of folk models of this (or perhaps any) kind is both possible and necessary. Indeed, the range of structural variability, which is the focus of comparative analysis, is predictably far less than the apparent cultural diversity, which, in itself, provides no basis for comparison. One might approach the matter by formally comparing the assumptions, elements, and structures of different folk models (cf. D'Andrade n.d.; Lock 1981). One might also center the comparative endeavor on concepts of personhood, as I have implied in this essay (cf. Shotter 1981), and Leenhardt (1947) and Read (1955), with different analytic problems, have done with respect to other Melanesian societies.

14. Particular catastrophic epidemics of influenza and other diseases introduced through European contact have temporarily raised infant mortality (normally about 26-31 percent previously) to heights of almost 45 percent over the last few decades.

15. Indeed, the ideal of full parenthood—an aspect of complete personhood—emphasizes having both a son and a daughter, and firstborn sons and daughters, whether or not they are also firstborn children, receive special ritual attention (see Poole 1982a).

16. There is some evidence that these male pseudohermaphrodites have incomplete masculinization due to disorders of testicular differentiation and function and, especially, disorders of function at the androgen–dependent target areas. Two known cases among Bimin-Kuskusmin during the time of field research were clinically examined, and analyses of their blood and urine samples were performed in Port Moresby. They probably represent instances of 5-alpha reductase deficiency, which is now relatively well known in terms of genetic pattern and biochemical milieu. Such cases, however, are never detectable in infancy, but only on the eve of puberty. The adolescent or adult 'male pseudohermaphrodite' (yomnok-min) then becomes the androgenous counterpart of the 'paramount female ritual elder' (waneng aiyem ser or afek-mun) (see Poole 1981b).

17. Pandanus nuts, taro, pork, and marsupial flesh, which are ritually important and endowed with aspects of personhood in their living states, are prominent among those 'male foods' believed to possess finiik 'spirit' and strengthen male aspects of the 'anatomy', both corporeal and noncorporeal. Indeed, the finiik can be transmitted only through male semen and male food. Thus, although the finiik develops in all proper male and female persons, young and old, it always has distinctively male connotations, and develops most forcefully in adult men and through male ritual experiences.

18. The designation of the infant as the 'mother's child' (aurfaat) has several connotations. First, the aurfaat is a social unit, which is referred to in the singular form. People interact with it, and it has particular rights and obligations vis-à-vis the community. Second, the aurfaat is a ritual unit, which is the focus of divination. Divinatory procedures recognize the mother's special sensitivity and insight with respect to her baby and may also acknowledge pathological problems of the dyad for which the mother is responsible. Third, the aurfaat is a more or less encapsulated interactive unit, in which intense protection, nurturance, play, "conversation" (in the form of baby talk that only the mother can understand), conflict, and even

eroticism take place. No other person may interact with the infant in any way that involves touching or close proximity without the mother's approval, and violations of this understanding are grounds for compensation. The attachment between mother and infant in the aurfaat is often referred to as the 'spirit' (*kusem*) of the umbilical cord. Nonetheless, other concepts suggest a clear recognition in many contexts that mother and infant are separate, if not autonomous, beings. Yet, it is said that no infant can survive apart from its own mother, and that the loss of an infant may sometimes provoke the mother to suicidal depression.

19. These divinations have diagnostic and prognostic characteristics. They focus both on the monitoring of normal development and on the detection of abnormal excesses, deficits, intrusions, extrusions, and imbalances that are signs of actual or impending illness or flawed development. Various behavioral traits of the infant, especially when they are believed to change suddenly (with respect to the infant's individual patterns) or to deviate gradually (from developmental expectations of normal infancy), are seen as symptoms of underlying malaise. Even with apparently normal infants (especially more vulnerable boys), there is more or less constant vigilance and frequent divination. Both divinatory and therapeutic measures are focused on the aurfaat dyad, for the quality of mother–infant relationships is often seen to provide directly, or fail to protect from, but also to remedy, misfortune.

20. Most of these polysemic terms represent quite complex ideas, and the English glosses presented here are only more or less global approximations of the meaning(s) of these terms.

21. The strongest connection of male blood, which is represented in notions of patrifiliation and lineage ties, is between the infant and its father and other close male agnates. The mother, however, is said to have the greatest understanding of the infant, for her bond of male blood is strengthened by umbilical connection, breast milk, intimacy, indulgence, familiarity, and so on. Yet, her menstrual capacity, if not properly shielded, may weaken this link of male blood and endanger the infant. Women are not believed to cease menstruating completely while breast-feeding a young infant.

22. Because the father is an adult, fully initiated man and his bond of male blood with the infant is the strongest, an infusion of his blood is believed to strengthen the male blood as well as the finiik of the child. This transfusion is also believed to enhance the efficacy of the father's preventive and curative rites for the child, which is important since the father is the ritual protector of the infant on most occasions.

23. Bimin-Kuskusmin conceive only vague and relative distinctions between the analytically separable notions of intellect and affect, cognition and emotion or feeling. No terms clearly differentiate these ideas, yet usage in context may indicate some relative emphasis on 'feeling/thinking' (*fudiiminaam, gaarankhaan*, etc.) or 'thinking/feeling' (*fukuuninaam, khuurkhaan*, etc.). But each aspect implicates and shapes the other in subtle ways. One cannot recognize a particular feeling without thinking about its etiology, context, and influence (on thinking). One cannot think clearly, forcefully, and significantly without the 'strength' (kitiirnam) of feeling (see Poole 1982b), which can also muddle thoughts if it is too forceful. What relative distinctions are drawn tend to stress myriad kinds of interdependencies and inter-

penetrations of these notions. Some mergings of 'thinking/feeling' may approximate the English connotations of, for example, "I feel that you are mistreating the baby."

24. The male blood of infants is inherently weak and must be constantly strengthened by ritual acts of agnatic and cognatic kin. But the mother's pollution and her occasional provocation of certain dangerous or extreme behavioral displays, often indicating an agitated finiik, exacerbate the weakness of infantile male blood, as do the attacks of female spirits and witches.

25. In this context, 'internal' (mutuuk) refers to anatomical parts that are either inside the body or connected to interior male organs, especially the heart. Thus, the apparently external penis and testicles are distinctively male organs by virtue of their 'roots' (kiimkiim) in the heart.

26. Sexual activity usually resumes about 6 to 8 months after the woman gives birth, but it often does not (and should not) involve vaginal penetration and may take the form of coitus interruptus or mutual masturbation. During early infancy, the child is reported not only to be present during parental sexual activity but also to be *held* by the mother.

27. At times of severe crisis, mashed taro coated with human or boar semen may be fed to the unweaned infant in small amounts.

28. In this context, 'external' (*bangep*) refers to anatomical parts that are either on or exposed to the surface of the body or are connected to exterior female organs, expecially the breasts and the vulval labia. Thus, the apparently internal vagina and womb are distinctively female organs by virtue of their 'roots' in the vulva.

29. In the infant boy, these more subtle signs of a lack of masculinity may include various kinds of erratic behavior, certain types of passivity, exaggerated fear of strangers and unfamiliar objects, failure to achieve penile erection when stimulated by the mother, and so on.

30. One might expect 'sadness' (*aget-buurnam*) to be implicated here, but sadness is *not* included within the folk psychology of infancy because it involves a kind of experiential reflexivity and is linked to 'compassion' (*kuguurnam*), which first appear as attributes of early childhood, after the ritual bestowal of female names at about two years of age (cf. Lutz, chap. 2). But see the conclusion of this chapter.

31. In any case, this protective ritual procedure is normally followed for boys of about 9 to 12 years of age at the beginning of the male initiation cycle to promote the acquisition of powerful male ritual knowledge (see Poole 1982*b*).

32. Important aspects of gender symbolism, however, do focus on androgeny, as represented by the 'male pseudohermaphrodite' (yomnok-min), the 'paramount female ritual elder' (waneng aiyem ser or afek-mun), and the original, founding ancestors (see Poole 1981*b*).

33. There are two basic kinds of control. The term *tuurakhaamiin* refers to an agency external to the person, and *faatebeemkha* refers to a more or less internal agency of the person. The latter is believed to be localized in the finiik or, indeed, to be an inseparable aspect of the developed finiik. This form of control, however, presumes a solidity, integration, strength, and force of the finiik which are not characteristic of infancy. Thus, intrusive spirits may easily exert 'control' (tuurkhaamiin) over the infantile finiik, which has no strong 'control' (faate-

beemkha) of its own (cf. later sections "Fear, Anxiety, and Boldness" and "Anger").

34. The term *tuuk-menaam* refers to weaknesses of the person and self, and the term *baruut* refers to weaknesses of the structure of objects or nonhuman beings or more or less "physical" parts of the person.

35. This recognition does not imply that Bimin-Kuskusmin have developed some clear notion of an unconscious, in any usual sense, although they do discuss internal states and processes and recognize problems of awareness and expression of them.

36. Note that the khaapkhabuurien cannot be equated with individuality in any simple sense, for even personal life experiences occur in a recognized sociocultural milieu and take account of significant other persons.

37. Ritual moiety and initiation age group identities are also reckoned in the idiom of finiik, but these social links require the special strengthening powers of male initiation rituals with respect to the finiik and the person and are only very loosely applicable to the social identity of the infant (see Poole 1982b).

38. In parallel to the case of sadness (see n. 30), the infant cannot be possessed of affection until other 'thinking/feeling' capacities develop, but the infant can be influenced by the affection expressed by others, notably the mother.

39. Possible psychoanalytic interpretations of such behaviors are complicated only in the folk model by Bimin-Kuskusmin views of the relevant fantasies concerning this admitted eroticism. In Bimin-Kuskusmin reckoning, this apparent eroticism is said to involve a pleasurable, but necessary, stimulation of the breast for lactation and of the penis for growth. Yet, there is some overt recognition that such fondling has a sexual significance, but a playful one only. Traditional understandings of this contact and its significance do not, of course, come to have explicit Oedipal form. On other grounds of dreams, tales, ritual constructions, "clinical" interviews, and so on, however, there is a substantial case to be made for the existence of a strong, complex, and poorly resolved set of Oedipal tendencies in Bimin-Kuskusmin males. It should be noted that these erotic acts are often somewhat rough. Mothers' stimulation of the penis may involve pulling, pinching, and twisting in a manner that produces struggling and crying in infant boys. Also, I have treated many women whose nipples had been bruised and lacerated by their infants.

40. In this context, 'seeing' is a more or less disorganized and primitive form of 'understanding', which requires more developed capacities of concentration and intention, appreciation of etiology and context, memory and recognition, general thinking/feeling organization, and, thus, finiik.

41. This distinction between a real and imagined audience is drawn from a common Bimin-Kuskusmin contrast between embarrassment in the context of an actual audience judging improper acts, which both older infants and more developed persons can understand in some sense, and narrative portrayals of similar scenes, which only older persons beyond infancy are said to understand clearly. Thus, stories that are often told with moral purpose to older children are never told to infants.

42. In this context, 'comprehension' is characterized as a more or less transitional state between 'seeing' and 'understanding' (see n. 40). Unlike 'seeing', it involves

some development of the capacities of concentration and intention, memory and recognition, general 'thinking/feeling' organization, and consequently, finiik. Unlike 'understanding', which involves a more advanced development of all the above traits, however, 'comprehension' does *not* include a developed appreciation of etiology and context.

43. For some quality to be 'planted' (kiimraakhiin) in the finiik or heart implies that such a quality is embedded or located (at least temporarily) in the structure of these phenomena. Thus, the internal aspect of shame is embedded in the finiik or heart when one 'feels/thinks badly'. In contrast, as previously noted, when the finiik is 'planted' (duurgaamiin) in a social community, it is integrated with and given shape by some aspect of that phenomenon; it is not embedded or located in the community. For example, ritual taro is 'planted' (kiimraakhiin) in a garden, but it is also 'planted' (duurgaamiin) in ancestral finiik.

44. There is some difference of opinion among Bimin-Kuskusmin about the centrality of prenatal influence in the development of mindless anger, but there is general agreement that postnatal experiences are the most important aspects of its formation.

GLOSSARY

aar-ker	on, on the surface of
abuurkhamiin	remember, recall; also imagine
abuusaarkha	reciprocity; also obligation
adetera'fefebaanam	attachment, linkage, bond
afaak ker	beneath, underneath
afek-mun	paramount female ritual elder, daughter or female uterine descendant of the primordial ancestress Afek
agaat fugooriinaam	recognition
agetaanok	surprise
aget-buurnam	sadness
agetnaam-kuraa	single-mindedness
aiyem khaa	meaning, significance, important meaning, sacred meaning
aiyepnon	spirit of unavenged dead (usually male warrior)
araang	stoicism, composure, unfeeling character
araar-taan	force, power
ataan takhaak	shadow

atuur aur kaar	infantile rage
atuur fagamiin	bravery, valor
atuur ket	short-tempered
atuur kunum	man of perpetual anger, killer
aur-abaarang	infantile revenge (usually directed against mother)
aurfaat	mother's infant or child, mother-infant dyad; also mother's favorite or most pampered child
aur-kiireng	infantile confusion
aur maamuruup muut	helpless and sucking newborn baby
aur-orsaak	infantile aggression (usually directed against mother)
babuuraan	infantile frustration
bangep	external, outside, environmental; also sometimes superficial or peripheral
baruut	weak (in reference to objects, nonhuman beings, or parts of persons); cf. *tuuk-menaam*; see n. 34
biriir saaninam	emotional stability
bubuuniinaam	withdrawal, retreat
bugumiin	pierced
bukhuum	type of white pigment (made from powdered or decayed limestone)
busaat	desolation
buukhrok	insult
buurgaang	social competence or skill
buur saaniin	calm, docile
daam	sense, truth; also essence
daib	path
daib abinaam men	umbilical path child
diikhraa	intention
dop aiyem	kernel meaning, primary significance; usually with the implication of secret or hidden or subtle
duubakha	irritability
duugamaan	trustworthiness
duugamiin	block, stifle

duunduun	matted together
duurgaamiin	planted (in the sense of integrated with or given shape by); cf. *kiimraakhiin*; see n. 43
duur-kha	strong (in a mystical sense); cf. *kitiir*
duur sakhiik mutuuk	depression
faaran	will
faatebeemiin/ faatebeemkha	control (in the sense of an internal agency of the person); cf. *tuurakhaamiin*; see n. 33
fen	true, real
fiitep	human, mortal
fiitom	shame
finganiinaan	fear
finiik	type of spirit or life-force (highly polysemic); see text
foguraar	infantile madness
fom	body
fom takhaak	body shadow-reflection
fudiim-duurkhanii	feel/think badly, reflect upon negatively
fudiiminaam	type of feeling/thinking; see n. 23
fukuuninaam	type of thinking/feeling; see n. 23
fuugamiin	twisted together
fuugamkha	boldness
fuugunaamiin	understanding; see nn. 40 and 42
fuukhaap	sorrow
gaarankghaan	type of feeling/thinking; see n. 23
giik	type of red pigment (made from ferrous earth compounds)
giitakhaa	fragments, shreds
guur	anger
guuraan	innate anger
guuriguuraaniin	flows
iboorkuun	type of retardation
iboorop	heart
iimtaar	distress

iraap ku-kaar	personality, character
iruum kamiin	wander
iruum-kiim khaamiin-kha	confused; with the implication of a lack of maturity
isaar	lust
kaar	skin
kaaragaam	desire
kaardaak	diffuse panic
kaar dugaamiin-khaaraak/kaar dugaamkhaa	self-centered, self-centeredness
kaar giisuup	arrogance
kaarkaar	hot (in reference to a mystical or ritual state)
kaar kiimkiim	skin root; also self
kaar kuureng-mamiin	embarrassment
kaar kitiir	strong skin; also strength of character or personality
kaasaknaam	solidity, firmness, cohesiveness
kakaat	happy
ken kuup	mundane, ordinary, everyday
khaabomnaam	stupidity; also a particular type of stupidity
khaakhuut	dull, lethargic
khaapkhabuurien	type of spirit or life-force (highly polysemic); see text
khaim-khraakkhaan	comprehension; see n. 42
khaim mighiir	black blood
khuurkhaan	type of thinking/feeling; see n. 23
khymin	covering, wrapping
kiim-fuugaar	concentration
kiimkiim	roots
kiimraakhiin	planted (in the sense of being embedded or located in); cf. *duurgaamiin*; see n. 43
kiinangkhaamiin fen-kha	understand truly (in the sense of diagnose or analyze)
kimerok	spongy

kitiir	strong (in both a general and a bodily sense); cf. *duur-kha*
kitiirnam	strength
kiyoorkuup	straight
kok abinaam	forehead, fontanelle
kugaar kemataak	moral character
kuguurnam	compassion; see n. 30
ku-iraask	affection
kumun abinaam	navel
kunum	person, adult person, human person, male person, Bimin-Kuskusmin
kunum iboorop weeng-karaak ker	male knowledge or meaning
kunum khaim	male blood
kunum yemen	male food; also male taro
kusem	spirit; includes both *finiik* and *khaapkhabuurien*
kutaang	unruly
kutem-gamiin	see; see n. 40
kuun aiyem	mystical power; also ancestral or ritual power
kuur-daam ken	justifiable anger
kuurkuuraak	balance
kwan ker tabiin	source in life, foundation in life experience
kwan werkhaak	fate, ancestral fate
maiyoob gom	semen
mamaak	impulse (usually with respect to matters of bodily forces or urges); cf. *yaamyaam*
mem	breath
mem gom	fertile fluids (female)
mem khaim	menstrual blood
men kikiis	new child
mighiir	black; also polluted or diseased
miing	bodily joints

miit	support, foundation, base; also sometimes origin
mutuuk	inside, interior
mutuuk kiin dugaamiin	see inside, understand (a person)
niimteywa	hidden, obscure
ogookaarem	responsibility
ok takhaak	reflection
oorkhraan	bodily desires; also urge to defecate
sakhiik	anxiety
sakhiikuur	anxious
suuniin	infantile envy
taak faraak	social encompassment, social constraint-support
tabiin-khraa duur	motivation
tamam	witch, witchcraft capacity
terotero	smooth, tight, taut
tiibaanam	loyalty
tiibisaak guur	mindless anger
tiinabiin	passive, inactive
tiinkaar	caution, wariness
tingiip gooran	antisocial
turuum	bridge, link, connection
tuuk-menaam	weak (in reference to the person or self as a whole or with respect to thinking/feeling capacities); cf. *baruut*; see n. 34
tuurakhaamiin	control (in the sense of an agency external to the person); cf. *faatebeemiin/faatebeemkha*; see n. 33
tuurun taamamiin	really know (as a person)
ugaam-kaar	social identity, status-linked reputation
unaankuur	direction (with the implication of purpose)
ungi-maan	dejection
utuung-khraan	intellectual acuity, intelligence; also foresightedness
uunaan	vapors (usually within the body)
uurfeng aur-weeng	baby talk
waasop waneng	promiscuous woman, wanton

waneng aiyem ser	paramount female ritual elder
waneng win	female name (bestowed on all children in a rite of passage at about the age of two years)
weeng	speech; also language
weeng ken	ordinary language
weeng magaam	root speech, speech of significance, speech addressing fundamental or important matters
weeng taan-kem	children's language
wernaam	crooked; also deviant
win boroorep aur	secret name
yaamyaam	impulse (usually with respect to processes of thinking/feeling); cf. *mamaak*
yabaar abinaam	forehead, fontanelle
yagaak	tantrum
yan tem	footprint
yegaar	judgmental capacity
yom kiin daakhamin ker	brought to the eye, revealed
yomnok-min	male pseudohermaphrodite, son or male agnatic descendant of the primordial ancestor Yomnok
yuguurgaamiin	consciousness, awareness

REFERENCES

Antaki, C., and G. Fielding
   1981   Research on Ordinary Explanations. *In* The Psychology of Ordinary Explanations of Social Behavior. Charles Antaki, ed. Pp. 27–55. London: Academic Press.
Caws, P.
   1974   Operational, Representational and Explanatory Models. American Anthropologist 76:1–10.
D'Andrade, R. G.
   n.d.   A Folk Model of the Mind. *In* Cultural Models of Language and Thought. N. Quinn and D. Holland, eds. New York: Cambridge University Press.

Fortes, M.
  1973   On the Concept of the Person among the Tallensi. *In* La notion de
          personne en Afrique noire. Germaine Dieterlen, ed. Pp. 283–319. Paris:
          Editions du Centre National de la Recherche Scientifique.
Frake, C. O.
  1969   Notes on Queries in Ethnography. *In* Cognitive Anthropology. Stephen
          A. Tyler, ed. Pp. 123–137. New York: Holt, Rinehart and Winston.
Geertz, C.
  1976   "From the Native's Point of View": On the Nature of Anthropological
          Understanding. *In* Meaning in Anthropology. Keith H. Basso and
          Henry A. Selby, eds. Pp. 221–237. Albuquerque: University of New
          Mexico Press.
Goffman, E.
  1955   On Face-Work: An Analysis of Ritual Elements in Social Interaction.
          Psychiatry 18:213–231.
Hallowell, A. I.
  1955   Culture and Experience. Philadelphia: University of Pennsylvania Press.
Harré, R.
  1981   Psychological Variety. *In* Indigenous Psychologies. Paul Heelas and
          Andrew Lock, eds. Pp. 79–103. London: Academic Press.
Harris, G. G.
  1980   Universal Elements in Concepts of the Person: The Taita Case. Paper
          presented at the 79th Annual Meeting of the American Anthropological
          Association, Washington, D.C.
Heider, F.
  1958   The Psychology of Interpersonal Relations. New York: John Wiley and
          Sons.
Leenhardt, M.
  1947   Do Kamo. Paris: Editions Gallimard.
LeVine, R. A.
  1977   Child Rearing as Cultural Adaptation. *In* Culture and Infancy. P.
          Herbert Leiderman, Steven R. Tulkin, and Anne Rosefeld, eds. Pp.
          15–27. New York: Academic Press.
Levy, R. I.
  1984   Emotion, Knowing and Culture. *In* Culture Theory: Essays on Mind,
          Self, and Emotion. R. A. Shweder and R. A. LeVine, eds. Cambridge:
          Cambridge University Press.
Lévy-Bruhl, L.
  1916   "L'expression de la possession dans les langues mélanésiennes."
          Mémoires de la Société Linguistique de Paris 19:96–104.
Lock, A.
  1981   Universals in Human Conception. *In* Indigenous Psychologies. Paul
          Heelas and Andrew Lock, eds. Pp. 19–36. London: Academic Press.
Mauss, M.
  1938   Une Catégorie de l'esprit humain: la notion de personne, celle de 'moi'.
          Journal of the Royal Anthropological Institute 68:263–281.

1969   L'âme, le nom, et la personne. *In* Oeuvres. Vol. II. Pp. 131–135. Paris:
            Editions de Minuit.
Poole, F. J. P.
1976   "Knowledge Rests in the Heart": Bimin-Kuskusmin Metacommunica-
            tions on Meaning, Tacit Knowledge, and Field Research. Paper pre-
            sented at the 75th Annual Meeting of the American Anthropological
            Association, Washington, D.C.
1977   The Ethnosemantics of YEMEN: Food Prohibitions, Food Transactions,
            and Taro as Cultigen, Food, and Symbol among the Bimin-Kuskusmin.
            Paper presented at the 76th Annual Meeting of the American Anthro-
            pological Association, Houston.
1981*a*   TAMAM: Ideological and Sociological Configurations of 'Witchcraft'
            Among Bimin-Kuskusmin. Social Analysis 8:58–76.
1981*b*   Transforming 'Natural' Woman: Female Ritual Leaders and Gender
            Ideology among Bimin-Kuskusmin. *In* Sexual Meanings. Sherry B.
            Ortner and Harriet Whitehead, eds. Pp. 116–165. Cambridge: Cam-
            bridge University Press.
1982*a*   Couvade and Clinic in a New Guinea Society: Birth among the Bimin-
            Kuskusmin. *In* The Use and Abuse of Medicine. Marten W. de Vries,
            Robert L. Berg, and Mac Lipkin, Jr., eds. Pp. 54–95. New York: Praeger
            Scientific.
1982*b*   The Ritual Forging of Identity: Aspects of Person and Self in Bimin-
            Kuskusmin Male Initiation. *In* Rituals of Manhood. Gilbert H. Herdt,
            ed. Pp. 99–154. Berkeley, Los Angeles, London: University of California
            Press.
n.d.   The Rites of Childhood. Unpub. MS.
Quinn, N.
1982   "Commitment" in American Marriage: A Cultural Analysis. American
            Ethnologist 9:775–798.
Read, K. E.
1955   Morality and the Concept of the Person Among the Gahuku-Gama.
            Oceania 25:233–282.
Rorty, A. O.
1976   A Literary Postscript: Characters, Persons, Selves, Individuals. *In* The
            Identities of Persons. Amelie O. Rorty, ed. Pp. 301–323. Berkeley,
            Los Angeles, London: University of California Press.
Shotter, J.
1981   Vico, Moral Worlds, Accountability and Personhood. *In* Indigenous
            Psychologies. Paul Heelas and Andrew Lock, eds. Pp. 265–284. London:
            Academic Press.
Smedslund. J.
1978   Bandura's Theory of Self-Efficacy: A Set of Common-Sense Theorems.
            Scandinavian Journal of Psychology 19:1–14.
Strathern, A. J.
1977   Why is Shame on the Skin? *In* The Anthropology of the Body. John
            Blacking, ed. Pp. 99–110. London: Academic Press.

  1981   NOMAN: Representations of Identity in Mount Hagen. *In* The Struc-
          ture of Folk Models. Ladislav Holy and Milan Stuchlik, eds. Pp. 281–
          303. London: Academic Press.
Strathern, M.
  1968   *Popokl*: The Question of Morality. Mankind 6: 553–562.
Waismann, F.
  1965   Verifiability. *In* Logic and Language. Anthony Flew, ed. Pp. 122–151.
          Garden City: Anchor Books.
Wittgenstein, L.
  1958   Philosophical Investigations. G. E. M. Anscombe, trans. Oxford: Basil
          Blackwell.

Part III

Person, Deviance, and Illness

7

Ghosts, Gossip, and Suicide: Meaning and Action in Tobian Folk Psychology

Peter W. Black

. . . individuals do not simply receive and spout out a cultural legacy. They live with it and through it, suffering it or evading it, perhaps even creating it at critical psychohistorical junctures.

—Belmonte, *The Broken Fountain*

INTRODUCTION

Early one morning in 1972 on the remote Micronesian island of Tobi there began a series of events which were so dramatic and unusual that they soon involved the entire population. A man I shall call Alfredo, a forty-two-year-old father of six, was the central figure in those events. Separated from his wife, who was living on another island, his love affair with a young girl had recently become a matter of public knowledge and discussion.

After intentionally wounding himself with a knife, he called together his children, bid them good-bye, and ran off into the uninhabited bush. Alerted by his terrified children, who feared he would kill himself, small groups of men fanned out through the bush looking for him. He was found sitting in a tree to which he had attached a rope with a noose in it. He came down out of the tree but soon ran away again. Thrice more during that day he acted in a fashion that seemed to indicate that he was suicidal. Once, he launched himself out to sea on a hastily constructed and completely unseaworthy raft, only to come ashore again. Later, he paddled a canoe out into the channel in the dark. Finally he returned home and once again turned a knife upon himself, this time inflicting a stomach wound. This last act ended Alfredo's sequence of "suicidal" behaviors.

In this chapter I report on that incident for methodological, ethno-graphic, and theoretical reasons. Its analysis will allow me to (1) dem-onstrate the utility of the case study method in ethnopsychological research, (2) explore one of the most potent metaphors of Tobian folk psychology, and (3) present some ideas about what Lutz has called "the ecology of ethnopsychological knowledge" (chap. 2). These three goals are interrelated and each can best be realized by an analysis of some of the statements that Tobians made in conversations both with each other and with me during and after Alfredo's attempted suicide. This procedure is based on the fact that, as Berger and Luckmann point out, "the most important vehicle of reality maintenance is conversation" (1966:152–153).

I begin with a consideration of the methods best suited for ethno-psychological research, given the several ways in which folk psychology enters into behavior. The body of the chapter consists of an expanded narrative of the case followed by an analysis in which the utility of certain methods for investigating important but often neglected issues in ethno-psychology is demonstrated. In the process "ghostliness" is shown to be one of the key organizing concepts in Tobian folk psychology, while gossip is shown to be an important feature of the islanders' social psychological landscape which is rather inadequately dealt with in their folk psychology. This leads to an investigation of certain elements of Tobian understand-ings about suicide which, when probed, prove unable to fully encompass Alfredo's behavior.

METHODS FOR THE STUDY OF FOLK PSYCHOLOGY

Folk psychologies are profoundly important in the social life of human communities. Their description and comparison form the heart of the ethnopsychological enterprise.[1] Unfortunately, folk psychologies are not particularly easy to study, largely because of the lack of an agreed upon vocabulary with which to map them.

It has often been pointed out that conceptions of personhood, as well as conceptions of relations between person, action, and meaning, are (to some as yet undetermined extent) culturally variable. Yet we still await an adequate vocabulary in which to express that variability. The difficulty arises from the fact that there are severe limitations on the use of academic psychologies in this task, because of their embeddedness in Western folk psychology. This is a serious problem, for if academic psychology is too badly contaminated with Euro-American folk notions to serve as an objec-tive, pancultural system with which to map folk psychologies, then how can we hope to even standardize our translations, let alone carry out comparative analysis?

Two possible strategies for doing comparative analysis come to mind. One can attempt to disentangle academic psychology from its Euro-American folk cousin by directly addressing the issue. (See Lutz's discussion of this point, 1982*a* and chap. 2.) Or, one can do the ethnography of one or more non-Western folk psychologies using as nontechnical a vocabulary as possible and providing as "thick" a description as is practical of the contexts in which such knowledge is salient. In this manner much that is usually left implicit by ethnographers can be made explicit. Essentially, what this second strategy calls for (and it is the one I have adopted here) is the translation of non-Western folk psychology in a very straightforward fashion.[2] Those psychologies can then await the outcome of the inevitably complex and difficult decontamination of academic psychology. The use of this strategy, which makes it necessary to take into account the full complexities of folk psychological systems, is also a way of meeting a second fundamental challenge for the doing of ethnopsychology—the necessity of moving beyond unidimensional methods.

In a statement that calls to mind Hallowell's notion of the behavioral environment (1955), Rorty notes that a "complicated biological fact about us . . . [is that] . . . humans are just the sort of organisms that interpret and modify their agency through their conceptions of themselves" (1976:323). A good part of that complexity is due to the fact that such conceptions are not mere representations. Therefore (and this is my point) they need to be studied with an assortment of ethnographic approaches.

Numerous scholars in the field of ethnopsychology have modeled their research and explanations on ethnoscience. In their conceptualization of what they are studying they draw a strict parallel between folk systems for classifying persons and behavior and folk classificatory systems dealing with plants, animals, colors, and other terminological "domains." Drawing on the research tradition grounded in the work of Pike (1954) and developed into a sophisticated methodological framework by Conklin (1962), D'Andrade (1965), Frake (1962), Goodenough (1956), and others, they investigate folk psychologies as though they were comparable to native botanies or astronomies. Although excellent work leading to intellectually polished descriptions has been accomplished within this paradigm, I think that ultimately it will prove inadequate to the needs of the field.

In a recent paper D'Andrade (1984) has discussed what he calls "cultural meaning systems." He convincingly argues that any given meaning system has three functions, which he calls the "representational," the "directive," and the "evocative." By representational is meant the role of the meaning system in mapping reality. By directive is meant the normative aspect of the meaning system, or its role in shaping human action. The evocative function refers to the capacity of meaning systems to stimulate affective response. Clearly these three functions are complexly interrelated and are also closely related to the constitutive character of culture in general and discourse in particular (Searle 1969). For example, it seems to me that, as well as stimulating affect, a cultural meaning system serves to organize it (see Gerber, chap. 4). It is important to recognize that while these three functions are part of the processes by which every system of meaning works, a given function may be more or less important in any particular meaning system. Further, since a system of meaning is itself complexly organized, its various functions may be unequally distributed across its elements.

Most of the domains analyzed by early ethnoscience were largely representational. Native taxonomies for plants, animals, and colors all dealt with domains in which the affective and normative functions were generally trivial. Therefore, the use of techniques for the elicitation and analysis of their representational features (classic ethnoscience) did not run the risk of omitting significant functions. When we turn, however, to meaning systems that have the person as their central focus (folk psychologies), we are faced with a very different and much more complex situation.[3]

Folk psychologies are not simply descriptions of the class of phenomena "people." They are also both evocative and directive; that is, they concern phenomena about which people feel deeply and which people also use to organize their feelings. Furthermore, folk psychologies are systems that guide and perhaps even compel behavior. To fully understand them, all three functions need to be investigated.

Broadly speaking, each of the three functions of folk psychology calls for methods from a particular research tradition. Naturally, the investigation of any one function will shed some light on the other two, but the point remains that each calls for distinct but complementary modes of investigation. Lexical techniques, with their roots in ethnoscience, are best suited, I think, for the investigation of representational functions.

The pioneering studies by White (1980), Gerber (1976), and Lutz (1982b) indicate that lexical and cognitive techniques can yield interesting and provocative descriptions of culturally structured representations of emotions, personal traits, and other elements of folk psychology. It could even be argued that such investigations should be done prior to any other, since a clear notion of the contents and boundaries of a system of meaning is required to investigate its evocative and directive functions. I think, however, that it will be more fruitful in the long run to investigate all three simultaneously to allow for feedback among findings. Furthermore, while

it is an advantage to have available an agreed upon set of relatively sophisticated methods to investigate the cognitive aspect of folk psychologies, we
should not, therefore, refrain from studying the other two functions simply
because we lack similarly elegant techniques. After all, the evocative and
directional functions are what make folk psychologies important in people's
lives. It would be a serious mistake to leave them unexamined just because
we do not have a well worked out set of methods for getting at them. The
question then arises: How can these two functions best be studied? In this
chapter I attempt to illustrate the utility of two complementary approaches
(briefly, empathy and the case study) to the task of studying these two
closely related functions. While either of these approaches can be expected
to illuminate both functions (and the representational as well), the first
(empathy) seems more appropriate to an investigation of the evocative
function while the second (case study) is most useful in getting at the
directiveness of folk psychology.

THE USES OF EMPATHY

It is no small irony that while we possess a variety of techniques for getting
at how people think about feelings, we currently lack any agreed upon way
of describing either how people *feel* about thinking and any of the other
elements of their folk psychology, or how they use those elements to
organize their emotional life. Yet, as ethnographers, we are heirs to a long
tradition of fieldwork in which the ability to comprehend (intuit may be a
better word) the emotional life of people is virtually taken for granted. I
am referring here to the notion of "empathy" which is widely regarded as
a prerequisite for successful participant observation.[4] Whatever else is meant
by this very slippery term, it always connotes an identification between
ethnographer and "native." This identification is built on past learnings at
the same time that it is used to develop further learnings. And most if not
all of these learnings have to do with feelings. Perhaps, therefore, a concentration of the emotional and affective substrata of the sustained dialogue
between ethnographer and informant can be made to yield otherwise inac-
cessible data on the evocative functions of folk psychologies. An example
from my fieldwork will serve to illustrate this point.

One of the central features of Tobian folk psychology is the use of
"ghost" as a powerful metaphor for people who demonstrate a lack of
concern for important social norms.[5] In a later section of this chapter I
present an analysis of this metaphor. My understanding of ghosts arises
from a number of sources, mostly conversations and actual ghost sightings
to which I was a party. One imporant element in my understanding grew

out of precisely the kind of interaction I referred to above—one in which empathy played a crucial role.

Very early in my first visit to Tobi I was incorporated into a large and complex family whose de facto head is a sensitive and intelligent elderly woman. This woman, who called me "son" and whom I called "mother," has been my main avenue into the world of Tobian women, and it is to her that I owe most of the insights into that world I have managed to achieve. It is also to her (or rather to our relationship) that I owe an important insight into the evocative function of the ghost metaphor, and how it might be undergoing a process of modification.

During my first stay on the island it was a matter of great pleasure to this woman that her favorite adopted son and I had become fast friends, fishing together to provide food for the household, making copra together, and, in general, spending much time with each other. She was especially pleased when her son and I began referring to each other as "brother." After I left the island, my "brother" died under very tragic circumstances. When I returned, my relationship with his adopted mother deepened and grew as a result of our mutual grief. During this time she engaged in a practice that her fellow islanders found unusual and disturbing, as did I until she finally "explained" it to me.

Every once in a while she would withdraw to the outskirts of the village. There she would sit for an hour or more with the black cloth of mourning over her head. Such behavior was not at all customary and it gave rise to much speculation and gossip. As the months passed she slowly let slip to me that during these occasions she was visited by her son's spirit, who was prevented from leaving for heaven because of his outstanding commercial debts. She told no one else this, largely, I think, because she did not want to gain the reputation of one who trafficked with ghosts. Out of the complexity of our relationship slowly emerged the joint understanding that for both of us I was in many ways the symbolic equivalent of her (almost) departed son, and that the debts that were tying him to us were not all monetary, nor were they all ones that he owed—some were owed to him.[6] Most impressive of all was the way in which she built on and transformed cultural understandings of ghosts to shape and structure her profound mourning. These insights, which taught me much about the connections between people and ghosts, especially one way of feeling about them and of using them to organize feelings, only became available to me because the relationship between my "mother" and I had developed a subtlety of communication unavailable in a mere subject-investigator relationship.

The most revealing interaction occurred one evening as she passed me on her way back to her house after having once more engaged in that curious behavior. I greeted her, as is customary on Tobi, with a stereotypic inquiry: "Mother, where are you coming from?" Instead of giving the formulaic reply called for by that question ("I am coming from over there"), she gave me a long, steady look and said, "You know, his money to the company is not yet finished." "Oh . . . I see," I replied.[7] And she walked on by.

There is nothing particularly mysterious about my immediate under-standing that she was in communication with her son's spirit. It arose from my (inevitably only partially successful) socialization into Tobian culture combined with our personal involvement with each other as well as my understandings of the mourning process both in America and on Tobi. These factors allowed the look she gave me to convey as least as much as her spoken words. That moment of insight sprang from and added to emotional as well as cognitive understandings. It was confirmed and amplified in the months that followed on both of those levels in equally indirect ways. That is, the spoken and semi-spoken but mostly nonverbal conversation that occurred during that brief interchange was characteristic of much that had transpired between us in the past and continued until I left the island.[8]

As an ethnographer, it would have been helpful if I could have directly explored these matters with her. If I could have explicitly confirmed or diconfirmed my understandings as they developed I would be much more confident today that they are accurate and complete. It would have been especially useful to formally "interview" her about the nature of the debts my "brother" owed as well as the nature of the debts owed to him. It was equally important to determine the exact shape of her communication with his spirit. Yet I never openly asked her about these matters. I do not think I was being overly delicate here; it was simply that I was very sure that if I did confront her directly she would be hurt and would withdraw. She is a very devout adherent of the Tobian version of Roman Catholicism, and her orthodoxy made her interaction with a dead man a matter of embarrass-ment and secrecy. She chose to leave much of our communication unspoken and I was forced to respect her wishes or lose the trust that had led her to reveal what was going on in the first place.[9] As with any of the methods used in anthropological fieldwork, a reliance on empathy has its drawbacks. In my opinion, its ability to generate important and otherwise unavailable insights into such things as the evocative dimension of folk psychology more than offset its weaknesses.

One is not forced to leave empathy as a methodologically primitive technique. Although it is not my intent here to offer a full-scale justification for its use, grounded in developed theory, I do want to indicate two schools of thought that can both rather easily serve to make of empathy a theoretically based method for the study of the evocative functions of folk psychology. I am referring here to the Freudian tradition on the one hand and hermeneutics on the other.

Both LeVine (1973) and Devereux (1978) convincingly argue that Freudian clinical techniques are uniquely suited (with some modifications) for use in ethnographic research. Indeed, LeVine's description of the method by which the psychoanalyst proceeds—continually presenting the analysand with tentative interpretations of his or her behavior, the response to which becomes the basis for further interpretations—well describes an important feature of my long-term relationship with my Tobian "mother." This technique also answers D'Andrade's (1984) call for the use of "small experiments" in the study of meaning systems—the Freudian process of continual interpretation and reinterpretation is, in essence, a process of continual hypothesis construction and testing.

Of course the Freudian justification for this technique is not available to ethnopsychologists who adopt a more cautious position vis-à-vis assumptions about internal psychic organization than do psychoanalytically oriented investigators. For a Freudian, the clinical technique works (and this is Devereux's point) because the analyst's unconscious *resonates* with that of the analysand. And for that transference-countertransference to occur in a cross-cultural context there must be an essential identity in the psychological processes of the two parties to the interaction. For those researchers who reject this assumption, hermeneutics offers, I think, an alternative foundation for empathy as an important technique in the investigation of folk psychologies.

In a thoughtful review of hermeneutical anthropology, Agar (1980) provides a useful summary of the work of a number of scholars in this field. It is apparent that in its focus on both parts of "the hermeneutic circle"—the investigator and the investigated (or perhaps the explainer and the explained) as well as the relations between them—hermeneutics offers ethnopsychologists a coherent way of grounding empathy in a reasonably developed theoretical structure. Indeed, much of what Rabinow has to say about reflexivity in his hermeneutically oriented *Reflections on Fieldwork in Morocco* is predicated on the achievement of a powerful mutual empathy with the various people he encountered in North Africa. He defines the hermeneutically crucial process of reflexivity as "a process of intersubjective construction of liminal modes of communication" (1977:153), a phrase that aptly describes what happened between that elderly Tobian woman and me.

Ricoeur's famous epigrammatic definition of hermeneutics as "the comprehension of the self by the detour of the comprehension of the other" (which Rabinow quotes approvingly) is well suited as a motto for research in ethnopsychology. And since, as Rabinow points out, the self referred to is not the "deep" self of Freud, but a "perfecty public" self, "culturally constituted and historically situated . . . which finds itself in a continually changing world of meaning" (1977:5), ethnopsychologists unwilling to accept the assumption of psychic universality which underlies Freudian-based fieldwork, may be able to rely on hermeneutics in their use of empathy to get at the evocative functions of folk psychology.[10] Whatever techniques are chosen, however, the larger point remains: to get at those functions, the investigator needs affect-sensitive methods. And, as I hope the example from my fieldwork demonstrates, we will do well as ethno-psychologists to pay them more attention.

We also need a language and an analytic style that can serve to make those methods, and the characteristic interactions in which they are appro-priate, intelligible. It is here that I think hermeneutics offers, *for our purposes,* clear advantages over a Freudian approach. Ethnopsychology takes the culturally constituted self as its topic and a hermeneutic approach makes that self more available than does the Freudian approach with its elaborate system of postulated internal processes, structures, and functions. Further-more, an empathy-based, hermeneutic approach is well suited to the in-terpretation of cases, which, in turn, is a productive way to investigate the second neglected function of folk psychologies, the directive.[11]

THE CASE STUDY IN FOLK PSYCHOLOGY

Just as with the use of empathy, the case study method rests on the obser-vation that spontaneously occurring statements and behaviors may provide rich insights into folk psychological material, even though contextual pre-cision is difficult to achieve. This is because concepts emerge in a form organized by the people themselves along lines that are meaningful to them.

The most ethnographically productive events are those which involve people in public attempts to generate explicit explanations. Since social explanations are nearly always negotiated, observations of their interactive construction can provide insight into their social and cultural principles of organization. When it is social reality itself—the behavior of individuals and groups—that is being explained, then ideas about what people are like become salient and more accessible. Furthermore, those events which are likely to call for some behavioral response by those doing the explaining are likely to bring into view the directive component of the underlying folk psychological system.

If one views social life as an ongoing stream segmented into meaningful chunks (commonly called "social events") by complex social processes, then the question arises: Which social events should we attend to? For the purposes of ethnopsychological research, especially research into the directive functions of folk psychology, I suggest we study *important* and *enigmatic* social events. By important events I simply mean those events which the people involved regard as nontrivial. They are events that engage people's attention, forcing them to come to grips with what is going on. Such events, which, by definition, people find difficult to ignore, are likely to lead to both commentary and action that can teach us much. This is especially true when those events are also enigmatic. By enigmatic events I mean those for which no widely shared indigenous explanations are immediately available. That is, either the culture contains no "prepackaged" widely known explanations of the meaning of such an event, or else competing explanations are available and people have to make choices in constructing their understanding and thus their action. As they negotiate these choices, much interesting cultural material is likely to be made available for study.[12]

The process of negotiating an explanation goes on both during and after an important, enigmatic social event (White 1985). Predictions about behavior very often need to be made during the event so that choices about behavior can be taken: "What is X going to do next? How should I (we, you, they) respond?" After the event, that which has transpired is converted into story and historical narrative: "Here is what happened when X did Y." Such stories often become guidelines for future behavior. Both operations involve people making sense out of people's behavior so that they can act. In the process of coming to a "sensible" explanation, the explainers draw on folk psychological concepts. As such events unfold, anyone interested in understanding what is going on is led to draw on the set of ideas about human behavior which are salient in that society. It is important to note that the ethnographer is no exception. For example, as the reader will learn, during Alfredo's case both the Tobians and I were preoccupied with trying to figure out the meaning of his behavior.

I have found that one of the benefits of attending to such social events is that to do so forces me as an ethnographer to confront behavior in great detail. And for me to understand that behavior, both while it is occurring and after, I must, like my hosts, draw on their ideas about human behavior. That is, since one of the factors that shape behavior is the set of understandings which the actors have about people, a knowledge of those understandings is essential for any kind of fine-grained analysis. At the same time, if the event meets the criteria of being enigmatic and important, it will be a good source of new information about folk psychology. Events of this type, then, are important to the ethnographer in three ways. First, they force him or her to utilize his or her understanding of the psychological concepts held by the actors in order to interpret what is going on. In doing this the ethnographer is led to systematize and make explicit much that may have been learned in other contexts. Second, the episodes themselves are prime sources for new insights into concepts held by the actors. And, third, important and enigmatic events often involve new ways of acting. There-fore, if one is interested in how folk psychologies change over time, such events are likely to prove particularly productive. In thinking about such events in this way one asks two questions: "What does this situation say about how the participants understand people?" and "How does organizing the material in this fashion help make sense out of these events?" Such situations, therefore, become *cases* for analysis.

The case study method has long been regarded as a valuable tool for preserving some of the immediacy and vitality of social life in ethnographic description. Max Gluckman called this the "method of apt illustration" (1961:7–10). However, some scholars, such as Van Velsen (1967), Gluck-man (1965), Turner (1968), and Garfinkel (1967), among others, have for their own separate purposes gone beyond this merely stylistic use of cases. I think ethnopsychologists can as well (Black 1978*a*).

Those scholars who use case material for analytic ends commonly see them as useful for revealing underlying reality. In Garfinkel's words, the case is taken as "pointing to" or "standing on behalf of" some social or cultural structure, pattern, or process of interest to the analyst (1967:116–185). Each of those who have used the case study method for more than illustrative purposes has sought to search out in his cases a reality appro-priate to his own theoretical or ethnographic interests—ritual, conflict, law, and so forth. For ethnopsychologists, interested in networks of assump-tions, beliefs, and attitudes about people, the relevant underlying phenomena pertain to indigenous understandings about persons. That in-terest dictates both the kind of case selected and the use that is made of it.

Two rather stringent conditions have been suggested to govern the case study method in social analysis. These have been put most clearly, perhaps, by Schwartz and Jacobs in their textbook *Qualitative Sociology:* "As long as this method is being used one must make assumptions about the underlying pattern in order to know what to make of the indicators. The assumptions will come from social context and common sense knowl-edge. . . . Second, one must know a great deal about something before he can find and competently interpret indicators of it" (1979:79).[13]

These are both reasonable conditions, and an attempt to deal with them returns us to the observation that the understanding of enigmatic, important cases both draws on and generates ethnopsychological knowledge, which in turn brings us back to hermeneutics. Agar (1980:270–276), for example, has a good deal to say about cases, especially what he calls problem cases and neglected situations. The discussions by Schwartz and Jacobs and by

Agar both hinge on the observation that what is most important to the actors in a situation is often left implicit by them. This may be especially true of folk psychological knowledge (Lutz, chap. 2; Tyler 1978; Hutchins 1980). In order for one to know what is going on, one must have at least the general outlines of this implicit material available. For example, "ghost-liness," a major construct used by the Tobians to make sense of Alfredo's behavior, was never made explicit by them during the case. It guided interpretation and action, both mine and theirs, but it never surfaced directly. It was available to me from previous learning. My comprehension of this aspect of Tobian common sense was amplified during the case, but if I had come into those events a stranger, I would have been much more puzzled by what was going on than I was. To put it another way: while it is true that the kind of case I am interested in is what Frake has called a "query-rich setting" (1981), considerable knowledge of the relevant folk psychology on the part of the investigator is necessary for those queries to be intelligently posed, let alone answered.[14] Clearly, empathy plays a very important role in the acquisition and interpretation of implicit material. I should also point out that my treatment of this particular case does not in any way exhaust its possibilities for developing insights into Tobian folk psychology. Much more could be done with it, but limitations of space prevent me from exploring its full richness. One of my programmatic intentions in this chapter is to demonstrate the utility of the case study method in ethnopsychological research. For tactical reasons I have chosen to make that point by focusing on the roles of the ghost metaphor and gossip in the organization of Tobian understanding and action.

At this point I turn to the full case. To do so without first providing "background" information no doubt violates standard practice in these matters. However, those features of the case's background which are relevant to my interpretation shade so imperceptibly into the analysis that to separate the two would be even more awkward. Perhaps this is inevitable in the use of cases for ethnopsychological research, since the knowledge of persons which the case is supposed to exemplify is the very knowledge upon which people's statements and actions during the case rests. In any event, for now it is enough to know that on the evening before he ran off into the bush, Alfredo had been severely and publicly reprimanded by his girl friend's mother. This was a kind of confrontation that Tobians think can lead to the shamed person acting in a ghostly, frightening fashion.

ALFREDO'S ATTEMPTED SUICIDE

Early on the morning after his scolding, already wounded in his social persona by his girl friend's mother, Alfredo wounded his body by cutting his right arm with his toddy knife. He called together all his children then resident on the island, and kissed each of them good-bye. Then he knelt beside the sick old woman he had been tending during what everyone feared was her final illness. She stood in the "mother" relation to him, and was his closest senior kin (actually, she was his maternal grandmother's sister's daughter).

"Mother, good-bye, I am going ahead of you. I shall be the first to die," he whispered, loud enough for at least some of his children to hear. Comatose and emaciated, she gave no sign that she had heard. Alfredo must have known that the gossip about him was sure to intensify as a result of last night's scolding and that the old woman was too sick to protect him (as a mother is supposed to) by circulating his defense in the gossip network. His social isolation was such that there was no one else he could count on for this service. He had no siblings on the island and no other close adult kin.

I am unable to say whether "I am going ahead of you" refers to an afterlife or merely to the act of dying. It is safe to assume that, as a Roman Catholic, Alfredo was well aware of his church's doctrine about suicide. In any event, since death is a necessary precondition to full ghosthood, this statement can be taken as an indirect reference to ghostliness. (I shall take up the ghost metaphor in a later section.) With rope and adze in hand, and dressed in his finest clothes, Alfredo then headed for the dense bush north of the village. As he left he is reported to have said: "Maybe I will climb to the top of my toddy tree and jump to the ground holding my coconut flower in my hand."

These words seem designed to create a powerful visual image, using symbols that have to do with masculinity and beauty. The production of coconut toddy is strongly evocative of male-linked traits of responsibility and generosity. It is the product of a dangerous twice-daily climb to the top of a coconut tree, and is either given to people whose health is thought to require it (the aged, pregnant, newly born, or ill) or is allowed to ferment into an intoxicating drink to be consumed by drinking parties. Both uses (as a kind of health food or as an excuse for a party) make it a highly valued substance, which reflects credit on its maker. Men covertly compete in its production, and the quality and quantity of a man's toddy is an important component of his social reputation. By calling attention to his standing as one of the premier toddy makers on the island, Alfredo called into play that aspect of his reputation of which he was perhaps most proud.

Flowers, however, are valued by both sexes for their beauty, their sweet smell, and their fragility. The image of Alfredo dressed in his finest clothes, leaping from his toddy tree, holding onto a flower is an idealization of masculine suicide. Whatever his intentions in making this statement, it did arouse a certain amount of sympathy, especially among the adolescents—but not much. For while they relish a skillful manipulation of such romantic and sentimental images, Tobians also seem to me to be a remark-ably tough-minded people who strongly resist acting on the basis of such images. That is, although they can and do appreciate stylistic skill in the construction of what can be called "sweet images" (especially in song), neither their actions nor their understanding of action often grow out of such images. There is a contrast here, I think, with the Ifaluk people who seem more willing to be swayed by such images (Lutz, chap. 2).

Even in this public announcement, the most direct expression of sui-cidal intent which he made, Alfredo left room for others to doubt his intention. By prefacing his declaration with "maybe," he gave those prone to other attributions a peg on which to hang their alternative understand-ings. The ambiguity may also have been intended to give himself room to maneuver. Perhaps this statement can be taken as a threat that if appropriate actions are not taken by (unspecified) others, he would dramatically kill himself, dying tragically like a beautiful flower. Taken together with his farewells to his children and mother and the self-wounding, this statement set the stage for all that followed.

Shortly thereafter, alerted by his terrified children to the fact of his impending death, I went to the magistrate's house. One of the island's few English speakers, this vigorous and forceful man seemed the appropriate person to turn to. I found him sitting over his food, unaware of the news. Near him sat is wife, and, as I told them what I had just learned, I heard her say, referring to Alfredo, "*Yar idea ichou*" ('That's just his idea'). This was the first formulation of one of the two competing interpretations of Alfredo's behavior which were to surface as people tried to come to grips with what was going on. The magistrate's wife's interpretation hinged on the Tobian category 'idea', which can best be glossed as "scheme." *Idea* is a loanword from English which all Tobian speakers now use in this sense. The *idea*-based interpretation is, in certain respects, the mirror image of the other interpretation, which hinged on the ghost metaphor. It implies that Alfredo was somehow *using* for his own selfish ends the beliefs that led people to respond to his behavior as though it was a genuine suicide attempt. Readers familiar with the ethnopsychological literature from Micronesia will recognize elements of the Trukese concept of "strong thought" in the Tobian concept "idea" (Caughey 1977, 1980).

The magistrate responded by asking, "What can we do?" With this statement he summed up the dilemma in which people found themselves. Until they figured out what Alfredo was doing, they could not decide how to act. The use of the pronoun "we" indicates that collective action is called for. It also (in good Tobian style) broadens the locus of responsibility from the individual to a group. Since he spoke in English he did not have to decide whether to use the inclusive or exclusive 'we', characteristic of his native language. The magistrate's statement also reveals that he was already thinking in terms of some sort of behavioral response. Given that his wife had just suggested that no action was necessary, perhaps the unspoken qualification of his sentence was: "if anything." In any event, he did act. He immediately went to Alfredo's house to speak with his children.

After speaking with Alfredo's children, the magistrate decided to attempt to find Alfredo and prevent his suicide. He and I went to join several small parties consisting of two and three men each which were combing the island for Alfredo. As we left the village he said to me: "I don't have a knife to take with us. . . . We need a knife to cut him down." There was a long pause between these utterances. The magistrate was making an implied reference to Alfredo's dangling corpse, and he was beginning to focus on weapons, although I did not know it at the time. Clearly, at this point he was speaking as though the suicide attempt might be genuine.

As we picked our way through the brush he showed me the wooden coconut husking stake he was carrying. It was about thirty inches long and two inches in diameter and sharpened at both ends. "I have the husking stick," he said in Tobian, "and I will use it to hit his arm if he attacks us with his knife." This statement surprised me. The fact that we might be in danger had not occurred to me until he said this. As an American, I was predisposed to think of suicidal people as being so inwardly focused that they posed no danger to anyone but themselves. The magistrate's words point to the second interpretation of Alfredo's behavior, and only make sense when considered in light of the set of unspoken assumptions organized around the ghost metaphor. A few minutes later he said: "Alfredo will throw his adze away." Here, the magistrate was adding to the sweet image constructed by Alfredo in his parting remark.

A man's adze is even more an indication of his masculine identity than his toddy knife. Reflecting its great utility as an all-purpose tool for everything from opening coconuts to building canoes, an adze is a very powerful symbol of masculinity. Long hours are spent sharpening it, and a work-bound Tobian man would no more think of leaving his house without his adze on his shoulder than an American executive would set off without a briefcase (see Csikzentmihalyi and Rochberg-Halton 1981 for a discussion of the relations between possessions and the self).

Many stories that recount a man's death include just the bit of behavior the magistrate was foretelling in this statement. Before a man drops, one of the last things he does, according to these stories, is to throw away his adze. For Tobians it is a powerful metaphor. By adding it to the set of symbols assembled by Alfredo, the magistrate considerably strengthened that sweet image. It is interesting that one of the most frequently told ghost stories relates the encounter between a man and the ghost of his father who had died in the bush. With eerie and mysterious gestures, the ghost led his son to the adze he had thrown away just before he died.

After we began to search, I asked my companion what we should do if we found Alfredo. "If we find him we should apologize [sic] him and tell him about his kids who are big enough now to be ashamed." To understand this statement, it is necessary to understand that in the magistrate's version of English the word "apologize" was equivalent to *parimarau* 'formal, respectful talk'. I did not think that the magistrate wanted us all to tell Alfredo that we were sorry he had been shamed. After all, we weren't the ones who had scolded him. Instead, I assumed he was indicating that an appropriate response (for which we had no precedent) would be for us to begin reenfolding Alfredo into the normal social world. By offering him the stereotyped formalities of respect we would indicate his importance to us and remind him of his place in Tobian society. To remind him of his children, and the shame they would feel if he killed himself, would accomplish the same thing and also engage his pity. Lutz presents a discussion of love/pity on Ifaluk which fits well with the Tobian material (1982*b*; chap. 2). The magistrate was formulating an approach that he hoped would bring Alfredo back from his ghostly state. He was hoping, I think, that in this way he could accomplish what either the island's chief or Alfredo's mother could have accomplished by their mere presence. Unfortunately the former was not on the island and the latter was too ill to act. He wanted to bring to Alfredo's attention his relations with his children and with the rest of society, relations in which respect and pity play fundamental roles. The idea that his children would be shamed by his suicide derives from the general notion that close kin can be shamed by each others' actions.

As we pushed our way through the bush in the remotest part of the island, the magistrate said in Tobian: "If I were to kill myself I would go far in the bush to a secret place where no one would find me until I swelled up and became unrecognizable and started to stink." The image he drew here contrasted strongly with the one created by Alfredo. It was typically Tobian that the magistrate should refer to bad smells. Odors, both good and bad, are very important in Tobian culture. They appear very often in stories and songs. The odor of rotting flesh is particularly offensive. There were no flowers and no beauty in this image, only death and decay. Also implied here, I think, was an indirect censure of Alfredo's 'pridefulness' (*tahiyatatep*). After all, he had publicly announced his intention and had managed to mobilize most of the population to stop him. Maybe the magistrate was criticizing him for not being serious. Certainly he implied that suicide is ugly, and that if he were to attempt to kill himself he would do a thorough job of it, not interrupted by anyone. Switching to English, he then made the following statement: "It is bad to threaten suicide. You say you are going to hang your neck and you don't and then someone get mad on you [sic] and you tell him that you are the really brave guy and he says you tried to hang your neck and you didn't and then you become very ashamed and go and hang your neck." This indicated a Tobian way of thinking about fearlessness and shame which I had not previously encountered. It was a statement of a general rule, drawn from understandings about feelings, behavior, and relationships. It indicated that the threat to commit suicide is a kind of holstered gun that can never be drawn except in earnest. The statement linked bravery, shame, aggression, and anger and demonstrated quite clearly why it is frightening to act in a disgraceful manner. If such behavior becomes public, the story can be used as a deadly weapon. This is one reason that interpretations of extraordinary behavior are a matter of interest to everyone, and may be a subject of negotiation and rhetorical maneuver. In the days that followed, the same sentiment was expressed by other people in a variety of ways. For those who held this view, if Alfredo's behavior was an *idea* it was not a very good one, for it left him vulnerable to the very understandings he was manipulating.

Not long after the magistrate referred to his own hypothetical suicide, we heard a whoop off to our right. We hurried toward the sound, not knowing what we would find. We discovered Alfredo sitting high above the ground on the branch of a big hardwood tree. Next to him could be seen his rope, which now had a hangman's noose tied to it.[15] Juan (an older brother of Alfredo's lover) and a couple of other young men were below him looking up. Juan quickly told us the conversation so far. Alfredo had greeted Juan by asking, "Why have you come here?" This was clearly a rhetorical question. Juan told us he had answered by saying, "Don't mind things." The absence of normal greetings in this interchange indicates the gravity and unusual nature of the situation. Juan's statement was quite vague. He simply encouraged Alfredo not to be distressed, leaving the cause of that distress undefined. Alfredo responded by asking, "How come every time two or three people sit together, they talk about me and say bad things?" Alfredo had singled out the gossip about his affair and not his public scolding as the "thing" he "minded." Juan responded with an admonition based on ideas of masculinity and social control. "Only little children mind what people say about them but you [Alfredo] are a man and should not let it stop you."

Shortly after we arrived, and without any further conversation, Alfredo climbed down out of the tree. After a brief, routine greeting he went with the group to the house of one of its members where we were soon joined by several others. Following a short period of casual conversation in which suicide was not mentioned, Alfredo left to join some people at one of the other houses.

The magistrate, Juan, and I moved to another house to talk with a group of old people who had not joined the search. Among them was the chief's wife. As we began recounting the events of the morning, she glanced over at two of Alfredo's young children who were sitting on the outskirts of the group and interjected: "It is bad to talk like this in front of his [Alfredo's] children." To some extent this woman shares in her husband's aura and she was acting as he would have done, calling our attention to the shame we would inflict on Alfredo's children by talking about his behavior.

Undaunted by this injunction the conversation continued. A young woman said: "It's too bad we didn't know where Nania [Alfredo's mistress] was this morning when he sent his son to find her because maybe he was trying to say good-bye." Everyone ignored this statement. I had not previously heard that Alfredo had tried to contact his lover before he set out. Later, after the events had become a known story, this part was always included, perhaps for the same reasons that the young woman brought it up. It directed attention to Alfredo's affair and raised the issue of "romantic love." And, it also made the events a better narrative, lending them dramatic structure. At the time, though, people were too preoccupied by the ongoing events to attend to aesthetics.

The magistrate continued the narrative. When he reached the point at which Alfredo had left us to go to that other house, he quoted him: "I am going to sit with Pedro now." The magistrate spoke these words in a grotesquely high falsetto, accompanied by a hideous grin. I did not take this remarkable exaggeration to be mockery, but rather to be an indication of Alfredo's liminal ghostliness. Next the magistrate turned to some general comments, one of which served to clarify things for me considerably: "I did not take a knife when I went looking for Alfredo. I only took a husking stick because I did not want him to think we had come to fight." In essence, when he said this the magistrate was testing to see if his behavior had been correct. The response "That is the right way to do things" was given by several of the old people (including the chief's wife). It indicated that he had chosen the appropriate behavior.

Suddenly someone from Pedro's house hurried over to tell us that Alfredo had again run off into the bush—knife, rope, and all. Again people (fewer in number this time) set out to search for him. By now I was with the group which had found him the first time and the magistrate had left, to finish his morning chores. As we walked through the bush, expecting at any moment to encounter Alfredo, one of the teenage boys with us said: "I have never seen any one kill himself before. This is my first time. I don't know what I will say to that guy." Despite all the detailed recountings of the morning's events which we had just sat through, and despite his membership in the group which had found Alfredo the first time, this person was still uncomfortable because he did not know how to interact with a ghostly person. Given Tobian understandings about ghostly behavior, he might very well have been frightened.

This time we found Alfredo on the beach. He had come across an empty oil drum that had drifted in overnight (a very unusual happenstance). As we sat down with him we saw that he was making a crude raft by using beach vines to lash driftwood logs around the drum. Again the conversation drifted along without mentioning suicide or any other intimate topic. Instead we talked about the drum and its properties. When his raft was done, Juan told the other young man to help launch it. Alfredo then climbed aboard and with a driftwood paddle began working his way out to sea. As he slowly disappeared around a bend in the beach, the people I was with showed no inclination of going after him. When I asked if they thought that Alfredo was trying to drown himself, Juan answered: "I don't know, and I don't care."

I think Juan's leading role in searching for Alfredo can be attributed to that fact that it was his mother who had done the scolding. No matter what the provocation, she had violated a very important prohibition on direct confrontation. So, if Alfredo attacked someone, Juan's mother would bear part of the responsibility. His participation also conveyed the message that Alfredo was still a valued member of society and that his relations with other Tobians (even the family of his lover) were still relatively intact. Now, however, if Alfredo genuinely meant to kill himself by sailing out to sea (an act reminiscent of pre-Christian burial practices), he was no immediate danger to anyone around him. Out of Alfredo's hearing Juan felt free to express disinterest in his behavior. By this time he and a number of other people were quite disenchanted with Alfredo's antics. Yet later, when it had become dark, it was Juan who tried to follow him. Juan's brief foray into the night was probably the most courageous act of the day: had Alfredo wanted to kill someone, that was his best chance and everyone knew it.

By this point, it was late afternoon. We walked slowly back to the village where we learned that Alfredo had come ashore at one of the houses and was sitting with people there. He remained sitting at that house until about eight o'clock that evening, when he appropriated his son's canoe and, in the growing darkness, paddled out into the channel. By this time many of the searchers were sitting together in a house, singing along with the island's one guitar. When we learned of Alfredo's behavior, only one person, Juan, left to see what was going on. He soon returned, announcing that it was too dark to see anything.

Everyone continued their activities, making no comments on Alfredo's behavior and showing no appearance of concern. Finally, it was learned that Alfredo had sung a song out in the channel and returned. He had then gone to sit with several of the old men who were gathered in the communal copra shed, smoking, telling stories, and singing songs. One of these old men asked him why he was doing what he was doing. He replied that there was too much gossip about him on the island. "Everyone is talking about me," he said, to which one of the old men replied, "Don't mind people talking." Once again gossip and the appropriate reaction of its subject were discussed by Alfredo and those around him. Alfredo was then told about a man long ago who, finding himself the subject of malicious gossip, made up a song attacking his accusers. The old men taught Alfredo that song and he sang it with them.

As the village began to go to sleep Alfredo finally returned home and began to do the chores that, along with his children, awaited him there. Later on the magistrate visited him. People in the vicinity of the house could hear the two of them talking about the ill-fated love affair and the intervention of the girl's mother. The one statement that was overheard was about gossip. Alfredo's complaint was loudly voiced. All the people in the area heard him say, "Whenever two or three people are gathered they talk about me."

After the magistrate left, we all heard a loud crash. Alfredo's eldest son then appeared in the door and announced that his father had cut himself in the stomach; the crash had been the noise of Alfredo's falling to the floor. We all rushed in (some muttering curses). The cut proved very shallow and no more life-threatening than the self-inflicted gash on the arm with which he had begun the day. "The cut is just a little one like the one on his arm because that guy is not brave," Juan said to me as we left Alfredo's house. He was indicating that he did not think Alfredo had ever become fearless enough to really do himself damage. In other words, he had never been shamed into ghostliness. This statement, if generally accepted, would free Juan's mother from any responsibility for either of those two cuts and from anything else Alfredo had done that day. Alfredo's stomach wound, which he cleaned and bandaged himself, was the last bit of "self-destructive" behavior in the sequence. For the next few days he kept himself hidden away, out of sight of most people most of the time.

That evening and the next day there were many intense discussions of these events. These discussions took place privately and never, so far as I know, included Alfredo. Among the more interesting of the statements I heard during this time was the following, made immediately after we had all left Alfredo's house. A teenage girl announced to the dispersing crowd, "Two big branches of Alfredo's mother's [the sick old lady] plumeria tree have fallen." Even though it turned out to be false, this item entered the story of the day's events as a minor feature. If Alfredo had indeed died that day, I am sure that it would have played a much larger role in the story. Plumeria trees are valued for their beautiful sweet-smelling blossoms, from which people make garlands. This is an example of a Tobian pathetic fallacy—drawing as it does a connection between the imminent deaths of Alfredo and his mother and the falling of branches from her special tree. I think the young girl created it on the spot.

This, then, is the account of Alfredo's behavior and the response it generated. My analysis of it begins with a discussion of the ethnographic setting, then moves to a consideration of previous suicide cases, next to relevant aspects of Tobian folk psychology, and finally to Alfredo and the interpretation of his behavior.

ETHNOGRAPHIC BACKGROUND

Tobi is one of the smallest and most isolated of all the inhabited islands of Micronesia. It lies in the extreme southwest corner of the old Trust Territory of the Pacific Islands, 380 miles southwest of Palau.

Tobian society, language, and culture betray close affinities to (and probable historical origins in) the array of low islands which lie between Truk and Yap to the east. Such Carolinian or Trukic atolls as Puluwat, Ifaluk, Woleai, and especially Ulithi share sociocultural systems whose broad outlines are also characteristic of Tobi (Alkire 1977; Black 1977). Politically, Tobi has been incorporated into Palau throughout most of its colonial history, even though Palauan society is markedly different from Tobi in language, social organization, and culture. It is from Koror, the capital of Palau, that the government ship that forms Tobi's main link to the outside world departs three or four times a year. This ship is the only way to get on or off the island. At the time of the case discussed here it was not due for a month or more—Alfredo could not leave and people were on their own in dealing with him. Tobi's economy is still largely a subsistence system, although there is a small but growing cash component. Copra is made, sold to merchants who come down on the field trip ship, and the proceeds are used to buy store goods from those same merchants. However, little if any cash is ever involved in transactions within Tobian society, whose main system of economic distribution involves a generalized reciprocity in which foodstuffs produced by men (mostly from the sea) are exchanged for foodstuffs produced by women (mostly garden grown taro and sweet potatoes). This system, which both reflects and organizes the relations between the sexes, underlies much of Tobian sociocultural organization (Black 1981). Alfredo, as a man with neither wife, sister, nor mother, had no one on whom he could count to provide him with woman's food. His girl friend was too young to have her own garden.

There are at the present time about 120 Tobians, approximately half of whom can be found on Tobi and the rest in Palau. Early in this century there were nearly one thousand people on the island, but a series of epidemics before and during the First World War drastically reduced their numbers (Eilers 1936). This meant Alfredo had no hope of finding someone to replace his wife.

A severe shortage of marriageable women exists on Tobi. It results from a number of factors. The demographic decline has brought the population to a level where random differences in the sex ratio of offspring no longer balance themselves out. Many more boys have been born over the last two generations than girls. Also, men remain in the pool of mate seekers to a much older age than do women. Thus, while widows tend to drop out of the search for a new mate, widowers do not. Finally, the combination of indigenous rules of clan exogamy (there are six exogamous matriclans) and the Catholic rules of incest (since the 1930s the entire population has been devoutly Roman Catholic) narrows down considerably the pool of possible mates for any one person. Thus, the fact that Alfredo had a love affair with a young single girl was a matter of great interest. Although premarital chastity is not seriously expected of anyone, and although the difference in age between the two lovers was neither unusual nor shocking, the affair did stir up substantial opposition.

Given the place of gender relations in the structuring of the Tobian sociocultural system, especially the fundamental importance of being married if one wishes to play an active political role, a proposed marriage is never the concern solely of would-be husbands and wives. Their families, and the families of any other people seeking mates, also have a stake in its outcome. And since one of the things men look for in a wife is sexual fidelity, everyone who was interested in the future marriage of Alfredo's lover was doubly interested in that affair.

Since religious doctrine rules out divorce for Tobians, the affair also angered people because it seemed to them that someone with a wife should not involve himself with a young girl when there were so many other men who could marry her. The public nature of their affair was a slap in the face for all these men and their families.

The other area of Tobian sociocultural organization which entered into the case has to do with political offices and morality. There are no police, judges, lawyers, or jails on Tobi. A traditional chief and an elected magistrate share leadership responsibility and have worked out a very subtle and complex system for dividing this task (Black 1983). The chief, a quasi-sacred figure, has primary responsibility for ensuring public morality, while the magistrate deals with administrative chores. On the day of the attempted suicide, however, the chief was not on the island. He was staying in the Tobi village in Palau and was unavailable. Had he been on the island, I am sure that the task of formulating a public response would have fallen on his shoulders. As it was, the magistrate took the lead (or maybe I thrust it upon him) by default. He had neither the experience nor the standing to bring the episode to a halt by his mere presence, as it is likely the chief would have done. Thus, Alfredo was left to act out his drama without the kind of intervention that the chief could have provided.

PREVIOUS SUICIDES

As Alfredo ran off into the bush that morning, one of the first things that happened was the activation and dissemination of knowledge about previous cases of suicide. For on Tobi, as elsewhere, when enigmatic important events occur people turn to the past for guidance. Stories of similar occurrences are activated and people begin referring to them as they construct their response(s). Therefore, to understand the things people did and said as the attempted suicide unfolded, it is necessary to understand what they knew about previous suicides.

All Tobians share a vast amount of knowledge about past events in their society's history. Much of this knowledge is contained in widely known narratives. There are, in addition, many stories that are not generally known, but are stored away in discrete segments of the social system. Most stories of this type date from the 1930s and are known only to older people. When current events make them salient they are told and retold, becoming part of the general corpus of knowledge and thus available as precedent for behavior. Folk psychological as well as other sociocultural variables clearly play an important role in shaping these remembered events.[16]

At the time that word spread that someone was apparently going to kill himself, two earlier suicide cases were known to everyone (with the possible exception of some of the small children). In addition, two other, much earlier cases were known only to the older people. All four cases were recounted again and again over the next few hours until everyone was familiar with them.

These four cases were all that were available to the Tobians for use as precedent. Each of the two previously undiffused cases involved old men who received an official document—a court summons in one instance and a bill from a store in the other (see also Berndt [1962] who describes suicides in New Guinea resulting from the receipt of official papers). Both cases took place during the Japanese mandate.[17] In one case the old man killed himself by hanging and in the other by drowning. The cases that were widely known happened much more recently. In one a man could not obtain his lover's parents' permission for a marriage, in the other a man feared he was losing his fiancée to a rival.

The first modern story has it that the frustrated young man wanted to commit dual suicide with his lover but that she convinced him otherwise, saying, "If we hang ourselves we will certainly die, but if we try to sail to the Philippines there is a chance we might be able to live. And if we drown that's o.k. too." Although neither of them knew how to navigate, they decided to try this plan. After secretly provisioning his sailing canoe, they slipped away one morning while everyone else was in church. The odds against a successful conclusion of this 400-mile voyage across open sea in a twenty-foot canoe were very high, which is why Tobians talk about it when they are talking about suicide. However, there is a rumor that they actually reached the Philippines, where they now can be found living in Davao City with their twelve children. The other recent case is equally ambiguous, even though there is no doubt that the central actor died by his own hand. He died of poison, consumed during a drinking party. It is possible that he meant the poison for a rival for his lover's hand. It might be that when the rival refused his invitation to the drinking party, he took the poison himself in drunken despair. Another possibility (and the "official" version of his death) is that he drank the poison by accident, unaware of its lethal qualities. Finally, I should note that I witnessed one case that in my mind was a suicide although Tobians never called it that.

A much-loved old man fell ill and died after starving himself. He had depended on his sister to provide him with taro because his wife had an allergic reaction to that very highly regarded staple. If she so much as touched it her hands would break out in a violent rash. Unfortunately for him, his sister fell ill and was unable to continue gardening for him. Rather than turn to rice as a replacement for taro, he simply stopped eating. His wife told no one of this until he died. She gave as the reason for his refusal to eat the fact that he had always eaten taro. That is, he had always been connected to some woman who had productive gardens (a prerequisite for any man who wished to play a full political and social role). He apparently simply refused to accept his demotion to the rank of those men, like Alfredo, who for one reason or another were forced to eat rice because they were not so connected.

Yet no one ever called his death a suicide.[18] Instead, they pointed to it as an example of how unreasonable pride could lead to disastrous consequences. When discussing this death, people commonly referred to several other old men. These men lived alone, but through careful management of their copra production were able to be self-sufficient, purchasing enough rice from the ship to feed themselves. People said that the old man who died was foolish not to have imitated these people, but they did not classify his death as a suicide.

There was very little in Alfredo's case which replicated details from any of these earlier cases. Although the full version of the story of the two lovers contains a description of a search of the island, there was overall very little in those four stories which people could use to directly guide their behavior. Several people found it particularly disturbing that there were no explicit guidelines available on how one should interact with a suicidal person. A number of the statements which I heard had to do with this issue. In one a young man indicated his uncertainty; in another the magistrate tested his theory of how a suicidal person should be approached on some of the island's elders. The lack of detailed precedent is one of the things that rendered Alfredo's suicide attempt enigmatic. It meant that people were forced to extrapolate from their understandings of what people are like in order to decide how to act. However, certain of the more general features of one or more of those earlier episodes were also characteristic of Alfredo's case.

Shame, which entered very deeply into the interpretations of Alfredo's behavior, did emerge as a minor theme in discussions about the two old men from Japanese times. There was some speculation that perhaps they were ashamed to have gotten themselves into trouble with the authorities, ashamed, that is, to have been proven incompetent to deal with new social structures. However, fear of the consequences of the paper they received was given far greater causal weight.

Thwarted love, another crucial component of Alfredo's case, was central to the two more recent cases. Both of these cases were also fundamentally ambiguous; it was just not certain if they were actual suicide cases. This, of course, is also true of Alfredo's attempt. Enough precedent existed so that suicide was a sensible reading to put on his behavior. Yet, in crucial respects that behavior was unique; people found it enigmatic. One reason for this was that it was highly public. He *announced* that he was about to kill himself. All the earlier cases had much more in common with the magistrate's hypothetical suicide—they were secret and hidden away. Indeed, the full story of the double suicide (if it was suicide) tells how the two lovers secretly made provision for their voyage over a period of weeks, only telling a single trusted confidant what they were about. Thus, Alfredo was trying something new that day. Like all innovators, he used preexisting material, perhaps changing it in the process. And some of the most important materials for him that day were folk psychological in nature. Thus, before I can consider Alfredo's behavior further, I need to discuss aspects of Tobian folk psychology.

TOBIAN FOLK PSYCHOLOGY

It is important to note that the following summary of the islanders' beliefs about persons is my model of their representation of their own psychology. This is the usual procedure for an ethnopsychological investigation (see Fajans, chap. 10; Lutz, chap. 2; White, chap. 9). At certain points, however, I augment this with an analysis of Tobian psychology (cf. Gerber, chap. 4). I do this because my understanding of Tobian psychology differs on specific points from the Tobians' understanding of these matters. In other words, since some of the things they believe about themselves seem to me to be inaccurate (although perhaps highly functional), I do not find it possible to grant them perfect insight into their own psychology. For example, as the reader will see, Tobians tend to say that the focus of the fear they think is necessary for social order is an extra-island authority figure; they severely minimize or even deny the fear of gossip as a motive for conformity. I think the actual situation is quite the reverse.

To attribute false self-consciousness to the Tobians is not, of course, to demean them; it is simply to refuse to idealize them as "primitive psychologists." The same critical eye with which we look at the statements of clinicians and academic psychologists should be used to examine folk psychologies for inaccuracies, distortions, and deliberate manipulations. It only remains to be said that, taken as a whole, Tobians do seem to have developed a remarkably hardheaded and astute folk psychology that, on most points, seems quite accurate, if perhaps appearing simplistic and unsystematic to an outsider.[19]

In Tobian folk psychology 'fear' (*metah*), 'shame' (*mah*), and 'anger' (*song*) are often mentioned together. Briefly, people are thought to be 'afraid' of 'shame' and 'anger' both within the self and within others. Shame is said to be feared for its unpleasant connotations of exposure and vulnerability and also because it is thought to have at least the potential of leading to dangerous behavior. Anger is said to be feared because it can lead to actions that are either shame-producing or dangerous or both. Fear and shame seem to be different in that the former is thought to be a permanent feature of a good person (see Lutz, chap. 2, for a similar conception on Ifaluk) while the latter is more situational, episodic, and avoidable.

"Fear is good," I was told, and "shame is bad." By "bad," this person did not mean evil, for shame is thought to be socially necessary. However, it is thought that fear (which is socially necessary) can be overwhelmed by intense shame. In such situations people are thought likely to directly express forbidden rage. Thus, for Tobians, fear, shame, and anger form a "functional cluster," that is, a set of constructs which ethnotheory holds to be closely interrelated on the basis of mutual behavioral implications. This notion is similar to Poole's discussion of the relations between shame and anger among the Bimin-Kuskusmin (chap. 6). In Tobian explanations of situations of deviance and/or conflict, fear, anger, and shame often appear together. As a functional cluster these notions serve to interpret and guide behavior, and thus assume special importance in the analysis of the directive function of Tobian folk psychology.

In her work, analyzing a set of Ifaluk emotion terms, many of which are cognate with Tobian terms (including the three discussed here), Lutz (1982*b*; chap. 2) presents five clusters. These clusters were generated by informants' judgments about semantic similarity. She calls the results of her research a "kind of average cognitive map" of Ifaluk emotion terms (1982*b*:118). The kind of operation the Ifaluk people were asked to perform involved judging which emotions were most similar in meaning. In contrast, the kind of data I am presenting concerns people's understandings of which emotions go together in interpretations of behavioral processes.[20] One important place in which notions of fear, shame, and anger cluster together is in understandings about suicide, a topic I shall return to in a later section of this chapter.

An important point to be made in an analysis of Alfredo's behavior, and the response to it, is that his motives in undertaking that extended, convoluted and finally irksome set of actions are a mystery (for us, as well as for his fellow Tobians). In a number of statements he offered hints about why he was doing what he was doing, but whether or not these statements should be taken at face value is another question. It is also a question that lies at the heart of the disagreement over what he was doing. However, it is not the kind of question often addressed by Tobians.

Ordinarily, Tobians do not hinge their public explanation of actions, problematic or otherwise, on motivations. Even in private conversation people are unlikely to speculate about such matters. They are much more likely to attend to the situation out of which behavior emerges, as well as its outcomes, both for interpersonal relationships and for possible goals of the actor. Therefore, it is difficult to speak of the Tobian attitude toward questions of motivation in any but negative terms. Tobians seem to believe that people are at any time capable of acting in any fashion, no matter how wrong, bad, or socially disvalued [*(e) tab*] it may be. From this it follows that any attention to the precipitating events or proximate causes of such behavior is fruitless, since virtually anything, no matter how small, can serve such a purpose. Instead, Tobian understandings of their own behavior, like many other elements of their folk psychology, are largely organized around their notions of 'anger', 'shame', and 'fear'. These are emotional states that receive the most social attention; and it is their organization, control, and expression that largely structure Tobian folk psychology.

Tobian everyday social life is pleasant in the extreme. People are highly skilled at constructing pleasant and rewarding interactions out of which can come the cooperative behavior on which life on the island, as it is presently constituted, depends. This pleasant tone is the product of strict adherence to the social norm that demands it while prohibiting direct expressions of hostility. It also depends, in this extremely small-scale society, on the intimate knowledge available to each person about the biography and personal attributes (especially those which are best called "foibles") of every other person. The first of these factors (adherence to norms of solidarity) involves the use of something very like "will" as well as various culturally constituted defense mechanisms. The second factor (knowledge of persons) is directly linked to the reservation of characterological assessments for those who move beyond the bounds of socially acceptable behavior. It is important to point out that the gentle and sweet tenor of everyday life which the Tobians value so highly, and which makes their island such an extremely attractive place for the visitor, is (as the Tobians recognize themselves) a cultural artifact, generated at least in part by conscious effort. It requires conscious effort because many of the people with whom a Tobian so pleasantly interacts during the course of his or her day are opponents, and some are even bitter enemies.

There exists on Tobi a large corpus of conflicts and disputes which divides and subdivides the population so finely that ultimately almost every person is opposed to almost everyone else. At the same time, cutting across all these divisions is an equally dense network of alliances which serves ultimately to tie almost every person to almost everyone else. Thus, each person is either directly or indirectly involved in so many crosscutting disputes that almost everyone on the island is simultaneously ally and opponent. These disputes, many of which have already spanned several generations and show no signs of dissipating, are generally organized around disputed resources, typically land, political offices, and marriages. The disputes and divisions are associated with a good deal of interpersonal hostility and other negative feelings, many of which arise from the inevitable frictions of a life lived in constant and inescapable intimacy. These feelings are crucial in Tobian folk psychology, and, in the Tobian view of things, their management is the main issue of social life. A number of mechanisms have been worked out to prevent these negative feelings from disrupting social life (see Black 1983 for a discussion of some of the more important of these). Most of the mechanisms for managing negative emotions are formal strategies of talk and interaction which combine with normative rules, such as those prohibiting public shaming and public confrontation, to produce a pleasant everyday atmosphere. Tobi contrasts markedly with both Hawaii (Ito, chap. 8) and Santa Isabel (White, chap. 9) in that there are no highly elaborated formal procedures such as the *ho'oponopono* of the former or the "disentangling" meetings of the latter for dealing with interpersonal hostility and conflict.[21] Yet the lack of formal procedures does not seem to prevent Tobians from minimizing overt conflict. Notwithstanding the success with which they live up to their ideals of interaction, however, Tobians perceive in themselves and in others a powerful hostility. Associated with this hostility is fear, which is both felt and used by the Tobians to explain why it is that people do not express that hostility directly.

Briefly put, Tobian wisdom has it that only fear keeps people from acting on their hostile impulses. This should not be taken as indicating that Tobians are an especially timid people, for they are not. It is just that they make fear the central element in their explanation of what social science has come to call social control. In this case it means the achievement of conformity to that basic norm of their society which prohibits the direct expression of hostility and which is, as I have said, the obverse of pleasant and cooperative interactions. The jokes, smiles, and mutual cooperation so characteristic of Tobian interactions are directly related to the ban on aggressive behavior. And when people disrupt the smooth, pleasant tone of everyday life, as Alfredo did with his suicide attempt, questions of fear and hostility (never very far removed) come to the fore.

Since it is fear, Tobians say, that prevents them from violating the prohibition on aggression, when someone acts aggressively or is thought to be likely to act aggressively in the near future, the focus of public discussion, and occasional public action, is the re-creation of fear in that person. The assumption seems to be that the reason a person has become fearless (what English speakers call "brave") is quite irrelevant and, given the widespread hostility assumed to exist, quite unknowable. Instead, attention is directed to the social relations endangered by the fearless one and to the task of protecting them from disruption—a task that involves the reimposition of a fear-based self-control.

Tobian common sense has it that the disputes that divide them from one another are inextricably linked one to another. A direct confrontation between two or more people is feared and sharply sanctioned precisely because people think that when such confrontations take place the whole fabric of social life is threatened by an eruption of all the disputes. Furthermore, during such a confrontation someone is likely to be badly shamed. Everyone commands everyone else's biography, and it is during the heat of public confrontation that a person is likely to shout out some extremely damaging bit of information about someone else, thus driving them beyond fear into a kind of liminal state in which anger might be directly, even physically, expressed. The Tobians think of this state as one in which a person has become a ghost.

GHOSTS AND GHOSTLINESS

'Ghosts' (*yarus*) are very important social actors on Tobi. As a cultural construct these malevolent supernatural beings are probably a post-Christian remnant of a much larger class of beings which once included such benevolent supernatural figures as ancestral spirits, lineage and clan ghosts, localized nature spirits, anthropomorphized and spiritually powerful birds, turtles, whales, and sharks, as well as a host of remote creator beings. Variants of such a religious system were widespread within the Western Carolines before the coming of Christianity and I have no doubt that Tobian religion fell well within that pattern.[22]

Since the conversion of the Tobians from their ancestral religion to Roman Catholicism, ghosts have maintained an uneasy coexistence with the Christian pantheon of saints, the Blessed Virgin and the Trinity. Like the humans on the island, they have lost much of their autonomy to powerful aliens. It was pointed out to me more than a few times that "now that we are Christian, the ghosts are not so powerful anymore." Tobians believe (perhaps "hope" is a more accurate verb) that Christian ritual protects their island and their society from the depredations of ghosts.

The impression of their home one gets from Tobians is that of an island infested by potentially highly dangerous evil ghosts. These beings are thought to have corporeal reality (eerie and horrible though it is) and to live in the sea off the reef edge. From there they come up onto the island, mostly at night and mostly to the cemetery. Occasionally they roam the entire length of the island and even can be encountered within the village. Most of them are unnamed and only vaguely defined. However, several of them are thought to be deceased islanders whose personal histories are known to everyone. The appearance of these "familiar" ghosts can be described in some detail. There is one, for example, whose presence is announced by the horrible smell of his decaying flesh. Another can be detected by the glowing tips of the three or more cigarettes that hang down from his mouth, ten feet above the ground (see Black n.d. for an analysis of this ghost). An encounter with either of these two beings, or with any other ghost, is extraordinarily terrifying for a Tobian. Although people are quite vague about the actual harm that may result from such an encounter, there is no doubt that it is one of the most frightening experiences of a lifetime.

I have seen self-confident, skillful people, ordinarily quite fearless in the face of physical dangers, cowering behind barred doors, reduced to a panicked and trembling state by a ghost encounter. And, as word of an encounter spread, I have watched the village transformed from a place of laughter and incessant talk to one of silent fear: an abrupt and dismal pall descends, children are scooped up, and everyone retreats indoors. There they sit transfixed and whispering until the manifestation ends.

The image of the ghost, a bizarre and terrifying figure which threatens anyone it encounters, well describes Alfredo on the day he ran away to the bush. The difference was that he could be dealt with, while ghosts must simply be endured. Also, the threat he represented was very specific, coded as it was in a script about shame and suicide which I shall take up shortly. Those who chose to act did so on the basis of that script, and shaped their interactions with Alfredo accordingly. In doing so, they acted to bring him back from ghostliness, to make him more ordinary.

From an ethnopsychological perspective, Tobian ghost beliefs are quite interesting. In common with many people who live in small, close-knit communities, Tobians label actions much more than they label persons (see, e.g., Shweder and Bourne 1982; Selby 1974). Perhaps because they understand one another well enough to know what complex, contradictory, and situationally dependent people their fellow islanders are, or perhaps for some other reason, Tobians do not talk extensively about "personality" or "character." Some Tobians have the reputation of being more or less intelligent (i.e., skilled at one of the various styles of learning or cognition which Tobians recognize), while others are thought to be perhaps more or less hardworking or good-humored, but the main focus of the folk psychology is on the analysis and labeling of behavior. This gives Tobian discussion of persons a concrete and highly specific character that fits neatly with the disinclination to engage in motivational analysis discussed earlier. Ordinarily, the closest Tobians come to such statements as "He or she is a lazy (stingy, good-natured, etc.) person" is to say that someone's behavioral pattern is 'just his or her way' (*fisirirah*). By this they mean some personal habit or custom or trait or idiosyncracy—in short, what I have called a "foible." For example, one man always insisted on speaking as pure a Tobian language as he could manage. He purged his speech of everything he could identify as a borrowing and even went so far as to coin neologisms for foreign words for which there were no Tobian equivalents. Another man made it his habit to rehearse arguments aloud, alone in the bush. Yet another introduced a great deal of Japanese into his speech and even strode about at what he and others imagined to be a brisk Japanese pace, a pace that contrasted markedly with the ordinary Tobian saunter. People would say about these and other foibles: "that is just his way." These foibles were neither morally evaluated nor taken as a reflection of some deeper, truer inner self. They were simply accepted as interesting attributes of the behavior of certain people. The same formulation was given and the same stance taken toward almost all other enduring behavioral tendencies—what are known in academic psychology as personality traits.

The only Tobian social actors whose reputations rest on beliefs about their essential natures are the supernaturals—the ghosts, the missionary who converted them, God, Jesus Christ, Mary. The ghosts are evil, the rest are good. It is important to note that much less social attention is given to the good supernaturals than to the evil ones. People are familiar (to various degrees) with Roman Catholic dogma, and can, if necessary, explain a good deal of it, including those parts about the beneficence of the Creator and His Son. Yet they do not ordinarily give these beings much attention. Ghosts, however, form an extremely important topic of attention. Of course, ghosts can also be encountered in daily life, while the benevolent supernaturals remain aloof from the island and its people.

Lutz (chap. 2) has noted that in the language of Ifaluk there is a much richer vocabulary for describing negative emotions than there is for describing positive ones. These findings indicate that Tobians are not alone in finding evil more compelling to think about than goodness. I think it is fitting to speculate here that, for the Tobians at any rate, this may be because the negative emotions felt in the self and attributed to others are highly problematic because of the threat they pose to social harmony and to individual survival. It is something in the nature of an existential tragedy for the Tobians that the social cooperation and good humor which are by far the normal state of social relations in their community are seen by them to be threatened by evil. The exigencies of their situation force them to be conscious of, and extremely sensitive toward, what their common sense tells them to be the very real possibility of evil, calamity, and disaster. Here lies the framework for their view of ghosts and 'ghostly' behavior.

Tobian ghosts are symbols of evil. Onto them is loaded the weight of all those features of their situation which people feel threaten them. As a symbolic and cognitive construct, the Tobian concept *yarus* can best be approached as organized along the lines of "prototypes" described by Rosch (1975). At the center of the web of meaning coded by the concept *yarus* are those supernatural, corporeal beings, who are regarded as hostile and ill-intentioned actors, embodying some of the most negative emotions in Tobian folk psychology. In psychodynamic language, then, ghosts represent projections of just those aspects of Tobian affective experience which are most threatening (cf. Spiro 1952).

As we move away from the center we encounter other beings, such as angels, fairies, and dwarfs, who have entered the Tobian religious world from such diverse sources as Catholic sermons and American comic book renditions of European folktales. Unlike the prototypical ghosts, these 'ghosts' are not the subject of intense emotional and intellectual concern. Instead they appear in stories and legends (some borrowed and some invented) as minor characters, able to engage in feats of supernatural ability such as size changing and flight. Finally, as we move out from the core meaning, we reach the point where the use of the term *yarus* becomes more completely a metaphor. As a metaphor it is a member of a small class of related items, all used to negatively label action and, in extreme cases, persons. All the items within this class constitute "moral benchmarks" (following Edelman 1977:29), which are used to establish and measure the degree to which behaviors (and in extreme cases, personhood) fall within socially acceptable boundaries. Ghosts are the most important benchmarks. The use of this metaphor evokes their mindless evil, unconstrained by the moral code that binds ordinary Tobians (just as their physical appearance and powers are unbound by the rules of ordinary existence). Other negative benchmarks include 'person of the jungle' (*manni fariworuwor*), 'Papuan' (*manni Papua*), 'Palauan' (*manni Panou*), and 'person of the remote past' (*manni mosuwe*).[23]

To call someone a 'person of the jungle' is to draw attention to their refusal to take part in communal activities, such as dances and cooperative work. To call someone a Papuan is to invoke Tobian conceptions of the cannibalistic habits and magical powers of the people who live in Papua New Guinea and its offshore islands, with whom the Tobians apparently have had some minimal contact over the years. A person who is said to be acting like a Papuan is usually someone whose behavior indicates incomplete socialization. On the few occasions when I witnessed violence (drunken and ineffectual as it was), the person engaging in it was uniformly said to be acting "like a Papuan." In addition to the prohibition on violence, stinginess and hoarding are also strongly condemned and their appearance avoided. A slanderous accusation of such behavior can be made by saying that someone is acting like a Palauan. Such an accusation builds on the notion of Palauans as a money-hungry and stingy people. Finally there is the phrase 'person of the remote past'. This is used if someone demonstrates less than complete competence in any of the new, borrowed social or technological processes that make Tobian culture a neo-Micronesian way of life rather than a completely traditional mode of existence.

These terms form a corpus of derogatory comments which can be made about someone's behavior. They are only rarely, if ever, used in face-to-face encounters, but they do appear in third party discussions (gossip) with some frequency. I need to restate here that it is not the case that these are used as fixed and enduring labels for what are seen to be personality traits. Rather, they are used to characterize particular behaviors: stingy, violent, antisocial, or ignorant, as the case may be. Even when they are used to refer to the person instead of to his or her behavior (as in "He is a Papuan," rather than "He is acting like a Papuan"), this is only a kind of shorthand for the longer form and must be understood as such. Only such an understanding can encompass the fact that a person referred to as a Papuan, or Palauan, or man of the jungle on one day, will be called something quite different on the next. Such examples are easy to find because the use of such terms is a mechanism of social control, and as a person learns that his behavior has been so criticized, he or she will act to rectify it, thus eliciting another and more positive evaluation from his or her audience (which in most cases is the entire population of the island).

The most profound of all such metaphors is that of the ghost. It may represent all the negative traits encoded in the others as well as several that are not. To apply it to someone implies that they have put themselves outside the ordinary moral system that makes life not only possible but orderly and meaningful as well. And in a vague and ill-defined way, it is more than a metaphor, for there comes a point when a person can be said to be a ghost in more than just a metaphorical sense. This occurs when, under the pressure of intense shame or for some other reason, a person is thought to have become fearless enough to be capable of violating any of the fundamental norms that structure and give meaning to life. They are then said to have become a ghost. This is a statement about the inner nature of such a person, and it is a statement that that inner nature is evil, danger-ous, powerful, and malignant. The public scolding given to Alfredo was precisely the kind of event which in many a story of past disasters led "human ghosts" (the term is mine) to become so fearless that they were a threat to everyone. And it was for that reason—the fear that Alfredo had become a ghost—that people acted to intervene in his suicide. Those who did not so act, but kept themselves aloof from the drama, did so not because they rejected that set of ideas about shame, fear, rage, and ghostliness but because they did not think Alfredo had really entered that state: they did not think of him as a ghost. However, this latter group of people had no equivalent metaphor to use in formulating their opinion.

Following Fajans (chap. 10) and Kirkpatrick (chap. 3), and using a linguistic model, we can say that ordinary behavior is unmarked in Tobian culture. The fearful, moral, cooperative, sharing (in short, 'good') behavior that is expected of everyone, and achieved most of the time, is not generally marked off from other kinds of behavior by a linguistic coding. Instead it is bounded and defined largely through contrast with the negative traits that are coded in the terms and metaphors standing for negative behaviors.

No one was of the opinion that Alfredo's actions were ordinary and usual ways of behaving. Those who rejected ghostliness as an explanation or at least a description for what was going on turned to the other major way of describing extraordinary, unusual, and cryptic behavior. They at-tributed it to what Tobians call an "idea." The cultural construct "idea" or 'scheme' plays an important role in Tobian understanding of behavior and social life. This English-derived word is used to describe what might be better called 'plans' or 'schemes'. The Tobian notion "idea" is used by one and all to describe the way people can go about achieving desired ends. I shall leave the interpretation of Alfredo's suicide attempt as *idea* behavior unexamined except to note that the major differences between it and the 'ghost' interpretation involved the degree of self-control which each attributed to Alfredo as well as the degree of goal directedness in his behavior.

Certain behaviors and statements that occurred during the suicide attempt made it evident that the ghost metaphor served a directive function in the interpretation of Alfredo's behavior. The implied use of the ghost metaphor drew on a number of clues in his actions and words for its formulation in this case. There were several initial features of the case which made the fear, shame, anger cluster salient for interpretation and brought the ghost metaphor into play. In the discussion after the episode, the magistrate at one point said: "When he [Alfredo] was scolded by Nania's mother he was really ashamed." This was just the kind of confrontation around which many stories of previous ghostly behavior are organized. Then there was that self-inflicted cut in the arm.

Self-mutilation, or indeed the intentional wounding of anyone, self or not, never occurs on Tobi. They have given up their ancient customs of tattooing and ear piercing, which were the sole previous contexts in which the cutting of the skin's surface was acceptable. Today, except for the occasional medicinal injection, people simply do not do such things. There is a very strict prohibition on using a sharp instrument in fighting. Spears, knives, axes, and adzes are all supposed to be reversed if they are used in either attack or defense. In the one such incident I witnessed, this did indeed happen. Therefore, when Alfredo turned his knife on himself he was acting in a highly unusual fashion. It was frightening because, given the beliefs about shame, no one knew if he would turn his knife on someone else.

The fact that Alfredo wore his finest clothes also lent credence to the ghost interpretation. They were the clothes he wore on Sundays to the regular church services. Such clothes are never worn during "regular time" and they could be taken as evidence that he had gone into a liminal, ghostly state. Finally, there was Alfredo's farewell to his children.

That evening one of the men who had been most active in the day's searches said to me: "I never believed Alfredo was fearless enough to kill himself, but after his son told me that this was the first time his father had called all his children together, told them good-bye and kissed them, I thought there might be a chance." Apparently this person thought that only a truly ghostly person would do such a thing. Farewells from dying persons to their close kin are an important cultural pattern on Tobi, for it is during these last moments that people dispose of their property. People speak of these times as extremely painful occasions and the speaker seemed to be saying that only someone so shamed as to be beyond either fear or pity would inflict such pain on his children. Those who held to the notion that he was simply engaged in some devious scheme thought that the farewell to his children was an extraordinarily callous act. At any rate, the scolding, the self-wounding, the fine clothes, and farewell were, taken together, enough to force at least some people to act as though they thought he was suicidal. That is, they acted as though they thought he had been so badly shamed he was no longer afraid and had become fearless enough to do any ghostly act. This meant they had to act. They were led to certain actions by the directive force of that element of their folk psychology which I have labeled the ghost metaphor. The next question is, in what ways were their actions shaped by that metaphor?

An examination of statements and actions that occurred during the searches for Alfredo indicates that the dread possibility of violence was never far from the searchers' minds. The magistrate's comment about using his husking stick to defend us is a direct expression of this fear. Later on he checked his reaction with the local experts—the old people. They agreed that, since a person in Alfredo's ghostly state is potentially very dangerous, one should approach him in a nonthreatening manner but prepared for self-defense. Thus, the magistrate carried no knife (even though one might be needed for cutting down the suicide), but instead carried a husking stick. Like the magistrate, all the searchers were caught in the frightening position of having to act—one cannot simply let a ghostly person run about in the bush, for you never know when he might spring out and attack. The beliefs about shame ensured that it could not be assumed that Alfredo would either kill himself or calm down. Instead he had to be brought out of that liminal, fearless ghostly state to which intense shame had driven him. To do that he was reminded of his position within society as a father with numerous dependents. It seems that for Tobians, as for the people of New Caledonia described by Leenhardt (1979), one's ordinary personhood is embedded within a set of relations with important others, and the recalling of an individual from liminal otherness (on Tobi, 'ghostliness') back to ordinary personhood is accomplished by making those relations explicit. Specifically, he was reminded that his suicide would cause his children shame. Thus, even though he may have reached his limit of excessive shame, his children (with whom he was assumed to share a sense of personhood) had not. Alfredo was also encouraged to feel that his relations with other people in his society, even the family of his lover, were still intact. Finally, he was reminded a number of times that gossip is not something which bothers people, especially men. Every time he "explained" himself after that initial dramatic flight into the bush, he talked about gossip, and each time he did he was told to ignore it. This is an interesting point and brings us to what I think is one of the major weaknesses in Tobian folk psychology.

GOSSIP AND FEAR

Culturally received wisdom has it that gossip (*hamangungu*: lit., whispering) is of no importance to adults; it is not something to be concerned about and certainly nothing to be afraid of. In this it contrasts strongly with public shaming. The hidden talk of people with nothing better to do than to comment on other people's behavior should simply be ignored. This holds especially true for men. Their stance as autonomous, responsible people, strong and independent, requires them to claim that gossip is of no importance to them. In my view (and Alfredo's case is one of the things that has led me to take it) that claim involves a certain amount of denial.

Tobians assert that fear is important in keeping people from engaging in prohibited behaviors. When asked what it is that people are afraid of, they mention extra-island authority figures with the power to punish them. They talk about Palauan policemen, the American and Palauan priests, and the Palauan district administrator. They also mention the long-dead missionary who converted them and who they believe will be their judge after death. However, the odds against any of these mortals actually intervening in Tobian affairs are very slim. In fact, a highly efficient set of mechanisms has been worked out to prevent even those who are most intimately involved in Tobian affairs (the priests) from learning that which people do not want them to know. So the threat that these authority figures pose to anyone violating norms is not very great, and the fear of their punishment is quite unrealistic. As far as I can judge, though, for some people at least it is quite real. I once saw an elderly woman hiding in the bush on ship day while a bored-looking Palauan policeman fruitlessly investigated a complaint, which she had made in anger and then been unable to retract, that someone had stolen her cooking pot. She was hiding because she was terrified that she would actually have to speak to this awesome personage. She was genuinely afraid, I think, but the reality of the situation was that she did not have any "objective" reason to fear that external figure of authority.

Fear is a complex issue in Tobian psychology, both in the islanders' understandings of themselves and in my understanding of them. A list of that which the Tobians regard as reasonable to fear would include extra-island authority figures, ghosts, anger (both in one's self and in others), and shame. There are interesting connections between the items on this list. When shame becomes too intense it can lead people to directly express their anger. Such people are then said to be acting like ghosts. Ghosts, in turn, straddle the boundary between extra-island authority figures and sources of fear which are endogenous to the island. They are of the island and not of it at the same time.

For a Tobian, it is both reasonable and moral to fear all these things. Gossip, however, is regarded as trivial. The ethos demands this. Yet, regardless of this stance, I do not think it can be denied that gossip is, in fact, one of the major loci of fear. It is for this reason that it can play such an important role in social conformity.

"How come every time two or three people sit together, they talk about me and say bad things?" Alfredo's plaintive question points toward the pain that a person feels when his reputation is continually being degraded by gossip. It is not difficult to understand why, in such a tightly bound society, gossip should be feared. After all, "whispering" is, in effect, the continual monitoring and reappraisal of persons. And, in a society like Tobi, in which so much of the self is located in relationships, negative gossip may be especially threatening.[24]

"Only little children mind what people say about them, but you are a man and should not let it stop you." When Juan responded to Alfredo's complaint with this admonition he was giving expression to an important component of the island's ethos. Gossip, in this view of things, is not an appropriate subject of adult fear. It should simply be ignored; one should refuse to allow oneself to be bothered by it. Yet Alfredo continued to mention gossip throughout the day. Even after the old men in the copra house taught him an appropriate response to gossip, he returned to it again while speaking with the magistrate.

By continually indicating that it was gossip which had driven him to act in such a bizarre and potentially self-destructive way, Alfredo was doing two things. He was pointing to a fact of life which other adults preferred to ignore, and he was ignoring what many assumed to be the "real" reason for this behavior. That is, by addressing himself to gossip whenever he was questioned about what was going on, he chose not to talk about his public scolding. This is important because the public scolding fit much better into Tobian ideas about suicide than did gossip.

SUICIDE AND TOBIAN FOLK PSYCHOLOGY

Suicide has proven to be one of the most interesting yet recalcitrant issues confronting social analysis, and one particularly relevant to contemporary Micronesia (Rubinstein 1983). One approach after another has cut (and sometimes broken) its teeth on this topic, beginning in the modern era with Durkheim's (1950) classic study and continuing right up through recent work in ethnomethodology and sociobiology.[25] What, then, can ethnopsychology bring to the study of suicide? Conversely, what benefits can the study of suicide offer ethnopsychology?

The outlines of answers to these questions emerge from the realization that in a suicide the actor acts upon his or her person in a particularly direct and often brutal fashion. Since the person acted upon is at least in part a cultural construct, the indigenous understanding of the person which is at the center of the local folk psychology must play an important role in the suicide. Ethnopsychological investigations can help to define (more precisely than other orientations perhaps) just what is being destroyed (or at least transformed) in an act of self-destruction. And by focusing on suicide, an act in which concepts of the person are inevitably highly salient, the ethnopsychologist is focusing on an act that necessarily involves crucial components of folk psychology. If dreams are the royal road to the unconscious, then suicide is a high road to folk psychology. Turning now to Tobian understandings about suicide, let us see how they help to make sense of the case.

Tobian understandings about suicide form a kind of social "script" (similar to, but much more complicated than, those described by Schank and Abelson 1977).[26] In this script, the fear, anger, shame cluster is linked to violence, withdrawal, and suicide. The episodic structure of these understandings has an important influence on how Tobians interpret and react to disorder and deviance, including Alfredo's suicide attempt.

Tobians say that it is vitally important to avoid any confrontation in which one or more persons will be badly shamed. Were this to happen, the shamed person would be likely to act in a ghostly fashion. He or she might (1) withdraw from the village and live in the bush, (2) take up a knife and run through the village killing everyone in the way, or (3) commit suicide. Any one of these outcomes—withdrawal, murder, or suicide—would be a social disaster.

The Tobian demographic situation is so extreme that the subtraction of the labor of any of the adults (a category that already includes people who in more populous times would be classified as either too young or too old to be productive) would make life very difficult, if not impossible, for the remainder. Therefore, even the most benign of the three outcomes, flight to the bush, could be a death blow to Tobian society. And since everyone knows that in the past badly shamed people have not simply retreated to the bush but instead have gone to Palau with their families, where they take no more part in Tobian affairs, the threat of losing a relatively large number of people is, perhaps, what is really meant when people talk about flight to the bush. There is more to it than that, however, for the bush is where ghosts are encountered.

The commonsense understanding that an intensely shamed individual might go on a rampage, stabbing whomever they come in contact with, is also related to the ghost metaphor. Like withdrawal, it is based, to some extent at least, on experience. In the early 1960s a man stabbed and killed the man who had refused to allow him to marry his daughter. The narrative of this event tells of an afternoon of terror when the killer stalked back and forth through the village, screaming curses and threats until he was finally talked into giving up the toddy knife with which he had done the killing. He was kept isolated from the rest of the population until the next field trip. He was then taken to Palau by the policeman on that ship, tried, convicted, and sentenced to Palau's rather relaxed jail, from which he was recently released. In addition to the searing memory of the horror of that afternoon, this killing also left an important imprint on daily life. It eliminated two of the most productive and cooperative adult men from the Tobian social system. And, although there is no way to be sure about this, a number of other case narratives indicate that people have been even more careful not to publicly shame one another since that incident.

Finally, there is the third alternative to intense shame: suicide. It seems clear that Alfredo's behavior was viewed by the Tobians, *and must be viewed by us,* as being importantly related to shame, and thus to the social script described above. This is because on the prior evening Alfredo had been publicly and severely scolded by his lover's mother. She had berated him in front of a large number of people and had forbidden her daughter to see him again.

"I am the mother of that girl and you cannot treat her like a chicken or a pig that just belongs to you. I am her mother. Why do you act this way?" This statement was widely seen as the precipitating event that led to Alfredo's disturbing behavior. He was publicly accused by a respected older woman of violating the fundamental norm that demands that people respect one another's personhood. Such respect is not required for such stereotyped nonhumans as chickens and pigs. By referring to them, she was drawing on the distinction between nature and society which structures Tobian (and perhaps all) culture. (See Seeger 1981 for a clear statement of why it makes sense to conceptualize the contrast as between nature and society rather than the more commonly used nature/culture opposition.)

A very important dimension of personhood on Tobi is the place of the individual in the network of hierarchical, dyadic, and interconnected social relations which I call the "in-charge complex" (Black 1982).[27] The girl's mother accused Alfredo of acting in a very antisocial fashion by treating his lover as though she was not embedded in this system, of acting as though the mother-daughter tie was of no importance. In fact, the phrase "that just belongs to you" could also be translated as "your ward and yours alone." Such an interpretation stresses the insult to the mother whose relation with the girl he has ignored. To publicly accuse someone of acting in this fashion, to call everyone's attention to this insult, is to do a number of things. It places the dispute within the public arena—a major escalation. It accuses Alfredo of social incompetence or worse—bringing into play the whole shame, anger, fear cluster. And of course it insults him, wounding his personhood by pointing out a flaw in his social persona. It should be noted that prior to this confrontation everyone knew of the affair, but this was the first time it had entered public discourse.

Each of the two competing interpretations of Alfredo's actions drew on the shame script. Those who 'believed' him and accepted the suicide attempt as genuine, felt they had to act even though they were badly frightened. This was because (a) they did not want him to die, and (b) they were convinced that he had become a 'ghost'. That is, they believed that under the impetus of the intense shame of having been publicly scolded he had become so fearless that suicide was only one of his alternatives, the others being withdrawal or lethal violence. The others, those who did not 'believe' him, assumed that he was trying to achieve selfish ends by manipulating society through the use of the beliefs about shame, anger, and fear coded in that bit of conventional wisdom which holds that an intensely shamed person will act in a ghostly fashion.

Part of the reason for the inability to reach consensus about what was going on and thus on how to act arose from widespread previous knowledge about Alfredo. There are two important points to make here. First, Alfredo had been known to act in a rather erratic fashion at times. Given to fainting and known to be quite excitable, he was also one of the island's most frequent ghost sighters. Very significantly for Tobians, he had rather strange eating habits. Second, he had also been known to attempt a leading role in almost every exciting event that occurred. No matter what the occasion—a marital argument, a turtle chase, the sighting of a ship, the approach of a bad storm, a public meeting—one could count on Alfredo not only to be there but to be highly visible as well. The self which Alfredo tried to establish was one of a competent, powerful adult man. He tried too hard, I think, and the Alfredo who emerged in the gossip about him even before his affair was a bit of a fool. Therefore, on that morning in 1972, when word spread that he had cut himself, kissed his children good-bye, and run off into the bush, it was easy for some of his fellows to denigrate the whole thing as "just his (rather foolish) scheme."

If it had not been Alfredo, but someone without his history of erratic and foolish behavior, I do not think people would have been so ready to discount the seriousness of the situation and there would have been much more unanimity about what was going on. Yet knowledge of Alfredo's past was not the only, or even the major, reason for the confused social reaction to Alfredo's behavior. More important by far was the fact that in certain crucial respects Alfredo was acting in a new way. I think it fair to speculate that this was a major element in the calculations of those people who decided that he had not become "brave enough" to kill himself.

In the discussion so far I have refrained from imposing my interpretation of Alfredo's behavior on the case. This chapter has now reached the point at which this is necessary in order to understand his behavior as an attempt at cultural innovation.

THE MEANING OF ALFREDO'S BEHAVIOR

The method I have adopted here (the search for directive functions of folk psychology through an empathy-based case analysis) has led to a more thorough understanding of the relations between Tobian knowledge of persons and Tobian action. This, in turn, has forced me to attend to the ways in which Alfredo's behavior was unique. By focusing on the directive functions of Tobian folk psychology as revealed in that enigmatic and important series of events which was Alfredo's case, I (like the Tobians) was led to a consideration of both previous suicide cases and the shame script. And it is in the ways in which Alfredo's behavior differed from both of these that we can see, I think, a new way of suicide (or at least suicide attempt) and, perhaps, a new way of thinking about ghosts.

I believe that (whether he consciously intended it or not) Alfredo was offering a new script to his society. When compared to the shame script, it is a script that has to do with gossip rather than shame, love rather than anger, and the reintegration of the person into society rather than personal destruction. As I have already demonstrated, gossip is a fact of social life rather inadequately dealt with in Tobian folk psychology. Alfredo brought this inadequacy to everyone's attention. The two most recent suicides in the corpus of culturally coded cases both revolved around thwarted love relationships. Alfredo expanded on that precedent. And instead of privately doing away with himself, as was true of all previous suicides, he acted in such a public fashion that he coerced the entire community into thinking about him and his problems, and a significant proportion of that community into spending the entire day revalidating his worth, bringing him back from ghostliness.

Like all cultural innovators, Alfredo drew upon preexisting ideas and understandings to construct his new behavior. The shame script, with its highly directive functions, and the two most recent suicides, especially the flight of the two lovers, were probably most important here. His attempt to create a sweet image and his two abortive trips out to sea make most sense when seen in the light of those two "romantic" cases. At least some of his fellow Tobians responded in kind. The two young women who talked about his attempt to bid his lover farewell and the falling branches of his mother's tree seemed caught up in this way of construing his behavior.

The shame script enabled Alfredo to mobilize people. They were afraid he had become ghostly; they needed to retrieve him from that dread condition. His failure to act out that script led to a steady decline in the intensity of the social response. People became convinced that he was not "brave" enough, that he was still under the influence of socially necessary fear. But by continuing to behave in a bizarre fashion, Alfredo acted to demonstrate that something other than shame was at issue. Romantic love was one of the things he addressed in his behavior, alienation was another.

Alfredo's lack of an effective senior relative to defend his reputation in the gossip network, his separation from his wife, and his lack of siblings all left him exposed and alone. It is true that he was the father of numerous children, but his relations with them were insufficient to firmly integrate him into society. This is rather poignantly illustrated in the episode of the case in which the chief's wife tried to prevent us from discussing Alfredo in front of his children.

The way that everyone ignored her admonition indicated not only the difference in moral authority between the chief and his wife but also the difference between children and parents and/or siblings in this respect. For, had one of the people in that group been Alfredo's close senior relative or his sibling, the chief's wife would not even have needed to make that admonition—no one would have spoken as they did.

While the shame script drew people's attention to the scolding Alfredo had received, he continually forced society's attention to the gossip about him and, by implication, the defenseless state in which he found himself by virtue of his social isolation. Seen in this light, the climax of the episode was his conversation with the old men in the copra house. Finally he found people who would take his complaint about gossip seriously. These old men, repositories of much of their culture's wisdom, even taught him a culturally appropriate answer, one of which younger people were unaware. The old men asked him what the trouble was. Up to this time no one had done that. Instead of exhorting him to ignore the gossip that he complained of, they offered him a historically valid response. In doing so, they acted to validate his complaint, if not his actions. If this interpretation is correct, then the self-wounding that followed was a kind of coda, which gave the day's events symmetry and underlined the seriousness of his concerns.[28]

Alienated and alone, perhaps aware of the negative light in which much of his behavior (and not just his affair) was viewed by the rest of society, he acted to force people to attend to him. In this respect his behavior is functionally similar to what has been described as "wild man" behavior in New Guinea Highland societies (Newman 1960; Salisbury 1964; Averill 1980), and to possession and illness in many parts of the world. For example, referring to a Burmese patient who was possessed, Spiro (1967:195) comments: "He can mobilize all the resources of his community to assist him in dealing with his problems."

Alfredo, caught up in a maelstrom of gossip, cut off and isolated, was like the person at the center of Ernest Becker's (1973) somber description of man's tragic destiny. And, like that person, he acted to "desperately justify himself as an object of primary value in the universe. . . . to stand out and show that he count[ed] for more than anything or anyone else" (p. 4).

An orientation such as Becker's is likely to make ethnopsychologists a little uneasy, for it attributes to others the alienation and existential crisis of industrial man. However, for Alfredo at least, I think it is appropriate to think in these terms. And as Tobian society continues to change, it is likely that more and more people will find themselves in his situation. Demographic and economic changes will increasingly make the interpersonally oriented Tobian self, validated through intensely meaningful traditional productive and exchange relations, more and more exposed. Perhaps people will build on Alfredo's precedent and use dramatic, public gestures to reveal hidden aspects of their selves and trigger integrative social responses.

The dramatic revelation of the self (or at least aspects of it) is nothing new on Tobi. The shame script, with its outcome of ghostly behavior, is a traditional statement about inner states. Rather than an evil aspect of the self, however, Alfredo revealed (or at least attempted to reveal) a beautiful, tragic aspect.[29]

CONCLUSION

The strategic value of the case method in the study of ethnopsychology lies in its ability to focus ethnographic attention on events that are themselves the focus of local interest and action. In the analysis of a case, the ethnographer may ask the related questions: Why are these events seen as socially significant? and How, in the local view, do they cohere as happenings that impinge on one another?

When people turn the ongoing flow of interaction into remembered events they draw on folk psychological assumptions that tie them together in webs of implication and relatedness. I argue, through the above analysis of Alfredo's attempted suicide, that cultural assumptions about persons are not only used in the interpretation of events but also provide a basis for evaluation and action. Crapanzano (1977:10) makes this point well in his discussion of the indigenous "articulation" of events, by which he means

> the act of construing, or better still constructing, an event to render it meaningful. The act of articulation is more than a passive representation of the event; it is in essence the creation of the event. . . . It gives the event structure, thus precipitating its context, relates it to other similarly constructed events, and evaluates the event along both idiosyncratic and (culturally) standardized lines. Once the experience is articulated, once it is rendered an event, it is cast within the world of meaning and may then provide a basis for action.

Stated in this way, the process of "articulation" clearly points to the multiple functions of folk psychology as representational, evocative, and directive (to use D'Andrade's [1984] terms discussed earlier).

The case method is well suited to the analysis of commonsense representations of events that frequently take the form of "scripts" or stereotyped sequences of emotion and action. In the case of Alfredo, I have argued that Tobian interpretations of his behavior were extensively structured by a 'shame' script that linked his suicide attempt with previous events in the community (specifically, a public scolding and gossip) and carried specific implications for emotion and possible future courses of action.

However, as this case makes clear, people's interest in Alfredo's behavior was not simply a matter of representation or comprehension. Rather, attempts at interpretation created an emotional experience that further became the basis for active responses to Alfredo. The evocative functions of the shame scenario can be seen in the intense fear that came to surround these events, based on the perceived resemblance of Alfredo's actions to ghostly behavior. The ethnographic usefulness of empathy in such a case is evident in the fact that I did not know how afraid people were until about halfway through the episode. As in my interaction with my Tobian 'mother', empathy involves close attention to subtle communications and analysis of one's own reactions to such communication. This reflexivity goes beyond what are commonly called "emic" techniques, and, in the end, comes down to the constant striving for openness to the experience of others. It is related to but not, I think, the same as empathy discussed by Kohut and other psychoanalysts of the self (Kohut 1971).

My discussion of this case also makes clear the directive functions of folk psychological interpretation. All through the case, people were positing their own explanations of what was happening, with distinct implications for inner experience and the appropriate actions to be taken in response. The process of posing and counterposing alternative interpretations, then, became a process of negotiating both meaning and action. If Alfredo's bizarre behavior was 'just his idea', it would be acceptable to ignore his actions. If, however, his actions signaled intense shame, they could be seen to resemble ghostly behavior, calling for preventive measures. As people sought to link Alfredo's behavior to prior events in the community, and to find analogous scenarios in the realm of Tobian psychology and action, they were at the same time negotiating their own responses and actions. The alternative interpretations that emerged in people's talk about Alfredo not only served to make his behavior comprehensible but ultimately created people's emotional and social experience during the episode.

The case study approach is likely to prove productive as ethnopsychology moves beyond the description and comparison of folk psychologies considered in vacuo to the development of a more contextual or ecological perspective. It should provide a rewarding avenue into fundamental questions about the relationships between human experience, knowledge, and action. And, for me at least, the hope for insight into those relationships provides the ultimate justification for attempting to understand folk psychological materials.

ACKNOWLEDGMENTS

The research on which this chapter is based was partially funded by an NIMH training grant administered by the Department of Anthropology, University of California at San Diego (UPHS 5 TO1MH 12766). A total of two and a half years has been spent with the Tobi people, six months in their community in Palau, and the rest on Tobi itself. Discussions with a number of people were all very helpful as I tried to clarify my ideas, although I alone bear responsibility for the errors and misperceptions that this chapter still contains. I particularly wish to thank Eleanor Gerber as well as the editors of this volume for their assistance. Otong H. Emilio gave much-needed help with Tobian vocabulary and psychological concepts. His is the only Tobian name that I have not changed here. Others whom I wish to acknowledge include K. Avruch, E. Brown, M. Fitzgerald, P. Levin, and C. Lutz.

NOTES

1. I am unaware of any systematic, exhaustive review of the field of ethno-psychology. Interested readers should see the introduction to this volume as well as Shweder and Bourne (1982) for an overview. A preliminary sorting of the various theoretical traditions represented in the field reveals two major (and complementary) orientations. One, which can be tentatively named the "cognitive," has its roots in ethnoscience and could probably be traced back to E. B. Tylor. The other, which I provisionally call the "social," grows out of the insights of (among others) Mauss (1938) and so reaches back to Durkheim. In this connection it is possible to note a historical irony. As is well known, Durkheim was at considerable pains to establish the autonomy of the social from the psychological and to exclude the latter from explanations of the former. "The determining cause of a social fact should be sought among the social facts preceding it and not among the states of individual consciousness" (1950:110). The irony lies in the fact that it is becoming more and more apparent that one social fact that plays an important role in sociological processes consists of the relevant folk psychology. While it may be possible to rule out our theories of individual consciousness as we attempt to explain sociological processes, even those working within the Durkheimian tradition increasingly recognize that we cannot exclude indigenous theories of such states.

2. Theodore Schwartz, personal communication, calls this the method of "trans-emicization." See Caughey (1980) and Lutz (chap. 2; 1982a) on the difficulties of translating Micronesian folk psychologies. For ideas on American folk psychology and its relation to academic psychology, see LeVine (1980) and Gaines (1982). The latter paper is particularly interesting, dealing as it does with the folk psychological notions of psychiatric residents. That Gaines found two competing folk psychologies at work should alert us to the fact that it would be a mistake to conceptualize American folk psychology as a unitary or monolithic structure. Both sides of the (in)famous "West vs. The Rest" formula are far too simplified to be useful.

3. In addition to D'Andrade (1984), see also Frake (1981) and Keesing (1979) for recent statements about the utility of cognitive approaches to the study of complex social processes.

4. An extended discussion of empathy would move beyond the usual treatment it receives in textbooks on field methods in anthropology and would take into account Weber (1964) on *verstehen,* Mead (1932) on the self and the other, and Cooley (1964) on the looking glass self, as well as other early social scientists who addressed themselves to the question of how one self knows another. In addition to the two approaches to empathy mentioned in the text, one would also need to address issues raised by Geertz (1976) and Lévi-Strauss (1978).

5. "Ghost" is the way that Tobian English speakers translate the term *yarus.* Both Lutz (chap. 2) and Spiro (1952) translate its Ifaluk cognate *alus* as "spirit." When (as in the present instance) no crucial dimensions of meaning seem to be involved, I tend to follow Tobians in the way they translate their native tongue.

6. The fourteenth-century French peasants of Montaillou also believed that a dead person's debts could prevent final departure from the world of the living

(Ladurie 1979:349). Apparently it is not only in American country and western music that one can say "I owe my soul to the company store."

7. The verbal part of our exchange occurred in Tobian.

8. Since my departure from the island this woman and I have attempted to continue our relationship by mail. She seems to have learned to live with her grief and continues to play the role of an active and vigorous adult. In a recent letter her daughter wrote (in a phrase that dates back to the visit of some American Seabees to the island) "Our mother STILL CAN DO."

9. It was not just tactical considerations that prevented me from confronting her. Mutual empathy binds both parties in a relationship to sensitivity to each other's feelings.

10. Perhaps this statement begs the question. It is unclear how "liminal" communication can be conceptualized except in a Freudian-based framework. Crapanzano (1981) has developed a partial reconciliation of the Freudian and hermeneutic systems, if "reconciliation" can be used for a process by which one theory (hermeneutics) is used to subsume another (Freudianism).

11. There is also a long history of the use of cases in the Freudian tradition. See Obeyesekere (1977) for a very thoughtful attempt to adapt that tradition to anthropological analysis.

12. See Frake (1981) for a provocative discussion of many of these issues.

13. This quotation ignores the question of *whose* common sense is salient in this process. In ethnopsychological research considerable self-consciousness is necessary on the part of the investigator about the commonsense notions both of his culture and the culture under study. The danger exists that without sufficient self-awareness, the investigator will at this point introduce unexamined biases into the research.

14. But see also Frake's (1981) critique of hermeneutics.

15. To my dismay I noticed that the rope ended in a classic hangman's noose. I had taught Alfredo and several of the other men how to tie that knot a month or so before. It should also be noted that Alfredo's use of this knot was an instance of his pride in his mastery of modern ways.

16. In an analysis of Tobian Catholicism (1978b) I describe changes that have taken place in the remembered teachings of the missionary who converted the island. It would be interesting to develop an analysis of the processes of remembering and storing folk psychological cases and the distortions that are introduced. The ideas of D'Andrade (1974) on the role of semantic structures in memory and of Keesing (1982) on the political economy of knowledge would be especially relevant here.

17. The Japanese epoch in Micronesian history lasted from the beginning of World War I to the end of World War II. It was followed by the American epoch, which has yet to end. The Japanese were preceded by the Germans, who in 1898 had replaced the Spanish who had ineffectually "owned" Micronesia since the time of Magellan and his fellow explorers.

18. Don Rubinstein, who has carried out a pioneering study of suicide in Micronesia (1983), has told me of a number of such cases among the Tobians in Palau. Perhaps there is an unspoken pattern here. If so, this raises important issues for both

ethnopsychology and the study of suicide. See Baechler (1981) for recent work toward a cross-culturally valid typology of suicide.

19. There is a danger in going to the opposite extreme and constructing an overly systematic representation of folk psychology. See Brunton (1980) for a cautionary account of how some ethnographers have fallen into this trap in the study of Melanesian religion.

20. It is possible to see hints of similar functional clusters in the material presented by Lutz (1982; and especially chap. 2 and 1983). Many of the items in her clusters are dyadic in nature and in some instances the item that is at the other end of the dyad is in another cluster. That is, emotion 'x' in cluster 'a' is said to elicit emotion 'y' in cluster 'b' so that if I feel 'x', he feels 'y'. It would be interesting to pursue this point using some of Bateson's (1958) ideas about schizmogenesis.

21. Formal institutions of conflict resolution may have existed in the past. I have four things in mind here: (1) In the past, a person who was *teuahi* (obligated by having caused illegitimate pain) to another would visit that person's house to exchange stereotyped gifts, thus normalizing relations; (2) at funerals different sections of the island (between whom hostility and competition is said to have existed) would engage in song contests in which each side would attempt to arouse anger in the other; (3) complex divination procedure used to be practiced to enlist supernatural assistance in identifying unknown culprits (Black 1978*a*); and (4) the disputing parties in a land fight used to walk the boundaries of the parcel of land in question, and, in the presence of large numbers of people, a spokesman for each contender would detail all the landmarks and their history. None of these practices are carried out today; nothing has replaced them. Tobians avoid the newly introduced institutions of conflict resolution, especially the courthouse in Palau, whenever possible.

22. See Alkire (1965, 1977), Lessa (1966), Goodenough (1974), and Spiro (1952) for discussions of Carolinian religion.

23. There are also a number of other ways of speaking negatively about people. Several English and Japanese terms have been borrowed. These are mainly used in situations of momentary irritation. A special case is the word *bush* 'crazy' (see Lutz, chap. 2). This term can be used to disvalue another's behavior but ordinarily it carries no negative evaluation along moral lines. It simply means, in most cases, that the person concerned seems to be acting in a very confused fashion. It was not used by the Tobians in discussions of Alfredo's case. And in the one instance in which I so used it, my listeners corrected me.

24. Gossip can be seen in a much more positive light. It is highly important, for example, in preventing direct confrontation between people. This is because it can be used to indirectly send messages between disputing parties. This use requires a good deal of skill in picking the right ear into which to drop an opinion and a high degree of knowledge of the gossip network—attributes that almost all adult Tobians possess.

25. See Douglas (1967) for ethnomethodological insights into suicide. For a sociobiological perspective, see de Catanzaro (1981).

26. For an application of Schank and Abelson's ideas to a Micronesian folk

psychology see Lutz (1983). See also Black (1977) for an application of Schieffelin's (1976) notion of "scenario" to Tobian materials.

27. Kirkpatrick's account of "extended agency" in the Marquesas (chap. 3) seems to bear a family relation to the Tobian in-charge concept.

28. It could also be that he was distressed by the answer the old men had given him. The ability to create a song is a highly valued trait, yet the songs are extremely complex forms and most people, including Alfredo, find them almost impossible to compose. Also, wounding himself in the stomach was perhaps analogous to using the hangman's noose; that is, it was a use of a "modern" form of suicide, in this case Japanese *seppuku* (see Lifton 1979).

29. Alfredo's behavior can be taken as an indication that not only shame but also thwarted love, isolation, and gossip can lead to ghostliness. But those who used the ghost metaphor to label his behavior after the case (and there were many who did so) were talking about a different kind of ghost than the traditional one predicted by the shame script. The ghostliness that Alfredo demonstrated had little in common with generally accepted notions of that frightening state. It was a thing of flowers and fine clothes, not of horrible smells and ghastly apparitions. Taken together with the extended and valued relations my 'mother' managed to retain with her dead son, this indicates that a change in Tobian ghost conceptions may be emerging. The metaphor may be in a process of extension so that it will increasingly summarize a variety of commonly hidden aspects of the person, not just forbidden rage. If this is correct, then Tobian suicide may also change from being solely a shame-based, hidden act, to a behavior with a variety of forms and a wide range of meanings. The fact that one of the ghosts which Alfredo reported he had encountered was in the form of a beautiful young woman probably should also be mentioned in this connection. His reaction was no different than the reactions of anyone who encounters a ghost (he was terrified), but the beauty of the ghost may indicate change in the direction I have indicated.

GLOSSARY

bush	insane, confused, crazy
(e)risamaruh	suicide; (he or she) kills himself or herself
(e)tab	(it is) forbidden, wrong
fisirirah	it is just his or her way; refers to idiosyncracy, personal habit, trait, or custom
hamangungu	whispering; gossip
idea	scheme or plan (loanword from English)
mah	shame
manni fariworuwor	person of the bush; social isolate
manni mosuwe	person of the remote past; old-fashioned person

manni Panou	Palauan; greedy and materialistic person
manni Papua	Papuan; incompletely socialized person
metah	fear
parimarau	formal, respectable talk (translated by English speaker as apology)
song	anger
tahiyatatep	pride, haughtiness, arrogance
teuahi	obligation owed to another who one has illegitimately harmed
yarus	ghost, spirit; supernatural being

REFERENCES

Agar, M.
1980   Hermeneutics in Anthropology: A Review Essay. Ethos 8:253–277.
Alkire, W.
1965   Lamotrek Atoll and Inter-Island Socioeconomic Ties. Urbana: University of Illinois Press.
1977   The Peoples and Cultures of Micronesia. Menlo Park: Cummings Publishing Company.
Averill, J.
1980   Emotion and Anxiety: Sociocultural, Biological, and Psychological Determinants. *In* Explaining Emotions. A. Rorty, ed. Berkeley, Los Angeles, London: University of California Press.
Baechler, J.
1981   Les Suicides. Paris: Calmann-Levy.
Bateson, G.
1958   Naven. 2d ed. Palo Alto: Stanford University Press.
Becker, E.
1973   The Denial of Death. New York: Free Press.
Belmonte, T.
1979   The Broken Fountain. New York: Columbia University Press.
Berger, P., and T. Luckmann
1966   The Social Construction of Reality. Garden City, N.Y.: Doubleday.
Berndt, R.
1962   Excess and Restraint: Social Control Among A New Guinea Mountain People. Chicago: University of Chicago Press.
Black, P.
1977   Neo Tobian Culture: Modern Life on a Micronesian Atoll. Ann Arbor: University Microfilms.

1978a   Crime and Culture: Tobian Response to Attempted Murder. Midwest
         Review 3:59–69.
1978b   The Teachings of Father Marino: Aspects of Tobian Catholicism. *In*
         Mission, Church and Sect in Oceania. J. Boutilier, ed. Ann Arbor:
         University of Michigan Press.
1981   Fishing for Taro on Tobi. *In* Persistence and Exchange. R. Force and
         B. Bishop, eds. Honolulu: Pacific Science Association.
1982   The "In-Charge Complex" and Tobian Political Culture. Pacific Studies
         6:52–70.
1983   Conflict, Morality and Power in a Western Caroline Society. Journal of
         the Polynesian Society 92:7–30.
n.d.   The Anthropology of Tobacco Use: Tobian data and theoretical issues.
         Journal of Anthropological Research (in press).
Brunton, D.
1980   Misconstrued Order in Melanesian Religion. Man (n.s.) 15:112–128.
Caughey, J.
1977   *Fa'a'nakkar:* Cultural Values in a Micronesian Society. Philadelphia: Uni-
         versity of Pennsylvania Publications in Anthropology.
1980   Personal Identity and Social Organization. Ethos 8:173–203.
Cooley, C. H.
1964   Human Nature and the Social Order. New York: Schocken.
Conklin, H.
1962   Lexicographical Treatment of Folk Taxonomies. *In* Problems in Lexi-
         cography. F. Householder, and S. Saporta, eds. Bloomington: Indiana
         University Research Center in Anthropology, Folklore, and Linguistics.
Crapanzano, V.
1977   Introduction. *In* Case Studies in Spirit Possession. V. Crapanzano and
         V. Garrison, eds. New York: John Wiley and Sons.
1981   Text, Transference and Indexicality. Ethos 9:122–148.
Csikzentmihalyi, M., and E. Rochberg-Halton
1981   The Meaning of Things: Domestic Symbols and the Self. Cambridge:
         Cambridge University Press.
D'Andrade, R.
1965   Trait Psychology and Componential Analysis. *In* Formal Semantic
         Analysis. E. A. Hammel, ed. Menasha, Wis.: American Anthropologist
         67 (pt. 2).
1974   Memory and the Assessment of Behavior. *In* Measurement in the Social
         Sciences. M. Blalock, ed. Chicago: Aldine.
1984   Cultural Meaning Systems. *In* Culture Theory: Essays on Mind, Self
         and Emotion. R. A. Shweder and R. A. LeVine, eds. New York:
         Cambridge University Press.
de Catanzaro, D.
1981   Suicide and Self-Damaging Behavior: A Sociobiological Perspective.
         New York: Academic Press.
Devereux, G.
1978   Ethnopsychoanalysis, Psychoanalysis, and Anthropology as Com-
         plementary Frames of Reference. Berkeley, Los Angeles, London: Uni-

versity of California Press.

Douglas, J.
    1967   The Social Meaning of Suicide. Princeton: Princeton University Press.
Durkheim, E.
    1950   The Rules of Sociological Method. New York: Free Press.
Edelman, M.
    1977   Political Language: Words That Succeed and Policies That Fail. New York: Academic Press.
Eilers, A.
    1936   Tobi und Ngulu. Ergernisse der Sudsee—Expedition 1908–1910 II. B, Band 9:2.
Frake, C.
    1962   The Ethnographic Study of Cognitive Systems. In Anthropology and Human Behavior. T. Gladwin and W. Sturtevant, eds. Washington, D.C.: Anthropological Society of Washington.
    1981   Plying Frames Can Be Dangerous: Some Reflections on Methodology in Cognitive Anthropology. In Language, Culture and Cognition: Anthropological Perspectives. R. Casson, ed. New York: Macmillan.
Gaines, A.
    1982   Cultural Definitions, Behavior and the Person in American Psychiatry. In Cultural Conceptions of Mental Health and Therapy. A. J. Marsella and G. M. White, eds. Dordrecht: D. Reidel.
Garfinkel, H.
    1967   Studies in Ethnomethodology. Englewood Cliffs, N.J.: Prentice-Hall.
Geertz, C.
    1976   "From the Native's Point of View": On the Nature of Anthropological Understanding. In Meaning in Anthropology. K. Basso and H. Selby, eds. Albuquerque: University of New Mexico Press.
Gerber, E.
    1975   The Cultural Patterning of Emotions in Samoa. Ann Arbor: University Microfilms.
Gluckman, M.
    1961   Ethnographic Data in British Social Anthropology. Sociological Review (n.s.) 9:5–17.
    1965   Politics, Law and Ritual in Tribal Society. Chicago: Aldine.
Goodenough, W.
    1956   Componential Analysis and the Study of Meaning. Language 32:195–216.
    1974   Towards an Anthropologically Useful Definition of Religion. In Changing Perspectives on the Scientific Study of Religion. A. W. Eister, ed. New York: John Wiley and Sons.
Hallowell, A.
    1955   The Self and Its Behavioral Environment. In Culture and Experience. Philadelphia: University of Pennsylvania Press.
Hutchins, E.
    1980   Culture and Inference: A Trobriand Case Study. Cambridge: Harvard University Press.

Keesing, R.
  1979   Linguistic Knowledge and Cultural Knowledge: Some Doubts and
          Speculations. American Anthropologist 81:14–36.
  1982   Kwaio Religion: The Living and The Dead in a Solomon Islands Society.
          New York: Columbia University Press.
Kohut, H.
  1971   The Analysis of the Self. New York: International Universities Press.
Ladurie, E.
  1979   Montaillou: The Promised Land of Error. New York: Random House.
Leenhardt, M.
  1979   Do Kamo: Person and Myth in the Melanesian World. B. M. Gulati,
          trans. Chicago: University of Chicago Press.
Lessa, W.
  1966   Ulithi: A Micronesian Design for Living. New York: Holt, Rinehart
          and Winston.
LeVine, R.
  1973   Culture, Behavior and Personality. Chicago: Aldine.
  1980   Anthropology and Child Development. In Anthropological Perspectives
          on Child Development. C. Super and S. Harkness, eds. San Francisco:
          Jossey-Bass.
Lévi-Strauss, C.
  1978   Tristes Tropiques. J. Russell, trans. New York: Atheneum.
Lifton, R.
  1979   The Broken Connection: On Death and the Continuity of Life. New
          York: Simon and Schuster.
Lutz, C.
  1982a   Depression and the Translation of Emotional Worlds. Paper presented
          at the annual meetings of the American Anthropological Association,
          Washington, D.C.
  1982b   The Domain of Emotion Words on Ifaluk. American Ethnologist 9:113–
          128.
  1983   Goals, Events and Understanding: Towards a Formal Model of Ifaluk
          Emotion Theory. Paper presented at the Conference on Folk Models,
          Institute for Advanced Study, Princeton, May 12–15.
Mauss, M.
  1938   Une catégorie de l'Esprit Humain: la notion de personne, celle de 'moi'.
          Journal of the Royal Anthropological Institute 68:263–281.
Mead, G. H.
  1932   The Philosophy of the Present. Chicago: Open Court.
Newman, P.
  1960   'Wildman Behavior' in a New Guinea Highlands Community. American
          Anthropologist 66:1–19.
Obeyesekere, G.
  1977   Psychocultural Exegesis of a Case of Spirit Possession in Sri Lanka. In
          Case Studies in Spirit Possession. V. Crapanzano and V. Garrison, eds.

New York: John Wiley and Sons.

Pike, K.
1954   Language in Relation to a Unified Theory of the Structure of Human
        Behavior. Part I. Glendale: Summer Institute of Linguistics.

Rabinow, P.
1977   Reflections on Fieldwork in Morocco. Berkeley, Los Angeles, London:
        University of California Press.

Rorty, A.
1976   A Literary Postscript: Characters, Persons, Selves, Individuals. *In* The
        Identity of Persons. A. O. Rorty, ed. Berkeley, Los Angeles, London:
        University of California Press.

Rosch, E.
1975   Universals and Cultural Specifics in Human Categorization. *In* Cross-
        Cultural Perspectives on Learning. R. Brislin, S. Bochner, and W. Lon-
        ner, eds. New York: John Wiley and Sons.

Rubinstein, D.
1983   Epidemic Suicide Among Micronesian Adolescents. Social Science and
        Medicine 17:657–665.

Sahlins, M.
1981   Historical Metaphors and Mythical Realities: Structure in the Early His-
        tory of the Sandwich Islands. ASAO Special Publications 1. Ann Arbor:
        University of Michigan Press.

Salisbury, R.
1964   Possession in the New Guinea Highlands: A Review of the Literature.
        Transcultural Psychiatric Research Review 3:103–108.

Schank, R., and R. Abelson
1977   Scripts, Plans, Goals and Understanding: An Inquiry into Human
        Knowledge Structures. Hillsdale, N.J.: Lawrence Erlbaum Associates.

Schieffelin, E. L.
1976   The Sorrow of the Lonely and the Burning of the Dancers. New York:
        Saint Martin's Press.

Schwartz, H., and J. Jacobs
1979   Qualitative Sociology: A Method to the Madness. New York: Free
        Press.

Searle, J.
1969   Speech Acts: An Essay in the Philosophy of Language. Cambridge:
        Cambridge University Press.

Seeger, A.
1981   Nature and Society in Central Brazil: The Suya Indians of Mato Grasso.
        Cambridge: Harvard University Press.

Selby, H.
1974   Zapotec Deviance. Austin: University of Texas Press.

Shweder, R., and E. Bourne
1982   Does the Concept of the Person Vary Cross-Culturally? *In* Cultural
        Conceptions of Mental Health and Therapy. A. Marsella and G. White,

eds. Dordrecht: D. Reidel.
Spiro, M.
  1952   Ghosts, Ifaluk and Teleological Functionalism. American An-
          thropologist 54:47–503.
  1967   Burmese Supernaturalism. Englewood Cliffs, N.J.: Prentice-Hall.
Turner, V.
  1968   Mukanda: The Politics of a Non-Political Ritual. *In* Local Level Politics.
          M. Swartz, ed. Chicago: Aldine.
Tyler, S.
  1978   The Said and the Unsaid: Mind, Meaning and Culture. New York:
          Academic Press.
Van Velsen, J.
  1967   The Extended Case Method and Situational Analysis. *In* The Craft of
          Social Anthropology. A. Epstein, ed. London: Tavistock Publications.
Weber, M.
  1964   Basic Concepts in Sociology. New York: The Citadel Press.
White, G.
  1980   Conceptual Universals in Interpersonal Language. American Anthro-
          pologist 82:759–781.
  1985   'Bad Ways' and 'Bad Talk': Interpretations of Interpersonal Conflict in
          a Melanesian Society. *In* Directions in Cognitive Anthropology. J.
          Dougherty, ed. Urbana: University of Illinois Press.

8

Affective Bonds: Hawaiian Interrelationships of Self

Karen L. Ito

INTRODUCTION

The Hawaiian concept of self is grounded in affective social relations.[1] These social relations are not confined to humans but include the spiritual and natural worlds as well. This conceptualization of self is a highly interpersonal one. It is based on the reflexive relationship of Self and Other and on the dynamic bonds of emotional exchange and reciprocity.[2] For Hawaiians, Self and Other, person and group, people and environment, are inseparable. They all interactively create, affect, and even destroy each other.[3] The Hawaiian folk psychology system of Self-Other has many commonalities with the symbolic interactionist model in which

> the most basic element in the image [of human beings] is the idea that the individual and society are inseparable units. . . . [T]he inseparability of the individual and society is defined in terms of a mutually interdependent relationship, not a one-sided deterministic one. . . . In the interactionist image human beings are defined as self-reflective beings. Human beings are organisms with selves, and behavior in society is often directed by the self. The behavior of men and women is 'caused' not so much by forces within themselves (instincts, drives, needs, etc.) or by external forces impinging upon them (social forces, etc.), but what lies in between, a reflective and socially derived interpretation of the internal and external stimuli that are present. (Meltzer et al. 1975:2)

What "lies in between" for Hawaiians is the bond of emotional affect. Hawaiians view themselves as bound together by affective ties—emotional bonds that support and protect each member.

The affiliative nature of interpersonal relations is central for Hawaiians (Howard 1974; Gallimore and Howard 1968). Group harmony and an egalitarian spirit are stressed. It is important to preserve harmony and the positive affective strength of affiliative bonds. A person is defined by and defines himself or herself by the affective quality of these interpersonal bonds. In their interactions with Others, Hawaiians formulate their concepts of Self and use them as conduits for the expression of self. A person's positive expression of self is through its extension in the open, expansive, *aloha* spirit. This generous giving of self is viewed as an altruistic exchange keeping the affiliative bonds flowing with 'love' (*aloha*), 'sincerity' (expressed as "heart" or *na'au*), and 'warmth' (*pumehana*). This is not so much a reciprocal exchange but a generalized one, in that the aloha and goodwill that one extends can return through any number of affiliative ties with others. Hawaiians like to view themselves as generous, gregarious, and hospitable. The affective connotation of these attributes of self is one of expansive release, a letting go, an 'easy' personality. Hawaiians enjoy and take pride in having people drop in, stay over, stay "for eat." The fact that people gravitate toward one and feel comfortable in one's presence is a testament to one's Hawaiianness: an interpersonal self-validation.

In contrast, the harboring retention of self, displayed in selfish behavior, 'jealousy' (*lili*), and the coveting of another's goods, goodwill, or interpersonal affiliations, will hurt and anger others.[4] These retentive, greedy acts block the exchange of positive affect and begin a cycle of negative exchanges of emotional retaliations. Here the affective connotation of self is one of smallness, a controlled, tight holding on, an inability to 'let it go'—be it a grudge, a possession, a beloved child, or another's superiority. Inexplicable illness, injury, misfortune, or even death are public evidence of negative acts of self-retention. They are interpreted as warnings, usually from God or *'aumākua*, 'family ancestors', of violations of the Hawaiian ethos. As one informant explained: "God doesn't want to hurt you. He is only trying to help you by warning you that you are on the wrong path." The "wrong path" is the involvement in negative exchanges entangling the affiliative ties.

To restore the positive affect between Hawaiians, and to end a cycle of illness and misfortune, Hawaiians go through a process of self and social analysis to try to pinpoint their specific error, so that restorative measures of apology and forgiveness can be taken (Ito 1982a). One method for the restoration of positive affect is called *ho'oponopono* 'to make things right, correct things', a form of conflict resolution which involves discussion, resolution, restitution (if appropriate), and mutual apology and forgiveness between parties. The final exchange reasserts both parties' expansive, giving, aloha nature by the mutual extensions of Self in apology and request for forgiveness. Furthermore, the gracious acceptance of this offering of Self is a reaffirmation by the Other. The relationship is freed of past negative, retentive, hurtful entanglements and opened to renewed exchanges of positive, or at least neutral, affect.

The Hawaiian interrelationship of selves, transgressions of affect, and the restoration of self, aloha, and positive affect through ho'oponopono will be detailed in this chapter. Throughout, the focus will be on "what people both say and do in everyday life" to discover the "cultural knowledge system for interpreting self and others" (Lutz, chap. 2).

SETTING

The material presented here is primarily from research conducted in Honolulu, Hawaii, during 1975–76. Additional fieldwork was done in Honolulu in 1974 and in South Kona on the island of Hawaii in 1973. The bulk of this research is based on case studies of six families in a Honolulu neighborhood given the pseudonym of Ka Pumehana (The Warmth).[5] The case studies focused on the central mother figure in the household. Ka Pumehana was chosen because it had the largest percentage of Hawaiians and Part-Hawaiians in Honolulu and it also reflected many of the socioeconomic problems of urban Hawaiians such as unemployment, poverty, and substandard or public housing.

In 1974, the state's resident population was estimated at 724,000 excluding 54,600 members of the armed services and 68,300 of their dependents (State of Hawaii 1975). Hawaii's multiethnic population (excluding military personnel and their dependents) consisted primarily of Caucasians (29%), Japanese (28%), Part-Hawaiian (17%), Filipino (10%), Chinese (4%), and Hawaiian (1%) (Hawaii State Department of Health 1973). In 1974, 82 percent of the state's population lived on Oahu and 50 percent of those were in Honolulu, the state capital (State of Hawaii 1975). Similar figures were found for the Hawaiian/Part-Hawaiian population, with 76 percent living on Oahu and about 46 percent of those living in Honolulu (Hawaii State Department of Health 1973).

In spite of this urban concentration, few published anthropological studies of urban Hawaiians exist. The last major works were in the 1930s (Lind 1930, 1939; Heen 1936; Beaglehole 1937) when the prognosis for Hawaiian culture surviving in the urban setting was pessimistic. Beaglehole (1937:53) bluntly declared: "In the course of migration to the town and dispersal among elements and slums, the Hawaiian has thrown off a large measure of community control and become a broken and disorganized group." Nevertheless, despite cultural commercialization, socioeconomic hardships, and a lack of any formal enculturation system, urban Hawaiians today, fifty years later, still maintain a shared system of values, morals, and etiological theories—a distinct world view that indicates a tough cultural resiliency.

The research data were collected in informal discussion sessions, called "talk story." A pitfall of doing research in Hawaii is that direct, constant questioning is considered intrusive and rude (*nīele*). If questions or expressions of interest are viewed as offensively invasive, this behavior is called *maha'oi*. Contact and responses will dissipate. To be rude is to violate, trespass on, or disregard someone else's boundaries, be they property, occupational, social, psychological, or emotional boundaries. Verbal breaches—the nosey question, the personal probe, a sharp word—are among the most disliked (Handy and Pukui 1972:189–190; Pukui et al. 1972:157–159; Ito 1978, 1982a).[6] One informant described the difference between the two words, *nīele* and *maha'oi*:

> "*Maha'oi* is inquisitive. Like you don't know me that well but you have a tendency to keep askin' me questions that are personal . . . [edited portion] . . . [KI: Is that like *nīele*?] *Nīele*—same thing: curious. *Nīele* is less. *Nīele* is more nice way of saying—curious. You see, curiosity gets the best of you. You want look only again. But *maha'oi*—when they say it—is rougher. They say, "Ooo, *maha'oi*!" Means you don't belong over there or you go over somebody's house you don't belong. You ask questions that don't even pertain [*sic*] to you."

Fortunately, "talk story" is a culturally appropriate conversational form. Usually it is a rambling, sometimes intense, exchange dealing with daily activities, gossip, or family happenings. Everyday activities or encounters are often embellished with a theatrical intensity. Individuals repeat in great detail the plots of movies, television stories, and novels. In the tradition of good storytellers, social entertainment is more the goal than narrative accuracy. Inquisitive questions that break the flow of the story are met with disapproval and irritation, although one can muse aloud about some area of wonderment. The revelation of details cannot be forced, only an interest indicated. A response is at the discretion of the storyteller and may occur then, never, or at some later unexpected time. Often others also will provide necessary details, but usually at some later date or in a private conversation.

Hawaiians are a gregarious and sensitive people. Once trust and friendship are established through a demonstration of sincerity and nonaggression, the "talk story" sessions become richly rewarding and dense with details. One informant became so familiar with my line of questions that she would finish some stories with a litany of self-posed anthropological questions such as: "Then you going say: 'How I know that?' 'When I first see this kine [kind]?' 'What it mean to me?'" Then she would either dismiss them or attempt to answer them, depending on her knowledge or interest.

THE INTERRELATIONSHIP OF SELVES

The bonds between people are very important to Hawaiians (Gallimore et al. 1974; Gallimore and Howard 1968; Howard 1974).[7] The establishment of interdependencies is much more central to the Hawaiian ethos than personal autonomy and achievement: "an individual alone is unthinkable in the context of Hawaiian relationships" (Handy and Pukui 1972:75). A person in Hawaiian culture is surrounded by social links: extending through time from one's ancestors through oneself, continuing to future descendants, and horizontally through one's own kin and friends. The liberal use of "aunty," "cousin," "bra" (brother), and "tutu" (grandmother) for non-consanguines reflects this centrality of kin ties.

Traditionally, all Hawaiian relationships could be expressed as bonds of kinship. The ali'i 'royalty', 'upper class' had extensive genealogies linking them to the gods and goddesses of Hawaii. The maka'ainana 'commoners' most probably felt kinship with the gods, goddesses, and spirits affiliated with their village land and their occupational and craft skills. Hawaiians felt kinship with the environment through the various natural forms of the gods and goddesses. Each of the gods and goddesses had multiple forms and natural transformations called kino lau. These were not representational forms but were thought of as actual transformations. For example, Ku, the god of war and patron of deep sea fishing, had many kino lau including a certain hardwood and specific adz used in canoe building, the ti plant (Cordyline terminalis), the noni tree (Morinda citrifolia), the red lehua flower from the 'ohia tree, the 'ohia tree itself, the sea cucumber, and the hawk. Pele, the volcano goddess, had kino lau of not only volcanic activity and lava flow but of a young, beautiful girl, an old hag, red-colored earth, fire, and tiny lava pebbles called Pele's tears. Belief in Pele's kino lau is still very much alive on the Big Island of Hawaii where volcanic activity remains vigorous. Adults and children tell of encountering Pele as an old woman on the road and children explain that Pele is still in the lava rocks they pick up on the ground (see also Ciborowski and Price-Williams 1982). In Honolulu, Hawaiians frequently cite Pele as an ancestor because they have a hot temper: a type of personality kino lau.

Therefore, traditionally, Hawaiians would see their ancestral relatives in a multitude of forms during their daily activities: in a particular sunset, a certain blossom, a distinctive breeze. People would respond to seeing these various kino lau as they would to seeing a kinsperson, friend, or acquaintance. Depending on the nature of the relationship, various affective responses would be generated: happiness, anger, suspicion, fear, devotion, wonder, or boredom. Currently, this affective response to kino lau is considerably less well defined. This is certainly true for urban dwellers who have little involvement with the natural environment aside from periodic beach camping, weekend fishing, or yard gardening. Nevertheless, belief persists in the consciousness and spiritual forces of certain places on the island, some elements of the sea, the sea itself, weather, certain foods, some plants, insects, and animals. Primarily, it depends on the context or conditions in which these elements are encountered whether or not they are treated as having spirits or being kino lau. Furthermore, interactions with 'aumākua 'family ancestors', 'gods', 'uhane 'ghosts', 'souls', 'spirits', and akua 'gods', 'goddesses', 'spirits', are commonly acknowledged. Therefore, Hawaiians participate in social relations even without human companionship. Social relations for Hawaiians are not limited to human interactions but include natural and supernatural interactions as well. People will deal interpersonally with elements of their natural and spiritual environment as parts of their social world (Ito 1978).

The affirmation of one's Self, the maintenance, the creation and re-creation of it, depends on interaction with these social Others. This does not have to be face-to-face interaction but can be one of observation, imagination, or memory. All offer interactive opportunities to formulate and express one's extension or retention of Self.

LINKS OF EMOTIONAL EXCHANGE

The linking dynamic of these Self-Other social relations is the reciprocal exchange of emotions. Reciprocity and exchange are, of course, recognized by anthropologists as important for the establishment and perpetuation of social relations. The focus has been on exchanges and obligations of a material or pragmatic nature. Exchanges of people, food, service, or ceremony—all can establish an obligation that perpetuates a cycle of reciprocity. However, for Hawaiians, the bonds of reciprocity and exchange extend to emotional exchanges between one's Self and Others.

> Ideally, in fact, all [commodity] transactions are viewed as metaphoric displays of relationship affirmation . . . [I]t is social rather than material capital that is the center of attention and in which individuals are expected to invest. . . .

[C]ommodities are perceived as being primarily in the service of affirming old relationships and consolidating new ones. (Howard 1974:207)

These emotional exchange links are not only of altruistic indebtedness but hostile, hurtful indebtedness as well. The dual quality of reciprocity is inherent in the Hawaiian word, *pānaʻi,* which means to reciprocate and revenge, as well as to "reward whether good or bad" (Pukui and Elbert 1971).

All relationships, past or present, human or nonhuman, are emotional conduits, connecting pathways of affective exchanges. There is always an affective dynamic in any Hawaiian relationship. As described by Howard, "All relationships are treated as personalized" (1974:206). Seeing someone again, talking with them, interacting with one of their relatives, passing their house, or remembering them, reaffirms and renews the social bonds. In the cultural milieu of the U.S. mainland, we speak of "breaking off" relations or "breaking up" with someone, as if the emotional ties of the relationship could be severed. We also feel that relationships which are not actively sustained by communication are no longer effective ones. We may remember such a relationship, like an old love or friendship, as past, not as continuing. Yet the reality is more complex than we like to admit. A recalled wound or slight can anger us anew even if we have not seen or heard from the other in years. Likewise, seeing a special place, hearing a familiar sound, or smelling a certain fragrance, refreshes a feeling of affection for an old, or even deceased, friend. The very remembrance reasserts the relationship. Hawaiians recognize and acknowledge that a relationship exists and is operational as long as the Other can still affect one's Self, that is, as long as one remembers them. The memory of the love, anger, loss, vindication, indifference, and so on, maintains the bond of the relationship. A remembered relationship is like an emotional souvenir that one carries about, sometimes taking it out, dusting it off, and reestablishing the affective bond.[8] The affect can be positive, neutral, or negative; it can change and be reformulated. Any sentiment, even neutral indifference, indicates that one is still engaged emotionally with that person.

Naturally, another's memory of one's self links one to that person, uncontrolled by or even unbeknown to one. In fact, we sometimes are startled to hear of someone who recalls us with some affective memory: a remembered kindness, a dislike of some personal characteristic, holding dear some personally forgotten intimacy, or seething over some perceived injustice. For this person, the remembered relationship has been an active part of his or her life, even without the remembered party's knowledge or participation.

Whether recalled or current, this affective link is manifest in good or bad rewards, reciprocity (pānaʻi) sent along the relational paths between selves. Therefore, the emotional valence of these active or recalled relational bonds is critical. Ideally, it is positive; minimally, it is neutral; and problematically, it is negative. When the bond is positive or neutral, 'the way is open' for positive exchanges and strengthening of the bonds.[9]

Ideally, people try to keep the relational paths flowing with 'altruistic' (*lokomaka'i*) exchanges of 'love' (aloha), 'sincerity' of feeling ('with heart', na'au), and 'warmth' (pumehana). A generous extension of self will be rewarded by a similar return from the recipient or through another relational pathway. So, helping a sick neighbor by cleaning her house and cooking for her family may result in one's husband getting an unexpected job offer or promotion.

These relational bonds are also protective. They protect individuals from negative intentions or attacks from hostile or offended people or spirits. The interpersonal relationships one has, when positive or neutral, build a protective netting around a person.

Children are more vulnerable to attack than adults because they are young and have not established an adequate net of protective social bonds. One informant explained that a child is defenseless until six or seven years of age because a child is still a spirit until this time "when their eyes open." Handy and Pukui (1972:100) state that from birth to seven years of age a child is vulnerable to spirits who will steal the child's life. This may be a representation of the child's decreasing parental contact and increasing shift to supplementary caretakers as the child matures (Gallimore et al. 1974; Gallimore and Howard 1968; Korbin 1978). "This 'shift' is the beginning of the child's active participation in a wider network of kin and peers" (Korbin 1978:17) and the establishment of their own protective relational ties.

Children are referred to as the 'weak link' in protective social bonds. They are likely targets of retribution for offensive acts of other family members. "It always hits the child" is a common saying among Hawaiians. There is also the belief that the innocent suffer the consequences of antisocial initiatives of kinfolk. There are no uninvolved parties, no innocent bystanders.

Obviously, these relational pathways are also dangerous. When they are negative, affective pathways become tangled by hostilities, hurt feelings, anger, revenge. Knotted relationships bunch up the protective netting, opening a hole in these ties, leaving one vulnerable to attacks of emotional retribution in the form of illness, injury, spiritual harassment, death, or other misfortune and bad luck (cf. White, chap. 9).

An interpersonal transgression begins the negative entanglements of a relationship. A transgression is called a *hala*. This term for error, transgression, or sin has the added connotation of missing the mark, that is, not up to standards (Pukui et al. 1972; Pukui and Elbert 1971).[10]

Traditionally, hala acts were *kapu* (tabu) violations that offended 'aumākua 'family gods', 'ancestors', or akua 'spirits'. Contemporary negative behavior that is abusive, disrespectful, or impolite to other people and, to a lesser degree, spirits or the natural environment, is best summarized as "behavior that impaired interpersonal relationships—greed, dishonesty, theft" (Pukui et al. 1972:38). Rather than using a standardized code of types of behavior which invariably are considered as hala transgressions, Hawaiians tend to interpret behaviors contextually, whether they are indicators of retentive affect or hurtful to others.[11] Several ethnographers have observed that it is the consequences of behavior rather than the rule violated which is important for Polynesians (Firth 1957; Gallimore and Howard 1968; Howard 1970, 1974).

The hurtful affect of retentive behavior entangles protective social relationships and leaves a person vulnerable to the retribution of misfortune. For example, one informant told me of another mother who stole money earned by their sons' Boy Scout troop and used it for a flight to the mainland. "'At's why now, she get hard times," declared my informant. She explained that since the theft the woman and her husband divorced and the woman has suffered financial difficulties. Her retentive self-interest expressed by the theft disregarded the trust and innocence of the Scouts and other parents. She thereby entangled her protective social relationships and left herself vulnerable to the retribution of misfortune.

> In the traditional understanding of *hala* as a transgression or offense, is a subtle but significant axiom of human relationships: that the wrong-doer and the wronged are linked together by the very existence of the transgression and its chain of after-effects. Mary Kawena Pukui suggests we visualize *hala* as cord. "It binds the offender to his deed and to his victim. The victim holds on to this cord and becomes equally bound." (Pukui et al. 1972:71)

However, it is not so much the hala or the original transgression that entangles offender and victim but the emotional exchange of hurt and pain (*'eha*), anger and revenge, which binds the two parties in a spiraling cycle of cumulative hurts and hostile retaliations called *hihia*.

> *Hihia* is an entanglement of emotions, actions and reactions, all with negative, troublesome connotations. . . . Emotions, actions and counter-emotions and counter-actions spread to the family or close associates. Soon everyone concerned is entangled in a network of resentment, hostility, guilt, depression, or vague discomfort. . . . The net tightens, yet expands at the same time. (Ibid., pp. 71–72)

Therefore, while rule violation (hala) is the precipitator in hihia, culpability is less the issue in resolution than is the unraveling of the hurt and pain inflicted. As one informant explained:

> "Well, to me, it doesn't make a difference whether who's right or who's wrong. It's a matter who's hurt and who's not. You know. Like if, uh, I felt hurt, because of, you know, something. I just like know why. You know, that person said that or did that knowing that it would hurt another person. I wouldn't, I wouldn't go too much on who's right or who's wrong but mostly, you know, who's hurt and who's not."

TRANSGRESSIONS OF AFFECT

It is the hurtful meaning of a transgression which is important to understanding Hawaiian interpersonal relations and concepts of self. Transgressions hurt and anger people and are affective messages to other Hawaiians. The disregard for another embodied in a hurtful or angering transgression is viewed by others as a self-centered, retentive act. It means one does not care enough about the other person to avoid the transgression. Or, even more painfully, the transgressor has forgotten about the other person and failed to consider the consequences for that person or others. This violation makes the victim doubt the affective value of the relationship for the transgressor. Furthermore, the altruistic intentions of the transgressor become questionable. The victim becomes suspicious of the other's goodwill, viewing the other as a retentive, selfish person, unconcerned about the feelings of friends and relatives. Out of hurt and anger for such disregard, the victim of a transgression will look to retaliate in a vengeful, defensive manner:

> "Let's say [my cousin and I] get into an argument—my cousin deny to me. But I know inside my heart he lied to me. And because he's close to me, even though we don't see each other regular because he live country now outside Honolulu, but because he's close to me—and for him to hurt me like that. It's going cause me great hurt. *Hawaiians, when they get hurt—they get hurt.* And can be something really minor sometime but it's just the principle of the thing *or what it represented.* And it going to hurt me and if this thing—let's say . . . you know, it might become, you know, the feeling just going grow. You know the mad or the hurt that going cause us. . . . Somebody going to have to pay for that mistake." (Emphasis added.)

The valence of the relationship is changed and the relationship is blocked to positive affect. The pathway of communication is entrapped with negative suspicions about intent and regard for the other person.

As both informants noted, hurt feelings are salient for Hawaiians. The vulnerable extension of selves leaves Hawaiians sensitive to being hurt by rejection or disregard. They feel they have exposed themselves in self-extension and, when rebuffed or ignored, they are deeply hurt—and then very angry. They become angry because they feel they have been taken advantage of or made to look foolish. For example, one informant was meeting her Caucasian (*haole*) boyfriend at his apartment. On the way over, she decided to bring a pizza. When she arrived, her boyfriend was lying by the apartment pool talking with a female neighbor who also was sun-bathing. In a gesture of hospitality and extension of self, my informant offered the woman, who was also haole, some pizza. The woman did not want any. My informant felt the woman refused a piece in a haughty and dismissing manner. My informant was initially hurt but quickly incensed by the refusal. She was further angered by her boyfriend, who thought there was nothing to be upset about. This is obviously a complex inter-change, for my informant felt some jealousy and competitiveness when she saw her boyfriend talking with this neighbor. She also may have felt some threat from their common bond as members of a culturally and economi-cally dominant group. To counter her culturally inappropriate retentive emotions, my informant extended herself in a gesture of giving and excul-pation. When the neighbor rejected my informant's apologetic offering, she indicated both the offer and my informant were neither appropriate nor adequate. In addition, by withholding herself from social interaction in this self-retentive fashion, the neighbor rejected the establishment of a relation-ship and further offended my informant.

In ongoing relationships, the rejection of offered hospitality or aid is seen as the hurtful sign that the other party no longer wishes to maintain the relationship. In these cases, the rejection blocks a repayment in the affective exchange of the relationship and begins a hihia entanglement of hurt and angry feelings. One informant told of a couple with whom she and her husband were good friends. When my informant was in the hospital for an operation this other couple took care of her husband and children by having the children stay with them. They also provided meals. Later, when this woman friend had to go to the hospital, my informant wanted to repay her and do the same for her children and husband. The woman said, "No, that's okay. Joe [her husband] promised me he'd stay home." My informant insisted and the woman again explained her husband's prom-ise and said that it was something between the two of them. My informant became quite angry and yelled at her friend, "What's the matter with you?" Was she too good for them? "Well," my informant said, "I hope we never see each other again." She told her friend to forget about calling ever again. The woman friend began to cry, but my informant said she was too angry to respond. She told her friend to forget it and hung up the telephone. My informant then felt bad that she said those things to her friend, so they talked again and my informant apologized. Her woman friend said it was okay (accepting the apology) and eventually the children did stay at my informant's house and she fed both children and husband. My informant said she later found out the woman was very jealous of her husband: this was her attempt to keep him at home while she was in the hospital. Nevertheless, my informant was unsympathetic and did not find this an acceptable reason for rejecting her offered hospitality.

An even more deplored and insulting act than the rejection of offered hospitality is the withholding of hospitality. The withholding of hospitality is considered 'stingy' (pī)(Pukui et al. 1972:7,9). Newton, working in the village of "Waikini" on the island of Hawaii, reports that not only is the unwillingness to be hospitable thought to be stingy but a village woman describing a family which was not hospitable "explained that 'There is no love in that house!' (that is, 'no aloha')" (Newton 1978:67).

The importance of affect for Hawaiian social relations and self concept is most clearly demonstrated in the concept of na'au which literally means one's innards and more generally refers to one's heart, mind, or affections. One's na'au is the seat of one's intelligence, feeling, and sincerity. It is important that a person act 'with heart': sincerely, affectionately, thoughtfully, and without reservation in the extension of self.

An insincere display of proper behavior will result in negative interpersonal entanglements and repercussions:

> "I have one, my sister. When my kids—when she give you something, she's not giving it because she wants to. Actually, she don't want to. So when my sister do thing that—we don't take it. Because it might not fall on us but fall on the kids. [KI: Like what?] Well, uh, I don't know how to explain it. The way—like if I was going to do a favor for you, you see. I not going do it because I want to, you see? I going do it because my heart is in my friend."

The total extension of self in heartfelt sincerity is expressed in this last sentence. The informant then explained that if her children ate this food given without 'heart', it wouldn't taste good and they would become ill. "What I do is I just throw 'em away." This also means she is attempting to throw away the distasteful affect accompanying the begrudgingly given gift. She was deeply hurt by her own sister's retentive unwillingness to give needed aid (kōkua) with sincere generosity or aloha.

If a person acts thoughtlessly or speaks rashly and offends or hurts others, but it is felt by others to be 'from the heart'—a sincere, emotional reaction of passion and principle—the individual will be protected from negative interpersonal entanglements. For example, one informant told of a man who spoke up at community meetings and would dominate the floor.

She said he would "talk rough" and offend people by his blunt, aggressive, and dominating speaking manner. But people excused this because everyone agreed that he spoke 'from the heart'.

Hawaiian tolerance for individual self-expression and personality types is expressed in the description of it as a person's 'ways' or 'style'. Newton (1978:127–131) mentions this as a method of characterizing and excusing or tolerating negative qualities such as dominance, combativeness, or drunken comportment as individual personality differences. In Honolulu, people also used these terms, 'style' or 'ways', for excesses in the opposite direction of overly generous or fun-loving natures. Newton further observed that once a person's negative 'style' was publicly established, people who fell victim to their excesses were not given sympathy and were told they "should have known better." The implication seems to be that the person's 'style' is not a voluntary expression. The person is not motivated to hurt any particular person. Therefore, he or she is not held responsible. It is the responsibility of the other parties not to take offense.[12]

Hawaiians feel negative thoughts or wishes are transgressions (hala) of affect as substantial and disruptive as are actions or words. Traditionally recognized forms of malevolent transgressions of affect were 'spite' (*mana'ao 'ino*), 'hate' (*mainaina*), 'jealousy' (lili), 'ill will' (*make ho'opilikia*) (Handy et al. 1934:5–6; Malo 1951:72, 89). Today, it appears that 'grudge holding' (*ho'omauhala*) and 'jealousy' are two primary types of retentive, self-centered thoughts and desires.[13]

The contemporary retentive thought of emotional 'grudge holding' is defined as meaning "to hold fast the fault. To continue to think about the offense" (Pukui et al. 1972:71). A person refuses to 'let it go', hanging onto the knotted emotional blockage in the relationship. This constantly renews the emotional hurt and anger of the original offense. Hawaiians often speak of the need to 'let it go' in a long-standing argument (*hukihuki*) or when an impasse is reached. Rather than stubbornly holding on for dominance in victory, it is felt that "one side gotta give"[14] or an innocent third party, usually a child, will be hurt.[15] The ability to 'let it go', and yield, is seen as a particularly Hawaiian trait:

> "And I'll tell you something. Any example, I've ever known—like Hawaiian and Portagee [Portuguese] or Hawaiian and one other nationality—the Hawaiians will always yield. (KI: Why is that? Because of the child?] Well, because they know what's going on—Hawaiians. Most of the time Hawaiians will yield."

While this character trait is valued, sadness and regret for things lost or given up are recognized.[16] However, the desire to keep relational bonds clear and free from the entanglements of conflict or bad feeling is paramount. Even at the cost of great personal pain and loss one is willing to extend one's self to another by giving the other the desired object or point of contention.

The self-centered, coveting nature of lili is evident in a story of the jealousy of the sisters of an informant's mother. My informant's aunts were envious of her mother's attractiveness and many male suitors. "They were enemies. They never talk to one another. You know Hawaiians get like that. Lili they call it—jealous. Lili means jealous." The selfish, retentive character of lili was demonstrated when one of the sisters had an affair with my informant's mother's husband. The mother, on discovering the affair, was hurt and angered by this malicious theft of the affections and loyalties of her spouse. She told her sisters, "You guys all going pay back (ho'opana'i)" for this and previous other hurtful, jealous acts. My informant explained that, indeed, the jealousy of one of the sisters was paid back when, some time later, she fell out of, ironically, a hala (pandanus) tree. The sister had climbed the pandanus tree to pick the lauhala (pandanus leaves) for her weaving. When she fell from the tree, she broke her leg. This occurred in an isolated area, and she despaired of ever being found. She called faintly for help. Coincidentally, my informant's mother was in the area collecting seafood when she heard a soft, distant cry for help in Hawaiian. My informant said that it was strange that she could hear the call at all because of the distance and placement of the hala trees. When my informant's mother went to investigate, she was surprised to see her jealous sister—who was similarly stunned to see who was her rescuer. Following their initial shock, the two sisters began to cry, fell into each other's arms, and forgave each other. When both sisters forgave each other, they jointly 'released' (kala) each other from the previous negative emotional entanglements, 'cutting' ('oki) the negative ties that bound them, and reestablishing the positive affective relationship.

It appears that the process of emotional release and mutual forgiveness actually began earlier than these embraces. A first step was heralded when the jealous sister fell out of the hala tree and perhaps metaphorically out of her transgressing (hala) emotions of lili. Then a second step was taken when the injured sister had to extend herself through her cries for help. At this point she was changing her behavior and thoughts from retentive ones to extensive ones: acknowledging her need for others. And finally, in the open extension of self in aid (kōkua) and comfort, the responding sister offers an accepting gesture of aloha. "My mom save her [sister's] life," declared my informant with finality—an act for which the sister was ever grateful.

This story exemplifies the escalating entanglements (hihia) of hurt and anger resulting from the affective transgression of the retentive, self-serving lili which locked the sisters in negative exchanges. The offending sister was embarrassed and defensive about her violations of the Hawaiian aloha ethos in her improper demonstrations of selfish attitudes and sexual indiscretions. The offended sister, responding in hurt and anger, cursed her sister and 'held fast the fault'. The jealous sister suffered her retribution when she fell out of the tree and broke her leg, a public confirmation of her transgressions. With her vulnerable cries for help, she extended herself outward and began to let go of her self-centered, retentive emotions. This was an initial step in clearing the tangled relational bonds, providing an opening for her sister to respond and reaffirm the bond with acceptance aloha. The responding sister rescued her not only physically but emotionally as she released her own cursing emotions by her accepting response. Both sisters acted openly, unselfconsciously, and without hesitation. This cleared the relational link and 'the way was open' for them to forgive each other and restore their aloha.

In contrast to functionalist models in which intragroup conflict is viewed as fragmenting and divisive, among Hawaiians people become more and more bound to each other as conflict develops, enmeshed in an exchange of ill will and hurt feelings of hihia. It is an emerging, escalating process; each transgression calls up a new or renewed response built on the memory of earlier hurts and actions. To break this cycle peacefully and reopen the tangled lines of interpersonal affect and communication, the two parties must come together, discuss the problem, resolve it satisfactorily, and 'forgive' (*mihi*) each other. This double forgiveness 'releases' (kala) each party from the vengeful cycle of old hurts and retaliations. The entangled affect is then 'cut' ('oki) "clearing the way" for renewed positive emotional exchanges.[17] Inherent in this process of conflict resolution (ho'oponopono) are many of the important dynamics between Self and Other.[18]

HO'OPONOPONO: TO MAKE THINGS RIGHT

In the Hawaiian community today, the term *ho'oponopono* is applied to a wide range of discussion formats for conflict resolution. The Hawaiian Culture Committee of the Queen Liliuokalani Children's Center developed a modern version as a culturally appropriate therapy for families of Hawaiian ancestry (Ito 1979). Other institutions also use ho'oponopono for conflict resolution involving Hawaiians. For example, the University of Hawaii and local community colleges use the format to help students of Hawaiian ancestry adjust to college life and to sensitize non-Hawaiian faculty to Hawaiian social interaction and nonverbal cues (Carse et al. 1977). Various churches of Hawaiian membership also use ho'oponopono as a form of family counseling to isolate and solve members' personal conflicts and problems (Aiona 1959; Ito 1979). In noninstitutionalized settings, ho'oponopono is used to refer to any discussion that has been convened to settle a conflict between two parties. There are variations in the amount of formal structuring in these ho'oponopono sessions, depending on the knowledge of the participants.

In daily life, ho'oponopono can refer to any discussion for the purpose of settling a conflict or dispute. One informant felt even our "talk story" discussions were a form of ho'oponopono because we were searching for answers to problems. But usually it is used to refer to discussions that lead to conflict resolution marked by double apologies and mutual forgiveness.

The conflict can range from a minor marital disagreement to a long-standing feud between neighbors or family members. In these discussions it is understood that in order to settle a dispute, there must be openness, honesty, the ability to 'let it go' (release the hostilities), and a readiness and willingness to forgive. Not all ho'oponopono sessions are successful, because of some lack of this ambience or agreement. One informant told of a ho'oponopono called by her aunt to settle a feud that my informant and her sisters were having with the neighbor's daughters. My informant's brother had married into the neighboring family and into the middle of the feud. The aunt said he was being pulled back and forth in the hukihuki and urged his sisters to "make ho'oponopono" for his sake. Although a truce was called, it was uneasy and temporary: "all of us looking daggers" during the session, laughed my informant. Often the ho'oponopono is called by an older, respected person, usually a woman, who acts as the mediator-leader in the discussion.[19]

The traditional use of ho'oponopono (Pukui et al. 1979) was to regularly clear away small hurts and hostilities before they developed into convoluted hihia (entanglements). In these sessions, the goal is to remove any blockage from negative emotions through mutual discussion, agreement, apology, and forgiveness.

The pivotal element in ho'oponopono is the apology-forgiveness exchange. The term *mihi* means to apologize with the concomitant affect of repentance and regret. A person extends himself or herself to another by offering an apology and, symbolically, the Self. Connected to any apology is a request for forgiveness. One opens up the Self in a vulnerable exposure of contrition by admitting error and asking forgiveness. Once this request for forgiveness is made, the Other is obligated to relinquish anger and to forgive the contrite person. Further, he or she must, in turn, apologize and request forgiveness for any reciprocal hurt or offense committed against the original offender, who must likewise accept and forgive. Aloha is restored with this sincere extension of Self in the mutual apology-forgiveness request and in the gracious acceptance of the Other's offering.

It releases and clears the affective bonds of the constricting ties of negative affect. Furthermore, it restores one's integrity of identity and soma (should there be retributive involvement of illness or injury), reestablishing that one is an expansive Hawaiian of generous aloha, healthful vigor, goodwill, and good manners. (See Ito 1982*b* for a brief discussion of Hawaiian etiquette and self-concept.)

Of course, this restorative apology-forgiveness exchange does not always go so smoothly. An offered apology-forgiveness request may be refused. There appear to be two interpretations of this refusal, depending on the history of the dispute and the personalities of the parties involved. First, if the original offender seems to have made genuine efforts to correct the 'entanglements', to have acted 'with heart', yet the offended person refuses to accept an offered apology and request for forgiveness, this becomes an offense of 'grudge holding'. This leaves the refuser vulnerable to the sanction of illness, misfortune, or even death. Second, if the original offender asks forgiveness too quickly, it is felt that the other person has not been given enough time or a chance to 'soften' his or her resentment. That person's hurt and anger are still too painful to forget. A person who requests an apology-forgiveness exchange before the other is ready or able is not considering the affective condition of the other. She or he is still acting in a self-centered manner. The requestor is felt to have made an error in judgment, and patience is counseled. In this case, no error or hala is attributed to the refuser. One informant told of a woman in her church who had a philandering husband. This woman had come to a church meeting "seeking help" or a solution to her problem with her unfaithful husband. This was the same problem my informant has long had with her own husband. At a church meeting, unaware of the nature of this woman's problem, my informant gave "testimony" about how she had to learn to love her own unfaithful husband "all over again" after her discovery of his infidelities. My informant spoke of how she now is "more mature" and even though she and her husband are separated, she hoped to "someday, try to make a go [of the marriage again]."

These meetings consist of church members giving testimony of their life's troubles and how they faced them. Other members with the same problems listen carefully, using the testimony as a source of a *ho'ailona* or sign of what to do or say in their own similar situations. The testimony is taken as God's method of "opening the way" to show the solution to one's problem. The woman thought that my informant's testimony was her answer, so after leaving the meeting, she returned to her husband.

Later, my informant saw this woman in the doctor's office with a broken leg. She asked what had happened to her. The woman explained that she had heard my informant's testimony that you had to love your husband again and try to make the marriage work. So she went back to her husband, but he beat her and broke her leg. My informant, instead of being sympathetic to the woman, was disgusted. She scolded the woman, telling her it was her own fault: "You didn't really understand what I was trying to say. But see, when you hurt a leg, when you break a leg, that's stepping on the truth. Your leg, when you hurt your leg, that's stepping on the truth of God." I asked my informant what was the truth the woman was stepping on and my informant replied, "The truth she wouldn't accept. She didn't go back the right way. She went home with her husband still having that hate in his heart for her. She, she didn't go with her self-defense first. And asking God to heal her husband, plant love in his heart." In other words, the woman should have prayed to God to put love in her husband's heart to "soften" his anger so he would be able to accept her forgiveness, see his own errors, and ask her forgiveness in turn. My informant saw this as a self-centered act on the part of the woman: "You know you ain't going get everything you want here." Therefore, one cannot initiate a conciliation on merely the basis of one's own affective condition, but must bear the responsibility for the affective disposition of the other party and his or her ability or readiness to accept and request forgiveness.

Hawaiians will also take a person's 'ways' into account in the completion of the apology-forgiveness exchange. Some people are thought to be incorrigibly bitter, irreconcilable sorts, and this will be seen as their 'ways' or 'style'. It is felt that these people are unable to act in an appropriate expansive, forgiving manner. It is assumed they will neither initiate nor return an apology. Therefore, it is the responsibility of those around to be cognizant of their 'ways' and to tolerate them as graciously as possible.

A formal or direct apology-forgiveness request does not have to be explicit to be acceptable as a contrite offering of Self to an Other. The extension of a friendly gesture can be sufficient:

> "You know how I told you how certain persons, one of my neighbors? You know. She accused me of turning her in [to the welfare office for an offense]. And I did . . . I didn't even turn her in. I didn't know what she was doing, you know. And we stayed bad friends for two years. But yet I never forgot her. I, I've always asked God to touch her heart. Cuz she'll realize that one day. And one day, I was washing the dishes, she came and knocked at the back door, said, 'This is New Year's, June. I'm having a party. Could you come over?' And the way, our minister always taught to us, they're washing your feet. In other words, she's asking forgiveness in her own way."

This woman viewed the affective change in their relationship as making them bad friends, not enemies. The friendship was still intact; it was the affect that had changed.

My informant did not talk with her friend directly because she felt the friend's heart was hardened by hostile feelings. Not until God 'softened' her friend's heart was she able to extend an apology-forgiveness in an offering of hospitality. Although this informant told of asking God to 'touch' her friend's heart, the more common saying is to ask God 'to put' or 'for to put love in their hearts'. This appeal to God to change another's feelings, to soften his or her hard heart, which blocks the exchange of positive emotions, is also used to influence a person to accept an offered apology-forgiveness request. As explained by another informant, one is

> "suppose to be forgiving in the right way. You know. Suppose to come to you, tell you, 'Sorry what I did. I like you forgive me.' If you say, 'Yes,' good. And what if he say, 'No'? Well. Then you can, they, you can—they know already, you know already we get one high Man above us. So that Guy you ask forgiveness. Now, He can do the impossible for you. So maybe He can put some thoughts in the one, uh, the one who you forgive. Can put some thinking or some thoughts in this, uh, lady. 'Cause you know already He just like one judge already. He know that you wen' go forgive and you want answer and then she no say and then you feel maybe she still hate you. So, well, you forgive to the Big Man that's the One and He can help you out. In some miracle way which you don't know. But then, yeah? You wen' forgive me and then I never say nothing. Maybe you think I still hate you. Yeah? See? Like that. So then you going know that, 'Oh, yeah, something was done,'—by somebody which you don't know—maybe you know. See? 'I think you change.' Change toward you. You laughing, she's laughing at you. You folks laughing, smiling. So 'at's why, right there, right off the 'fat,' forgive already. [KI: But it won't work if she won't forgive you?] Yeah. Because you know why? If she don't forgive you, her conscience going be the one bothering. But—if the Big Man can do something—the: 'Oh, yeah. I gotta forgive her. I go talk to her. Talk nice.' She going talk like that: 'Hey!' And when she see you tomorrow: 'Hey, howzit? How you?' All that kind, yeah? And, 'Oh, we all right,' you going tell like that. Um hum. 'What you going do today?' Tell, 'Oh, I going to school.' And, and then you just drive the car. You just go. You used up plenty words already."

This affective change in the relationship ("You laughing, she's laughing at you. You folks laughing, smiling.") is interpreted as an acceptance of an extended offer of apology and a granting of forgiveness. Also, as in the previous example, the extension of a friendly gesture, this time in a conversational exchange, is viewed as a return request for forgiveness. More explicit expression is not necessary, particularly following an extended conflict and/or apology process: "You just go. You used up plenty words already."

When the appropriate joint apologies, restitution, and forgiveness have occurred, there should be a 'letting go' and release of the negative affect knotting the relationship (kala). Implicit in the word kala is the releasing or loosening of the grudge bonds of hurt and anger. When this is completed, the hihia 'entanglement' is said to be 'cut' ('oki). This does not involve a "forgive and forget" attitude. In fact, the incident is not forgotten, only removed or neutralized from the entangling cycle of reciprocal animosity.

As described here, ho'oponopono is a method for resolving transgressions of affect. It is used to clear relationships from the entanglements of negative affect through discussion, agreement, and an apology-forgiveness exchange. This apology-forgiveness exchange 'opens the way' to renewed exchanges of positive affect. There is not only a restoration of the positive affect of the relationship but also a restoration of one's positive self-concept. This is done by the extension and offering of one's Self to an Other through an apology and request for forgiveness. The acceptance of this offer and the return offer of Self in apology and forgiveness reestablishes both parties as giving, accepting, open Hawaiians of altruism and aloha. Further, this mutual humbling and exposing of Self, extension and acceptance of the Other's apologies and forgiveness, reestablishes the relationship on an equal footing, albeit on a different plane from that before the 'entanglement'.

CONCLUSION

For Hawaiians, the Self is intimately linked to the affective quality of one's relationships with Others. The affective quality of a person's relationships will determine how others view him or her and how they will interact with and respond to that person. Self is a socially interactive concept tied to correct social behavior (*hana pono*) between Self and Other.[20] Correct social behavior is based on the Hawaiian ideal of extending one's Self in generous, sincere aloha to cooperate with and mutually 'aid' Others. The negation of this ideal, and a transgression of affect, is found in greedy, jealous behavior that is self-centered and retentive.[21]

The Self-Other relationship is an affective pathway for emotional exchanges. It offers a protective netting when open to positive exchanges, and dangerously exposes the Self when entangled by negative exchanges. Negative exchanges begin with some violation (hala) of correct social behavior—which is a violation or disregard of the Other. This precipitating hala so 'hurts' ('eha) and angers the Other that he or she will reciprocate in kind, further entangling the relationship. If the original hala was committed intentionally, it inflicts pain on the other person because it indicates the transgressor felt such ill will toward the person that he or she wanted to demonstrate this by hurting them. If the transgressor committed the hala unintentionally, it is equally, if not more, painful because this lapse of consideration meant one had so little meaning to them that they forgot about one. In this disregard is a negation of Self, of one's existence.

These conflictual entanglements of negative emotional exchanges (hihia) are not disruptive in a schismatic, fragmenting way but actually bond people closer together as the exchanges escalate and others are drawn into the situation. Social relations in Hawaiian culture do not break down, they "jam up." Relationships are always in force—just their affect changes.

Ho'oponopono and elements of this procedure, such as mutual forgiveness and apology, are used to clear the paths of negative affect and to 'open the way' to renewed exchanges of positive, or at least neutral, affect.

> The problem, then, is not a conflict between personal identity and social-cultural identity, for they are both personal and socio-cultural. The problem is, rather, the empirical one of discovering the bonds of feeling that hold people together or tear them apart, and what their interrelations and conditions are. (Singer 1980:500)

ACKNOWLEDGMENTS

Financial support for this research was generously provided by the Carnegie Foundation and the UCLA Kona Research Project, a UCLA Behavioral Anthropology NIMH Predoctoral Traineeship, and the Socio-Behavioral Group of UCLA's Neuropsychiatric Institute's Mental Retardation Research Center. Much inspiration and generative support was gained through correspondence and discussions with John Kirkpatrick, Geoffrey M. White, and David J. Boyd. Thanks to Jill E. Korbin who read and commented on an early draft. Thank you to Lynette Paglinawan and Rev. Roxanne Craig-Rodenhurst for their special help in understanding aspects of ho'oponopono. And a special thank you to all my "lady friends" and other *kama'aina* for their *aloha* and *kōkua*.

NOTES

1. See Pukui et al. (1979) for a discussion in greater detail of the traditional elements of Hawaiian personhood and more current influences on self-image. Holt (1974) has written a highly personalized account of his search for an ethnic consciousness and pride. See Newton (1978:127–131) for a discussion of Hawaiian acceptance of individual personality types.

2. In this chapter, the terms "Self" and "Other" are capitalized when they refer

to situations which specifically involve their reflexive interaction in the social construction of the Hawaiian Self.

3. As Devereux has pointed out, our Cartesian separation of Self and Other,
Individual and Society, is a spurious Inside-Outside dualism since "at any moment,
the person is a 'subject' to himself and 'environment' to the Others; all that is inside
for the subject is outside for the Other" (1978:49). See also Singer (1980); in contrast,
see Myers (1979).

4. See Kirkpatrick, chap. 3, for contrastive Marquesan concepts of envy.

5. See Ito (1978) for background details on each of these women and their
households.

6. In a reversal of most anthropological fieldwork, direct questions in an interview format were not asked until the very end of the fieldwork when informants
felt at ease and understood that the questions were not rude violations of their
privacy.

7. See Werner and Smith (1982) for the importance of extended kin relations in
socialization.

8. See Devereux (1978) for a discussion of "souvenir" as part of the Self-Other,
Inside-Outside unity.

9. The term 'open' is used by Hawaiians to mean 'to release' or 'to free'. For
example, people 'open' their clothes or slippers, that is, take them off or 'free' their
bodies from confinement. They 'open' the television: by turning it on they release
the electrical energy or electronic image. Heighton (1971, cited in Howard 1974:159)
mentions the medicinal use of purgatives to 'open' the body. People use the
metaphorical phrase 'the way is open', meaning one's plans will meet no obstacles
(ālai). One informant noted pragmatically, "The way is always open, Karen. But
it's the money." If people leave the house forgetting something, they will not return
for it. Returning tangles the direction of good intentions and luck, thereby blocking
success. For this reason, people may inexplicably arrive for a court appearance or
other official meeting without their documents or identification, much to the con-
sternation of the authorities. It also is considered bad luck to call someone back
once they have started out (Handy and Pukui 1972:186), although this may be more
because the call back is considered a warning or omen that the 'way' is not clear of
obstacles rather than an entangling of good fortune. Other related examples are the
ʻahaʻaina māwaewae ceremony for a firstborn to clear life's path for this and all
subsequent offspring (Handy and Pukui 1972; Pukui et al. 1979) and 'clearing the
way' prayers performed before any task is undertaken (Pukui et al. 1979).

10. This most likely is a cognate of the Tahitian hara, which has the same error
entanglement and missed target connotations of the Hawaiian hala (Levy 1974).
Firth also mentions sara for the Tikopia, "which I have translated as 'done wrong'
. . . the idea of conduct not in accord with the social harmonies, and therefore
subject to supernatural sanction" (1963:164). This hala/hara error of a below par
performance has implications for the 'shame' expressed by Hawaiians and Tahitians
in feelings of performance inadequacies. See Piers and Singer (1953) for a discussion
of the shame response to feelings of failure or incompetence.

11. See Malo (1951:57) for a statement about traditional Hawaiians' lack of a
codified system of rules or laws.

12. See also Levy's (1973) discussion of the Tahitian *'a'au*.

13. Pukui et al. (1979:226) give a more inclusive category, *mana'o 'ino* 'hurtful thoughts', under which they list such examples as grudge holding, 'bad' thoughts, and fault finding. A further illustration of this retentive quality is the word *ho'ohihi* meaning 'to cause entanglement, to entwine' and 'to take a fancy to' (Pukui and Elbert 1971), which connotes the effort to draw an object of desire closer to one's self.

14. Here again is a reference to the need to extend rather than retain one's self.

15. As one informant explained:

> Because sooner or later, what happens is the feelings is so strong, it's like two families getting together and they start clashing like this [clap] and the kid is in the middle and the kid is the one get hurt, gets sick. For, the, for the problem. See? One side gotta give or not . . . not, you know. The child suffers. See? Or suffers the burdens or whatever the problem was (Ito 1982:389).

16. Sadness for lost chances or irreplaceable items is expressed in the word *pohō*. People will say, "Pohō the land" or the children, a lover, an opportunity, a job. *Minamina* is an even more regretful and poignant term.

17. Another use of the process to 'oki or 'cut' the entanglements of negative affect can be found in the Hawaiian treatment of emotionally upsetting dreams. There is the potential for trouble from the affect of negative thoughts expressed in dreams, since dreams are omens and precognitive warnings. A dream about the endangerment, injury, or death of someone or one's self is particularly disturbing. In order to 'cut' the dream power the dreamer must 'open' or tell the dream to someone as soon as he or she awakens. The negative thoughts or wishes expressed in the dream need to be 'cut' by a confessional expression (an 'opening up'), thereby releasing the ties of dangerous affect.

18. See White's discussion in chapter 9 of the A'ara "disentangling" session which has striking similarities to ho'oponopono.

19. See Howard (1974) for the importance of the mediator function of a Hawaiian leader.

20. See Ito 1982*b*.

21. Shore (1981) discusses a similar distinction for Samoan behavior and the Self-Other relationship. The term *aga* describes socially approved and other-directed acts while *āmio* refers to self-oriented and socially disapproved acts. Aga represents mature thoughtful acts, āmio acts of impulsive abandon. Shore emphasizes these are not distinctions between two polar types because āmio can be a socially approved, group-oriented behavior, conforming to aga and reflecting ("proper teaching (*a'oa'oina*) or socialization, and the ability to 'think' (*mafaufau*) properly").

GLOSSARY

'aha'aina māwaewae   a "clearing the way" feast given for a firstborn to clear misfortune from life's path for this child and all subsequent children

akua	a god or goddess, a spirit
ālai	an obstruction or blockage
aloha	love, affection
'aumakua (pl. *'aumākua*)	ancestor, family god, or spirit
'eha	hurt, pain, suffering
hala	transgression, error; also the pandanus tree (*Pandanus ordoratissimus*)
hana pono	correct behavior, good manners, etiquette; leading to harmonious relations between people, spirits, nature
haole	Caucasian
hihia	an entanglement, snarl; knotted
ho'ohihi	to become captivated by, to take a fancy to; to entangle, entwine
ho'omauhala	grudge holding
ho'opana'i	to pay back
ho'oponopono	to correct, to make right; a method of conflict resolution
hukihuki	to pull back and forth
kala	to loosen, release, pardon, excuse, let go; to forgive
kapu	tabu, prohibition
kino lau	the many forms and bodies of spiritual beings
kōkua	help, cooperation
lauhala	pandanus leaves
lehua	red flower of the *ohia* tree
lili	jealous; jealousy
lokomaka'i	altruism, generosity, goodwill, kindness
maha'oi	tactlessly intrusive, nosy; offensively rude
mainaina	anger; hate
maka'ainana	commoner
make ho'opilikia	ill will; to cause serious trouble
mana'ao 'ino	spite; hate; hurtful affect, thoughts
mihi	apology; repentance
minamina	regret, sorrow; especially for what is lost

na'au	innards, heart; seat of intellect, emotions, sincerity
nīele	annoying or senseless questions; inquisitive
noni	*Morinda citrifolia* tree
'oki	to cut
pāna'i	revenge; reward; pay back; reciprocity
pī	stingy
pohō	loss; associated sense of regret, sadness
pumehana	warmth, affection
ti	*Cordyline terminalis* plant
'uhane	ghost, soul, a person's spirit

REFERENCES

Aiona, D.
  1959   The Hawaiian Church of the Living God: An Episode in the Hawaiian's
          Quest for Social Identity. Master's thesis, University of Hawaii.
Beaglehole, E.
  1937   Some Modern Hawaiians. Honolulu: University of Hawaii Research
          Publication.
Beckwith, M., and L. Green
  1924   Hawaiian Customs and Beliefs Relating to Birth and Infancy. American
          Anthropologist 26:230–244.
Carse, W., E. Libarios, M. Mossman, and P. Wahilani
  1977   An Ancient Therapy—Revisited. Paper presented at the Meetings of the
          Western Psychological Association, Seattle, Washington.
Ciborowski, T., and D. Price-Williams
  1982   Animistic Cognition: Some Cultural, Conceptual, and Methodological
          Questions for Piagetian Research. *In* Cultural Perspectives on Child
          Development. D. A. Wagner and H. W. Stevenson, eds. Pp. 166–180.
          San Francisco: W. H. Freeman.
Devereux, G.
  1978   Ethnopsychoanalysis. Berkeley, Los Angeles, London: University of
          California Press.
Firth, R.
  1963   We, The Tikopia. Boston: Beacon Press. Abr. ed.
Gallimore, R., J. W. Boggs, and C. Tharp
  1974   Culture, Behavior and Education: A Study of Hawaiian Americans.
          Beverly Hills: Sage Publications.
Gallimore, R., and A. Howard (eds.)
  1968   Studies in Hawaiian Community: Na Makamaka O Nanakuli. Pacific

Anthropological Records 1. Honolulu: Bernice P. Bishop Museum.
Handy, E. S. C., and M. K. Pukui
1972   The Polynesian Family System in Kaʻu, Hawaiʻi. Tokyo: Charles E. Tuttle Co.
Handy, E. S. C., M. K. Pukui, and K. Livermore
1934   Outline of Hawaiian Physical Therapeutics. Bernice P. Bishop Museum Bulletin 126. Honolulu: Bishop Museum.
Hawaii State Department of Health
1973   Population Characteristics of Hawaii. Population Report 5. Department of Planning and Economic Development.
Heen, E. L.
1936   The Hawaiians of Papakolea: A Study of Social and Economic Realism. Master's thesis, University of Hawaii.
Heighton, R.
1971   Hawaiian Supernatural and Natural Strategies for Goal Attainment. Ph.D. diss., University of Hawaii.
Holt, J. D.
1974   On Being Hawaiian. Honolulu: Topgallant Publishing Co. Ltd.
Howard, A.
1970   Learning to be Rotuman. New York: Teacher's College Press.
1974   Ain't No Big Thing: Coping Strategies in a Hawaiian American Community. Honolulu: University Press of Hawaii.
Ito, K. L.
1978   Symbolic Conscience: Illness Retribution Among Urban Hawaiian Women. Ph.D. diss., University of California, Los Angeles.
1979   Hoʻoponopono: Structure and Meaning. Paper presented to *Ala Hou*: Conference on Hawaiian Awareness in the Pacific Northwest, University of Washington, Seattle.
1982a   Illness as Retribution: A Cultural Form of Self Analysis Among Urban Hawaiian Women. Culture, Medicine and Psychiatry 6(4):385–403.
1982b   Hawaiian Etiquette and Self Concept. Paper presented to the 81st Annual Meeting of the American Anthropological Association, Washington, D.C., December 6, 1982.
Judd, H. P.
1930   Hawaiian Proverbs and Riddles. Bernice P. Bishop Museum Bulletin 77. Honolulu: Bishop Museum.
Korbin, J. E.
1978   Caretaking Patterns in a Rural Hawaiian Community: Congruence of Child and Observer Reports. Ph.D. diss., University of California, Los Angeles.
Levy, R. I.
1973   Tahitians: Mind and Experience in the Society Islands. Chicago: University of Chicago Press.
1974   Tahiti, Sin and the Question of Integration between Personality and Sociocultural Systems. *In* Culture and Personality: Contemporary Readings. R. A. Levine, ed. Pp. 287–306. New York: Aldine.

Lind., A.

1930   The Ghetto and the Slum. Social Forces in Hawaii 9:206–215.

1939   Social Disorganization in Hawaii. Social Process in Hawaii 5:6–10.

Malo, D.

1951   Hawaiian Antiquities. N. B. Emerson, trans. 2d ed. Bernice P. Bishop Museum Special Publication 2. Honolulu: Bishop Museum.

Meltzer, B. N., J. W. Petras, and L. T. Reynolds

1975   Symbolic Interactionism: Genesis, Varieties and Criticisms. London: Routledge and Kegan Paul.

Myers, F. R.

1979   Emotions and the Self: A Theory of Personhood and Political Order Among Pintupi Aborigines. Ethos 7:343–370.

Newton, F. N.

1978   *Aloha* and Hostility in a Hawaiian-American Community: The Private Reality of a Public Image. Ph.D. diss., University of California, Los Angeles.

Paglinawan, L. K.

1972   *Ho'oponopono* Project II: Development and Implementation of *Ho'oponopono* Practice in a Social Work Agency. Hawaiian Culture Committee, Queen Liliuokalani Children's Center, Liliuokalani Trust. Manuscript Report.

Piers, G., and M. B. Singer

1953   Shame and Guilt: A Psychoanalytic and Cultural System. Springfield, Ill.: Charles C. Thomas.

Pukui, M. K., and S. H. Elbert

1971   Hawaiian Dictionary. Honolulu: University Press of Hawaii.

Pukui, M. K., E. W. Haertig, and C. A. Lee

1972   *Nānā I Ke Kumu* (Look To The Source). Vol. I. Honolulu: *Hui Hanai,* Queen Liliuokalani Children's Center.

1979   *Nānā I Ke Kumu* (Look To The Source). Vol. II. Honolulu: *Hui Hanai,* Queen Liliuokalani Children's Center.

Shore, B.

1981   Sexuality and Gender in Samoa: Conceptions and Missed Conceptions. *In* Sexual Meanings: The Cultural Construction of Gender and Sexuality. S. B. Ortner and H. Whitehead, eds. Pp. 192–215. Cambridge: Cambridge University Press.

Singer, M.

1980   Signs of the Self: An Exploration in Semiotic Anthropology. American Anthropologist 82(3):485–507.

State of Hawaii

1975   Data Book: A Statistical Abstract. Honolulu: Department of Planning and Economic Development.

Werner, E. E., and R. S. Smith

1982   Vulnerable But Invincible: A Study of Resilient Children. New York: McGraw-Hill.

9

Premises and Purposes in a Solomon Islands Ethnopsychology

Geoffrey M. White

INTRODUCTION

Recent decades have seen a resurgence of social science interest in common-sense understandings of social life. During the 1950s, Hallowell (1954), in anthropology, and Heider (1958), in social psychology, developed significant empirical approaches to the phenomenology of social experience which are frequently cited in current research. But their approaches, like much subsequent work in each discipline, tended to treat the problem of ordinary thought as one of mapping abstract symbolic structures and general principles of reasoning, separating the study of cognition from the everyday contexts of social experience. In this chapter, through a discussion of ethnopsychological data from a Solomon Islands society, I argue that folk models of person and social process are bound together by cultural ways of thinking about the concerns and purposes of persons in daily life.

The analysis discussed here began as a study of an indigenous theory of personality among A'ara-speaking people in Santa Isabel, Solomon Islands. I set out to investigate the cultural organization of a Melanesian ethnopsychology with methods drawn from approaches to "person perception" in social psychology (e.g., Hastorf et al. 1970; Rosenberg et al. 1968; Schneider 1973). One of the assumptions behind this approach was that cultural understandings about personal characteristics are encoded in linguistic terms for behavioral dispositions: by reviewing the range of trait terms available in a language and analyzing their meanings, one could begin to understand cultural interpretations of social behavior. If, however, the analysis is restricted in scope to a predetermined lexical field, with the presumption that one may glean concepts of personality independent of other sorts of ethnographic data, severe limitations are placed on understanding. I argue instead that the very structure of folk models is shaped by their application to the interpretation of events—events that are themselves embedded in wider systems of cultural significance.

The meanings of ethnopsychological vocabulary, such as linguistic expressions for personal characteristics or emotions, are an important avenue to understanding indigenous modes of thought and action. However, with a topic as complex, affectively charged, and socially significant as this, analysis of language quickly moves from the study of referential semantics to questions of inference and pragmatics (D'Andrade 1984b). Terms descriptive of personal and social processes are meaningful not as labels but as signposts to an underlying body of cultural knowledge about matters of shared importance (see Rosaldo 1980:24; Quinn 1982). It is possible to derive a corpus of key terms as I have done with A'ara person descriptors (1978, 1980a), and explore their range of meanings through informants' exegesis and semantic judgments. But these procedures provide only a glimpse of the thematic organization of cultural knowledge about persons and of social activity.

In this chapter I seek to explore more fully cultural themes that emerged only in the barest outline in previous analyses of lexical structure. This more broad-ranging analysis reveals an A'ara model of social experience which is extensively concerned with personal (and community) well-being, a model that postulates an intimate link between well-being and interpersonal processes. The premises of this model are perhaps most evident in folk theories that explain misfortune in terms of social conflict and associated emotions. The discussion examines a variety of linguistic data (words, metaphors, discourse) in order to indicate some of the ways personal harm and well-being are conceptualized, particularly in relations between persons, spirits, and chiefs, where ideas about power and vulnerability find their clearest expression. I then go on to argue that much of A'ara talk about persons and emotions acquires meaning and moral force on the basis of these cultural models or conceptualizations about matters of shared concern.

SETTING

Fieldwork for this study was done in the Maringe area of Santa Isabel, one of the five largest islands in the Solomon Islands. The language of this region (spoken by about half of the island's more than 12,000 people) is referred to as *cheke holo* 'bush language', and specifically as A'ara in the villages where fieldwork was carried out. A'ara is an Austronesian language related to other languages in the Western Solomons.

In the past, residential patterns were characterized by small, shifting settlements composed of a few households pursuing swidden gardening in the interior of the island. But after a disruptive period of increased head-hunting and internecine warfare in the late nineteenth century, most of the island population embraced Christianity and moved down to larger villages (ranging between 50 and 300 residents) in coastal areas (White 1979a). Despite Christianization and modernizing changes that led to independence for the Solomon Islands in 1978, people continue to depend primarily on subsistence horticulture.

Indigenous patterns of sociopolitical organization resemble those de-scribed for other islands in the Western Solomons (Oliver 1955; Scheffler 1965). Kinship relations and regional alignments were the important bases of cooperation and competition among peoples scattered throughout the island in small hamlets. The idiom for tracing descent is clearly matrilineal. Exogamous matrilineal clans are found in all parts of the island. Major forms of cooperative enterprise in the past included raiding, making pro-pitiatory offerings at the shrines of deceased ancestors, and staging feasts. These activities were organized by local leaders (*funei*) whose power was based on personal reputation and accomplishments in feasting and warfare, somewhat similar to the model of the Melanesian "big man" portrayed by Sahlins (1963), but with some of the features of the Polynesian "chief" as well.[1]

Despite the slow pace of economic development (the island was with-out roads or motor vehicles, except outboard canoes, at the time of fieldwork), the last century has seen extensive cultural transformations and social reorganization. The most fundamental sociocultural changes have followed from conversion to Christianity through the Anglican Melanesian Mission. By 1920, conversion of the entire population was essentially com-plete. Furthermore, the population was converted by a single church, which is highly unusual for a Melanesian society as large and diverse as Santa Isabel. Accompanying the conversion process, cultural ideals of social be-havior have been extensively recast in the framework of a Christian social ideology and the rhetoric of brotherhood and cooperation (White 1980b).

THE SELF: DEFINITION AND DEFENSE

Sorcery, Magic, and Spirit Doings

From the time of Tylor on, systems of magic, sorcery, and supernatural belief have provided the prototype for portrayals of "primitive" thought.

In developing his notion of "mystical participation," Levy-Bruhl (1975:69) pointed specifically to instances of sorcery and sympathetic magic:

> for example, to strike a spear into the footprint of an enemy or animal who is out of range. They think that the wound made in the imprint strikes simultaneously the man or animal who left it. . . . We interpret these procedures by the conviction, established among the natives, that the appurtenances *are* the individuals themselves. . . . The footprint is the foot itself; the foot . . . *is* the animal or man himself. (Emphases in original.)

As Levy-Bruhl rightly notes, this type of practice assumes that the action directed at the footprint will affect the person who made it. However, the statement that the footprint *is* the person infers a relation of identity between footprint and person which is not necessary in the native theory of sorcery and illness. The cultural significance of the footprint, in this case, is that it is a vehicle for sorcery attack, an effective medium for harming the target person. In other words, the footprint becomes a symbol of the person only in the context of theories of illness and the practice of sorcery, in which it constitutes an important link in the causal chain from malevolent act of the sorcerer to the pain, illness, or death of the person attacked. Levy-Bruhl and others repeatedly cite this type of practice as evidence of more *general* and *abstract* conceptions of self among "primitive" peoples, but this type of characterization is unwarranted by the data, and is probably more of an artifact of the ethnographer's interest in mapping an abstract concept of the bounds of selfhood than an indication of actual processes of cultural reasoning.

Consider This point is similar in some respects to Needham's (1976) discussion of theories of head-hunting which have consistently postulated indigenous beliefs in some kind of "soul substance" or "life-force" as the mediating link between the practice of taking heads and its perceived benefits, such as increased fertility and strength. Needham notes a general lack of ethnographic evidence for such mystical substances in head-hunting ideologies, and suggests that errors in description stem from a failure to recognize alternative conceptions of causality which may operate without a mechanistic mediator between cause and effect. In like fashion, Levy-Bruhl's description of sorcery beliefs postulates an identity between personal vestiges and the whole self in order to make sense of cultural practices of reasoning which are at variance with our causal models.

Perhaps because of the long history of Western philosophical interest in self-awareness and self-consciousness, ethnographers have frequently posed the question "What are the boundaries and limits of self-definition?" just as Hallowell does when he emphasizes the importance of understanding the way in which cultures organize "the emergence of the self as a perceptible object" (1967:75). The focus on the symbolic size and shape of self-concepts has led ethnographers to interpret data such as the pierced footprint as evidence that, in "primitive" thought, "the self is not rigorously delimited by the external surfaces of the body" (Levy-Bruhl, cited in Leenhardt 1979:13). This perspective portrays the cognitive structure of folk conceptions in overly abstract, generalized terms, and misses the more interesting question, "What are the contexts in which objects such as footprints, fingernails, or feces represent vehicles for affecting persons?" In other words, what are people *doing* when they conceptualize these objects as tokens of the person? A recent review reached a similar conclusion in noting disagreements among ethnographic interpretations of cultural "modes of thought":

> Crucial disagreement among anthropologists has turned on exactly this point—disagreement about what it is that people are doing in the task under study. In the modes of thought discussion, disagreement about task takes the form of arguments between "intellectualist, neo-Tyloreans," and those who claim that the native task is not to explain the world in causal terms, but to exert social control. (Laboratory of Human Cognition 1978:66)

I have cited the example of the pierced footprint because the same procedure occurs in the A'ara arsenal of sorcery procedures (which, although very much alive in cultural belief, are probably practiced very rarely in contemporary Christian society). The sorcery technique known as *churumala* 'pierce footprint' involves stabbing a person's footprint with a sharp implement to cause that person pain and sickness—specifically, swelling of the legs often associated with filariasis (elephantiasis). Outside of this context, it would make no sense to assert that a person's footprints represent the self or the whole person. They acquire personal significance as symbolic links in culturally constituted activities of attack and defense from attack. In other words, their conceptual role in thinking about persons or selves is framed more by concerns with self-*defense* than with self-*definition*. The meaning of footprints as tokens of the person derives from their position in cultural reasoning about sorcery attack, rather than from a general relation of identity.

By thus broadening the focus of ethnographic analysis and linking it more closely to indigenous concerns, it is possible to see that understandings about sorcery are one type of conceptual schema among others that interpret misfortune (illness, injury, failure) as caused by malevolent spirits or persons who enlist supernatural assistance in accomplishing their destructive purposes. To use Hallowell's term, the A'ara "behavioral environment" is populated by a variety of powerful spirit forces which may be regulated with the proper ritual knowledge, but which pose an ever-present threat to personal well-being (cf. Schwartz 1973). For example, serious illness is frequently interpreted as the work of malevolent social actors, hostile persons, or spirits. I argue here that the spirit realm and interpersonal processes are largely conceptualized in terms of concerns with personal harm and community misfortune (as well as their obverse, well-being and prosperity, discussed below). These concerns may be glimpsed in the use of analogous metaphors to conceptualize encounters with both spirits and other persons perceived as damaging to the person.

Pain, Penetration, and Protection

The human body is a potent symbol of personal well-being. A'ara speakers extend certain core concepts of bodily experience to the domain of social experience, saying, for example, that moral transgressions 'cause pain' and 'hurt' others (see Lakoff and Johnson 1980). Terms for 'pain' (*khabru*) and 'sickness' (*fogra*) are among the most basic expressions for personal harm. Conditions of illness or injury, or even bad feeling, evoke explanations in terms of folk theories about the various sources of harm. In the A'ara case, these sources range from malevolent social actors (both persons and spirits) who may intentionally 'damage' one (lit., 'make bad', *fadidi'a*) to moral transgressions and disruptions in social relations. The notion of 'pain' is used as a metaphor for suffering and unhappiness caused by others who have 'hurt' someone, as in failing to fulfill kinship obligations. In this sense, the term is used in a transitive form, *fakakabru* 'cause (someone) pain'.

The concept of 'causing pain' is further elaborated in an array of metaphorical expressions which describe harmful actions as 'digging', 'poking', or 'jabbing' a person with a sharp implement of some kind (White 1985). Furthermore, attempts to coerce someone into revealing information (such as knowledge of wrongdoing) are described as 'prying out' (*suisukhi*), as one would pry out a splinter lodged beneath the skin. Another example of penetration comes from contact with a 'forest spirit' (*na'itu mata*) which may result in one being 'speared' (*fada*) by the spirit. Being 'speared by a spirit' (*fada na'itu*) is believed to cause a type of serious illness, probably that diagnosed as pneumonia in Western medicine. In addition to the method of 'pierced footprints' described above, another sorcery technique that reflects these images of penetration involves 'staring'. Those who have the appropriate power (assumed to derive from spirits) are able to cause sores or ulcers simply by looking intently (*toetoe,* from the verb *toe,* 'stare or gaze') at someone. And, as is the case with most sorcery beliefs, the knowledge and power to cause a certain kind of illness are assumed to be effective in curing those same kinds of disorder.

A'ara theories of powers and dangers associated with the supernatural and malevolent persons have important behavioral consequences. Specifically, the proliferation of perceived threats to personal and community well-being leads to a heightened sense of vigilance about possible contact with harmful persons or spirits. So, for example, certain individuals are said to have special abilities to sense whether or not cooked food has been the object of sorcery, *gamunitu,* literally, 'eat something imbued with spirit-power', and thus should not be eaten. The ability to perceive the invisible threat of sorcery is termed *t'haboghano* (from the words 'touch' *tabo,* and 'food' *gano*). Another example of preventive measures taken to ward off sorcery attacks is that of dancers at public occasions and feasts who are believed to be vulnerable to harm from the stares or looks of people in the audience. Thus, dancers will frequently carry magical potions or wear charms to defend against possible harm from ill-intentioned others in the audience.

Much of the traditional religion involved pragmatic procedures for regulating transactions with the supernatural, to gain power or mana (*nolaghi*) to succeed in daily activities and, especially, to protect oneself from dangerous spirits or sorcerers. In the past, people would commonly wear amulets containing ginger root (*khogu*) or other magical substances to provide protection from spirit attacks or dangerous stares and the like. The process of imparting magical power to a protective amulet is termed *babana* (from the root 'build' *bana*)—a term that figuratively describes building a barrier.[2] (Another use of the term refers to a camouflaged screen used in hunting.) The aim of this kind of countermagic is conceptualized figuratively as making one 'hard' (*maku*) and hence less vulnerable to penetration by dangerous forces. According to one informant, such an amulet is regarded as 'preparation' (*tarabana*) in the same sense that taking paddles along in an outboard motor canoe is preparation for possible misfortune. In contemporary society, Christian symbols and ritual function to provide people with this kind of daily insurance against possible threats in the behavioral environment. Crosses worn around the neck are a new kind of protective amulet, whereas prayer in church before Communion ceremonies is termed 'preparation'.

In a general way, Christian belief and ceremony in Santa Isabel function in much the same way as the old religion to regulate transactions with powerful supernatural forces in the context of pragmatic concerns with personal well-being and community misfortune. Many contemporary religious practices may be seen as symbolic and behavioral consequences of these culturally constituted concerns—as institutionalized attempts to protect against perceived threats or deal with their destructive consequences (as in curing illness through prayer and hymn singing). Concerns with personal well-being are conceptualized in folk theories that explain the social and supernatural sources of power and prosperity, harm and misfortune. In the next section, I deal with some of the ways in which these concerns provide an important context for understandings about persons and spirits as social actors.

PERSONS AND SPIRITS

Perhaps the most general or basic sense of the A'ara term 'person' (*naikno*) derives from its contrast with the term for 'spirits' (*na'itu*). These two opposed terms encompass the A'ara world of social actors, of beings who do things that affect oneself and others. *Na'itu* has a complex array of meanings and uses. It may label inchoate or uncertain perceptions, as well as various types of supernatural forces and actors. This discussion will be concerned primarily with spirits as social actors, such as the spirits of deceased ancestors and various forest spirits, both of which, in addition to acting independently, may enter into relations with persons who possess the appropriate magical knowledge with which to regulate the interaction. In the contemporary view, persons and spirits are conceptually distinct, but interact almost continuously. The category of 'person' is coextensive with human beings. Persons have bodies and hence are visible. More important, they are more or less predictable and accountable in their actions (cf. Redfield 1953). Spirits, in contrast, are unseen (or only partially glimpsed, as in the form of fireflies in the night), unpredictable, and unaccountable to society's moral constraints. As shown by other authors in this volume, the degree of participation of ancestral spirits, or ghosts, in the moral community is an important theme in ethnopsychological interpretation, and one that is variable across cultures (cf. Tobian and Ifaluk ghosts, chaps. 7 and 2).

It is likely that this contemporary view of spirits, which appears to be generally shared, represents a shift from that of pre-Christian Santa Isabel. Traditional religious practices were largely formulated as ritualized transactions with ancestral spirits who could enter into reciprocal relations with the living, and who frequently acted as guardians or sources of assistance in worldly affairs. I take one old informant's kindly reference to his deceased ancestors as 'our kin' (*kherami*—a term now also used in the sense of 'friend') as evidence that traditional views of relations between the living and the dead were more balanced than they are today. At the present time, the Christian God is the source of beneficial power and hence is the object of ritual activities designed to tap that power and maintain harmonious relations. Ancestral spirits (ghosts) are, along with other types of spirits, generally now regarded as uncontrolled and dangerous. The modern attitude is reflected in the common use of the Pijin term *devol* ('devil') to refer to spirits of all kinds, including ancestral spirits. The historical process of Christianization has literally *depersonalized* the notion of 'spirit', making the categories of 'person' and 'spirit' more exclusive.

Whatever the case in the past, Christianization has pushed ancestral spirits outside the moral community. It is not meaningful to evaluate their actions as either "good" or "bad." What is important about spirits in the local view is their potency or causal efficacy. The cultural reality of spirits is manifest particularly by their role in the interpretation and manipulation of a broad range of matters of personal and community importance. The actions of spirits acting independently are usually perceived as either mischievous or malevolent. An unplanned encounter with a spirit is likely to cause a person harm, whether in a minor way by disorienting the person, or more seriously by causing sickness or death. The experience of disorientation is frequently interpreted as the result of mischievous actions by spirits which have caused one to become confused. Thus, whether confusion occurs while traveling or while conversing with others, it is often attributed to the actions of na'itu. For example, a person who becomes temporarily lost while walking in the forest may infer that he or she has been affected by spirits, making the disorientation a frightening experience—frightening because spirits may also cause illness, injury, or death (cf. Fajans, chap. 10). The A'ara language includes a variety of transitive verbs which describe the experience of a person who is disoriented, confused, or frightened by an active agent. At least one of these verbs, *fahiba,* applies only to the actions of 'spirits'.

Much of traditional religion and contemporary magical knowledge is concerned with regulating and controlling transactions with spirits to gain access to their extraordinary powers or to protect oneself from their injurious effects. Thus, persons with the appropriate magical knowledge are able to cause or cure specific illnesses, succeed in hunting or fishing, woo a lover, win arguments against their adversaries, change the weather, and perform many instrumental tasks with greater effectiveness. Although nearly everyone possesses some kind of specialized magical knowledge, persons with publicly demonstrated skills and abilities are said to have access to the most potent sources of spirit power. In the past, priests and chiefs possessed the ritual knowledge as well as the sacred artifacts, such as bits of hair or fingernails from deceased ancestors, necessary to 'awaken' (*fadodofra*) the spirits for assistance in gardening, paddling canoes, raiding enemies, or other purposes. Demonstrated accomplishments and access to powerful spirits are mutually validating sources of a reputation for personal effectiveness or mana, and hence prestige.

Since traditional leadership by chiefs (funei) was largely based on personal accomplishments and reputation for success in sociopolitical activities, the most renowned chiefs were also those perceived to have access to powerful spirits which could strengthen and protect their chiefly 'owner' and his followers. The transformation of conceptions of the supernatural through Christianization, with the concomitant discrediting of ancestral spirits, was associated with a general decline in the legitimacy and influence of traditional funei as regional leaders. However, persons who possess or control diffuse spirit powers—now primarily through Christianity—continue to be attributed with mana (nolaghi).

The A'ara concept of mana pertains to the personal abilities of one who manifests some of the potency and causal efficacy associated with spirit-doings. In the past, a 'man of mana' was one who could perform dramatic feats, and who also acted as an intermediary with the spirit world in performing propitiation rites at the shrines of deceased ancestors to ensure prosperous gardens, ward off illness, or otherwise enhance life. (Hence the term for 'priest', *mae fafara,* is, literally, 'propitiation man'.) Nowadays, Christian priests and catechists most exemplify mana by virtue of their actions and status in the church. It is important, however, to note that mana is demonstrated through personal action and accomplishments, and thus is not attributed equally to all priests. Rather, it is associated particularly with a few individuals renowned for performing miraculous feats.

The participation of renowned chiefs, and especially of priests (both traditional and modern), in the power of the spirit world is reflected in the use of the term 'person' (naikno) to refer to people as 'followers' or 'common persons', as distinguished from 'chiefs'. There are a number of terms which differentiate the elevated status of chiefs from that of the 'common man', *mae khomabro,* such as the contrast of 'big man' (*mae bi'o*) and 'small man' (*mae sitei*) in addition to the word 'person' (naikno), which, when contrasted with 'chief', takes on the sense of 'common person'. This usage represents a narrowing of the 'person' category to differentiate people from chiefs, and especially priests, as distinct types of social actors. (An interesting historical footnote illustrating this sense of the word *naikno* is the translation given by the first Spanish explorers in 1568 to the cognate term *nakloni,* which they rendered as "vassal" [Amherst and Thomson 1901].)

This opposition of the categories 'chief' and 'common person' is an example of linguistic marking as discussed by Greenberg (1966) and others. This is so because a single term, *naikno,* is used to refer to one category ('common person') in the oppositional pair as well as to the more inclusive category, 'person', which encompasses both members of the opposition. Thus, 'chiefs' are marked in the categorical sense that they are referred to by a distinctive term, while the term *naikno* is retained for 'common persons'. However, in addition to this referential marking, notions of 'chief' and 'priest' are marked in relation to unmarked 'common persons' in a broader social ideological sense on the basis of their greater degree of participation in the spirit world and associated attributes of personal power. Just as the category 'chief' is lexically marked in opposition with that of 'common person', so chiefs, past and present, are marked in social discourse as topics of particular interest and discussion. In a society where there is relatively little talking about personal behavioral characteristics, the personal actions and behavioral qualities of local leaders are frequently the focus of both conversation and ceremonial discourse.

Chiefs, then, occupy a middle position in the conceptual opposition of the social and moral world of 'persons' and the world of 'spirits'. They are certainly 'persons' in contrast with 'spirits', yet their knowledge and control of spirits makes them more spiritlike in comparison with 'common persons' (cf. Howard n.d.). Traditionally, renowned chiefs said to possess powerful spirits were both feared and respected by others as a source of protection for the community. These mixed emotions of fear (*nahmaghu*) and respect (*gatho tahu* 'think heavily'; *filo fahaghe* 'look up') also characterized relations with familiar spirits. Both chiefs and priests were, and continue to be, regarded with considerable ambivalence as social actors who are at once powerful and potentially dangerous, capable of effecting extraordinary changes in the social and natural world. The ambivalence that characterizes views of chiefs is also evident in perceptions of their personal and behavioral characteristics, which will be taken up further below in discussion of the "dilemma of dominance" affecting traditional leaders whose legitimacy is based in part on images of personal power and strength.

The above formulation of the significance of the two senses of the word *naikno* (as 'person' and 'common person') can also be applied to another, third sense of the word. One of the most common uses of the term *naikno* is to refer to women, in contrast with men. Thus, an adult male is often referred to as a 'big man' (*mae bi'o*), whereas an adult female is termed, literally, 'big person' (*naikno bi'o*). Retaining the term *naikno* to designate the category 'adult female' creates an opposition of marked and unmarked terms which neatly reverses the marking of gender in English, and presents an exception to the cross-cultural tendency for marking female categories noted by Greenberg (1966).

Like the opposition of 'chiefs' and 'common persons', this third sense of the word *naikno* (as 'adult female') is produced by a contrast in social categories (with 'adult male') which differentiates the more inclusive concept of 'person'. Both of these narrower senses of the term *naikno* ('common person' and 'adult female') could be defined on the basis of criteria for category membership, such as leadership status or sex. However, more relevant for the present discussion, this linguistic marking of social categories appears to express parallel cultural notions about contrasts in personal abilities and actions. Among the large number of behavioral differences which contrast the categories of 'adult male' and 'adult female', one of the most salient is the difference in power based on personal strength and participation in the spirit realm. Although women participate fully in local sociopolitical life, the most public positions of leadership and the most visible demonstrations of power belong to men. This difference in degree of publicly demonstrated power is most evident in beliefs about the spirit world in which women are regarded as anathema to the personal potency to be derived from spirits. A typical example is the belief that if men on a turtle hunting expedition have sexual contact with women, they risk becoming powerless (*sapu*), a condition opposite to that of being imbued with power (nolaghi, mana). Another belief that reflects the A'ara view of relations between women and the spirit world is that women and children are regarded as most vulnerable to the dangerous spirits which inhabit burial grounds and other tabu sites. There is a restriction (which does not need enforcing) against women or children visiting the now overgrown ancestral shrines and burial sites associated with the old religion. Violation of the tabu is believed not only to cause illness for the transgressor but to cause natural disturbances such as thunder as well.

These three senses of the term *naikno* may be represented as a set of interrelated oppositions in which the superordinate category 'person' encompasses 'chiefs' and 'common persons', and the latter are further differentiated into 'adult males' and 'adult females'. When viewed in this way, these categories form a hierarchically ordered series of oppositions which progressively narrow the 'person' category through contrasts with the marked identities 'chief' and 'adult male', as depicted in figure 1. Representing these contrastive identities in a single branching structure draws attention to the fact that each opposition plays upon the theme of potency, such that 'spirits', 'chiefs', and 'adult males' carve out successive degrees of participation in the spirit realm. In like fashion, each opposition points to the quiet, orderly, rule-following behavior that is ideally characteristic of the unmarked identities of 'persons', 'common persons', and 'adult females'.

Figure 1 highlights the fact that cultural models used to think about spirits and spirit-related action also extend into the world of interpersonal relations where they are used to define social identities and interpret interaction. Hallowell noted this general point when he observed, "The relation of the self to [spiritual beings, deities, ancestors] may, indeed, be characterized by the same patterns that apply to interpersonal relations with other human beings" (1967:92). Having noted that spirits are invoked particularly

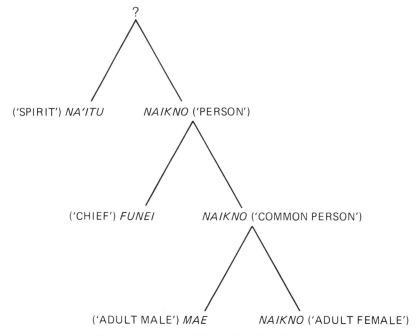

FIGURE 1. Marked/Unmarked Social Categories.

in interpreting experiences that are threatening or damaging to the self, I next examine some of the ways in which these concerns shape interpretations of interpersonal processes.

PERSON DESCRIPTION

Ordinary A'ara descriptions of people, and ways of talking about emotional experience, emphasize processes of interpersonal interaction and the state of relations among people in the community. This interpersonal emphasis reflects the basic premise that a person's actions, talk, and feelings reverberate throughout a web of social relations, with consequences for the well-being of self, others, and community. These assumptions about the relational implications of feeling and action are particularly evident in folk theories of illness and misfortune in which perceived hostility and conflict play a key conceptual role. The account below describes some of the language used to talk about persons and attempts to explicate its interpersonal meaning in terms of certain contexts and concerns that engender ethnopsychological discourse.

Interpersonal Lexicon

As stated at the outset of this chapter, I set out in my own fieldwork to investigate the conceptual organization of implicit theories of personality in one Melanesian society. My basic strategy relied on vernacular terms and phrases as meaningful cultural symbols that can provide a window onto indigenous concepts of personality. Thus, I began in open-ended fashion by cataloging linguistic expressions culled from my efforts at compiling an A'ara dictionary and from recordings of conversation or story telling.[3] This corpus of person descriptors was then used to derive a smaller, representative set of frequently used terms and phrases. Having arrived at a set of thirty-seven descriptive terms and phrases that seemed salient in ordinary talk about persons, I attempted to explore their meanings by asking several informants to define them and give examples of appropriate usage. In addition, I asked twenty-five informants to perform a sorting task, judging which terms were the most similar in meaning (for details of the elicitation procedure, see White 1978:336). This procedure produced a set of data showing relative degrees of similarities among all the terms in the corpus—data that could then be analyzed with multivariate techniques such as cluster analysis and multidimensional scaling to search for clusters of similar terms and for dimensions formed by terms arrayed in conceptual opposition to one another.

The model of person description which resulted from this analysis reveals as much about the conceptualization of the domain as a whole as about relations among particular terms. My attempts to interpret these data led increasingly to the realization that academic notions of personality are themselves a cultural construction, rooted in more fundamental understandings about social life.[4] Examination of the lexicon of person descriptors, of informants' exegesis of the terms, and of the structure of the model of semantic similarities suggest that A'ara descriptions of personal behavioral traits are basically about *interpersonal* process rather than the characteristics of individuals as social isolates.[5] The interpersonal themes that structure A'ara person perception are evident in informants' discussions of the meanings of descriptive terms as well as in the structure of lexical models.

Representation of the judgments of similarity among the thirty-seven terms using multidimensional scaling shows them to be structured by two primary conceptual dimensions that cross-cut each other. Based on knowledge of the meanings of the terms which form these dimensions, I have interpreted them as reflections of the themes of solidarity versus conflict and dominance versus submission (for a more detailed account, see White 1978, 1980*a*). The dimension of solidarity-conflict is represented by the opposition of terms such as 'sympathetic' (*kokhoni di naikno* 'sympathetic with people') and 'kind' (*nahma*) with 'quarrelsome' (*mamagra*), 'recalcitrant' (*huhughu*) and 'individualistic' (*nogna sopa puhi* 'his own way'); while the dimension of dominance-submission consists of the opposition of descriptors such as 'strong' (*hneta*) and 'bold' (*frane*) with 'fearful' (*nahmaghu*) and 'poor' (*kmo'e khame gna na* 'his hand is short').

The structure and meaning of this dimensional model suggest that A'ara vocabulary for describing personal behavioral traits is essentially *inter*personal in nature. This result was somewhat surprising, given that my study began as an investigation of personality concepts generally. Similar research with American personality trait terms has derived a variety of factors or dimensions representing basic types of personality concepts. While two of the dimensions which emerge from the American studies resemble quite closely the dimensions of solidarity-conflict and dominance-submission (see, e.g., Wiggins 1979), the striking difference is that the American lexicon includes a wide range of terms that describe individual qualities not closely tied to interaction, such as the factors "culture" ("intellectual," "refined," etc.) or "conscientious" ("persevering," "careful") (D'Andrade 1985; Goldberg 1981).

The interpersonal significance of A'ara person descriptors emerges even more clearly in informants' exegeses. When informants discuss the meanings of terms or give examples of their use, they do so by describing interactive behavior in specific social contexts. For example, one informant, discussing the meaning of the word 'knowledgeable' (*glalase*), said that a person with 'knowledge' is able to win out in argumentation and influence others. Inferences about the interpersonal significance of the attribution 'knowledgeable' are not just peripheral but central to the term's meaning.

Understanding the meanings of A'ara language for describing personal behavior (and of the themes of solidarity and dominance) requires a closer look at some of the culturally constructed contexts for social interaction, as well as some of the occasions for ordinary talk about persons and their behavior.

Power and the Dilemma of Dominance

One of the most fundamental features of ordinary descriptions of persons is that they are almost always *evaluative* in nature. In other words, ethnopsychological or social discourse carries moral force—it implies that actions are good or bad, desirable or undesirable. In commonsense formulations, behavior is not simply measured or represented, it is evaluated in terms of its significance for self, others, and the community. The evaluative connotations of person descriptors are especially prominent in informants' exegeses that inevitably characterize behavior as 'good' (*keli*) or 'bad' (*di'a*).

The evaluative connotations of A'ara person descriptors appear to be well represented in the lexical model by the dimension of solidarity versus conflict, with traits of solidarity ('kind', 'sympathetic', 'willing') regarded as the most positive and traits of conflict ('quarrelsome', 'recalcitrant', 'individualistic') regarded as the most negative or undesirable types of behavior.

The lexical model also poses an intriguing picture of the evaluative *ambiguity* of traits of dominance (e.g., 'strong', 'bold', 'commanding') and submission ('fearful', 'poor'). Informants judged these traits to be as semantically similar to the positive traits of solidarity as they are to the negative traits of conflict. It is for this reason that the lexical model shows traits of dominance and submission to form a distinct dimension that cross-cuts the more evaluatively polarized dimension of solidarity-conflict (White 1978, 1980*a*). The theme of dominance and its evaluative ambiguity are related to uncertainties surrounding cultural construals of power—personal, political, and spiritual—and the roles of chiefs (*funei*), as outlined in the prior discussion of personhood.

Many of the terms for traits of dominance are used primarily in the contexts and activities of leadership: speaking at meetings or feasts, directing and organizing work activities, engaging in transactions with spirits, and, in the past, raiding and fighting. For example, the term for 'strength' (either social or physical), *hneta,* is also used to form the term for 'warrior' (*mae hneta* 'strong man'). The meanings of terms such as 'strong', 'commanding' (lit., 'always speaking' *checheke khoba*) or 'bold' are embedded in cultural understandings about the contexts of chiefly activity. Indeed, notions of social strength and interpersonal dominance can hardly be separated from the particular arenas of political action, lest they lose their cultural meaning. This embeddedness is reflected in the fact that, when asked to discuss terms for traits of dominance, informants repeatedly made spontaneous reference to chiefs and their roles. For example, one informant described the term *faheaheta* 'aggressive' by linking it to the contexts of leadership ('making feasts', 'talking about plans for working') on the one hand, and to expressions of conflict ('fighting or stealing') on the other:

> "A man can be faheaheta in talking, in working, or in the bad ways of fighting. Chiefs can be faheaheta in making feasts, or in talking about plans for working and leading people. Another meaning is the way of fighting or stealing. A person may be faheaheta not because he is really bold but because he is fearful or angry."

Note that this bit of exegesis ranges across both positive and negative meanings of 'aggressive'. Chiefly identity is invoked to legitimate 'aggressive' behavior in the context of activities such as 'making feasts' or 'talking about plans for working'.

It is not an accident that most of the ethnographic discussions of Melanesian theories of personality or perceptions of personal traits have focused on the personalities of traditional leaders, Big Men (e.g., Oliver 1955; Read 1959; Sahlins 1963; Valentine 1963). As mentioned earlier, much of this interest derives from the importance of personal abilities and reputation for political legitimacy—a subject that has long attracted the attention of social anthropologists. However, the character and behavior of Big Men is also a salient *indigenous* focus for Melanesian discourse about persons. A reading of the ethnographic literature shows a surprising degree of convergence in accounts of cultural understandings about the ideal traits of legitimate leaders, with numerous writers citing the model of personal traits and ideal types of leaders developed by Read for the Gahuku Gama of Highlands New Guinea. In its simplest form, Read (1959:427) proposed that Gahuku Gama understandings about personality are organized in terms of two basic dimensions or orientations: "equivalence" and "strength," which he characterizes as somewhat "antithetical" since "equivalence" represents notions of fairness and compromise which may be overridden by unrestrained "strength" or "bigness." He noted particularly that traits of "strength" are regarded with some ambivalence and pose a problem for aspiring Big Men who, ideally, exhibit both types of qualities:

> As a rule the ideal masculine type is found toward the extreme of "strongness" and "bigness." Yet it is not the men who most closely approximate the stereotype of the "strong" man—not the truly "big"—who tend to be the most successful leaders. Indeed, extremes of "strength" and "bigness" are probably incompatible with the role of leader . . . the truly "big"—if we accept the descriptions given by informants—are characteristically aggressive, somewhat compulsive and overbearing. These may be valuable assets in warfare and raiding. . . . But the precipitate, compulsive individual may be a constant source of irritation or disruption in his own group, where the use of force or the threat of force is proscribed under the ideal of group consensus. (Ibid., pp. 434–435)

Watson has described a similar ambivalence in perceptions of traits of dominance or "strength" among the Tairora, another Highlands society: "the political ideal rather calls for the leadership of men of strength but, when they arise, the Tairora often experience with them the moral conflict expressed in characterizing them as 'bad'" (1967:103).

There is a close parallel between the model articulated by Read and the dimensions of dominance and solidarity in the model of A'ara person descriptors (although Read, like many other ethnographers, generally assumes a convergence between actual Gahuku Gama personalities and their *perceptions* of personality). The semantic linkage of dominance with both solidarity and conflict reflects the potential for alternately positive or negative evaluations of dominance. And, as in many other Melanesian societies, the contexts of leadership and the activities of aspiring Big Men are the arena for these ambiguities, shifting evaluations, and ambivalences.

The "dilemma of dominance" posed by leadership activities is evident in the ambiguous evaluative status of many of the metaphors used to conceptualize dominance. A recognized traditional leader is one who is said to be the 'first man' (*mae ulu*). A powerful funei is not only 'big' (bi'o), he is figuratively 'on top' (*au fakligna*) or 'high' (*au fahaghe*). Accordingly, followers of such a person show respect by 'looking up' (*filo fahaghe*), as in the English idiom. However, where a person is not regarded as a legitimate funei or representative of others (which is likely to be a highly variable judgment), 'strong' or 'aggressive' behavior is usually evaluated negatively, and described with the same metaphors used to conceptualize chiefly dominance. Without the legitimation of public recognition, dominance connotes self-aggrandizement at the expense of others. Indeed, one who inappropriately assumes a leadership role (as in taking a directorial role in a work task, and not actually performing any work) is said to be one who 'makes himself big' (*fabibi'o*), 'puts himself high' (*fahaehaghe*), or 'makes himself chief' (*fafuefunei*). As if to counter the problem of self-aggrandizement, A'ara speakers reverse the metaphors of dominance to say that a leader ideally 'puts himself behind' (*au faleghu*) his followers.

The cultural importance of the theme of dominance is reflected in the frequent use of these spatial metaphors of size (BIG/SMALL) and position (ABOVE/BELOW, IN FRONT/BEHIND) to express the relative positioning of social actors. A person whose behavior is described as 'putting himself above' (*fakliakligna*) others is, by implication, 'putting others below' (*fapaipari*). The relational structure of these spatial oppositions provides a convenient way of conceptualizing the premise that social actors are fundamentally interdependent.

In general, construing a person's behavior as 'putting oneself high' is a very negative attribution. The negative connotations of the term *fahaehaghe* 'put oneself high', glossed as 'haughty', are depicted in the lexical model that shows the term to be judged most similar to traits such as 'quarrelsome' or 'possessive' which are regarded as highly undesirable. One informant's explication of the term 'quarrelsome' (mamagra, from *magra* 'fight') illustrates the type of cultural reasoning which associates aggression and conflict with images of dominance:

"A quarrelsome man can fight about land, about food, about almond trees, breadfruit, or anything. He thinks that he is high, above others; that he is boss; a haughty and aggressive man. In the past he might be the one to give orders to go and raid people somewhere. A man who is strong can do anything because he is strong, that's how he can fight. He isn't sympathetic, he's a fighter."

The chain of association in this exegesis moves from talk about fighting to talk about effective action ("can do anything") characteristic of those with personal 'strength' or power. The reasoning illustrated in this passage reflects the kind of cultural understandings in Read's statement about the "antithetical" relations of "strength" and "equivalence," and in Watson's reference to "moral conflict" in perceptions of Big Men cited earlier. The "dilemma of dominance" faced by aspiring traditional leaders, then, is to demonstrate 'strength' and the 'ability to do anything' without being cast as 'haughty'—a dilemma that constitutes the ethnopsychological counterpart to what Sahlins (1963:293) called the "Melanesian contradiction." (The problem is not only Melanesian, as shown by Kirkpatrick [1981] for the Marquesas.)

These ethnopsychological formulations of strength and dominance point to the ambiguous position of chiefs (funei) as a marked category of 'person' which mediates between the moral order of persons and the amoral world of spirits. And, in fact, the dilemma posed by chiefly dominance was probably more acute prior to pacification and conversion to Christianity when the most renowned funei derived their power (personal and political) from access to potent ancestral spirits. With that power came all the fears and ambivalence associated with the traditional world of spirits.[6] As organizers of cooperative activities and representatives of social collectivities (lineage, clan, or village), traditional leaders are an important focus for ordinary talk about social events. In particular, however, the moral and evaluative uncertainty surrounding perceptions of dominance probably contribute to making Big Men more pertinent topics of discourse about personal or behavioral traits than others.

The image of the "strong man" or warrior is prominent in legendary accounts of warfare, and is caricatured as excessively violent and belligerent in ritual dramatizations of raiding and fighting during pagan times. However, when the descendants of a renowned funei, even one notorious for his role in raiding and killing, talk about their ancestor, they will usually portray him in images of solidarity. Perhaps because of the "dilemma of dominance" and the potentially harmful powers of chiefs and priests, people deliberately articulate their traits of solidarity, thus implying that their strength and supernatural potency are not a threat to others in the community. Characterizing a prominent funei in this way provides a conceptual resolution of the problem of dominance by associating traits of strength with more clearly positive traits in idealized images. As an example, consider the narrative account given by one old man about his maternal grandmother's brother (whom I will call Sorumola) who had been known as one of the most active warriors in the region:

> "When Sorumola was grown up and could understand things, his father decided to teach him how to fight. But he was certainly not taught to kill indiscriminately. Sorumola didn't think, 'I can simply attack and kill people.' His kinsmen, offspring, and sisters were all his friends. Sorumola didn't kill anyone needlessly. He didn't look for compensation payments or attack unprovoked anyone who passed in front of him. If he was eating and someone went to defecate or urinate, or were to speak harshly or swear, he would not get angry with them. Sorumola was like that. He didn't kill or harm others needlessly. He was sympathetic with people, with his relatives [friends]. It was Sorumola's way to take care of people. He was a strong man and he did kill. But other chiefs would summon him before he would do any killing. He wouldn't simply say, 'I am going (along on a raid) in order to kill.' Before he would go out on raids, chiefs from other places would say, 'Come along on a raid against this village, friend. You accompany us and we'll all go attack these people.' It was not the way of Sorumola to simply say, 'I am going to attack the people of that place.' But in standing as a pagan, Sorumola was one man in this area who was strong in times past." [7]

Given the stories I had heard about Sorumola as a warrior, I was initially surprised by the fact that these recollections focus primarily on Sorumola's moderate and sympathetic qualities, and only secondarily on his reputation as 'strong man' (which is presupposed). While Sorumola is presumed to be 'strong' (and this is asserted twice), the primary conceptual work done by the above narrative is to construct an image of a person who was 'sympathetic', would 'take care of people' related to him, and did *not* 'kill or harm others needlessly'.

It might be that this portrayal was shaped to fit the context of tape-recorded remarks elicited by an anthropologist. There is, however, more to it than this. The elicited description is not unlike more natural characterizations of deceased ancestors who are periodically memorialized in ceremonial occasions. Ancestors such as Sorumola are an emblem of social identity for their descendants and exemplify, in their person, culturally valued postures for living and acting in the social world. If Sorumola is seen as an extension of the old man doing the remembering, it is not surprising that he portrays Sorumola as a person who showed solidarity with his kin relations, was restrained, and only engaged in violent actions when there was a deliberate purpose in cooperating with allies to attack mutual enemies. Sorumola's 'strength' and aggressiveness, then, were directed outside the boundaries of immediate kin and neighbors. By contextualizing aggression in this way, it becomes more acceptable, at least in the pre-Christian moral code (cf. Read 1955).

Solidarity and Conflict

Important personages, past and present, play an important cultural role as emblems of social ideals and social identity. Renowned ancestors are periodically commemorated in feasts and church celebrations marked by speeches and/or sermons about that person in character images representing sociomoral ideals. As an example of a characterization typical of public speeches, consider the following description of a famous ancestor offered at the end of a commemorative ceremony:

> "The funei whom we remembered today was a good man. He was unassuming and had nothing to do with fighting and quarreling. He never talked back. He was a good man and a good leader who was sympathetic with people . . . sympathetic with children and others alike."

The most prominent aspect of the above description is its positive, evaluative character, with multiple references to the 'good man' and the 'good leader'. Big Men and renowned ancestors not only represent the social identity of those related to them but they also stand as symbols of social ideals: as examples of valued behavior. What, then, are some of the social meanings expressed in talk about solidarity?

The theme of solidarity expresses a social ideal in which the goals of the self and those of the community are in alignment. In the A'ara view of conflict, not only may individual desires and actions come into conflict with those of others but the independent actions of a person as an individual per se are generally evaluated negatively. To 'follow one's own mind' is, at the least, to be perceived as 'lazy' and, at worst, as 'disobedient' and 'selfish'. The traits 'individualistic' and 'haughty' are central to the cluster of person descriptors which defines the dimension of conflict. One of the most negative things which could be said about someone is that the person 'follows his own way'—the literal meaning of the phrase glossed as 'individualistic'. This phrase is semantically similar to another person descriptor, *ghamu hnoto* 'eats alone', which may be glossed as 'selfish'. Both phrases point to an overvaluation of the goals of the self and an undervaluation of the goals of others in the community.

Individualism in A'ara views of social behavior is not just undesirable, it poses a genuine risk to person and community alike. The negative evaluation of self-emphasis, self-elevation, and selfishness reflect a folk theory that interprets social behavior in terms of its interpersonal consequences. This logic can also be extended to the actions of groups, as expressed in a speech by a village representative to a local political council. He declared that since his village seemed to be receiving no benefits from tax revenues, they would no longer pay the local tax. However, he deliberately stated that this action was not an attempt by his village to 'put themselves above' others and that they would continue to listen to and cooperate with local chiefs.

Perhaps the most explicit articulation of the theme of solidarity (other than in sermons) is in speeches by local leaders at feasts and other social gatherings. The rhetoric of solidarity is used to exhort people from different villages and clans to participate in cooperative projects that will help to develop and strengthen the region. People are encouraged repeatedly to be of 'one mind' (*kaisei gaoghato*) and to 'work together' (*loku fodu*). These themes are expressed in metaphoric images of 'fullness' or 'bigness' which connote prosperity, success, and well-being. In the passage cited below, from the speech of a chief recorded at a large feast, the speaker reasons rhetorically that cooperation leads to success and accomplishment, whereas individual action results in one becoming figuratively smaller ('narrow' and 'thin'):

> "I want very much for these villages to be together. If you all are together, you will be well; you will be able to make feasts, build houses, do well in traveling, meetings, discussion, in any of these things. If you are separate and speak separately, it will not be so. . . . If that is your way then it is like your body, your speech, and your manner become narrow and thin. . . . One way is well for all of you. We mustn't take separate ways."

In this context, a leader's exhortation to his audience to act in specific ways is clearly moral discourse—it recommends a course of action by articulating the positive outcomes of cooperation, and the negative consequences of independent action. The speaker is describing the *purpose* of being or acting in a certain way, specifically, to achieve desired goals of making feasts or building houses, and so on. The evaluative connotations of person descriptors rest in part on inferences about the personal and social consequences of behavior—a kind of "ethnofunctionalism." Similarly, Lutz (chap. 2) discusses the way in which interpersonal interpretation in Ifaluk obtains moral force through its links with cultural values and goals. The evaluative force of social discourse derives from the implications of social conflict or of moral transgression for personal and social well-being. Just how these implications are inferred in cultural reasoning about fortune and misfortune, health and illness, success and failure is examined further below.

EMOTIONS AND THEORIES OF MISFORTUNE

Conflict and Hostility

Social relations play a central role in A'ara interpretations of significant personal and social events. It is not so much the actions of individuals, but interactions and relationships that have direct and immediate consequences for persons and communities. As argued earlier, A'ara cognition of self is structured in part by concerns with sources of harm and misfortune in the social and supernatural environment. The spectrum of potential *social* threats to personal and community well-being includes hostile actions by others (ranging from sorcery and cursing to gossip or slander), moral transgression by oneself or by significant others, strained relations between self and others, and bad feelings harbored by self or significant others. These alternative routes to personal or social misfortune are all charted through the terrain of interpersonal relations. For example, not only may hostile actions of others, or one's own actions or feelings, make one sick but one may suffer illness directly from social conflict and/or bad feelings among significant others. Thus, it is said that if a husband and wife are continually arguing and fighting, it is likely that their child will suffer persistent illness. Children are regarded as particularly vulnerable to the social causes of illness.

Interpersonal causes are generally implicated in cases of accidental injury or death, in persistent or serious illness, and in unexpected failure in important tasks. The use of explanations concerning interpersonal conflict in these more serious cases lend greater moral weight to the ideals of social solidarity. In other words, social action that is interpreted as out of alignment with community goals and the moral rules that express them may result in serious harm to the person, to significant others, or to the community as a whole. Thus, when a man was killed by a wild pig, one explanation contended that his death was the result of his 'following his own way' (i.e., he was 'individualistic') and living outside the moral strictures of the Church. The latter point presupposes the belief that adherence to Christian moral rules provides one with protection associated with the power of the Christian God.

The most direct source of harm in the social environment is associated with hostile actions of other persons. An examination of the meanings of verbs describing social actions regarded as 'bad' shows that almost all forms of undesirable social behavior are perceived to cause personal harm to others (White 1985). Thus, whether it is open aggressive confrontation, covert forms of verbal aggression ('curse', 'slander'), deception or passive non-cooperation, the behavior may be said to 'hurt' or 'spoil' others. When asked to make judgments about a corpus of such interpersonal verbs, the word most frequently selected by informants as similar in meaning to other verbs was a term for 'hurt' (*faneinei*)—somewhat like the expression for 'damage' or, literally, 'make bad' (fadidi'a). The perceived damage may vary from annoyance, when someone does not cooperate or 'talks back', to the more serious consequences of malicious gossip or a 'curse' (*tibri*), which may cause illness or death. There appears to be little room for notions of unintended actions or unforeseen consequences in A'ara interpretations of behavior. Intentionality or purposefulness is attributed to most social behavior, such that there is no sharp difference between loose talk and malicious slander or between incorrect speech and lying. And gossip can be a serious threat to personal well-being.

As outlined earlier, the vulnerability of the self to hostile actions or feelings is conceptualized in vivid metaphors of penetration and pain. The term for malicious gossip, *buiburi,* evokes the metaphor of the painful bite of a *buri* fly (a large horsefly). It is said that the appearance of a buri fly in one's house is a sign that, somewhere, one is being slandered at that moment. Intentionality is expressed or intensified by reduplication of the verb stem and addition of a causative prefix, *fa.* Thus, for example, *khabru* 'pain' becomes *fakakabru* 'cause (someone) pain'—a form that requires an active agent. Many transitive verbs, constructed in this way, are used to describe the causation of personal harm in metaphors of being 'stabbed' or 'poked' by a sharp implement. Examples include *fajiojito* from *jito* 'poke fire with a hot ember'; *fajaija'i* from *ja'i* 'plant with a digging stick'; *juijuli* from *julu* 'pluck fruit from a tree with a long pole'; *fakhoakhonga* from *khonga* 'a hooked pole for snaring nuts from a tree'; or *fachacha* from *cha* 'poke, stab, or stick'. In each case the directed, purposive quality of the destructive behavior is represented metaphorically as some kind of instrumental, goal-oriented action employing a sharp implement as a tool.

Describing behavior as actively causing pain characterizes that behavior as aggressive: it is an attack. Many such forms of aggressive behavior are described by informants as motivated by the agent's 'anger' (*di'a tagna*), usually directed at a person or group who evoked that 'anger'. 'Anger' is sometimes, but not always, attributed as a motivation for sorcery (*neilehe,* lit., 'make death'). Among the various types of actions regarded as expressions of hostility are those which involve open confrontation (e.g., 'shout back and forth') and those which involve some form of *covert* verbal aggression (referred to generally as 'hidden talk' *cheke pouporu*). When asked to judge which types of harmful behavior were the most inappropriate for a 'Christian person', informants ranked covert forms of verbal aggression such as 'slander', 'swear', 'lie', and 'curse', as the most serious and undesirable (White 1985). These findings provide a more finely tuned look at the types of interpersonal conflict which are regarded as the most personally damaging, revealing the cultural importance of hidden forms of anger and hostility. In contrast, the positive meanings of the A'ara concept of the 'Christian person' condense and express social ideals of solidarity and submissiveness in personal traits such as 'kind', 'sympathetic', and 'humble' (White 1980*b*).

'Anger' is both a motivator of aggressive actions and a likely *response* of the individual threatened or affected by hostility or social conflict. Rule violations such as 'lying', 'deceiving', or 'stealing' are seen as causes of 'anger' in the person affected by those actions. However, sociomoral ideals proscribe expressions of anger and aggression, at least among closely related persons, thereby posing a cultural dilemma in moral reasoning: responses to a rule violation ('anger') may themselves constitute a moral breach (expression of hostility or aggression). A'ara society offers a culturally constituted solution to this dilemma, in the form of a type of social activity known as 'disentangling' which provides an occasion for ritualized expressions of 'anger' and other types of bad feeling. A description of some of the cultural premises underlying 'disentangling' illustrates the working of folk theories of misfortune and the role of emotion concepts in reasoning about interpersonal relations.

Emotion Concepts and Social 'Disentangling'

In addition to 'anger', almost any type of 'bad feeling' associated with social conflict (such as 'sadness', *di'a nagnafa,* or 'jealousy', *gogotu*) is regarded as a potential source of personal harm, such as illness or failure, or of community misfortune. The A'ara word for emotion or feeling is, literally, 'heart' (*nagnafa*), although there is no sharp separation of this notion and that for 'thought' (*gaoghato*). Troubled or bad feelings are often described with the metaphor 'tangled' (*firi*) or 'knotted' (*haru*). In particular, the notion of 'tangled' or 'knotted' emotion expresses the moral conflict associated with 'anger' or ill feeling among closely related persons. A whole range of metaphorical oppositions is used to express complementary notions of conflict and harmony. These oppositions include:

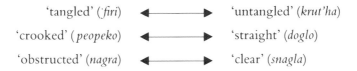

       'tangled' (*firi*) ⟷ 'untangled' (*krut'ha*)

       'crooked' (*peopeko*) ⟷ 'straight' (*doglo*)

       'obstructed' (*nagra*) ⟷ 'clear' (*snagla*)

These may be used to conceptualize either psychological or social types of conflict and harmony. Bad feelings and social disputes may both be described as 'tangled', 'crooked', or 'obstructed' conditions.

The concept of 'disentangling' refers to the undoing of 'tangled' emotions associated with social conflict or moral transgression in order to resolve or avoid their negative consequences. 'Disentangling' is aimed at 'speaking out' (*cheke fajifla*) about conflictful events so that one may 'reveal' (*fatakle*) bad feelings, which, if 'concealed' (*tutufu*), may threaten both the person and the community. 'Disentangling' sessions are a social occasion for talking about bad feelings and social conflict in a context that is defined as an antidote for problematic emotions, rather than as a forum for dispute settlement which might provoke, rather than eliminate, further confrontation and bad feeling. The recognized function of 'disentangling' as a means for dealing with problematic emotions related to interpersonal conflict is evident in one informant's comparison of 'disentangling' with village Holy Communion ceremonies. Both types of activity symbolize a kind of moral purification of closely related persons, that offers protection from misfortune.

There are two general forms of 'disentangling', both of which are based on the same assumptions about sources of personal or community misfortune. 'Disentangling' is used as a treatment for cases of illness, and it is used preventively to 'disentangle' bad feelings lest they interfere with important social tasks. The therapeutic use of 'disentangling' bears some resemblance to Western psychotherapy or group therapy. Like the Western theory of psychosomatic disorder which attributes psychosocial causes to maladies that show no obvious somatic causes, or that do not respond to conventional medical cures, the 'disentangling' theory attributes socioemotional factors in cases of illness which persist despite the application of usual treatments. For example, in the case of a woman suffering from uterine pains and bleeding who had been treated without success with a variety of traditional remedies over a period of six weeks, a village leader finally said that he could 'see' that ordinary treatments were not working because of problems between the woman and her husband. In the leader's words, it was "their thinking which blocked the work of the other treatments," and thus they needed to 'disentangle' their thoughts and feelings.

The most significant difference between the 'disentangling' theory and Western theories of psychosocial disorder is the distinctly interpersonal or social character of the A'ara model. For example, the 'disentangling' theory includes the premise that one person's socioemotional entanglements may cause illness or misfortune for third parties—for significant others or for the community as a whole. Ito's discussion of the Hawaiian ho'oponopono (chap. 8) provides an important example of a similar theory of illness (see also Turner 1964). One informant illustrated this belief by saying that "if two people, husband and wife, are always arguing, then their child will continually be sick."

The explanatory efficacy of emotions extends beyond illness to various kinds of social misfortune. The failure of an important community enterprise such as fishing or hunting may be attributed to some lingering 'bad feeling' that obstructed or blocked success, similar to a 'curse', which could have the same effect. One of the most common examples involves domestic pigs that become lost in the forest. Domestic pigs are usually not kept penned, but are allowed to forage in the forest, where they establish well-known feeding places and can be located and retrieved when needed. On occasion, however, a pig cannot be found, despite the efforts of several men. If, after one or two days, the pig is not located, the searchers will conclude that something is 'obstructing' their attempt to find it, just as something was 'obstructing' the medical treatment of the woman's illness mentioned above. In one case where two brothers and their sister were preparing (together with their respective households) to host a memorial feast for their father who had died a year earlier, one of their pigs could not be located after a day and a half of searching. So they decided to hold a 'disentangling' meeting in which the three siblings, their spouses, and their mother gathered to 'talk out' any bad feelings that might be blocking their efforts. The topics discussed at the meeting included: (1) the mother's regrets about her children's failure to take good care of their father in his old age, (2) a previous argument between the brothers about their responsibilities in preparing for the feast, and (3) a dream by the sister that her father's ghost was playing tricks on the party searching for the pig. Since the pig was located the next day, it was generally inferred that this airing of bad feelings associated with social conflict served to overcome the obstructions.

The preventive uses of 'disentangling' can be seen as an extrapolation of the premises of this theory of illness and failure. Given the premise that bad feelings can cause misfortune or obstruct social activities, 'disentangling' *before* important social ventures is a way to avoid accidents or injuries and help ensure success. A series of intervillage meetings are usually held before significant collective enterprises such as turtle hunting or fishing for major feasts. Before any major feast that demands group fishing or hunting, those involved will first meet in one or more 'disentangling' meetings to air any bad feelings.

In both the therapeutic and the preventative forms of 'disentangling', talk about emotional responses to social events is an important way of signifying close social relations between persons and between person and community. Illness and social failure stand as symbols of dysfunction (the former personal, the latter communal in nature), for which explanations are sought ultimately in the fabric of interpersonal relations. Both types of event—harm to the person in the form of illness and harm to the community in the form of, say, a bad catch of turtle—may be explained in terms of an underlying folk theory that attributes misfortune to social conflict (e.g., quarreling, cursing, or a violation of sexual mores) or to bad feelings engendered by social conflict. The theory is usually invoked for serious or unexpected problems, for which notions of chance or fate almost never play a role. If, for the moment, social and moral transgressions can be subsumed under the rubric of social conflict, the general structure of cultural reasoning about the causes of misfortune may be represented as follows:

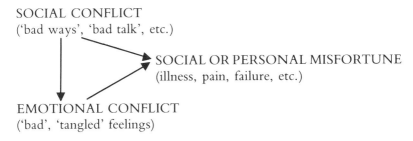

SOCIAL CONFLICT
('bad ways', 'bad talk', etc.)

SOCIAL OR PERSONAL MISFORTUNE
(illness, pain, failure, etc.)

EMOTIONAL CONFLICT
('bad', 'tangled' feelings)

This representation of cultural interpretations of misfortune makes clear the inferential role of emotion concepts as symbols that link social conflict with personal and community well-being. In this light, emotion concepts, which might otherwise be regarded as the quintessential province of the individual person, can be seen to express important interpersonal meanings. A close examination of the meanings of emotion talk in 'disentangling' discourse shows that emotion attributions serve to express and reaffirm a speaker's interpretation of conflictful events (White 1979b). The model above illustrates this by showing that talk about emotional conflict ('bad feelings') would presuppose some kind of antecedent social conflict.

A significant proportion of the topics of 'disentangling' narratives in four meetings I attended focused on the ways people managed or *responded* to some prior transgression or conflictful event. Thus, one long sequence at a 'disentangling' meeting involved accounts by two brothers whose sons had been in a fistfight. The focus of their exchange was not the fight at all, but one brother's decision to report the incident to the police rather than attempt to find a solution by talking with his brother and village leaders. Accounts of how people respond to conflictful events typically highlight the social relations between participants, and then indicate appropriate types of response. In the typical case, close social relations imply that anger, aggression, or other signs of conflict (e.g., acting 'separately') are not appropriate. These relationships are ideally characterized by solidarity. For example, in one meeting, a man said that he was angry at his sister's son for stealing betel nuts from one of his trees. But because he simply expressed 'anger', without acknowledging the close relation of kinship between himself and his nephew, two others at the meeting chose to comment on the uncle's expression of 'anger' toward his nephew, rather than on the act of stealing. One of the listeners spoke to the uncle, saying:

> "This kind of talk that you are making is as if you are all separate people. It is better to speak to your nephew to teach him, like I do with my nephew. . . . That kind of [angry] talk can be aimed at other people, but to our own nephews, our own children, it is very bad."

'Disentangling' accounts frequently foreground social relations important to the speaker, and refer to emotions that emphasize the value and importance of those relations. The following excerpts from one speaker's narrative account at a 'disentangling' meeting are quite typical of 'disentangling' discourse, which moves from talk about emotions to talk about social relations among actors involved in conflictful events, and back. In this case, the speaker's younger brother had been told by the parents of a young woman with whom he was having illicit sexual relations not to set foot in their village again. When the speaker was originally told about the incident, he went to the parents' village and angrily told them that if that is how they speak to his younger brother, then they also should not visit his village. In his account, the speaker acknowledges that his younger brother had brought the trouble on himself, but goes on to report his feelings about the banishment of his brother by the girl's parents, who were related to him as aunt (mother's sister) and as husband of his aunt:

> "It was the statement, 'Don't set foot in [the village] that made me ashamed with him [the father] . . . but he is our father. The two of us [the speaker and his younger brother] would go into the house [of the parents], the sweet potatoes were our food, these houses and these beds. . . . We took care of our mother who had married our father. . . . That's what made me sad.

> "It's just that when my real father ['uncle'] came out and said that [Don't set foot here.] that I was sad and came to talk to the old lady here [the mother].

> "Now I'm in front of my mothers and my sisters. These houses are for entering, for drinking water. It was when that talk [Don't set foot here.] started coming from my father that I was sad."

These fragments are excerpted from a much longer narrative to illustrate the integral role of emotion attributions and images of solidarity in formulating a plausible interpretation of conflictful events. Not only does the talk about emotional response constitute 'speaking out' about bad feelings (the purpose of 'disentangling') but the social meaning of the emotions implicitly reaffirms the value of important social relations. The speaker's repeated reference to his 'sadness' in response to the banishment of his younger brother presupposes closeness or solidarity in the relations among those involved. The solidarity appropriate to these relations is characterized in images of sharing food and shelter with the parents who are referred to as 'our mother' and 'our father'. By talking about 'sadness' rather than, say, 'anger', the speaker articulates an interpretation that foregrounds his concern with the damage done to valued social relations (between the parents and both himself and his brother). The entire narrative notably excludes any mention of 'anger', which, according to informants, was expressed during the actual confrontation. In the context of this account, the attribution of 'anger' would not have been consistent with either the speaker's rationalization of his own actions, or with the implicit agenda of 'disentangling' meetings which involves the symbolic repair of damaged social relations that might otherwise bring harm to the persons involved and to the community.

As can be seen from the brief excerpts cited here, these occasions are an extremely rich source of naturally occurring discourse about social and emotional experience. It is not within the scope of this chapter to examine in detail the complex meanings expressed in 'disentangling' discourse. Rather, the discussion has been aimed at placing 'disentangling' within the wider context of A'ara ethnopsychology, indicating the role of cultural models in lending it meaning as a specific type of social activity, a culturally constituted solution to the moral dilemmas of conflict and ill feeling among closely related persons. It is through inferences about the social meanings of emotion and the consequences of hostility and conflict that talk about social events and responses to them acquire cultural meaning and moral force in this context. By focusing on an occasion in which participants are engaged explicitly in posing and counterposing interpretations of events, the moral weight of ethnopsychological discourse becomes especially clear. In this case, the use of emotion language to symbolically repair damaged social relations (and thus achieve the valued state of solidarity in close relations) illustrates the pragmatic force of 'disentangling' as a social performance.

CONCLUSION

This chapter began by noting signs of renewed interest in the phenomenology of social experience. In anthropological circles this interest focuses on the culturally variable ways in which social realities are constructed using understandings about persons and interpersonal ties. Various and often complementary approaches—cognitive, psychological, symbolic—to this task share a common concern with the interpretive processes people use to perceive, talk about, and actively shape their lives. For example, LeVine (1983:291) writes that an important trend in the "new empiricism" of psychological anthropology is "the descriptive ethnography of indigenous concepts of the person, the lifespan, the self and behavior and mental function in normality and deviance." The writings of Hallowell are frequently cited as an important precedent for much of this work. Hallowell's approach is especially provocative because his interests did not lie in the structure of symbols for their own sake, but for what they reveal about the cultural organization of experience—of the ways people handle mundane interactive problems (such as aggression) and pursue their purposes in everyday life. However, the analysis given here suggests that indigenous concepts do not only, as Hallowell (1967:91) put it, "become psychologically significant" in relation to "motivations, goals and life adjustment," but that they are in fact *conceptualized* in relation to such matters of personal and social concern.

In trying to learn about the underlying premises that give ordinary talk about persons and behavior its meaning and moral force, one is drawn into culturally constructed worlds of identity, action, and emotion. Thus, for example, A'ara informants explicate notions of personal strength with a set of ideas about chiefs, spirits, feast making, knowledge, forms of talk, fear, accomplishment, and anger. Cultural or linguistic items—a word, a metaphor, or natural discourse—may depend on just such a set of interconnected understandings for their meaning and social significance. The task of ethnographic description, then, becomes one of articulating cultural practices of inference which interconnect such notions in coherent interpretations of social experience. This chapter has argued that inferences about matters of shared importance and personal concern are a connective tissue giving shape and durability to the body of ethnopsychological interpretation.

My approach to ethnopsychology has been to identify some of these culturally formulated concerns and examine folk reasoning that is brought to bear on them. The analysis suggests that processes of inference may produce *layers* of cultural concerns by linking, for example, notions of harm and well-being with interpersonal processes such as conflict or dominance, or the actions of spirits. Folk theories that find the roots of illness, failure, and misfortune in interpersonal conflict tie the well-being of persons and communities to a web of social relations and interactions. The personal consequences of conflict and hostility in everyday life are expressed in metaphors of pain and penetration, similar to the images used to conceptualize the damaging effects of contact with powerful spirits. In this way, a broad range of experiences in the social and spiritual environment acquire personal significance and moral force through their connection with basic concerns with health or prosperity.

The attempt to identify some of the important concerns that engender cultural reasoning about social experience is akin to asking what it is that people are *doing* with ethnopsychological discourse. Attempting to answer this question leads the ethnographer into the purposes that shape ordinary discourse about persons, and the social occasions for talking about them. Having been lead into the realm of purposive action, it is not surprising to discover that much of ethnopsychological discourse is moral in nature. Talk about persons can be used to sanction or direct behavior by interpreting it in a way that draws out its implications for personal or community well-being. To a large extent, the social control functions of A'ara interpretations rely on the theme of social conflict, and its perceived negative consequences for persons and communities.

One of the methodological arguments of this chapter has been that an important avenue to the study of ethnopsychologies is through close attention to ordinary occasions for social and moral discourse. Where such occasions exist, they may offer a rich source of naturally occurring conversations about selves and social events which depend on ethnopsychology for their coherence and force. One of the most significant occasions for talking about social experience in Santa Isabel is an indigenous form of therapy and conflict resolution termed 'disentangling'. The cultural rationale or meaning of 'disentangling' as a distinct type of activity derives from the folk theory that attributes misfortune to hidden bad feeling engendered by conflict within the community.

The account of ethnopsychology offered here has been deliberately broad rather than narrow, attempting to point up interconnections, common premises, or metaphors that reveal something of the underlying concerns and contexts that structure thought and experience in a Solomon Islands society. The diversity of the material brought together within this chapter suggests that the task of investigating cognitive structure from the perspective of everyday concerns and social contexts is not a neat or easily managed task. As Robert Abelson (1981:1) has written from the perspective of a discipline usually much more "neat" than cultural anthropology:

> The study of knowledge in a mental system tends toward both naturalism and phenomenology. The mind needs to represent what is out there in the real

world, and it needs to manipulate it for particular purposes. But the world is messy, and purposes manifold. Models of mind, therefore, can become garrulous and intractable as they become more and more realistic.

ACKNOWLEDGMENTS

This chapter is based on fieldwork carried out in Santa Isabel, Solomon Islands, between December 1974 and April 1976. Support for that work by the Social Science Research Council Foreign Area Program and by the Wenner-Gren Foundation for Anthropological Research (Grant No. 4021) is gratefully acknowledged. I would like to thank the members of the ASAO Symposium on "Folk Psychology in Pacific Cultures" for an inspiring exchange of ideas that has contributed to this chapter, and especially Peter Black, Reuel Denney, Jane Fajans, John Kirkpatrick, and Catherine Lutz for particularly helpful comments.

NOTES

1. In discussing traditional A'ara leaders (funei) I will use the term "Big Man" (in capital letters to indicate that the concept is borrowed from general anthropological usage, not an indigenous phrase), as well as "chief" (which is frequently used by local speakers of English and Solomans Pijin) with no particular significance for the ideal types of Melanesian "big men" and Polynesian "chiefs" (Sahlins 1963).

2. Along the same figurative lines, the phonologically similar term for 'fence' (bara) is also used in active, verbal form (fababara) to describe defending against attacking enemies.

3. A copy of my card-file A'ara dictionary is lodged with the Pacific Collection, Hamilton Library, University of Hawaii.

4. My awareness of the problem of determining what A'ara talk about persons or "personality" is all about only emerged gradually from the lexical study, spurred on by observations such as one by Melford Spiro. After listening to a presentation of this material, he commented to the effect, "That's all very interesting, but what does it have to do with personality?" His question points to the fact that there is no distinct A'ara domain of "personality" terms distinguished from vocabulary for social roles, emotions, or other types of ethnopsychological vocabulary, as indicated by the inclusion of terms such as 'fearful', 'jealous', 'manager', or 'mediator' in the corpus of thirty-seven terms mentioned above.

5. In a similar vein, A'ara pronouns can be seen as giving as much or more weight to concepts of interpersonal relatedness as to individuality. As in other Austronesian languages, certain possessives are used for "intimate" relations—to one's body, house, land, and, notably, consanguineal kin—and others for more "distant" links. Analysts have discerned a degree of "identification" or "blending" in such usages

in relation to other persons (see, e.g., Levy 1973:213–214). Indeed, the remarks of Levy-Bruhl cited earlier followed on a similar analysis. Again, it is my impression unsupported by any systematic observation, that A'ara speakers make proportionately greater use of plural subject pronouns in describing their thoughts and actions (i.e., use 'we' instead of 'I') than is the case among English speakers. A'ara speakers seem to spend more time talking about events, plans, actions, and reactions, and so on, in which the agents are social collectivities rather than individuals. For example, when some children were playing on the porch of my house and began to make excessive noise and commotion, an old woman with whom I was talking yelled at them, "Be more quiet! We (you and I) are ashamed." (See Lutz, chap. 2, for an analysis of similar data.)

6. One of the apparent cultural transformations associated with conversion to Christianity has been that a new, more uniformly positive (and hence less feared) spirit realm has been opened up. Christian ceremony has been used to eliminate or defend against the most dangerous aspects of the traditional spirit world (sorcery and 'forest spirits', see White 1979*a*), while at the same time providing a source of personal power (mana) for success in worldly activities. One of the ethnopsychological consequences of these changes has been the apparent domestication of mana through its association with the Christian ideals of passive and cooperative behavior. These conceptual associations are shown in the lexical model where the term for mana (*nolaghi*) was judged most like traits of solidarity such as 'kind' and 'sympathetic'.

7. The reference to Sorumola as a "pagan" in this last sentence creates a context for his actions in raiding and killing, since pagan times (the 'ways before') are closely associated with warfare in images of the past.

GLOSSARY

au	be, have, exist; have the property of
bana	build; impart protection to
bara	fence
bi'o	big
blahi	tabu, sacred, forbidden
buri	horsefly; gossip about
cheke	talk; language
churu mala	pierce a footprint to work sorcery
di'a	bad
di'a nagnafa	sadness
di'a ta(gna)	(his) anger

fada	spear, shoot
fa	causative prefix
fadidi'a	cause to be bad, damage, harm
fadodofra	awaken
fafara	propitiate
fahaehaghe	raise up; haughty, make oneself high
faheaheta	assert strength, aggressive
fahiba	confuse, disorient (spirit agent only)
fajifla	outward
fakligna	above, on top; proud, arrogant
faleghu	behind; humble
faneinei	hurt (someone)
fatakle	reveal, appear
fa'ulu	in front; leading
filo	see, understand
fodu	full, together, unified
fogra	sick, illness
frane	bold
funei	chief, leader, important person
gaoghato	thought, mind, meaning, plan
ghamu	eat
gamunitu	eat food which has been bespelled by a sorcerer; the illness derived from this practice
glalase	knowledge, knowledgeable
gogotu	jealousy, envy
graurut'ha	disentangling, a ritual encounter to air emotions related to social conflict
haghe	high
haru	tied in knots; pent-up (emotions)
hneta	strong
hnoto	alone
huhughu	recalcitrant, disobedient

keli	good
khabru	pain
khera(mi)	(our) friend, kin
khogu	ginger root; protective amulet
khomabro	common (in social status)
kokhoni	have sympathy for
mae	adult male, man
magra	fight, conflict
nagnafa	heart; feeling
nahmaghu	fear
naikno	person; common person; adult female
na'itu	spirit, ghost
neilehe	sorcery
nogna	his, her, third-person singular possessive
nolaghi	mana, spirit power
pouporu	hidden, secretive
puhi	action, manner, way
sapu	rendered powerless from tabu violation
sitei	small
sopa	separate, singly, divided
suisukhi	pry out
tarabana	prepare, give protection to
t'habogano	power to sense "poisoned" food through touch
tibri	place a curse on
toetoe	injure by staring
tutufu	hide wrongdoing, refuse

REFERENCES

Abelson, R. P.
   1981   Constraint, Construal and Cognitive Science. *In* Proceedings of the

Third Annual Conference of the Cognitive Science Society. Berkeley, California.

Amherst of Hackney, Lord, and B. Thomson (eds.)
1901   The Discovery of the Solomon Islands. London: The Hakluyt Society.

D'Andrade, R. G.
1984   Cultural Meaning Systems. *In* Culture Theory: Essays on Mind, Self and Emotion. R. A. Shweder and R. A. LeVine, eds. New York: Cambridge University Press.
1985   Character Terms and Cultural Models. *In* Directions in Cognitive Anthropology. J. Dougherty, ed. Urbana: University of Illinois Press.

Goldberg, L.
1981   Language and Individual Differences: The Search for Universals in Personality Lexicons. *In* Review of Personality and Social Psychology. L. Wheeler, ed. Beverly Hills: Sage Publications.

Greenberg, J.
1966   Language Universals with Special Reference to Feature Hierarchies. The Hague: Mouton.

Hallowell, A. I.
1967   The Self and Its Behavioral Environment. *In* Culture and Experience. New York: Schocken Books. (Originally published in 1954.)

Hastorf, A. H., D. J. Schneider, and J. Polefka
1970   Person Perception. Reading, Mass.: Addison-Wesley Publishing Co.

Heider, F.
1958   The Psychology of Interpersonal Relations. New York: J. Wiley and Sons.

Howard, A.
n.d.   History, Myth and Polynesian Chieftainship: The Case of Rotuman Kings. *In* Transformations of Polynesian Culture. A. Hooper, ed. Auckland: Polynesian Society (in press).

Kirkpatrick, J.
1981   Appeals for 'Unity' in Marquesan Local Politics. Journal of the Polynesian Society 90:439–464.

Laboratory of Comparative Human Cognition
1978   Cognition as a Residual Category in Anthropology. Annual Review of Anthropology 7:51–69.

Lakoff, G., and M. Johnson
1980   Metaphors We Live By. Chicago: University of Chicago Press.

Leenhardt, M.
1979   Do Kamo: Person and Myth in the Melanesian World. B. M. Gulati, trans. Chicago: University of Chicago Press. (Original French edition published in 1947.)

LeVine, R.
1983   The Self in Culture. *In* Culture, Behavior and Personality. Rev. ed. Chicago: Aldine.

Levy, R.
1973   The Tahitians: Mind and Experience in the Society Islands. Chicago: Chicago University Press.
Lévy-Bruhl, L.
1975   The Notebooks on Primitive Mentality. New York: Harper & Row. (French edition published as *Carnets* in 1949.)
Needham, R.
1976   Skulls and Causality. Man (n.s.) 11:71–88.
Oliver, D.
1955   A Solomon Islands Society: Kinship and Leadership Among the Siuai of Bougainville. Boston: Beacon Press.
Quinn, N.
1982   "Commitment" in American Marriage: A Cultural Analysis. American Ethnologist 9:775–798.
Read, K.
1955   Morality and the Concept of the Person Among the Gahuku-Gama. Oceania 25:233–282.
1959   Leadership and Consensus in a New Guinea Society. American Anthropologist 61:425–436.
Redfield, R.
1953   The Primitive World View and Its Transformations. Ithaca: Cornell University Press.
Rosaldo, S.
1980   Knowledge and Passion: Ilongot Notions of Self and Social Life. Cambridge: Cambridge University Press.
Rosenberg, S., C. Nelson, and P. Vivekenanthan
1968   A Multi-Dimensional Approach to the Structure of Personality Impressions. Journal of Personality and Social Psychology 9:283–294.
Sahlins, M. D.
1963   Poor Man, Rich Man, Big Man, Chief: Political Types in Melanesia and Polynesia. Comparative Studies in Society and History 5:285–303.
Scheffler, H.
1965   Choiseul Island Social Structure. Berkeley: University of California Press.
Schneider, D. J.
1973   Implicit Personality Theory: A Review. Psychological Bulletin 79:294–309.
Schwartz, T.
1973   Cult and Context: The Paranoid Ethos in Melanesia. Ethos 1:153–174.
Turner, V.
1964   An Ndembu Doctor in Practice. *In* Magic, Faith and Healing. A. Kiev, ed. Pp. 230–263. New York: The Free Press.
Valentine, C. A.
1963   Men of Anger and Men of Shame: Lakalai Ethnopsychology and Its

Implications for Sociopsychological Theory. Ethnology 1:441–447.

Watson, J. B.
1967   Tairora: The Politics of Despotism in a Small Society. Anthropological
        Forum 2:53–104.

White, G. M.
1978   Ambiguity and Ambivalence in A'ara Personality Descriptors. American
        Ethnologist 5:334–360.
1979a   War, Peace and Piety in Santa Isabel, Solomon Islands. *In* The Pacifica-
        tion of Melanesia. M. Rodman and M. Cooper, eds. Ann Arbor: Uni-
        versity of Michigan Press.
1979b   Some Social Uses of Emotion Language: A Melanesian Example. Paper
        presented at the 78th Annual Meetings of the American Anthropological
        Association, Cincinnati, Ohio.
1980a   Conceptual Universals in Interpersonal Language. American Anthro-
        pologist 82:759–781.
1980b   Social Images and Social Change in a Melanesian Society. American
        Ethnologist 7:352–370.
1985   'Bad Ways' and 'Bad Talk': Interpretations of Interpersonal Conflict in
        a Melanesian Society. *In* Directions in Cognitive Anthropology. J.
        Dougherty, ed. Urbana: University of Illinois Press.

Wiggins, J. S.
1979   A Psychological Taxonomy of Trait-Descriptive Terms: The Interper-
        sonal Domain. Journal of Personality and Social Psychology 37:395–412.

10

The Person in Social Context: The Social Character of Baining "Psychology"

Jane Fajans

INTRODUCTION

The most challenging and interesting thing about the Baining (of New Britain, Papua New Guinea) from the point of view of ethnopsychological studies is that they appear not to have a folk psychology. The Baining exhibit a pervasive avoidance of modes of discourse about psychology. If we understand the latter to be a domain of culture which includes a concern with affect and emotions, concepts of person and self, theories of deviance, interpretations of behavior, and ideas about cognition and personality development, the Baining manifest very little interest in these areas. They are reluctant to speculate about the personal motivations, actions, and feelings either of themselves or others. They do not offer interpretations of the meanings of the behavior and events around them in these terms.

Baining concepts of personal feeling, expressive behavior, and affective relationships are embedded in accounts of general cultural patterns and social events. The ethnopsychological structure of the Baining, in other words, is not culturally distinct from their sociocultural structure. Through analysis this domain can be factored so as to make possible a description of ethnopsychological processes, but such a description is essentially meaningless without the structural underpinnings of the sociocultural system. This chapter is an attempt to analyze Baining ethnopsychological processes in the context of other social and cultural processes to show how all these domains are related in the Baining system. The interrelationships intrinsic in this analysis provoke a theoretical confrontation with Western ideas of psychology (see Lutz, chap. 2) as an essentially isolable domain. The Baining data thus force us to focus on the problematic nature of our own domains of cultural knowledge.

I propose to describe the interrelationships in this culture by means of a hierarchical model of a generative system. Each level of this system is composed of patterns of relations between features and actions. The more complex the relations in a set, the higher in the structure that set is found; those sets with less complexity are found on the lower levels. This analysis describes psychological processes in a manner consistent with the rest of the Baining sociocultural system, most notably kinship and household organization (Fajans 1979, 1984). Within this schema, the normative psychological state is composed of elements tightly integrated and socially coherent; it is defined as being on a high level. Instances of deviance represent breakdowns in these patterns of integration and are at a lower level. Such behavior is frequently perceived as lacking the key relationships and patterns that define sociality for the Baining; consequently, these states are conceived as being outside of the social order, and essentially natural in character. This boundary between inside and outside is generated by the relations within the system and in turn generates key dimensions of the system. It is processes such as these to which I refer when I call my model generative.[1]

Baining culture emphasizes the role of the person, which I analytically oppose to concepts of self and individual. It is in the construction and action of the person that daily activities, relationships, and symbols are integrated into a self-reproducing system. For the Baining, people act predictably and coherently when they function as social *personae*. When they deviate from these expectations and thus cease to behave as social beings, they become culturally unpredictable. In this state action is considered to emanate more directly from the actor's natural side than at other times. In such conditions people are not integrated into the normative social patterns and relationships around them and thus perforce act in an isolated fashion.

The concepts of person and patterns of normal social behavior that I present here do not correspond to single Baining terms or expressions. They are not, in other words, overtly expressed in the Baining language. The analytic abstraction of these concepts is derived by the author's inference from assumptions Baining make about themselves and others, and are built up from other domains of culture. These domains include perspectives on industriousness as the cardinal virtue of the normal social person; key social relationships created through food exchanges; the value of these relationships created through and by the work that is invested in them; and people defined in terms of their relations with others, as they are in a system of kinship relations. If pressed to put a label on people or actions that they consider within the normal social range, they rely on terms such as *atlo* 'good', 'industrious', or *abu* 'bad', 'lazy', but they do not generally evaluate people or personalities. There is, however, a general term for all deviations from the normal social state: *akambain* 'crazy', 'wild', 'drunk', 'lost'. Normal social behavior as such may thus be said to be "unmarked" while asocial behavior, as a contrasted, residual category is "marked" (Greenberg 1966). Here I am using the terms "marked" and "unmarked," not in their normal sense of denoting contrasting lexical categories but in an extended sense to denote the contrast between an unlabeled category comprising what is taken to be the normal state or general condition as a whole and a labeled category that refers to a residual class of deviations from this.[2] The logical relationship between these two categories is identical, I would argue, with that between lexical pairs such as man:woman; the difference is that in the case I am discussing labeling itself is the marking device.

This chapter is an attempt to describe and analyze the normative ideas and behaviors associated with the social person among the Baining, and to show how these are generated through particular values and sentiments. These values and sentiments define the underlying processes in the social and cultural as well as psychological domains. Deviant or asocial behavior is then described and analyzed in contrast with the normative state. The relations between these two conditions then become a model for understanding and analyzing the Baining sociocultural system as a whole.

Person, Self, and Individual

To begin my discussion, I would like first to elucidate my concept of the person. Drawing heavily on ideas presented by Mauss (1960*a*, 1960*b*), I distinguish between the individual, the self, and the person, although my analytical use of these terms differs significantly in some respects from Mauss's. I make these distinctions not to insist they are always isolable or culturally segregated categories but to underscore the need to define the sector(s) under discussion for greater clarity in comparative analysis.

Mauss analytically categorizes the concepts of person and self in a historical perspective. He traces the evolution of Western notions from personage into person and through that stage to a self-conscious and autonomous entity, the individual. As an intellectual progression, this transformation is undoubtedly accurate, but as Mauss himself points out in his conclusions, while the concepts of self and individual become progressively more culture bound throughout history, his model becomes more specifically that of Western history. I would suggest that in borrowing Mauss's historical stages in the development of consciousness, we remove them from their temporal progression, and examine them as foundations for an atemporal set of analytic categories.

Mauss traces the concept of person as it emerged from that of person-age. Historically, the personage consisted of a set of characteristics represented by a mask or, in my usage, a role; each wearer took on the same set of attributes or statuses as his or her predecessor upon assumption of the role. From this set of fixed characteristics, the "person" gradually acquired individuality and corporeality that existed apart from the mask or role. The person thus boasted an enduring body and a juridical status composed of rights and duties in a network of relationships. The next historical stage, according to Mauss, was the attribution of moral character to the person, thereby investing him/her with independence, freedom, and responsibility beyond the more stereotypic rights and duties. The final stage of development arrived when one attributed consciousness to the moral being, and established the location of consciousness, rationality, and individual unity in the concept of the self. These three stages, while not exactly congruent with the categories I want to call person, self, and individual, are closely related.

I want to distinguish between the person as a bounded entity invested with specific patterns of social behavior, normative powers, and restraints, and the individual as an entity with interiorized conscience, feelings, goals, motivations, and aspirations. I propose to show how the former is the entity around which Baining society and culture revolve, while the latter is relatively underemphasized in Baining values, and becomes important essentially in opposition to the former.

Although the person is most commonly conceived as the entity associated with a particular corporeal body (see Mauss 1960a), this body need not be identical with the social entity I am here calling the person. Parts of the physical body might be socially elevated to stand for the person (e.g., the head for the mind or soul), whereas at other times the body might not be considered part of the person at all, but merely a physical vessel (e.g., a person referred to as a "vegetable"). Sometimes the body must be modified to make it more social. This may be accomplished through processes such as circumcision, scarification, or body painting. By these means, people are saying that the physical body is only coterminous with the social being after it has been transformed through cultural patterns and social action (Turner 1980:112). In an even more extreme way, the boundaries of a person may be conceptualized as extending far beyond the physical body. For example, all members of a nuclear family might be assumed to share an essence distinct from those outside the family, which in turn binds them as a unit in relation to those others (Turner 1979a). As I will show for the

Baining, circumstances can determine patterns of sharing and thus perceptions of boundedness that are context related and not permanent. Certainly
in different societies, the sociocultural boundaries of the person vary widely
(as shown by Lutz, chap. 2; Kirkpatrick, chap. 3; and Poole, chap. 6), but
even within a society the boundaries of the person may alter and transform
from one context to another. This can be true over the life cycle, over
shorter time periods, in relation to geographic or social space, or because
of social relationships.

I am concerned about these distinctions and definitions because I want
to emphasize that my analysis focuses on a discussion of the person and not
the individual or self. In this respect, my analysis, while not an indigenous
model (the Baining are not explicit about these matters), is in keeping with
the Baining emphasis on external behaviors and relationships, and their lack
of interior, emotional, subjective explanation.

SOCIAL CONSTRUCTION OF THE PERSON

The Baining are not prone to describe themselves or explain others in terms
of personal experience or subjective states; their descriptions are much
more dependent on aspects of social roles, interpersonal interaction, and
the nature of social behavior and action. This perspective heightens the
relevancy of the concept of person among the Baining. In consequence, I
am led to the conclusion that my analytical emphasis on the person is in
keeping with the Bainings' own perspective and perception of themselves.
In this chapter, however, I will examine instances and accounts of more
idiosyncratic, even deviant, personal experiences as phenomena beyond the
category of the person; these cases will allow me to look at the relations
between person and self in a particular cultural context. I believe that these
exceptions only emphasize the predominance of personhood in Baining life
and the relative inaccessibility of subjective and emotional attitudes and
orientations. The absence of expressions of emotion or subjectivity does
not imply the absence of all affectivity. The Baining project and experience
certain affective states through sentiments. Sentiments are culturally constructed patterns of feeling and behavior which define, extend, and contract
the boundaries of the self, and which can be socially interpreted by others.

The Baining

The Baining of Papua New Guinea inhabit the inland mountainous
regions of much of the Gazelle Peninsula. They speak a non-Austronesian
language, which sets them off linguistically and culturally from their

Austronesian-speaking neighbors, the Tolai (see Epstein 1968). They are swidden horticulturalists for whom the staple crop is taro. They live in nuclear family households often within an extended family hamlet. The traditional settlements were dispersed hamlets that were often located near garden sites. Although the Baining now sometimes group into villages under the influence of administrative or mission programs, they manage to spend much of the year scattered among their gardens or cocoa plantings.

The Baining are an extremely amorphous and loosely structured society. This relative lack of structure is also reflected in a lack of elaboration in cultural or symbolic domains. Kinship is reckoned generationally and bilaterally, and genealogical memory is shallow. There are no corporate kin groups. People are recognized as belonging to geographical districts (now denoted by village names) within which they have access to land and resources on a first come, first served basis. There are no big men or chiefs, and almost no specialist roles or statuses. The primary subsistence and social unit is the household, most commonly consisting of a nuclear family. Adoption is quite prevalent among the Baining, and adopted children are valued very highly.

The Baining see the development of the person during the life cycle as a progression defined by the gradual acquisition of important social characteristics and powers, and then by the erosion of these characteristics during aging and dying (Fajans 1984). Throughout the life cycle, each Baining is constantly negotiating his or her status vis-à-vis the natural world. At birth, a Baining infant is a relatively natural creature who is not automatically considered a "person" (*defined as a social entity*) but is only accorded this status after attaining certain social characteristics and behaviors. Gradually, through the labors of his or her parents, the child is socialized. From the age of about six months, a person gradually emerges with more social attributes and greater and greater control over social action. Socialization is accomplished through the giving of food and the teaching of work.

The Baining person is characterized primarily by his or her engagement in (1) social relationships predicated on food giving and food taking, and (2) productive labor. As a child grows up she or he is continuously nurtured as a "social" being by being given food from the gardens, and by being taught to participate in daily tasks such as getting water or firewood, gathering food, and working in the gardens. On reaching adolescence, a child is a full social being capable of performing virtually any garden work; he or she also attains growing independence in social relationships. The culmination of this growth occurs at the point when the person pivots between the roles of food taker and food giver. At this moment in the life cycle people engage in communitywide relations of a reciprocal nature. They are now fully social. As married people, and subsequently as parents, they are not only full social actors but have also successfully reversed their childhood roles and dependencies, and have become the inverse, providers and food givers. The attribute of food giver is of tremendous significance in the status of the person. The giving of food, which is produced by human activity, transforms natural relationships such as those extant at birth into relationships that are progressively more defined and determined by the values of exchange, reciprocity, production, and industry. A food giver is a person who is once again engaged in asymmetrical social relationships, but now he or she has succeeded to the dominant position. Such people are the actors in this society. The processes that culminate in the role of socializer are reversed during the phase of aging, and individuals become progressively "desocialized" as they become older, more helpless, and increasingly dependent.

The whole life cycle is perceived in terms of the social and cultural values of food giving/food taking, production/reproduction, and reciprocity. These values form the criteria on which judgments about the status, effectiveness, and behavior of others are made. For example, the Baining say: she is a 'good' (atlo) prospective bride because she is industrious; he is my child because I give him food; she is my mother, my wife, and my mother, because she cooks and gives me food; he works hard, so he is ready for marriage; she is lazy, so no one wants to marry her; I scold her so she will work hard and people will think well of her; I give them food, and later they will look after me. These are the sorts of personality descriptions and motivational statements the Baining spontaneously give. Occasionally one can elicit other descriptions or judgments by offering information as a provocative stimulus. For instance, if I reported "So-and-so told me this," an informant might respond, "Oh, he is a liar"; or if I announced "my rooster disappeared," someone might volunteer that "those boys were hanging around yesterday," or "X's wife was caught stealing a rooster last week." But without such contextual incentives most personal descriptions reflect judgments not on the "personality" of the subject but on his or her social, relational, and productive characteristics.

As described above, the culturally patterned phases in the life cycle alternate between the natural and the social. In addition to these broad cycles, people move between nature and society at many points in their daily lives. These movements are related to and influenced by spatial, geographical, or social criteria. For the Baining, the village is the social space par excellence. It is clear, warm, easy to move about in, and it is where visiting, food exchanges, and dances occur. The bush is the opposite: obstructed, visually unclear, cold, and filled with natural and supernatural beings. People are said to have to keep their wits about them in the bush or they become akambain 'crazy' (Pidgin: *long long*), and get lost or trapped by bush spirits (cf. White, chap. 9). The bush is a place where you can only walk or roam during the day; at night it becomes impassable. It is the source of many raw materials for bark containers, mats, cane belts and dyes, and dance masks. It is not a place for prolonged social intercourse. In fact, it is where people test their wits and strength against asocial, animal, and supernatural forces. The garden is an intermediate place. It is a clear space produced through human labor and sweat which is surrounded by the forest with its antisocial agents and forces continually threatening to penetrate (e.g., pigs breaking into gardens and stealing food). The garden produces the raw materials that people take to the village and transform into social food. The garden is transformed from forest to clear space through two agencies that the Baining consider socializing, fire and sweat. The Baining believe that sweat makes humans productive (it is not just a sign of productive labor), while fire is seen as a nurturer ("fire is our mother because it cooks our food").

The contexts of village, forest, and garden are seen as affecting the internal states of people located within them. Thus, hunters are thought to be vulnerable to the disorienting properties of the forest and may *kambain*, that is, become inwardly as disoriented as the world around them. There is some idea, although it is not explicitly expressed, that men are better able to survive and hunt in the bush. Women, especially when burdened with children, are more vulnerable. Women are not barred from any forest domain (except some ritual places) but are less likely to frequent them alone. By contrast, inside the village people are surrounded by social products and the agencies of social transformation, such as fire. This environment protects them, to a degree, from their own internal "natural" properties. This is why the village is an apt place for children and old people to spend the day, while those who are more fully social can brave the natural elements. Adolescents and adults have enough social and transforming properties, such as 'heat', to act as buffers against the forces of nature. Old and young contain elements of nature in their own being and thus have little resistance to similar forces from the outside.

The symbolic properties of old and young, natural and social, hot and cold, night and day (discussed elsewhere, Fajans 1984) are important as defining characteristics of the Baining person. They are the properties that mediate the boundaries between internal and external. They help define the boundaries and nature of the entity, and they work to expand or contract these boundaries in different circumstances. As mentioned earlier, sentiments are another class of phenomena which also act on the boundaries of the person, helping to define, expand, mediate, and contract these boundaries.

The Role of Sentiments in Defining the Person

Sentiments are culturally constructed patterns of feeling and behavior which demarcate the boundaries of the person. As such they provide forms of affective interaction of the person with his or her environment (which, of course, includes other people). These standardized affective patterns include both reactive and active forms of feeling; that is, responses to events and motivations which are projected outward from the individual onto the social order.

> But there are two sorts of social sentiments. The first binds each individual to the person of his fellow-citizens: these are manifest within the community, in the day-to-day relationships of life. These include the sentiments of honour, respect, affection and fear which we may feel towards one another. The second are those which bind me to the social entity as a whole. (Durkheim 1972:219–220)

It is the movement between internal and external domains which acts to formulate and demarcate the boundaries of the person. The person is not a fixed entity but one whose attributes and positions evolve as much through particular contexts as through enduring "human" qualities. The acquisition and projection of sentiments during the process of socialization is one process by which an asocial (natural) individual is transformed into a socially and culturally defined person.

When things are flowing smoothly, the process of creating and sustaining the social milieu and its relations to individual behavior excite little attention. When problems arise in the demarcation of domains, however, so do conflicts in interests and expectations. Sentiments are stereotyped patterns of feeling and acting which are used to negotiate such confusions. Not all sentiments mediate the same types of problems. They, therefore, may be differentially weighed in importance. Among the Baining, 'shame' (*angirrup, akalup*) appears as the most important sentiment in the sociocultural system. The particular salience of shame for this culture is related to its role in delimiting the underlying structure of the system. Shame exists on the edges of the structure. It functions to maintain the separation between the natural and the social. In this analysis, the presence of shame indicates a disruption of some of the key processes of transformation and coordination within the Baining sociocultural system. Shame is, therefore, an important mediator in the structure. In other studies, shame is frequently analytically perceived as a form of negative sanction and constraint (Piers and Singer 1953), but it may just as well be viewed as a positive means of

reasserting the normal order of relations. Such a positive value is also visible
in accounts of similar sentiments among Marquesans (chap. 3) and the
Ifaluk (chap. 2).

Not all sentiments are equally powerful in ordering and motivating
the actor in this sociocultural system; they are not equally weighed, but
sentiments in general play a structural role of motivating and generating
acceptable behavior. The other sentiments discussed here, hunger and
awumbuk 'lassitude', extend and contract the boundaries of the self within
a smaller domain. While not as salient as shame, they complete the set of
sentiments which adhere in kin and food-giving relations. As I have written
elsewhere (Fajans 1979), the construction of relationships through kinship
and food giving is central for generating the Baining sociocultural system.

THE PLACE OF SHAME IN THE SYSTEM

Through my study of adoption (Fajans 1979, 1984), I became aware of the
importance of shame in Baining culture. Shame adheres in certain relations
and actions, many of which are situated in the nuclear family. The members
of a nuclear family usually work, eat, and sleep together in a relatively social
milieu. It is when the relations within the unit are contrasted with external
relations, predicated entirely on social ties, that the naturalness of family
ties are emphasized and become shameful. Since shame crops up where the
interaction between two or more people relies more on natural bonds than
on socially determined ones, it reflects the differential weight and value of
these ties. Those which do not elicit shame are valued more highly than
those which do.

The Baining say that their adopted children are their 'true' (*araik*)
children, and that they are 'ashamed' of their natural children. Similarly,
they say it is 'good' (*amuris*, atlo) to use kinship terms reciprocally with
their adopted children, but are 'ashamed' to use kin terms with their natural
children. They are prepared to support and come to the defense of adopted
children in public arenas, but would not defend a natural child because they
are 'ashamed' of what their natural children do (Fajans 1979). While friends
and some relatives of a deceased person may undertake food taboos to
express their sorrow, members of the nuclear family would feel shame at
this. However, adopted children and more distant relatives would find such
expression appropriate. Although examples of shame between family members
led me to investigate this subject, it is not restricted to family contexts.

Other contexts producing shame are: to come upon a person of the
opposite sex bathing; to be discovered in the act of intercourse; for a man
to discover that a woman is menstruating; to enter someone's house without

being invited (visitors often lurk, out of sight, near a house they want to visit until they are glimpsed or some slight noise is overheard and they are invited in). People also feel shame in requesting food or gifts from people not related in any way. Because of this, people are reluctant to travel to places where they have no kin or close friends. Despite the range of these examples, key aspects of the sentiment are constant throughout. Briefly, shame inheres in contexts where natural and social relationships, and the boundaries between them, are constructed and contrasted, and where private and public spheres are delimited.

The dichotomy between natural and social in the Baining family parallels similar distinctions between private and public spheres. Nuclear family relations (except for adoptive relations) are natural; they are also private and ideally not made explicit. Direct reference to the nature of the relationships, as, for example, through kin terms, is avoided. Within the private domain people are connected, but such connections are not socially formed or transformed. It is here that shame inheres. Shame is evoked principally in contexts where the untransformed, natural connections are juxtaposed with other types of relations, those which are socially and culturally defined. Thus, speaking up for a close kinsperson in public produces shame by intruding the private into the public. In much the same way, shame is felt by people who want to visit someone, a social act, but are stopped from entering the other's house without invitation because of the shame of intruding into the other's private sphere. People arriving at another community are ashamed because they see before them a social nexus with which they have no ties, neither natural nor social, and therefore no means of entrée. They are outside the system. After a death, when a person's social network is disrupted, people following food taboos are ashamed to speak of them because they are a private matter, not to be discussed in public.

Shame is expressed when aspects of the private sphere are extruded into the public domain or, conversely, when those of the public domain are intruded into the private sphere, just as it is when a person is outside the system entirely. Shame is a reaction to a disorder of the boundaries of margins, whether potential or actual. Strathern (1975) has reported that shame is said to be "on the skin" in another New Guinean tribe. While the Baining are not so explicit about the bodily locus of the sentiment, it is clear that the cultural locus is also on the boundary of a social entity, the "person," the household, or the community. Shame is, however, more than just a reaction to a transgression of boundaries between equal domains. The domains here are not structurally equal.

The Baining sociocultural order is a hierarchical system (Fajans 1984). The hierarchy is generated when the natural is transformed into the social. The natural order exists at a lower level of coordination and complexity because its components have not been acted on and coordinated by transformational principles. The sociocultural order is a more complex domain because it consists not just of isolated elements but of elements and interconnections between them. This complexity raises the domain to a higher level of structure. Within this system of separate levels, shame results when a set of relations normally opposed or separated is contradicted by relations or actions that deny that separation or collapse the opposition. It is, in short, the juxtaposition of a higher with a lower level of structure, where the higher level forms the context and the lower level the intrusive element, which is accordingly the focus of the shame. As a result of this definition, it is no longer enough to see shame as a negative sanction and constraint on behavior. Shame also functions positively to reassert the normative order; to restore the separateness of the levels of structure; and to reinstate the relative value of these opposed domains. Consequently, shame is the principal sentiment in the Baining repertoire. That is why it can be opposed to atlo, 'good', in the particular examples cited above. Other sentiments also negotiate boundary and category oppositions, and I class them with shame as part of a set of sentiments which locate people in natural and social space.

HUNGER

One particularly important sentiment in Baining attitudes and orientations is that of *anaingi* or *airiski*. This is literally translated as 'hunger'. It might seem that hunger should be classed as a physical state and not as an emotion or sentiment, but I would argue that for the Baining it is both. The experience of isolation and hunger are the subject of a number of Baining songs.

> *Ngu muwun aira dama airiski kyia vulung ngua*
>   I sit here and hunger is killing me
> *Ngu muwun aira dama airiski kyia vulung ngua*
>   I sit here and hunger is killing me
> *Sa ngua muwun aira mura ma hinga na nda kuri ngua*
>   And I sit here and there is no one, and I am here
> *E ra mit semani sup ma* Kavungum *sa dama* Misseit *nari*
>   Already they have gone down to Kavungum and Misseit here.

> *Ngu muwun nda ngu knak lunguakaka*
>   I sit here and cry, there is no one around
> *Mra manaingi kyia vulung ngua*
>   Hunger is killing me

Sa ngu muwun nda ngu knak
    And I sit here and cry
Mra manaingi kyia vulung ngua
    For hunger is killing me
Bra manaingi kyia vulung ngua
    For hunger is killing me
Sa ngu tu ngua akavuk sangul umga
    And I think of him
Ambrutka na ka, ambrutka na ka
    The dead man, the ghost [a ghost who has died violent death]

Ambiowa kyi knak savra ngua
    The ambiowa [a bird] cries for me
Ambiowa kyi knak savra ngua
    The Ambiowa cries for me
Kyi knak savra ngua nda airiski kyia vulunga ngua
    She cries for me and hunger is killing me
Naut gulavu ta me ra mit savut ma Malasait
    My parents and all of them, they went to Malasait

People left alone feel their loneliness as hunger. Often they recount hearing birds sing or call since, when alone, it is so quiet that the bird cries stand out, whereas the other times they are masked by human noise. At such moments Baining become acutely aware of the nature that surrounds them. The individual removed from her or his social milieu is identified with nature by being outside society.

Since food is the primary cultural medium of sociality, it is fitting that the absence of people is associated with the absence of food (hunger). The Baining concern with food is related systematically to sentiments. What is good and valued (atlo) in social relations is based on using food as a medium for bond formation. The absence of these elements is problematic, contrastively marked and mediated by sentiments. The person experiencing 'hunger' is one whose expectations are still attached to a higher level of social order but who is suddenly plummeted to a lower, more natural level. The transformation is expressed by the sentiment.

To assuage the isolation and sadness that accompany travel, a visitor arriving in a Baining community is given food immediately. The social form that demands the giving of food is a response to the threat of 'hunger'. Here the sentiment indirectly motivates behavior, and the desire to incorporate the newcomer into the social order is accomplished through social transaction. The presentation of food to visitors also addresses a second social dilemma. Since food sharing is ideally based on social relationships, asking for food is, for an outsider, an extremely difficult and shameful undertaking. Baining express shame in having to ask for food, and describe people who do ask for it as 'shameless'. Even when food is presented to a visitor, he or she might be too ashamed to accept it at first. The eventual acceptance leads to social bonds that have ramifications in other ways, as will be seen below.

AWUMBUK

Another sentiment in Baining culture is *awumbuk*, a lassitude that people feel after the departure of visitors, friends, or relatives who have resided with them. If people come to visit, sleep in one's house, and eat one's food, one will feel awumbuk on their departure. (This is also true when co-residents leave to visit elsewhere.) The Baining say that awumbuk is caused by the 'heaviness' that the departed visitors leave behind. They go off lightly and leave this weight behind. The experience is conceptualized as a physical indisposition. The symptoms of awumbuk are tiredness (sleeping late in the morning, and an inability to get started), lack of success in activities (failure to find game or get a garden weeded), and some degree of boredom. It is a social "hangover." I do not believe it has an encompassing gloss in English, and therefore leave it untranslated. Awumbuk lingers for three days after the departure. Awumbuk is also experienced at the death of a person, particularly before a death is announced and mortuary practices are initiated.

This peculiarly Baining sentiment exists on the boundaries of social events. Visits are social occasions during which people share food, shelter, and friendship. The shared experiences erase the barriers between individuals and connect them to one another. When the social group disbands, these connections are served. The socially extended persona is destroyed and individuals must reconstitute their boundaries. They experience this loss in the form of awumbuk. The departure induces a loss of social vitality and leaves the home party feeling relatively weakened and diminished, experienced as an additional weight or burden. The more people who have left, the greater the awumbuk. Activities in which sociality is esteemed, for example, hunting and gardening, suffer most acutely from awumbuk. Baining often seek to escape awumbuk in behaviors and activities contrasted with it. One potential antidote for the remaining residents of a household is to get up very early the morning after the departure and toss outside the house a dish (originally a coconut shell) of water that has been left out all night and is believed to have absorbed the awumbuk. If this is properly done, life proceeds normally. It is atlo, 'good'. A second response to the problem is for the remainder of the household also to leave their home.

Typically, they will spend several days living and sleeping in their garden houses, but they also have the option of leaving to go visit elsewhere. Both solutions have the indirect consequence of promoting the very characteristics that awumbuk undermines. They encourage alertness, industrious productivity, and sociality.

Both anaingi 'hunger' and awumbuk 'lassitude' are concerned with the creation and maintenance of sociality. They mediate and modify the boundaries of the person in particular contexts. These boundaries are expanded or retracted through food. Food is both a model of and a model for (Geertz 1966b:7) the bonds that unite people in social relations. Food provides the individual with the natural vitality that underlies the social order. It is through food that natural relations are transformed into social relations, but this process can also be reversed. The threat of this reversal, through either a lack of food or the breaking of social relations, is the social dilemma that the sentiments awumbuk and anaingi express and seek to control. Anaingi and awumbuk show clearly the structural processes of the system. In the normal order of events, social activity predominates and transformations are performed; it is a 'good' state. When the system is upset, the normal directionality of these processes can be altered and reversed. These transgressions are reflected through awumbuk and anaingi. Each state, however, is countered by specific actions and practices that alleviate these problems.

From the examination of this set, we see that Baining sentiments are an expression of the interdependence between a social actor and her or his social environment. Sentiments are not needed to mediate every situation. It is in contexts where the boundaries between individuals and their social environment are problematic, where sets of expectations are in conflict, and where new roles are being negotiated or old relations are threatened or transformed, that sentiments are called upon to express and mediate the situation. The social actor is not a rigidly defined and delimited entity in the Baining world. The boundaries of the individual and the definition of the person are neither permanent nor immutable, but alter and adapt in specific contexts. Often these changes are so subtle and mundane as to excite no particular notice. Occasionally, however, there is a disturbance of the fundamental structural relations of the system. Sentiments are responses to the boundaries of the extension of the person into the arena of social action; the processes by which the self is augmented or diminished; and the contradictions created by the juxtaposition of incompatible levels of relationships.

The sentiments described in this chapter are a particularly salient set in the organization of Baining personal, social, and cultural domains because they negotiate the transformations between the natural and the social. They are the means for bringing into focus and articulating important values of

Baining society. Through the examination of shame, awumbuk, and hunger, I have defined the structural elements of nature and society, the transformative value of socially created bonds, the importance of food as a mediator of social bonds, and the role of the social person in experiencing, negotiating, and contextualizing these relations. The sentiments examined adhere to the boundaries of this social and cultural system and come into play when the system is threatened or penetrated. Sentiments act not only as sanctions against behavior but also as vehicles to motivate acts that maintain and transform the system.

The sentiments described here are not merely reflections of states that exist within a predetermined social system or cultural order; they are created by and participate in the generation and maintenance of key aspects of the system. It is in the process of social activity that the social domains are defined. The activity or work that goes into separating the domains and levels of the system is repaid through the value attributed to its products. Thus, adoption, visiting, and food exchanges are highly valued activities for the Baining. In contrast, the processes that seek to undermine the system are devalued and made problematic. Sentiments are not a symbolic domain apart from the dynamic functioning of the system. Rather, they are an integral part of a dialectical system that includes social action, symbolic domains, values, and relationships. The integration of these entities into a holistic system defines the system's generative and functional structure.

The concept of person is a social construct that articulates aspects from both the social and cultural domains. The Baining articulation focuses on social relations, food exchanges, production and reproduction, and the dynamic contrast between nature and the social. A social analysis involves more, however, than the definition of person and relationships. It is necessary to go beyond this static model and analyze the dynamics of the person in a range of social and cultural contexts.

Sometimes the dynamics of social actions involve behavior that is defined as outside the social system proper. This includes instances in which the behavior, attitudes, and values of the participants fall beyond the net of ties and balances described above. Such behavior is considered deviant, and represents a collapse of the system in some of its dimensions. This breakdown can be either permanent or transient. In the Baining system, the pattern of deviance is socially stereotyped, and its occurrence reflects major values and patterns of the system. In this system deviance does not simply mirror normative values and patterns, but actually creates, defines, and articulates those values through opposition and contrast. For this reason, an analysis of social actions becomes the key to the analysis of the system. In the following section these problems will be discussed and analyzed.

THE PERSON IN DYNAMIC SOCIAL ACTION

The Person versus the Individual

I have portrayed the Baining as being person oriented. By this I mean that their views of themselves, their experiences, and those around them are not predominantly individualistic. Informants do not readily speak or proclaim personal opinions about either their own actions or those of others. Evaluations of events do not invoke an internal, emotional explanation. The most common response to questions such as "Why did he do that?" is "I don't know about him." While not speculating on others' subjective attitudes is common in many non-Western societies, the Baining reluctance to utter even their own opinions seems extreme.

I have heard teachers, missionaries, and government officers comment on the lack of individualism among the Baining. These comments range from their lack of entrepreneurial motivation (compared to their neighbors, the Tolais, who have been called "primitive capitalists" [Epstein 1968]) to their lack of success in vocational or educational training. Students are increasingly leaving the Baining area to pursue secondary education in the neighboring towns under the auspices of church or government programs. Although I have no data, the number of Baining is said by administration sources to be quite low compared to other groups. The success rate has also been quite low. Almost all of the educated people have returned to the village and again taken up the life of subsistence gardeners. I can think of only one Baining, not still at school, who continues to live and work away from the Baining area. This is not to say there are not others, but few Baining thrive outside their community. For those who return home, these special skills and experiences are left almost unmentioned and are not displayed in any way.

There is another facet to the tendency of the Baining to return to their community. There are no Baining laborers or residents in Rabaul, the nearest town and one filled with *wantok* communities from all the Papua New Guinean provinces.[3] When Baining go into town to sell their cocoa beans or garden produce they do so for the day only. At night they insist on returning at least as far as the beach twenty miles out of town where their transport boat docks. They will sleep there, on the beach if the boat is unavailable. If they fail to sell all their produce, they might resort to sleeping right in the marketplace. These measures are necessary because they have no wantoks in town with whom they can stay. As described above, they would be 'ashamed' to visit or ask for food from nonkin.

Among other Papua New Guinean peoples, at least some youths migrate to town for wage labor. While it is true that the Baining have a source of wage labor closer to home on the plantations that line their coast, and most males spend at least three months of their bachelorhood working as plantation laborers, they are not a reliable labor force according to local plantation managers. They do occasionally seek work, and frequently respond when there is a need for sudden or massive labor input, but do not contribute a steady supply of plantation labor in the district. They tend to sign on for only three months at a time instead of the two-year contracts the managers prefer. Plantation managers in the Baining area still resort to old-fashioned recruitment of Highland and Sepik youths who are anxious to leave home and work for wages. The Baining have no resentment toward these migrant laborers and occasionally, even increasingly, adopt them into their families, intermarry, and sell them land.[4]

What emerges from these examples is the notion that the Baining personality is social in more than the ordinary sense, and the particular Baining are unusually dependent on the surrounding sociality of their own group and the customary patterns of behavior for their self-definition (cf. Leenhardt 1979:155). They have been relatively unable to step outside the matrix of community roles and social expectations in order to succeed at or enjoy other endeavors. I attribute this to the relative weighting that the sociocultural system gives to the development of the person rather than that of the individual or self.

Personal Experiences and Individuality

Despite the emphasis on the person described above, idiosyncratic behavior is fairly easily tolerated among the Baining. People's habits and styles are accepted, usually without comment. This is in keeping with the low tenor of gossip in the society. Everyone might know of someone's idiosyncrasy, but few people would have the curiosity to ask about its origin. A very simple case was that of my adopted father in Lan, who refused to eat pig. I asked him about this and he said that when his (adopted) father died he tabooed pig and never started eating it again. The tabooing of a foodstuff is a Baining custom at death, and is not remarkable or surprising. What was surprising to me was that neither his wife nor his grown daughter had any idea why he did not eat pig. The wife simply answered that she did not know, while the daughter said, when asked separately, that maybe he did not like it—and this in a culture where pig is the most valued foodstuff available. They showed no curiosity about his individual behavior.

In Yalom, the old woman Pinam was unique among all my informants because she neither chewed betel nor smoked, while virtually everyone else chewed betel. On one of my first evenings, while trying to create rapport, I asked why. She responded with a story from her youth:

> "When I was young, I went with some women to the bush. We went to a certain tree [*arandunaka*, a tree with white sap which in times of scarcity was used as a substitute for betel nut]. We took this sap like betel nut and chewed it with leaves [pepper leaves] and lime. We chewed and chewed and chewed. Then I vomited and vomited and vomited. I said I would never chew betel again. I left behind me a large packet of the sap, but the other women went back and fought over it and took it."

Similarly, she told why she does not smoke:

> "Once when I was little, my parents went to the garden and left all the young girls and children at home. There was tobacco drying from the house rafters and the children took it all down and wrapped it in leaves, one after another, after another, after another. We smoked and spit balls of tobacco until the house was full. I got very, very dizzy and sat down and vomited and vomited. When my parents came back they scolded us because we had finished all the tobacco and leaf wrappers in the house."

These stories were told in a house occupied by three generations of Pinam's descendants. All of them knew well that she neither smoked nor chewed, and said so when I would offer her betel nut or tobacco. However, no one in the house had ever heard these stories before. People laughed and enjoyed the stories, which had never arisen spontaneously. This was so even though everybody knew the tree she mentioned, and had seen the cuts in the bark where the sap had been drained.

These stories illustrate what seems obvious, that the Baining acknowledge some personal experiences and recognize their influences in determining the later behavior of the person. Individuals retain memories of at least some such experiences and can produce them in anecdotal form on certain occasions for telling stories of this type. The great majority of such incidents told to me were elicited by direct questions or produced for tape recording when I solicited stories. They were rarely produced spontaneously. The infrequent use of narrative for presenting personal experiences contrasts sharply with the use of song for the same purpose. Composing songs, about oneself or another, is the primary mode by which Baining (predominantly males) encode idiosyncratic experiences and behaviors. Although a recognized forum for personal expression, songs are frequently performed and enjoyed by participants who lack prior knowledge about the incident or person they describe. I do not believe it is an accident that these experiences are relegated to ritual and not daily occasions, since both forms intrude on the normative flow of social intercourse and activity.

Experiences Outside the Social Order

In contrast to the scarcity of narratives about personal experiences involving people, there is an abundant flow of accounts involving encounters with *aios* ('ghost', 'forest spirit') and other forest creatures. I was amused with stories of this sort in numerous contexts. Some stories were spontaneously told as I was sitting with an informant; some were elicited for tape recording; several were inserted into life histories; a few were included in the reminiscences of Pinam; and a number were recounted shortly after they occurred. These stories all allude to the ongoing negotiation between the natural and social milieu. The vast majority occur in the bush or forest, and the remainder occur at night, either in a house or the village. As a pattern, these experiences involve single men or small groups of women and children who, when walking through the forest, see creatures who look like real persons but who do not speak or behave socially. Sometimes these creatures chase the victims, but often they just watch them. The victims always escape or keep the attackers at bay. Occasionally the aios appear at a house at night, commonly when only children are home, and chase the victims. In these cases, the aios disappear at dawn. Sudden deaths of young children are frequently attributed to aios.

A more interesting and profound experience with aios is that of people who have run wild in some way (Baining *kambain,* verb; *akambain,* noun), or have encountered spirits in illness. Kambain experience seems to span a range from intoxication (*ka surup nda ka kambain,* he drinks and is crazy), to disorientation due to being lost in the bush, to antisocial behavior. The one real idiot in the village was also described as *akambain pra ka* (the crazy one). The effects of being kambain can be of very short duration, or they can be permanent attributes. The antihero in a whole series of stories, the man who does everything wrong is called *Kambainium,* in which *kambain* is the first part of his name, and which informants translated as the "crazy one."

In an analysis of how akambain behavior represents an inversion of aspects of personhood, the more permanent cases seem less interesting than the cases of temporary craziness. Nevertheless, they are an extension of the category and should be mentioned. In Lan there was an eighteen- or nineteen-year-old boy who was obviously retarded and could barely walk or talk. He frequently fell into fires and was covered with burns. He was always surrounded by a swarm of flies which were attracted to the sores on his body. Informants said he did not feel the pain of the fire. Apparently he had once been normal and even attended school and was said to have learned English. His craziness was attributed to a forest spirit of a type called *akumgi* (Pidgin *masalai* 'forest spirit'), which lived in a tree by a water hole. He encountered it when his family was clearing land for a garden and became very sick and emerged akambain from his illness. He died about six weeks after my arrival in the field (although many years after being stricken).

In Yalom there was a man in his forties named Ingi, whom a number of people treated as a crazy person. I was warned by Tovi early on to avoid frustrating or antagonizing him. His craziness had started when he was almost an adult: "he was almost married, but he became crazy and now all the women dislike him." He lived at some distance from the main village and only came in on Sundays to go to church and socialize. He was perhaps the most regular attendant at church. Ingi was still able to support himself, but grew no cash crops and did not work for wage labor. Tovi once speculated that maybe he did not pay Council taxes because he had no money. He managed to acquire other store-bought goods by asking for them. Tovi explained,

> "If you give him a new laplap, then he is all right until the laplap tears, then he might go crazy. People give him laplaps, tobacco, and betel nut so that he does not get frustrated and go wild. You can not scold him for anything wrong lest this set him off. If he gets violent he could kill a man, he runs around with a knife or axe. He hasn't killed yet, but he once attacked his father."

I think this latter incident marked the initial onset of his craziness. Nobody knew why he was crazy, but when questioned and pressed for an answer most people mumbled *aioska* 'ghost'. Despite his reputation for craziness, Kusak, an older man who was a very open, good informant, disclaimed knowledge of any akambain people in Yalom. I had a visit one weekend from the East New Britain regional psychologist. He was curious about *long long* (Pidgin for 'crazy') men in the village and how the community cared for them. We talked to the older informant who denied any knowledge of 'crazy' men. At that time I knew of three instances of crazy behavior in the community (the two besides Ingi will be discussed shortly) and finally introduced them into the conversation. The old man knew nothing about the other two, despite his presence in the village on both occasions. At the mention of Ingi, he registered a bit of recognition, but said he did not know the story. I mentioned that I believed he had tried to kill his father with an ax, and Kusak nodded, but said that if I wanted to know the story I should ask Ingi himself.

This incident affirms my belief that the Baining have very little interest in and curiosity about the behavior of others, in distinct contrast to other groups discussed in this volume. In particular, they do not consider it a proper subject for discourse. As a consequence they are not prone to label or categorize known incidents. Although the label and category of akambain exist, people do not readily associate events and experiences with the terms. They are not actively classifying actions and events. Instead, this category exists as a residual domain for behavior or experiences that deviate from the norm. In this sense the greater success I had eliciting labels and categories from a younger informant like Tovi might be indicative of his greater education and experience outside his society. For example, Tovi explained that sometimes a dancer will run wild, as if he were drunk. The wild man might run off along a path out of the village or break straight into the bush. The others will have to go after him to restrain him (similar to the Tobian response to a man striking off into the bush to attempt suicide, chap. 7). This had happened to Kangmani once, a few years before my stay, when he was dancing with a *akavuganan,* a piece of dance regalia with a shield atop a pole. He went wild and started to run out of the village toward the cemetery. They went after him and brought him back. Somewhere on route, he grabbed a raw taro and started to eat it.[5] They did not know where he had obtained the taro but he said a 'ghost' had given it to him. He held it by the stalk with the leaves pointing to the ground and started to eat it from the bottom. The men took the taro from him and threw it away, then they carried him back to the house. Later he recovered completely. During my stay we had another dance, and Kangmani decided to participate again. This time nothing went wrong.

After the dance, all the dancers who had danced with an *akipka,* a long spear tied to the back by a rope that is sewn into the flesh of the lower spine, were laid low by the sore this rope caused. Inangaiyi was particularly sick. I went to see him and he told me that *tumbuna* (Pidgin word for 'ancestors', often used in Baining) used to die from these sores. Tapalat had died in this way. A long time before, when Inangaiyi was just a boy and Tapalat was sick with such an infection, he told Inangaiyi to go to the river and catch and kill an eel for him. Inangaiyi went that night and caught and killed one. Apparently, however, it was not a real eel, it was an akumgi 'forest spirit'. He brought it to Tapalat who cooked and ate it, and shortly afterward died. Inangaiyi said that, although others said the sore killed him, it was really the spirit which had gotten him. Several days after the dance I attended, but before Inangaiyi's sore had swelled up, he saw Tapalat in a dream. In the dream, Tapalat said, "You are my younger brother, and now I am coming to get you."[6] He showed Inangaiyi an eel in a small pool above the place the village got its drinking water. The next day Inangaiyi's sore swelled up, became infected, and his sickness worsened. Inangaiyi told me he was not going to send someone to go catch the eel, because it was really a 'forest spirit' and not an eel. A spirit can go inside and inhabit a snake or eel. My young informant, Tovi, expressed relief at not being sent to get the eel for Inangaiyi since he was sure it was a spirit. Inangaiyi was sure that he would die if he ate the eel, because Tapalat and the other 'bad ones' (*avungut*) had marked him to die. He told me "I am finished now," and was afraid he would die from the sore even without eating the eel. Despite this fatalistic attitude, Inangaiyi accepted penicillin and recovered.

About six weeks after this, Inangaiyi ran amok (*akambain pre ka* 'become crazy'). This event followed a very tense period when Inangaiyi had taken a second wife, and his first wife, Uras, had left and gone down to live on the family cocoa block on the coast. After about six weeks, Uras returned, and on the night in question she called on Inangaiyi and they talked. Uras said she wanted to give Inangaiyi some money, and then she would leave and go 'wandering' or visiting on the coast. Inangaiyi said, "You can't give me any money," but Uras said she wanted to shake hands over the money (come to an agreement) while she went off and he stayed in the village with his other wife. While they were talking Inangaiyi became 'foggy' or 'dizzy' and saw the 'ghost' of his dead son, Supsis, through the door (which was closed). Supsis said "Come," so Inangaiyi said, "All right." Suddenly it was not night, but day. They went into the bush and found some ripe bananas. Supsis gave him three and took two himself. Then they wandered onto the "village green" where they met Tovi and another adolescent and exchanged greetings. Supsis said "Let's go," so they broke into a run and ran straight into the bush. Tovi followed them and suddenly Supsis disappeared and Tovi was holding Inangaiyi. Inangaiyi saw he was holding a hard, green banana, whereas before it had been soft and ripe. It was also night again.

Tovi described finding Inangaiyi standing in a soaking laplap alone on the green eating unripe bananas. When Tovi approached him, he ran off, and Tovi chased him for a while before finally catching him. He brought him to his brother's house where they talked to him for at least ten minutes before he seemed to hear or to be able to answer.

Inangaiyi recalled that Supsis said that he would return, and that next time he and his father would sleep in the bush for several days. He said he would pull his father to the place of the aios, but he did not set a time. Inangaiyi took this as an omen that he would die soon. Both Inangaiyi and Tovi, when questioned, recognized the tension between Inangaiyi and his first wife, Uras. Both thought that Supsis had appeared to try to resolve this problem. Neither of them suggested how he might do it.

When I was recording life histories three months later, I tried to get Inangaiyi to reconstruct these two incidents.

> We danced with the spears, and they pierced us. When it was finished I was very sick, my back swelled up, and I was sick. I stayed with my two wives.

One wife went to the cocoa block, and I stayed with the other, and she looked after me during the sore and the sickness. And Uvian[7] (the anthropologist) used to come and she dressed the sore for me. She brought medicine and I drank it, and now I am alright. If it had not been so, I would have died. I danced with the akipka [dance spear], and I almost died after the *asarai* [dance name] from the sickness.

Anthropologist: What caused the sickness?

The sickness came from the aios. I saw the aios and they said later I would die. My back swelled up and they said I would die from the sore on my back, just like Tapalat did. Then later I got better, Uvian gave me some medicine and the sore dried up.

Anthropologist: You saw another aioska [ghost]?

Yes, after this one, I saw another aioska, who came with me and gave me some leaves. He said he would go with me and we would sleep somewhere together. I am afraid of aios. I saw him, and I was afraid since I had seen them bury him, the aioska [*aioska* here means corpse]. He made me eat leaves as if they were green vegetables. And later I saw they were just leaves. We talked to each other, and we ate food; we went to the bush, the aioska and I, and we ate food. We ate their food, their taro, Singapore taro, and vegetables. It seemed like taro, but when I came up to the village it turned out to be just a seed pod. The seed was taro there, but when I came up to the place it was just a seed. The seed was not taro. I saw the aios, Tapalat, Misaigi, and Kariongi, I saw these three aios. They said that later they would get me, they would take me and I would stay with them [would die too].

Anthropologist: Had you seen aios before?

No, it was my first time. The second time I saw Supsis here.

Anthropologist: What caused this?

I don't know about these aios. I think they saw me making trouble like this [oblique reference to his two wives]. I don't know about them, I think only that I don't know. I made all this talk, this trouble. Yes, I think it was this, but I did not ask them enough, those aios.

Three months later Inangaiyi's memory of the experiences are quite detached. He failed to make any mention of the instances spontaneously, and only commented on them after my direct questioning. The reality of the experiences, the fear of death, the personality and presence of the aios are all greatly diminished in the above recollections. What remains are the cultural remnants of the akambain experiences, the prediction of death and the reversals of normal social behavior such as eating raw food or bush materials instead of cooked food.

The last instance of a person running wild is the least elaborated of this set, but it is the only one to which I was a witness. Several young men were having a song rehearsal, staged for my benefit so I could hear the song that had been composed about me, my stay, and my impending departure. In addition to this song, I was recording other songs recently composed by young men of my acquaintance. After several hours of very intense singing in a house turned over to the occasion, the group broke up, although I was not sure whether it was just a break. Tovi got up and asked to borrow my flashlight. He and several young men went outside. The next thing we heard were several whoops, rapidly getting further and further away. Tovi had started to run and whoop. He ran outside the village, past a clearing with one house in it, through another abandoned clearing, and fell down at the foot of some rocks on the path out of the village. Another boy was right behind him and a trail of others followed. I came running up with two young married men while Tovi was still lying face down in the mud. He was trembling slightly. Marukawa told him to get up and he slowly stood up and walked back to the village, leaning on Marukawa. Back at the house he lay down on the platform bed with his head half over the edge, and stayed there in a stupor for about fifteen minutes. Then he called for water and said his stomach was hot. Marukawa poured water over his stomach. People resisted my attempts to cover him, but agreed he should move over to a dry spot. When we told him to move he did, but continued to just lie still. After another fifteen minutes, he started to snore. Then a few minutes later he sat up, took off his wet shorts, and wrapped himself in a blanket. After sitting for a few minutes, he lay down to sleep. During all this time, the young men sat silently. His mother and some girls came into the house and also sat silently. When his mother saw him sitting up, she said "He's gotten up" and she left. When Tovi lay down to sleep, people told me to leave. Shortly thereafter everyone became quiet and slept.

Tovi and all the other young men were up very early the next morning reroofing a neighboring house. After this work was done I questioned him, and he said he was all right. He certainly appeared normal. He said he did not know why he ran; he went crazy and ran without knowing why. It was as if someone was holding his hair and pulling him up. He felt so light that he ran. It was like someone was leading him and pulling him. When another boy held his arm he felt his touch, but it did not stop him. This was the first time he'd ever behaved like this. When asked he said he thought it was connected to the singing, but then lapsed into silence.

Despite a large number of witnesses, this incident was not widely discussed. Because of the low level of gossip and the readiness to forget such incidents, it is difficult to ascertain how common they are. All of my examples deal with men, but informants said it could happen to women too, and some mentioned a woman in another village as an example.

In these examples of akambain behavior and confrontations with aios, the Baining do not seem to see themselves as agents in their own right. In these contexts, their behavior is attributed to the influence of another force that brings them under its direction. It thus seems that deeply emotional, idiosyncratic behavior is conceived as being outside the control of the person it affects.

The emotions and behavior that erupt in these situations resemble Mauss's *"l'emoi envahissant"* (Mauss 1960b:385). These "invading emotions" (or better translated as encroaching emotional chaos) are seen as dangerous but potent forces that pull the person away from his or her social milieu. As such, they are a threat to the social order, and are therefore perceived by the Baining as being outside the social order. "This resistance to the invading emotions is something fundamental in social and mental life" (Mauss 1960b:385; my translation). For the Baining these emotional experiences are opposed to normative social action as instinct is to learned behavior and nature is to culture. These oppositions are, however, culturally constructed and not a priori. They are intrusions from nature and are not transformed by social action. The ability to transform these experiences and encounters is what ultimately reasserts the dominance of the social order and erodes the potency of the emotional base. Mauss says, "It is thanks to society that there is an intervention of consciousness [including the conscience] it is not thanks to the unconscious that there is an intervention of [by] society" (ibid., p. 386; my translation). In most of the cases presented here, the actor regained control over his emotions and proceeded to reinterpret the experiences in ways more compatible with social norms and expectations. People did this by attributing the events to outside agents, and not to internal factors. This is one more piece of evidence for my claim that the Baining deemphasize concepts of interior states.

The Baining tend to minimize this sort of experience. Although they recognize its occurrence, they do not give it any permanent or transforming place in the social order. For example, there is no special role or status, such as shaman or warrior, that is assumed as a result of these experiences. Consequently, people are not concerned with retaining the individuality of their experience. Rather, they are likely to subsume it under cultural stereotypes.

There are two aspects of note in the relationship of akambain states to the normative system. The first is that running amok or being kambain is clearly the marked state. It is differentiated from normal behavior and labeled as deviant. In contrast to the clear marking and labeling of akambain, the normative state is not explicitly named and categorized; it is all that is not marked. Terms such as *atlo* 'good' may be used to describe this state, but they do not denote it in the same way that the term *akambain* denotes its state. Atlo is not an encompassing label. This is true both linguistically and by extrapolating psychologically. The unmarked is implicit and assumed.

This brings us to the second point. Although the unmarked is implicit and consists of generally accepted behaviors and perceptions, the marked state, akambain, is very stereotypically defined. It is a composite of traits which are symbolically meaningful as the antithesis of proper social behavior. On the occasions when people break from the social web, they express this departure in antisocial ways. These ways are better classified as antisocial rather than natural since I use natural to stand for a residual category of everything that is outside society and untransformed through social action. Nature is not a set of elements which can be directly contrasted with their cultural counterparts. The elements defining the akambain experience, however, consist of just such a set of direct oppositions to social activities and values. Akambain elements are, therefore, a coherent and transformed set, intended to be antisocial, but not natural in the way I have been using the term. From a normal Baining perspective, reality is inverted during these experiences. People leave the social space of the village and head for the forest, but they think the forest is clear like the village; they see night as day; they see the dead as alive; they see unripe, raw, or inedible foodstuffs as good food; they fail to respond to social relationships or encounters. Their antisocial activities symbolize the disappearance or penetration of the barrier between the person and the natural world and place them temporarily on the other, opposed side.

This same perspective is advanced by the Baining explanation of their akambain behavior in terms of external agents. The victim deflects the origin of the feelings and subsequently acts outward onto external agents such as aios and akum 'spirits'. It is as if the internal emotional aspects of the self are in some way continuous with external nature, and can be located outside the corporal body. The person is the social skin (Turner 1980:112), the boundary between these two realms, which is therefore vulnerable to attack or penetration from both inside and out. But it is strengthened by its locus within the social order. It is in situations of marginality, which may be ritual, social, or spatial (such as the forest), that the social persona is most vulnerable and the "invading emotions" most powerful.

CONCLUSION

In this chapter I have analyzed Baining behavior and orientations ranging from the normative to the deviant. In the Baining system, normative behavior is characterized by participation in certain key activities and relationships, notably, food giving and food taking, which are part of productive and reproductive cycles in the society. This pattern is opposed to the domain of nature which consists of material and relationships that are untransformed by the sorts of social action just mentioned. Nature and society are ideally kept quite separate by continuous activity on the part of the actors in the system. There are, however, a number of types of situations where such activity is insufficient to maintain the separation of these domains or levels. When these situations are external to the actor, the actor experiences the ambiguity of the situation as his or her own vulnerability to the elements of nature, barriers that are normally maintained socially. These experiences are mediated through a culturally meaningful set of sentiments, of which I have discussed shame, hunger, and awumbuk.

When situations are not external to the actor, but arise from internal emotions, perhaps anger, jealousy, frustration, or fear, which are not socially transformed by work, food, reciprocity, or most important, social relations, the actor falls victim to these conflicting values and experiences akambain disorientation. Akambain is also a product of the opposition of natural and social forces. In this case, nature consists of the untransformed aspects of the individual. Through the akambain experience these disruptive elements are transformed from natural into "antisocial" elements and are thus defined in relation to the sociocultural system. In most cases, the victim of akambain reverts to his or her former role and status in the society. Only very occasionally is someone unable to readjust to the normal activities and associations of the group. Sometimes, as in the case of Ingi, they can sustain certain activities such as subsistence while being unable to engage in normal social relationships such as marriage.

This range of personal and psychological behavior cannot be represented as a static classificatory schema, but is rather the product of a dynamic range of situations and responses on different levels of conceptual integration. People do not consistently fall into one category or another, or even one level or another, but move between levels and categories as situations change. For these reasons, the Baining generally do not categorize people in stereotypic modes. They recognize the diversity of behavior and affect which can affect anybody in particular contexts. Thus, analysis of ethnopsychological processes among the Baining requires looking at the totality of context and action.

ACKNOWLEDGMENTS

I wish to acknowledge the help of John Comaroff, John Kirkpatrick, Catherine Lutz, Michelle Rosaldo, Renato Rosaldo, Milton Singer, Terence Turner, Geoff White, and Sylvia Yanagisako for their comments on earlier drafts of this paper.

NOTES

1. A generative model is one in which the relations within a system or structure are defined as the products of a set of transformations. These take social form as concrete processes of production and reproduction, but are culturally expressed as rules defining and regulating those processes. Such rules may be expressed as formal operations of transformation or the coordination of transformations in a way that conserves some invariant parameter of a system (cf. Lyons 1968:156).

2. I use unmarked here to refer to the implied, normal, or basic condition, and marked as the relatively unusual or abnormal condition.

> Viewed psychologically there is perhaps justification for seeing a similarity between the implied, fundamental characteristic that is the unmarked member . . . and the Gestalt notion of ground, the frequent, taken-for-granted, whereas the marked character would answer to figure in the familiar dichotomy. (Greenberg 1966:60)

3. *Wantok* is the Pidgin term for speakers of the same language. It is used colloquially to refer to those who are members of the same group, linguistic or social, and to express mutual solidarity.

4. Although at times the Baining have been more dependent on wage labor from the plantations for cash to pay taxes, and so on, they were only occasionally more involved than at present, according to earlier patrol reports and mission documents.

5. Raw taro burns the mouth, throat, and stomach, and can be very irritating. Therefore, it is never eaten raw.

6. Inangaiyi was not biologically Tapalet's younger brother, but was a classificatory brother.

7. My name among the Baining was Uvian.

GLOSSARY

abu	bad, lazy
aioska (pl. *aios*)	corpse, ghost, spirit
airiski	hunger

akalup	shame
akambain	crazy, wild, lost, drunk, or disoriented
akambain pra ka	a crazy person (lit., craziness on him)
akavuganan	piece of dance regalia with shield mounted on a pole
akipka	spear tied to the back of a dancer
akumgi (pl. *akum*)	forest spirit (Pidgin, *masalai*)
amuris	good, fine, industrious
anaingi	hunger
angirrup	shame
araik	true
atlo	good, fine, industrious
avungut	the bad ones, evil people
awumbuk	lassitude felt after people have left one
kambain	become crazy, wild, lost, drunk, or disoriented
long long	crazy (Pidgin)
tumbuna	ancestors (Pidgin)
wantok	speaker of the same language, member of the same group (Pidgin)

REFERENCES

Durkheim, E.
  1972   The Conception of Religion. (Review of Guyau's L'Irreligion de l'ave-
          nir.) *In* Émile Durkheim: Selected Writings. Anthony Giddens, ed.
          Cambridge: Cambridge University Press.
Epstein, S.
  1968   Capitalism, Primitive and Modern: Some Aspects of Tolai Economic
          Growth. East Lansing: Michigan State University Press.
Fajans, J.
  1979   Adoption, Sex and Shame Among the Baining. Paper presented at the
          78th Annual Meetings of the American Anthropological Association,
          Cincinnati, Ohio.
  1984   They Make Themselves: Life Cycle, Domestic Cycle and Ritual Among
          the Baining. Ph.D. diss., Stanford University.
Geertz, C.
  1966a   Person, Time, and Conduct. New Haven: Yale University Press.

1966*b*   Religion as a Cultural System. *In* Anthropological Approaches to the Study of Religion. ASA 3. M. Banton, ed. London: Tavistock.

Greenberg, J.
1966   Language Universals with Special Reference to Feature Hierarchies. The Hague: Mouton.

Leenhardt, M.
1979   Do Kamo: Person and Myth in the Melanesian World. B. M. Gulati, trans. Chicago: University of Chicago Press. (Original French edition published in 1947.)

Lyons, J.
1968   Introduction to Theoretical Linguistics. Cambridge: Cambridge University Press.

Mauss, M.
1960*a*   Une catégorie de l'esprit humaine: la notion de personne, celle de 'moi'. *In* Sociologie et Anthropologie. Pp. 313–364. Paris: Presse Universitaire de France.
1960*b*   Les techniques de corps. *In* Sociologie et Anthropologie. Pp. 365–388. Paris: Presse Universitaire de France.

Piaget, J.
1970   Structuralism. New York: Basic Books.

Piers, G., and M. B. Singer
1953   Shame and Guilt: A Psychoanalytic and a Cultural Study. New York: W. W. Norton.

Schieffelin, E.
1983   Anger and Shame in the Tropical Forest. Ethos 11:181–191.

Strathern, A.
1975   Why is Shame on the Skin? Ethnology 14:347–356.

Turner, T.
1979   Kinship, Household and Community Structure Among the Kayapo. *In* Dialectical Societies. David Maybury-Lewis, ed. Cambridge: Harvard University Press.
1980   The Social Skin: *In* Not Work Alone. J. Cherfas and R. Lewis, eds. London: Templesmith.

Part IV
Epilogue

11

Ethnopsychology and the Prospects for a Cultural Psychology

Alan Howard

The chapters in this volume are "pioneering" in the literal sense of the term. As a group, they open up several new lines of inquiry for psychological anthropologists to follow, and raise important questions concerning theory and methods. Like most pioneering efforts, each essay represents its own form of groping, of seeking to get an intellectual handle on the issues the endeavor brings to the fore. The preparadigmatic nature of work on the topic is much in evidence in the diversity of viewpoints represented. Indeed, at the meetings of the Association of Social Anthropology in Oceania (ASAO) which spawned the project, much discussion was devoted to attempts to define or circumscribe the domain of ethnopsychology— attempts that, not surprisingly, did not reach closure. Still, one senses that something of more than ordinary importance is at stake, that the effort strikes at the heart of some fundamental epistemological issues in the pursuit not only of anthropological research but in the general conduct of inquiry into the human condition.

HISTORICAL PERSPECTIVES

In pondering the project, after having read initial drafts of the papers included in this volume as well as others not included, plus transcripts of discussions and a selection of already published materials on related topics,

I was reminded of an exchange I had as a graduate student at Stanford with Alfred Kroeber, who consented to meet with a group of us while he was visiting the Center for Advanced Study in the Behavioral Sciences. His talk consisted mainly of reminiscences associated with the development of anthropology as a discipline in the United States. He was frail in his dignity and was clearly approaching the end of his distinguished life. I can still remember my sense of self-congratulatory exuberance when I asked him about the future of anthropology—the ill-disguised implication being that he would be an active participant in shaping that future. He wisely deflected the question back to me. "The future," he said, "will be determined by people like you. What are you interested in?" I answered that I was interested in culture and personality, to which he replied something like, "Oh that's too bad. Culture and personality is a dead end." He went on to relate how early in his career he had envisioned the development of a field within anthropology he called "social psychology," but commented that what he had in mind was very different from the field that had come to be known by that name.

I would like to believe that Kroeber would have been pleased by the chapters in this volume. I suspect that he had in mind a psychology that was truly sensitive to cultural contexts, that was capable of reflecting the diverse patterns of personal experience in a less ethnocentric way. To be sure, the results still leave us far from a satisfactory formulation of such a social psychology, or more properly, a cultural psychology, but at least the challenge has been joined.

Perhaps the main concern that forms a common ground for the contributors to this volume, and unites them in spirit with Kroeber, is a shared dissatisfaction with Western psychology as pretender to a universal analytical framework for personal experience. To begin with, several of the participants explicitly question the conceptualization of personhood in Western psychology, with its strong emphasis on individualism, that is, on isolating the individual as the basic unit of analysis. Dramatizing the deficiencies of this approach stands as one of the more important contributions of this volume. By describing "folk theories" of human conduct in a variety of settings, even though limited to one geographical region, the authors make us aware of the wide array of alternatives available for categorizing human experience and for making sense of it. In particular, they have demonstrated the necessity for framing such efforts in their appropriate cultural contexts.

But as with all efforts to establish culturally sensitive frameworks, the task is fraught with profound obstacles. For one thing, the mere acts of selection and translation require a theory of psychological significance. Thus the very problem of delimiting a domain of ethnopsychology brings us squarely up against the issues of how *we* define "ethno" and "psychology," which are themselves of a theoretical nature. For the most part such theory has been implicit, and has included as an operationalized premise contrast with idealized (only occasionally documented) Western forms. One reason for this is that Western culture constitutes the common referent for professional anthropologists, and it is by reflection against this template that we establish the bases for our communication with one another. This is a shortcoming that can be overcome, or at least ameliorated with time, as we and our audiences become more familiar with the true range of human variation (so that questions about American experience with the New Guinea Hagener's emotion of *popokl* and the Ifaluk emotion of *fago* can be meaningfully discussed, as Lutz implies). The papers in this book thus provide us with a modest step toward the goal of introducing into the Western frame of reference an expanded range of concepts and theoretical propositions, so that an increasingly inclusive array of experience can be incorporated into its repertoire. The aim is to release "scientific" psychology, which should be universal, from the shackles imposed on it by Western "folk" psychology, which is culturally constricted.

In this respect the authors follow in the time-honored tradition of their anthropological predecessors, begun in earnest by Malinowski, whose field data challenged the universality of the Oedipus complex, and Mead, who challenged received wisdom in American psychology concerning adolescent crises and the linkage between sex and temperament. Appropriately, as far as this volume is concerned, the trail was blazed in the Pacific Islands. Contemporary anthropologists, in conjunction with such culturally sensitive psychologists as Michael Cole and his associates, continue to test and correct Western misconceptions about the patterning of human behavior, cognition, affect, and other aspects of experience. For the most part, however, such studies are conducted in a verification mode. They take propositions derived from Western psychology and explore their validity in a variety of cultural contexts, sometimes modifying the form of the proposition in the process. What distinguishes the papers in this volume is the goal of minimizing reliance on Western psychological notions in favor of exploring the cultural premises other people use to explain their experience as sentient human beings to themselves and to one another. In contrast to verification research, which strives toward delimiting acceptable scientific propositions, the immediate aim of ethnopsychology is to expand the repertoire of possibilities. The underlying logic is that only by examining a range of folk models from different societies will we come to see the limitations imposed on academic psychology by our cultural presuppositions.

Lutz alludes to one such presupposition, which is reflected in our preoccupation with scaling and ranking, particularly in trait psychology.

The assumption is that all people are containers for the same basic qualities, but in differing degrees. If a quantitative imbalance occurs, such that an individual has too much X and/or too little Y, it makes a qualitative difference, that is, they are labeled differently as psychological types. Many of the categories we use in psychological analysis have this semantic shading.

It remains to be seen whether this perspective is widely shared or whether it merely signals a Western obsession with quantifying and ranking. While some cultures seem to share aspects of this perspective (e.g., portraying individuals in terms of degrees of maleness and femaleness), others seem to be less disposed toward quantifying the "substance" of humanity.

The contrast between Western "scientific" psychology and "ethno" psychology falls along dimensions of current debate that give the volume timely significance. The dimensions to which I refer are those of universalism versus particularism and its corollary (human) nature versus (cultural) nurture. These are, to be sure, ancient debates that seem to be resurrected in each generation and brought to center stage, only to fade again into the background of supposition for the majority of social scientists. Two recent publications have brought these issues squarely into focus within psychological anthropology. I am referring to Melford Spiro's (1982) reanalysis of Malinowski's Trobriand data relating to the Oedipus complex, and Derek Freeman's (1983) disputation of Margaret Mead's interpretation of adolescence in Samoa. Following in the wake of bitter debates focusing on sociobiology, these works are especially important challenges to cultural relativists.

In *Sex and Repression in Savage Society*, Malinowski analyzed relationships with the Trobriand family and concluded that the data did not support Freud's contention that the Oedipus complex was universal, rooted in the biology of psychosexual maturation. Freud appeared to take the European form of nuclear family for granted, which led Malinowski to question its applicability to societies, like the Trobriands, that were matrilineal in organization. According to Malinowski's description, it is the mother's brother who is the disciplinarian in Trobriand families, and it is toward the maternal uncle that hostility is directed. Fathers, in contrast, exert no special authority over children and there is, in Malinowski's view, no significant friction between father and son. Instead of libidinous desires within the family being directed toward the mother, Malinowski finds them to be directed toward sisters. Thus, he writes, "We might say that in the Oedipus complex there is the repressed desire to kill the father and marry the mother, while in the matrilineal society of the Trobriands the wish is to marry the sister and kill the maternal uncle" (1951:80–81). While not completely discounting the Freudian view of instincts—indeed he concedes that his research confirms the teaching of psychoanalysis on several points— Malinowski concludes that sociological considerations drastically modify the expression of primal impulses. The main sociological forms he mentions in this regard are the regulation of infantile sexuality, the incest taboos, exogamy, apportionment of authority, and the type of household organization (1951:277).

Early criticisms of Malinowski's analysis came from psychoanalysts Jones (1925) and Roheim (1950), but as Spiro (1982:1) points out in the introduction to his critique, the main thesis was generally accepted by interested scholars of every persuasion. On the basis of his reanalysis of the Trobriand data, Spiro argues that not only are there no convincing grounds for Malinowski's contentions, there are grounds for believing that the Oedipus complex is even stronger in the Trobriands than it is in the West. Spiro concludes with a cross-cultural assessment in which he maintains that the evidence supports a view of the Oedipus complex as being universal in "structure" (i.e., consisting of the boy, his mother, and his father in every known society), while variable in "intensity" and ultimate resolution, or "outcomes."

Whereas Malinowski's interest in the Oedipus complex was tangential to his dominant sociological concerns, Mead went to Samoa specifically to address the question of whether the disturbances that vex adolescents in Western society are due to the nature of adolescence itself, derived from the physiological changes that occur at puberty, or are the consequences of particular social and cultural conditions. Following nine months of fieldwork, she concluded that adolescence in Samoa is not characterized by tension, emotional conflict, or rebelliousness. Her book, *Coming of Age in Samoa* (1928), became a key weapon in the arsenal of cultural relativists despite the well-founded skepticism of virtually everyone who knew something about Samoan society.

If any lingering doubts remained about the veracity of Mead's findings, they have been laid to rest by Derek Freeman's devastating critique, *Margaret Mead and Samoa: The Making and Unmaking of an Anthropological Myth* (1983). Using primarily behavioral data, Freeman makes a compelling case for a stressful adolescence in Samoa. He presents the case in part as a counter to cultural relativism, and reasserts the importance of taking into consideration biological universals as an underpinning for ethnographic interpretation. The main lesson to be learned from the case in Freeman's eyes, however, is the danger of taking into the field theoretical dogmas that result in such pronounced data selection that objective conclusions are virtually precluded.

It is of some interest that in neither of these instances has significant attention been paid to the indigenous people's perceptions of their own psychological states. Gerber (chap. 4) gives us a glimpse of the insights into a more complex Samoan psychology to be derived from an ethnopsychological investigation of the ways people themselves construct their social and emotional lives.[1] Even though Malinowski and Mead assumed a theoretical posture of cultural relativism, their psychological frames of reference never shifted from their Western roots. They observed behavior and recorded verbal accounts in order to obtain evidence to "test" propositions explicitly formulated in Western psychological theories. Their critics examined the results and found them unconvincing, but they, too, have presented conclusions within the same psychological frameworks. Why, one is led to ask, have anthropologists, and psychological anthropologists in particular, been so reluctant to explore their subjects' views of such phenomena, whereas we readily recorded their theories of religion, kinship, and other social phenomena? Attempting to answer this question may help us to appreciate the significance of ethnopsychology as an intellectual endeavor. Is it perhaps a reflection of our own view of behavioral causality, a view that postulates mysterious inner forces beyond the awareness of the actors themselves? It seems to me that while we readily accept the notion that a people's religious concepts and beliefs affect their behavior (or at least help to explain ceremonial and ritual practices), and that social and political theories influence forms of social organization, we do not make the same assumptions vis-à-vis our subjects' psychological theories. I am reminded of a dictum I heard as a graduate student in psychological anthropology: the investigator should not ask the natives to explain their own behavior, this was his job as a scientist. At that time, during the late 1950s, the major concerns of both psychodynamic and behaviorist psychology, as well as psychological anthropology, were with explaining *behavior*. Cognition was rarely mentioned, and almost never as a valid object of study in and of itself.

Another reason ethnopsychology may have been delayed is that anthropologists in general were preoccupied during this period with documenting intracultural regularities, which led to ignoring issues of individual variation, a natural focus of psychological inquiry from a Western point of view. The major exception to these generalizations could be found in the writings of A. I. Hallowell, whose articles on the self and world view were read with great interest and admiration. But it was Hallowell's work with projective techniques that really caught our fancy as graduate students, for such techniques—especially the Rorschach and Thematic Apperception Test—would allow us, so we believed, to see beyond the cultural veneer into that "true" psychological domain, hidden from our subjects' own perceptions, of mysterious inner processes and symbolic forms. Thus, after receiving a modicum of training from George Spindler in the use of these techniques, I went to Hawaii in 1957, located a small sample of third generation Japanese-American (Sansei) women, administered Rorschachs and TATs, and wrote a master's thesis.

I brought Rorschach and TAT cards with me when I began fieldwork in Rotuma in 1959, but my interest in them had waned somewhat and I quickly became disillusioned when Rotumans showed so little interest in playing my games. Besides, I became more and more interested in making sense out of their behavior by attempting to apprehend the logic of their culture. This reflected my exposure, just prior to going into the field, to the developing cognitive approach in cultural anthropology, especially as reflected in the early works of Ward Goodenough and Anthony Wallace. My goal, however, was still to make sense of Rotuman *behavior,* and I paid attention to Rotuman concepts and theories only insofar as they helped me to formulate my own theory of Rotuman culture. To a considerable extent, I was motivated by an aversion to psychiatric concepts, and other formulations, that portrayed subject populations in the same terms used to describe the mentally ill in Western society (e.g., shallow affect), for I was strongly convinced that Rotuman culture was an admirable one, and that the vast majority of Rotumans were models of mental health.

When I undertook my next research project, among Hawaiian-Americans on Oahu, this concern for avoiding ethnocentric misapplication of Western psychological theories was central to my research strategy. Hawaiian-Americans were portrayed by a variety of social agencies as a "culturally deprived" population whose extraordinarily high incidence of social problems derived from failures in proper socialization and other forms of deprivation. It was apparent that the stereotypes of Hawaiian-Americans were cast almost entirely within a framework of deficiency formulations, that is, the ways in which they failed to live up to Middle American value norms of achievement and success. There was virtually no appreciation for the possibility that alternate cultural values might be at work; indeed it was an explicit assumption by most people who advised me prior to entering the field that Hawaiian culture had been "dead" a long time, and that I would be dealing with "just another impoverished minority group."

As was the case with Rotuma, I was motivated to conceptualize Hawaiian-American behavior in other than deficiency terms, to describe it as much as possible in terms consistent with *their* perception of *their* goals and *their* strategies for obtaining them. My reason for rejecting deficiency formulations was the distortion that comes from using constructs that derive their substantive meaning from normative patterns within one group to characterize patterns in a group with quite different norms. By focusing on the ways in which culturally divergent groups deviate from mainstream Western patterns, such accounts generally fail to provide systematic information about the normal, everyday aspects of social life and how they *are* organized; indeed, they generally contain far more information about the values and presuppositions of the middle-class American (and/or European) groups within which the constructs were developed, tested, and substantiated. In an article addressed to these issues which I wrote with sociologist Robert A. Scott, we reviewed the social science literature on minority groups and concluded that

> a central objective of social science research must be to provide a clear sense of how the social life of a group is ordered. Even though profound frustrations exist, minority group members pursue various goals and sometimes achieve them; they actively engage in interpersonal relations from which they derive satisfaction; and they organize their activities in ways that are meaningful to themselves and those with whom they associate. A major flaw of deficiency formulations is that they neglect to document such behavior and activities and thereby fail to provide a firm basis for understanding the nature of social life among minority populations. (Howard and Scott 1981:114)

Still, I do not regard my research among Hawaiian-Americans as ethnopsychological in the sense used by the authors of this volume. In fact neither I nor my associates attempted to systematically explore our subjects' concepts of personhood or theories of behavior. We focused instead on aspects of behavior that were of most interest to *us,* rather than to them, and these in turn were dictated by the interests of such agencies as schools and the Department of Health, and although we did spend a great deal of time doing participant observation, our systematic data were elicited through the use of formal interviews and social psychological experiments. Nevertheless, we did aim our inquiries at identifying coping strategies—a distinctly cognitive concern—and we were explicitly concerned with the patterning of intracultural diversity (see Howard 1974). In these respects I see my Hawaiian research as headed toward an ethnopsychological perspective, although it was still very much tied to a Western psychological framework, albeit one that was far more accommodating to cultural diversity than previous versions.

At the time we began the Hawaiian research I formed a close personal and professional relationship with Robert Levy, who was in the midst of analyzing his Tahitian material. We shared many of the same biases and presuppositions, although I dare say we enjoyed debating finer points. I see his book, *Tahitians* (1973), as a vital link in the historical chain leading toward ethnopsychology. Levy made extensive efforts to elicit indigenous categories of thought and expression, and much of his analysis is based on exploring the implications of these concepts for Tahitian systems of thought, feelings, and action. Yet his interpretations are also explicitly informed by Western psychological and cultural theories.

I see both my own work in Hawaii and Levy's in Tahiti as attempts to contribute to the formulation of a culturally sensitive, though universally applicable, "scientific" psychology. Neither of us was prepared to surrender those tenets of Western psychology we felt might form the foundation of such a universal framework. What distinguishes ethnopsychology from our approaches is a commitment, in theory at least, to loosening the grip of Western construct on psychological theorizing. From this standpoint ethnopsychology falls much further toward the particularistic end of the universalism-particularistic continuum. It also falls within the broader camp of social science inquiry described by Howard and Scott (1981:143) as "naturalism," which they contrast with the hypothetico-deduction approaches that have dominated social science for the past century. According to Howard and Scott:

> When a naturalistic approach is adopted, concepts are derived differently. The commitment of naturalism is to remain as true as possible to phenomena and their nature. Its loyalty is to the experiential world (Matza, 1969, pp. 1–10). The aim of naturalistic accounts is to describe a phenomenon in a manner that maintains the phenomenon's integrity rather than the integrity of a particular theoretical viewpoint. A basic assumption of the naturalistic approach is that human behavior is purposeful, and that persons participate in defining social reality in an active way. For this reason humans are seen as transcending the physical realm in which conceptions of cause, force, and mechanical reactivity are readily applicable. When approaching the study of humans, therefore, naturalism compels the adoption of a subjective view and consequently requires supplementing more rigorous scientific methods with the distinctive tools of humanism—personal experience, intuition, and empathy. The descriptive aim of naturalism is a faithful rendition of human activity, even though only an approximation of that ideal is ever actually possible.

> Whether or not they utilize terms employed by the people they describe, social scientists with substantive concerns require a good deal of input from their subjects before arriving at descriptive categories. Their concern is that the categories contain a high density of information, rich in meaning for the people being studied. To be suitable vessels for describing how people manage their lives, such concepts must necessarily take into account the principles by which those persons organize the information they acquire about the world in which they live. It is important for the naturalist to know what contrasts in the overall stream of events are meaningful to those being described, so that an excessive amount of information is not lost at conceptual boundaries. To do this requires intensive interaction with the subjects of study, the use of open-ended questions, and opportunities to observe people in natural settings.

THE "ETHNO" OF ETHNOPSYCHOLOGY

Despite such commitments, one can legitimately question just how "ethno" ethnopsychology can be. If the criterion for a study to be strictly "ethno" in character is that only those data that are spontaneously produced by our subjects in natural contexts can be considered, the subject matter would be rather barren, it appears, for one of the most striking differences between "the West" and "the rest" is that "they" are generally much less likely to publicly elaborate those areas than are "we."

To clarify this issue it may be necessary to distinguish propositional levels, the assumption being that certain levels are more readily susceptible to ethnoanalysis than others. In reading the chapters in this book, I found it useful to distinguish between three levels. At the level of least complexity are those propositions that underly conceptual distinctions, that is, that group phenomena as the same or distinguish them as different. Many, if not most of these propositions are encoded in the lexical and semantic structures of the language and can be explored through inquiry into these areas. This is the ethno of ethnosemantics, or more pretentiously, ethnoscience. While virtually all such inquiry involves intrusion into normal routines by the investigator, it aims at coaxing informants either to formulate acceptable propositions themselves or to verify our formulations of them. The methodological procedures of ethnosemantics have tended to be formal and prescribed, which is its greatest strength. But this level of theory has proved less than satisfying as a means of gaining insight into other cultures' world views. What is gained in methodological rigor is lost in comparative relevance. Not all domains, or all concepts within any given domain, are equally important to cultural constructions of reality. The ethnographic trick is to pick out those domains and key concepts that are central to a people's theoretical understandings and to elucidate them. This the authors in this volume have attempted, much to their credit. Efforts are made to isolate key constructs, then to relate them to a variety of phenomena for which they are deemed relevant to the people involved. Concepts are thus related to actions, events, thoughts, and feelings, as well as to other concepts. The propositions underlying these perceived relationships are often explicit in statements of association, correlation, causation, and so on, ranging from simple statements such as "x affects y" in some indeterminate way to highly formalized, specific propositions relating multiple variables in precise ways.

At this second, more complex level ethnological research presents a formidable methodological challenge. While people, during the normal course of social life, enunciate commonsense propositions all the time, they generally seem to be so context specific, and so dissociated from one another, that the logic underlying the relationships between them remains a mystery. It appears, in short, that explicit statements of association, correlation, and causality are but a pale reflection of an implicit set of organized presuppositions that order social behavior. The question then, is just what do we mean by ethnotheory? (I presume ethnopsychology to be a particular kind of ethnotheory; precisely what kind is another thorny issue to be taken up shortly.) If we were to adhere strictly to our subjects' formulations, we would likely be stuck with a rather unsatisfying hodge-podge of propositions, many of them contradictory, at least when removed from their contexts. So the question is, what do we do about it? To the extent that we demand a coherent, logically consistent theory from our informants, we restrict the possibilities for a genuine ethnoanalysis. We all know how difficult it is to get our graduate students (or our colleagues), who have been exposed for years to the principles of science, to clearly formulate coherent theories. Indeed, we regard it as an outstanding achievement and reward it accordingly. So, unless we are fortunate enough to come across a most extraordinary native synthesizer, the task of making coherent logical sense of what we have recorded falls on our shoulders. However, to the extent that we do intervene with propositions of our own and force the strands of our observations into a coherent package, we subvert the intent of ethnopsychological analysis.

The endeavor is therefore of a clearly different nature from that of producing an acceptable theory within the Western psychological scientific tradition. Instead of logical consistency and systemic coherence, order must be sought in praxis, in the ways our subjects *do* psychology. A minimum responsibility for an ethnopsychologist is thus to provide an adequate account of the conditions under which propositions are enunciated, the degree to which they are contextualized, and perhaps most important, the specific grounds for the particular interpretation offered, or even better, for competing interpretations.

Ideally, ethnoanalysis would be based entirely on data that occurred in natural contexts, but we all know it is unrealistic to expect a richness of data without intrusion. Just how much badgering of our informants is acceptable is an open question. In part the problem is one of distinguishing the effects of the interview context on assertions. (It is clear that informants will sometimes make assertions to anthropologists they would virtually never make to compatriots, while there are others they are loathe to make to outsiders.) In part the problem is one of sampling, since we may be getting idiosyncratic rather than culturally shared views. One of the dangers is that we may set the frames for conceptualizations through elicitation, and may therefore lose important information about the meaning of concepts, since context so often implicates meaning. The problem is made even more acute when it comes to translating native concepts into English, for it is through the contextualized usage of terms that we gain our best sense of meaning.

When concepts are used metaphorically or metonymically, or otherwise condense a rich symbolic content, we are especially vulnerable to misconstrual if deprived of usage within natural contexts. Certain key concepts (e.g., 'blood') may implicate a broad array of propositions and be powerfully charged with emotion. As is generally the case with such symbols, associated propositions are likely to be implicit (unconscious) and poorly articulated. We therefore run the risk of eliciting only superficial, rationalized assertions about human experience and miss the underlying theories.[2]

Yet another level of complexity has been labeled metatheory, which refers to propositions about the formation of propositions and about their acceptability, truthfulness, and the like. It is necessary to consider this level because ethnotheories are never static. They invariably have a generative aspect to them, as the ranges of possibilities are explored and applied to new circumstances (new, at least, for the individuals experiencing them). They therefore implicate the degree of intracultural variability that occurs in each community. That is, to the extent that assertions are subjected to a rigorous and coherent set of metapropositions before being accepted, variability is likely to be reduced, while lack of a well-specified metalogic breeds diversity. The latter condition complicates the problems of an analyst since he or she may have ethnotheories to contend with, or at least significant variations on the major themes. For this reason it is important to investigate the manner in which a people seek to validate assertions, to understand the grounds on which acceptability is based. Failure to do so removes an analysis one step further from being "ethno," since the investigator must fill in his own assumptions to the extent that he ignores those of his subjects.[3]

An excellent example of the importance of investigating metatheoretical dynamics is provided by Borofsky's (1982) recent work in Pukapuka. Borofsky points out that status rivalry underlies the processes involved in making assertions, asking questions, and providing responses. Whereas deference to those in authority apparently leads to convergent public knowledge in hierarchical Polynesian societies, in egalitarian Pukapuka individuals are concerned that they do not appear deferential to others, and are motivated to question, qualify, or disagree with other's views, at least within the bounds of social propriety. This, combined with a lack of concern for explicit verbal agreement, leads to considerable variability with regard to "knowledge," and gives Pukapukan ethnotheory in all domains a dynamic character.

THE "PSYCHOLOGY" OF ETHNOPSYCHOLOGY

Let us turn now to the second part of the problem of circumscribing the domain of ethnopsychology, which involves defining the scope of psychology. It is apparent from reading these chapters that psychology is employed to encompass a broad range of possible concerns. It incorporates anything that affects the way persons think, feel, or behave; includes material and symbolic environments; and refers both to processes internal to the organism and those with stimulant value that are external—so how are we to distinguish ethnopsychology from ethnophysiology from ethnosociology, and the like? This question arose during a discussion that followed presentation of the papers at an ASAO meeting. Some participants were inclined to leave the issue open, to allow the parameters of the domain to be defined programmatically, by what scholars interested in the topic researched and reported. Others wanted to allow the contours of ethnopsychology to vary from culture to culture, in line with the formulation of native domains of personhood and the like. But Ward Goodenough, who was in attendance at the session, wisely pointed out that without some consensus about a focal area there would be no basis for comparison. Of course, since the domain of psychology in Western culture is so expansive, any attempt to delimit it for comparative purposes will necessarily be somewhat arbitrary. Nevertheless, there is something to be gained by narrowing the focus somewhat and building out from there.

Since, in my view, the nature of personhood is so central to a useful conception of ethnopsychology, and since it is so problematic, it is a good place to initiate a discussion of the problems of comparative analysis. To begin with, I think it important to recognize that a concept of person is necessary if we are to avoid the risk of merely applying psychological labels to culture rather than actually doing psychological analysis. However, the preceding chapters highlight the fact that defining personhood is no easy task for any given cultural group. The distinctions which some investigators found useful, for example, between "self" and "person," or between personal and social identity, were perceived as being inappropriate by others, given their particular concerns or those of the people they had studied. If every cultural group utilized a singular term in reference to a social (as distinct from physical) entity universally recognized as "person" there would be no problem, but such is not the case. As it is, "person" is an abstract conception everywhere that must be derived through analysis of multiple terms. It invariably has meaning at several contrast levels: human/nonhuman; infant/adult; live human versus dead human, and so forth. Exploring these usages requires deriving semantic content through contextualization, which may require a good deal of investigator intrusion.

Since the presuppositions on which such concepts are normally based are deeply implicit, the investigator may be required to formulate his or her own propositions to make sense of the multiplicity of usage. The problem is made even more acute when terms are used analogically as well as digitally. Thus, while "person" may be readily contrasted with "spirit" in many contexts, there may be intermediate concepts such as "chief" or "dead person," so that what appears to be a polar opposition in one context may be perceived as part of a continuum in another. In other words, personhood may be (and is in most of the societies dealt with in this volume) a matter of more-or-less rather than either-or.

Another problem in dealing with the concept of person has to do with the distinction between persons as individuals and persons as parts of relationships. It is evident, and has been for some time, that American culture is at the extreme end of a scale. Our folk psychology conceptually isolates individuals as actors to a degree that seems in stark contrast to the Pacific peoples studied by the participants in this symposium. The point is made again and again, as it was made by Leenhardt (1979) many years ago, that in these cultures personhood is inextricably woven into the fabric of social life, that the unit is better conceived as persons-in-relationships than as persons as discrete entities. The dissatisfaction with Western "scientific" psychology mentioned earlier is in large part a reflection of precisely this type of bias (see also Geertz 1976; Straus 1977; Rosaldo 1980; and Lutz, chap. 2).

As compelling as this contrast is at first glance, however, I would like to inject a bit of caution into our tendency to rush headlong into making this a cornerstone of comparative ethnopsychology. Thus, I wondered, as I was reading the papers, what kinds of evidence one could come up with to support the proposition that we, too, extend personhood beyond the skin, though perhaps in somewhat different ways. Just a moment's reflection brings to mind a variety of behavioral indicators of personal extension. All those phenomena associated with the concepts of empathy and identification could be included, as well as the more obvious example of personal space extension documented so well by Hall (1966). One could, I am sure, find a good deal of verbal evidence in ordinary discourse to support such an assertion. The other side of the coin could also be made problematic. That is, despite compelling evidence that most Pacific Islanders do not normally distinguish themselves as individualized entities in ordinary discourse, does this mean they do not have a clear conception of themselves as unique individuals? If so, how do they deal with the corporal reality of the body—the fact that it urinates and defecates and experiences hunger, thirst, and sexual urges? It seems to me that we have here an issue as to whether the submersion of individuals within broader, more inclusive categories of relationship represents a prior notion of individualized selves, extended outward through socialization, or whether it represents a cultural conception that does not allow for self-differentiation. The point I wish to make is that it may be more fruitful for comparative analysis to accept the proposition that all people extend personhood beyond the skin than to begin with a "they do it and we do not" framework. What would then be problematic—the focus for comparative analysis—would be the ways in which extensions occur and from what conceptual base. Along these lines, I am sympathetic with the suggestion by Poole, made during one of the discussion sessions, that we explore how the inside-the-skin/outside-the-skin distinction is handled in different cultures, and how it relates to various notions of personhood.

Viewed from this perspective, what seems to distinguish Western folk psychology is the degree to which our notions of an inner self are elaborated and made central. For us the "real" self is conceived as that inner core of thought and emotion that is only partially displayed in behavior. It is not that our complete sense of personhood excludes interpersonal relationships, just that they are further removed from this central core. For the islanders described in this volume the reverse seems to be true. They have elaborated the public, relational aspects of their selves and seem to be much less preoccupied with the inner components. In some of these cultures people apparently allocate the inner domain to the realm of private experience and make no effort to account for it, whereas we provide multiple public models for inner experience (through popularized psychology as well as dramatic media) that encourage elaboration and accountability. In other cases, people appear to interrelate their private and public experiences into a shared framework for interpretation and action. That is, they integrate significant situational and/or relational contingencies with subjective experience when conveying their understanding of relevant occurrences.

Another cultural variable that may come into play, and significantly affect the way in which personhood is conceptualized among different cultural groups, has to do with the relative importance of boundaries. It appears that some groups are virtually obsessed with keeping phenomena conceptually distinguished from one another, while others are extremely tolerant of ambiguity and overlap. One need only look at textbooks within the Western academic tradition to gain an appreciation for the degree to which we have expended energy and effort to clearly distinguish one kind of phenomena from another. This preoccupation with isolating units of analysis seems to have reinforced ideological individualism in Western society, resulting in a psychology, of both academic and folk varieties, that isolates individuals as cornerstones for interpretive analysis. Pacific Islanders, as the chapters in this volume clearly show, more readily accept the interrelatedness of phenomena and incorporate it into their social and psychological perspectives. The point is that natural boundaries (such as skin) can as readily be seen as mediators between domains as separators.

A related issue has to do with degrees of complexity and coherence. Are there notions of persons, or selves, as composed of discrete parts, and if so, how do these parts relate to one another? The division of personhood into corporeal and spiritual components is extremely widespread, if not universal, but elaborations vary. Body parts may or may not be included in conceptions of self, or certain parts (e.g., head, heart) may be considered central while other parts (e.g., feet, hair) may be thought of as marginal. Contextual variation may also be involved, so that on certain occasions particular body parts take center stage in self-conceptions (as when they are injured in our society) while on other occasions they are peripheral. Likewise, we are all familiar with the possibilities for elaborating models of the psyche from the professional psychological literature. The Freudian model comes readily to mind as an example of a differentiated mind whose components (ego, id, and superego) are quasi-independent of one another, and even have conflicting interests. From a comparative standpoint, therefore, we might ask about which areas are elaborated in different cultures, and follow with questions about the reasons they occur in specific ways under particular conditions.

The contributing authors provide a groundwork for comparative analysis by focusing on another type of universal phenomena—the transition into and out of personhood. The primary means of becoming a person is, of course, to be born and socialized. At just what point from conception to adulthood personhood is achieved is variable from culture to culture. In the Roman Catholic view personhood begins at conception, hence abortion is equivalent to murder; in other cultures a child might not be considered a person, and given a name, until well after birth. Infanticide in these societies is equivalent to postpartum abortion. Personhood may be achieved in stages, as Poole so nicely demonstrates for the Bimin-Kuskusmin, and it may be sharply demarcated by ritual acts such as initiations. The point is, however, that by examining the process of becoming a person we have a ready-made framework for comparison. A second way in which a nonperson can become a person is through adoption into a group, as when a stranger, particularly an ethnically distinct stranger, is transformed through socialization. An examination of the conditions under which this takes place should shed further light on comparative aspects of personhood.

Yet another way in which personhood is rendered problematic is through behavioral deviance, including interpersonal conflict as well as individual aberrations. Several of the chapters focus on such disturbances of "normal" social life as a means of illuminating basic cultural premises.

The great advantage of focusing on deviance is that it is precisely in such circumstances, in which the rules of cultural order are violated or threatened, that fundamental propositions concerning personhood are frequently made explicit. Inasmuch as ethnopsychology leans heavily toward a naturalistic methodology, and places a heavy emphasis on verbal utterances as primary data, the stimulus value of deviance is considerable. However, to the extent that we rely on such data, we must temper enthusiasm with caution, for the propositions about human experience posed at such times may be specialized and skewed; they may constitute a subset and not accurately reflect underlying conceptions of normal, everyday behavior. The classical psychoanalytic model, which was based on concepts designed to explain pathology and portrayed virtually everyone as deviant from an unobtainable ideal, provides an example of the distortion that can occur when deviance or illness is the center of concern. Despite this caution, it seems clear that we have here an area that will provide ethnopsychology with some of its richest data and most illuminating insights into comparative folk psychology, as the foregoing chapters demonstrate.

The question of what types of phenomena are to be included in the investigation of personhood is itself a thorny issue. On the one hand, it would be possible to relate virtually all of social life (and much else in addition) to concepts of personhood; on the other hand, not everything is as interesting or as important as everything else. In doing analytical work I consider it important to keep indigenous notions of self and/or personhood in focus, lest we drift into a form of description that is indistinguishable from normative social structural analysis, as Kirkpatrick has cautioned. It is this concern that makes Lutz's suggestion, that ethnopsychology focus on indigenous conceptions of personal variation, so appealing. One way to make strategic choices concerning the parameters of study is to let the people being studied determine what is important, either directly, by prescription if they are so inclined, or indirectly, by virtue of how much time they devote to various topics. But while this is always important information, I believe a truly comparative ethnopsychology requires more, and in the end it will be up to us to make informed choices. We cannot expect, of course, an equal density of information from each group that we study. Groups vary with regard to the degree of elaboration they provide in any area, but that in itself may prove grounds for comparison.

CONCLUSION

To summarize, it appears that from both the universalistic and particularistic perspectives ethnopsychology faces a formidable array of theoretical and methodological problems. Obtaining valid accounts of indigenous theories without significantly altering them by virtue of our intrusion may be an unobtainable goal. Perhaps the best we can do is to arrive at compelling inferences about the ways our intrusions affect the texts we interpret. Sensitivity to the complementarity involved in data collection is doubtlessly more important for ethnopsychological analysts than for nomothetically inclined theorists. We must also be especially alert to the presuppositions we employ in translating texts into ethno*theory*. The problems of comparison—the only road to a universalistic cultural psychology—are likewise monumental. The Boasian credo, that extensive data collection must precede theory, has proved to be a barren prescription for cumulative understanding. Delimiting domains for comparison will, at the very least, be necessary for generating theories about ethnotheories; evaluating their validity and utility will require *us* to commit ourselves to metatheories (see Lutz, chap. 2, for further discussion of these issues).

Eventually, theoretical sophistication can be expected to emerge through an iterative process between increasingly competent contextualized descriptions of particular cultures on the one hand, and increasingly refined nomothetic formulations on the other. Radical relativism is as unacceptable a framework for the anthropological endeavor as is reliance on parochial "scientific" theories. The ultimate quest must be for an appreciation of the human condition in all its complexity, and this requires comparison. But the human condition cannot be properly understood as long as we resort to a language, couched in universalistic scientific garb, that is ethnocentric, value laden, and often pejorative. An examination of the literature that applies psychological analysis to non-Western peoples, and minority groups within Western societies (see Howard 1978; Howard and Scott 1981), reveals the extent to which such accounts are demeaning and dehumanizing. The worst abuses involve those instances in which cultural context is ignored, for it is precisely context, including the intentions and goals of the actors, that we use to attribute meaning to behavior, and by so doing attribute humanity—personhood—to people. When we ignore context and explain behavior on the basis of psychological abstractions derived from alien cultures, we deprive people of their humanity and reduce them to objects. In so doing we provide a rationale for disregarding their sensibilities and using political power to restructure their lives in ways that we see fit. If anthropology has indeed been handmaiden to colonial oppression in the past, psychology has provided one of its most pernicious tools.

It is to the credit of the authors of the chapters in this book that they aspire to reform scientific psychology so that it provides for cultural context. Perhaps it was an awareness of the difficulties involved in developing a universal cultural psychology that led to Kroeber's pessimism concerning the future of culture and personality. The challenge is indeed formidable, but it also seems to lead us into the very heart and soul of human experience. These essays are but first shaky steps in what may be an unending quest, but the issue must be joined, and the sooner the better.

NOTES

1. The value of exploring the native viewpoint is also well demonstrated by Shore's account of Samoan culture in *Sala'ilua* (Shore 1982). His analysis of personhood falls squarely into the domain of ethnopsychology.

2. In his thesis on Pukapukan knowledge, Borofsky provides a specific instance of the consequences of investigator intrusion. Whereas Pukapukans were content to leave a discussion full of ambiguities and unresolved discrepancies, as an anthropologist concerned with providing an intelligible account of Pukapukan culture to Western audiences, he tended to push discussions toward consensus and closure. In the spirit of ethnoanalysis Borofsky analyzes the effects these alternate metatheoretical approaches have on forms of knowledge (Borofsky 1982).

3. It is in this area, by the way, that anthropologists have much to gain by familiarizing themselves with the achievements of ethnomethodology within the field of sociology.

REFERENCES

Borofsky, R.
   1982   Making History: The Creation of Traditional Knowledge on Pukapuka, A Polynesian Atoll. Ph.D. diss., University of Hawaii.
Freeman, D.
   1983   Margaret Mead and Samoa: The Making and Unmaking of an Anthropological Myth. Cambridge: Harvard University Press.
Geertz, C.
   1973   Person, Time and Conduct in Bali. *In* The Interpretation of Cultures. Pp. 360–411. New York: Basic Books.
Hall, E.
   1966   The Hidden Dimension. New York: Doubleday.
Howard, A.
   1974   Ain't No Big Thing: Coping Strategies in a Hawaiian-American Community. Honolulu: University of Hawaii Press.
   1978   An Arsenal of Words: Social Science and Its Victims. Comparative Studies in Society and History 20:469–482.
Howard, A., and R. A. Scott
   1981   The Study of Minority Groups in Complex Societies. *In* Handbook of Cross-Cultural Human Development. R. H. Munroe, R. L. Munroe, and B. B. Whiting, eds. New York: Garland.

Jones, E.
  1925   Mother-Right and the Sexual Ignorance of Savages. International Journal
            of Psycho-Analysis 6:109–130.
Leenhardt, M.
  1979   Do Kamo: Person and Myth in the Melanesian World. B. M. Gulati,
            trans. Chicago: University of Chicago Press. (Original French edition,
            1947.)
Levy, R.
  1973   Tahitians: Mind and Experience in the Society Islands. Chicago: Univer-
            sity of Chicago Press.
Malinowski, B.
  1951   Sex and Repression in Savage Society. New York: Humanities Press.
            (First published in 1927.)
Matza, D.
  1969   Becoming Deviant. Englewood Cliffs, N.J.: Prentice-Hall.
Mead, M.
  1928   Coming of Age in Samoa. New York: Morrow.
Roheim, G.
  1950   Psychoanalysis and Anthropology: Culture, Personality and the Uncon-
            scious. New York: International Universities Press.
Rosaldo, M.
  1980   Knowledge and Passion: Ilongot Notions of Self and Social Life. Cam-
            bridge: Cambridge University.
Shore, B.
  1982   *Sala'ilua*: A Samoan Mystery. New York: Columbia University Press.
Spiro, M.
  1982   Oedipus in the Trobriands. Chicago: University of Chicago Press.
Straus, A.
  1977   Northern Cheyenne Ethnopsychology. Ethos 5:326–357.

Index

Designer:	UC Press Staff
Compositor:	Prestige Typography
Printer:	Cushing–Malloy, Inc.
Binder:	John H. Dekker & Sons
Text:	Bembo 10/12
Display:	Ad Lib